THE ATLANTIC ARCHIPELAGO

A Political History of the British Isles

Richard S. Tompson

Studies in British History
Volume 1

The Edwin Mellen Press
Lewiston/Queenston

Library of Congress Cataloging-in-Publication Data

Tompson, Richard S.
  The Atlantic archipelago: a political
  history of the British isles.

  (Studies in British History; v. 1)
  Bibliography: p.
  Includes index.
  1. Great Britain--History. I. Title. II. Series.
DA 30.T66 1986   941   86-21684
ISBN 0-88946-455-3

This is volume 1 in the continuing series
 Studies in British History
Volume 1 ISBN 0-88946-455-3
SBH Series ISBN 0-88946-450-2

The Edwin Mellen Press   The Edwin Mellen Press
Box 450   Box 67
Lewiston, New York   Queenston, Ontario
USA 14092   CANADA L0S 1L0

Printed in the United States of America

6-1-87

Preface

The idea of a comprehensive view of the British Isles has a solid pedigree in the social sciences. But historians have succumbed to powerful Anglocentric tendencies for most of the modern era. Some years ago I began to work on a comprehensive legal history of the islands and the absence of a general survey became painfully clear to me. It was then that I decided to try my hand at a remedy. To work in a new conceptual framework is both challenging and intimidating. Nevertheless, there is a genuine need to recast the outline of political history in the British Isles, if only as an experiment. I am grateful to those scholars who listened patiently to my early and ill-formed proposals.

The composition of this work is much less dependent on original sources than I would like, but the general reader will not regret the absence of the customary ranks of footnotes. I had to choose between a lifetime of research and a modest preliminary survey, and the choice was easy. My debt to others, therefore, is greater than ordinary. For those who were generous of their time and talent in reading drafts, I particularly want to thank Gordon Donaldson, John Pocock, Glenn Olsen, and Lindsay Adams.

The Research Committee of the University of Utah and the Dean of the College of Humanities have been kind in their support, and I thank them for their confidence in the primitive stages of this work.

Richard S. Tompson
Salt Lake City

CONTENTS

INTRODUCTION

THE ATLANTIC ARCHIPELAGO

> The British Isles form an archipelago, at its south-east corner within sight of the continent of Europe.... English history is part of the history of the British Isles, and the history of the British Isles is part of English history.
>
> (Sir George Clark, *English History: A Survey*, 1971, pp. 4-5)

The group of islands between the North Sea and the Atlantic Ocean has no universally acceptable political name and in recent times it has not had an adequate comprehensive political history. The name "British Isles" gives precedence to the largest island and its population. But "Great Britain" does not satisfy the reader in Ireland, Man, the Orkneys or Shetland. As for that which is called "British" history, the discrepancy is even greater, and it is unlikely that Scots or Welshmen will find in it much of the history of their ancestors, and even less likely that they will find an integrated account of English political events and their parallels around the archipelago.

In order to tackle this problem, I have deliberately chosen to use the somewhat ungainly "Atlantic Archipelago,"[1] not in any sense trying to invent an artificial political entity, but simply to recognize a physical reality which was and is a community of island-dwellers whose political lives have ever been closely related. Indeed, the political names in the archipelago are an integral part of the problem which this book addresses.

---

[1] I have borrowed the term from J.G.A. Pocock, with his kind permission. See "British History: A Plea for a New Subject," *Journal of Modern History* 47 (1975): 601-28.

Peoples and Places

The names we use to identify political and cultural groups each have a history. These histories are poorly understood and partly unrecoverable. Most names were labels made by aliens and then used by historians. The political names in the Atlantic Archipelago were created during the first Christian millenium. We can reconstruct the process in a general way, from names which existed at the time of Roman occupation, through the Germanic and Danish invasions of the fifth to tenth centuries, to the Norman Conquest, by which time the major nomenclature was complete.

The Romans invaded an archipelago inhabited by Celtic tribes whose ancestors may have arrived six centuries earlier. "Celt" is the earliest proper name used by modern scholars for the inhabitants of the archipelago, but it was not a name used by the ancients. In fact the name comes from the scholarly work on the languages common to these European peoples. The Romans referred to the natives by tribal or generic names. The tribal names were either Latin translations of native words, or words which the conquerors thought were appropriate symbols. More general names were used for peoples not under Roman control, for instance the "scotti" (attackers) to the West, or the "picti" (painted men) to the North. The Roman name for the archipelago (or for its largest island) was "Britannia." This word was probably a transliteration of the old Greek geographers' name "Pretannic Islands."

The political names in the archipelago become much harder to trace once the Romans leave under pressure from both indigenous "scotti" and "picti," and Germanic invaders. During the fifth and sixth centuries these groups, and the surviving "Britons," (Celtic and Roman inhabitants of the former colony) all had petty warrior kingdoms. No doubt they also had names for each other, which names have apparently not survived. The invasion of Germanic peoples has been called "the coming of the English," which usage is an anachronism. As we shall see, contemporary sources of the fifth to eighth centuries do not support that usage.

In all likelihood, the earliest wide use of "England" or "English" came in the ninth century. The conventional etymology begins with Tacitus, the Roman historian, who reported a tribe called *Anglii* in the vicinity of the lower Danish peninsula. They migrated to the archipelago in the fourth

2

century and later (with Saxons, Jutes and Frisians). The "Angles" did not always use the name in their new home (see "Northumbria", Mercia") and their tribal power was paralleled by that of several Saxon kingdoms. It was one of those, Alfred's Wessex kingdom, which withstood the great ninth century Danish invasions and began recovery of the occupied areas. Thus the Saxon kings became *rex anglorum*, their language by the ninth century was refered to as "englisc," and soon they were known on the continent as "Anglo-Saxons" to distinguish them from the continental Saxons.

This pattern of name-production through the crisis of invasion can be seen in varied shapes elsewhere in the archipelago. Those Britons who resisted or fled from Angles and Saxons tended to concentrate in the western parts of Britannia. They referred to themselves as the "cymreig" (the folk, people); their foes, the "Saesneg" (Saxons) in turn called these natives "wealh" or "foreigners" (hence "Welsh"). Besides the continental invasions, there were movements of warriors from Ireland ("scotti") into the northwestern parts of Britannia ("Scotia"). Gaining hegemony over Picts, Angles and Britons, the Scots created a kingdom whose name was imported from Ireland.

In Ireland's case, "Hibernia" was the Latin translation of the Greek "Iveriu." The essential difference for Ireland was the absence of large-scale invasion until the ninth century, and in its place there was a long period of trade and cultural contacts with the continent and with "Britannia." In the absence of invasion, Ireland's case seems to fortify the idea that people's names come from without. Here is how one Irish historian explains it?

> The usual word for the free population in the laws is *Feni*, and the traditional law itself is called *fenechas*. The normal word elsewhere for the Irish is Goidil 'the Gaels'--a borrowing from the Welsh *Gwyddyl* suggesting that the Irish had no common word for themselves until they came into contact with foreigners.

The "contact with foreigners" was the catalyst for name-giving. The making of records (and their survival) was what preserved these fragments of information about early names. That same process was the means by which we have received the early history of the archipelago.

---

[2]F. J. Byrne, *Irish Kings and High-Kings* (1973), p. 8.

The English Hegemony in Archipelago History

The fact which is central to this book is that English political hegemony has been followed, from the earliest times to today, by English domination of historical writing. The early English pre-eminence, based upon ample chronicles and legal and administrative documents, was less than overwhelming. Irish high-kings, Welsh princes and the Scottish royal court sponsored their own histories until the later middle ages. But in the 16th and 17th centuries, an English history of the archipelago became supreme. There were three vital developments which made the hegemony possible. (1) The English Reformation established a national church which assumed primacy in the archipelago and encouraged English royal aggrandizement at the expense of its rivals. (2) By 1603, or 1707 at the latest, there was an English imperial regime in the islands. In the same period, historical writing began to move in an Anglocentric direction. (3) The English-dominated regime joined the expansion of European political power overseas in the 17th century, and though the process involved all archipelago communities, it served to enhance English power at home and abroad.

In the 18th and 19th centuries, English hegemony was emphasized by industrial and further colonial growth in spite of defeat in America. In its influence on historical thinking, the empire encouraged a sense of virtue, progress and the inevitable "expansion of England." At the same time, historical writing became more of a professional occupation, with associations, journals and a canon of scholarly practice, a development which reinforced the English position of power. The 19th century historians were absorbed with an Anglocentric view which obscured non-English events and eschewed comparisons between the nations of the archipelago. But the late 19th century saw political changes which began to prepare the ground for changes in historical writing.

The advances of liberal democracy, ubiquitous reform movements, and material and intellectual improvements put increasing pressure on the old political structure. From the 1870s, signs of nationalist agitation increased in Ireland, Scotland and Wales. Each form of protest threatened the United Kingdom, awakening both unionist and nationalist reactions. Both impulses fostered the recovery of historical records and traditions, and by the early

20th century there were signs of new life in national and pan-Celtic studies, alongside the growing English and imperial fields.

By the middle of the 20th century, some authors were experimenting with a wider view of archipelago history. Lewis Warren described Henry II's "Lordship of the British Isles" as it existed in the 12th century. Geoffrey Barrow explained the spread of feudal institutions to Scotland and Wales. David Quinn detailed colonial parallels between Ireland and Virginia in the Tudor era. Dame Veronica Wedgwood offered a panoramic view of the dominions of Charles I on the eve of "The King's War" in the 1630s. These authors and others breached the Anglocentric tradition in their own special subject areas.[3] The general concept of "British History" was discussed by J. G. A. Pocock in what he called a "Plea for a New Subject" in 1975. It is of course an old subject, even an old interpretation. For there has always been a wider approach to prehistoric and Roman Britain, and historians before 1700 were inclined to write histories which encompassed the archipelago. The phrase "British history" strikes the student of historiography as an odd echo from the popular but discredited medieval account by Geoffrey of Monmouth. What is wanted today, when for the first time there is a distinguished collection of academic histories for each of the major parts of the archipelago, is a new comprehensive history. Its goal will not be to supplant the excellent surveys already available, but rather to combine, correct and supplement them.

The Value of Archipelago History

A wider view of the archipelago will add to our historical understanding in a number of ways. Although the illustrations used here are taken from political history, there are many equivalent opportunities in other fields.

In the first place, all English political decisions were made in the context of the archipelago, not just those which directly addressed the "Celtic fringe." The principle here has long been recognized and observed by Anglocentric historians who feel obliged to acknowledge the continent of Europe (even while they ignore Wales, Ireland and Scotland). Thus, for example, we

---

[3]W.L. Warren, *Henry II* (1973); G.W.S. Barrow, *Feudal Britain* (1956) and *The Anglo-Norman Era in Scottish History* (1980); D.B. Quinn, *The Elizabethans and the Irish* (1966); C.V. Wedgwood, *The King's Peace* (1955).

know that King John's decisions in 1215 were formed in a matrix of French, papal and baronial pressures. But do we realize that John had also been trying to create (or enhance) integrated feudal rule in the archipelago, that his confrontation with the barons was a sign that he had failed there too, and that Magna Carta also addressed problems in Wales and Scotland, and was separately transmitted to Ireland in 1217? (see below, Chapter 3).

The archipelago also offers a prolific source of comparisons. There were many situations where the same policy was applied in different areas with very different results. For example, in the reign of Edward I (1272-1307) the conquest of Wales, the succession and war in Scotland, and the colonial regimes in Ireland and Gascony display a fascinating range of royal policy and action. Careful comparison and correlation of the developments in these areas should deepen our understanding of this period (chapter 4).

The several national areas were connected by varied means of political communication. On one level there was military and diplomatic contact; on another, representation and delegation. The 16th century was notable for the emergence of what some recent scholars have termed the "unitary state." The concept was nourished in the court of Henry VIII, and it was probably involved in the statutory measures for Welsh annexation (1536-42), the attempt to create the new Irish kingship (1540-42) and the effort to conclude a second Tudor dynastic connection with Scotland (1543). Exploring these modes of political communication or linkage will strengthen our understanding of Tudor constitutional change (chapter 5).

The most interesting aspect of archipelago history lies in its potential for correcting existing interpretations. Several orders of magnitude are involved, the lowest being simple modification. One example might be taken from what Wedgwood called *The King's War* . For some time, the historians of the English Civil War have been accustomed to credit the Scots with generating formal opposition (1639-40) and the Irish with triggering a general panic (1641), which both preceded fighting in England. As J. C. Beckett has aptly named it, the "War of the Three Kingdoms" was far more than an English affair, and it deserves to be studied more fully in its multinational dimension (chapter 6).

More important correction will be made by the reversal of some older interpretations. The "Glorious Revolution" of 1688-89 was an English event by most accounts. William of Orange was invited to "preserve English

6

liberties." But while the revolution grew out of an English plot, it went on to have major impact on the rest of the archipelago and the colonies as well. One of the main products of the revolution, by older accounts, was the passage of the Mutiny Act of 1689. This was supposed to have assured parliamentary control over the royal army. Such a result was disputed long ago by the leading army historian,[4] but the idea persists in liberal and Whig historiography. In March 1689, we may doubt that William's view contained any such notion. He faced an army forming under James in Ireland and a mutiny by a Scottish regiment in Ipswich. William needed tough new powers of military justice as part of his campaign to stabilize the new regime. These powers were provided in the Mutiny Act, limited to a term of six months because the legal implications were serious, and the measure was not intended to be permanent. When we understand William's insecure position in the wider setting of the archipelago, we have a much better explanation for the Mutiny Act.

In a few cases, the archipelago approach will help to break new ground. The most striking example comes from the 19th century. There is no history of the United Kingdom of Great Britain and Ireland, which was a political reality from 1801 to 1922. There is every reason to expect that modern historians would have studied this entity, its political structure and operation, and the manifold ways in which its corporate existence developed. An Anglocentric historiography helps to explain this oversight, but the void remains astonishing in view of the amount of effort devoted to the single subject of Anglo-Irish relations in the 19th century (chapter 8).

There were three broad phases in the historical development of the Atlantic Archipelago. First, the islands were peopled by a variety of continental immigrants and governed by rulers with continental political power until the 13th century. In the second phase, a long process of national identification established distinct traditions by the late medieval and early modern period. The Welsh, the Scots and the Irish were unable to sustain political independence, and instead they were drawn into a dynastic union with an imperial parliament, by the end of the 18th century. In its third phase, the archipelago's internal imperial character was paralleled by global

---

[4]J. W. Fortescue, *A History of the British Army* (1899), v. 1, p. 337.

expansion, which masked the diverse national and cultural features of the United Kingdom. The imperial power was undermined by World War One and ended by World War Two, leaving the archipelago with a fractured political and constitutional foundation. To understand that condition and its background, we have to reconstruct the way in which England and its archipelago have developed over time.

PART ONE

COLONIAL ARCHIPELAGO

If there is a political theme in the early history of the Atlantic Archipelago, it is the repeated entry of outside groups which, for lack of a better term, we may call "colonists." In prehistory the patterns are dim, in the historic era there are written records and clearer political consequences. The Celts, Romans, Saxons, Norse and French seem to share the character of colonial conquerors. At least the origin of their power lay outside the archipelago. But when settled, each colonial group exercised power in keeping with its own tradition. In no case did a colonial people sweep over the whole archipelago. Seldom were their governments unaffected by merging with those already present. Few were able to sustain formal imperial contact with their homelands. After all, in most cases we are dealing with personal and local political power. Only gradually did organs of government grow and develop, and then at very different rates in dissimilar circumstances around the archipelago. This variety reinforced a basic vulnerability which a stronger continental power could exploit, at least until the 13th century.

The first defining feature of the Atlantic Archipelago was its geological formation. About 10,000 years ago the end of periodic ice ages allowed the rise in water level to form channels in and around the new islands, and the melting so reduced the pressure on northern and western sections that the earth's internal forces lifted large coastal zones while rising water began to form their rugged contours. More than 5,000 islands of all sizes were formed, as the remains of the former northwestern European plain and hills were now largely submerged.

Humans had traversed the area in warm inter-glacial intervals, and the "Swanscombe Man" (in fact a woman), found in 1935, is the earliest evidence, being about 250,000 years old. Hunting parties surely visited the islands in their pre-archipelago state, and evidence such as the "Red Lady of Paviland" (actually a male) dates from about 16,000 years ago. Only with the last retreat of the ice was continuous habitation possible. Forest replaced tundra, and hunters found ample prey. The early human inhabitants were joined about 7000 years later by people we believe to be the first identifiable immigrants--the Neolithic farmers who introduced techniques of cultivation. These farming methods had first appeared thousands of years earlier in the Middle East. The migrants probably made their way up the Atlantic coast to Ireland and across the North Sea to Britain. The earliest dated archipelago farm settlement is in Ireland at Ballynagilly (4600 B.C.)

In addition to evidence of farming and habitation, stone age man left extensive monuments and burial sites which still puzzle prehistorians. Stone circles, henge monuments and chambered tombs testify to large social groups with organized structure, strong beliefs and advanced mechanical skills (3000-1500   B.C.). We also know that they too were hosts to new immigrants, the "Beaker People," so named because of the distinctive cups deposited with their dead in single burials. These Bronze Age colonists were equipped with metal weapons and tools. Scholars have identified a number of subgroups, but relations between them are not clear. For instance, a distinctive Wessex culture in the south of England has been described as one of warlords who controlled the trade in metals between Ireland and the continent, but this idea is now in dispute.

In what was once seen as an even clearer episode of colonization, Iron Age Celts arrived some time after 600 B.C. Prehistorians now are having doubts about earlier attributions to these colonists. What were once thought to be "Celtic" features are now seen to date from earlier periods. Iron swords appeared before the seventh century B.C., hillforts may have been in use by 1500 B.C., and mostly in the west and north, and in Ireland. Even worse for the archaeologist, the last prehistoric millenium saw a decline in hoards and funerary sites. This is offset by increasing evidence of settlements, but that evidence becomes harder to interpret as the time scale shortens and the population grows. Still, the entry of those we call Celts is generally accepted by scholars, even if its description has become more difficult as research becomes more extensive.

What we do know is that the archipelago's inhabitants at the arrival of the Romans were a far cry from the early hunters. To Caesar they were "barbarians," by which he classed them with all other non-Romans. The Roman army was victorious in Britain and ruled the province for four centuries. But this was the atypical archipelago colonial experience. When the Roman legions were withdrawn, growing numbers of German tribes migrated to and settled in southern and eastern Britannia. They uneasily coexisted with native Celtic neighbors and with "Britons," those who descended from a mixed Roman and Celtic ancestry. This mixture of inhabitants was visited by a militant migration of Scandinavian origin in the 9th to 11th centuries, and then by a Norse-descended French invasion in the late 11th. For two centuries after William the Conqueror won the Battle of Hastings, the most powerful political force in the Atlantic Archipelago, the English crown, was linked to French aristocratic political roots and issues. Only in the 13th century was this link broken and a new political phase begun, the first in which basic political definition and direction were conceived and carried out within the archipelago without significant outside interference.

In this section we will follow the sequence of colonial action in detail, and it will become clear that while movement into the islands was the main theme, it was paralleled by the sub-themes of contact and conflict within the archipelago, and consequent differential development which produced an increasingly complex colonial polity.

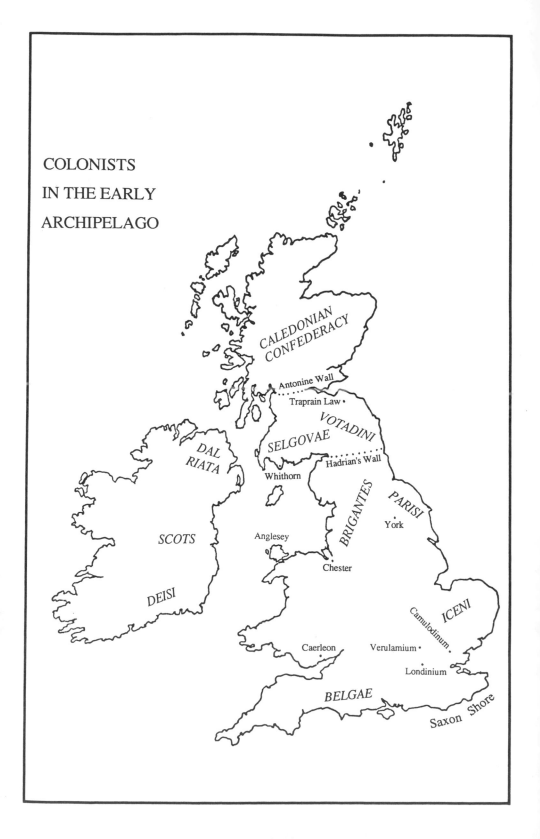

COLONISTS
IN THE EARLY
ARCHIPELAGO

CALEDONIAN
CONFEDERACY

Antonine Wall

Traprain Law •

VOTADINI

SELGOVAE

DAL
RIATA

Whithorn

Hadrian's Wall

BRIGANTES

PARISI

York

SCOTS

Anglesey

Chester

DEISI

ICENI

Camulodinum

Caerleon

Verulamium •

Londinium

BELGAE

Saxon Shore

CHAPTER 1

COLONISTS IN THE EARLY ARCHIPELAGO

> The Romans first with Julius Caesar came,
> Including all the Nations of that Name,
> Gauls, Greeks, and Lombards; and by Computation,
> Auxiliaries or slaves of ev'ry Nation.
> With Hengist, Saxons; Danes with Sueno came,
> In search of Plunder, not in search of Fame.
> Scots, Picts, and Irish from the Hibernian shore:
> And Conquering William brought the Normans O're.
>
> All these their Barb'rous offspring left behind,
> The dregs of Armies, they of all Mankind;
> Blended with Britains, who before were here,
> Of whom the Welch ha'blest the Character.
> From this Amphibious Ill-born Mob began
> That vain ill-natured thing, an Englishman.
> (Daniel Defoe, *The True-Born*
> *Englishman*, 1701)

The ancient world knew the Atlantic Archipelago through the maps of Ptolemy and Strabo, which were based on the reports of sailors like Pythias of Massilia, who had circumnavigated the islands in the third century B.C. There were trading contacts with the Mediterranean during the Iron Age, though there was undoubtedly more regular travel and communication with Atlantic communities, both into the Irish Sea region and along the eastern coasts of the archipelago. Some geographers and prehistorians have mapped the sites of stone monuments, graves and other finds which create a picture of numerous small coastal communities, probably linked by maritime contacts.

Celts

The first colonists for whom we have any historical evidence are the Celts. Their arrival surely predates 100 B.C., perhaps by as much as five centuries. There is archeological evidence which prompts us to equate the early Celts in the archipelago with the continental La Tène and Hallstatt communities.

How and when the first Celtic settlers arrived, and who greeted them, we may never know. The "Arras" culture in eastern Yorkshire probably marks one of the clearest incursions (fourth century B.C.) and the Belgic tribes who were located in the south, had direct contact with the Romans. Their material remains are ample, but we cannot reconstruct a full view of their political experience. The Celts kept no written records, hence all our information is second-hand, either from contemporary Roman observers, or from much later transcriptions of the Celts' oral traditions.

It is likely that when Julius Caesar first landed there were several distinct zones of Celtic settlement: near the channel or the Irish Sea there were trading communities; inland there were farming areas, and further north there were areas of pastoral society. These assumed differences indicate the risk attendant on simple general descriptions of Celtic social order, but we must put together some of the sketchy sources to try to understand the society which Rome was about to conquer.

The social, legal and political order of the Celts, as far as we can tell, was based on kin groups. The descendants of a four-generation group (*derbfine*) made up a typical family unit in the Irish laws. The group shared property and was legally responsible for its members. A number of family groups made up a *tuath*, or people. While not a tribe in the linguistic or customary sense, the *tuath* is commonly so called in political discussion. It was usually headed by the leading member of a royal *derbfine*, sometimes a woman. The ruler of a *tuath* (*rí*) had specific, limited duties--the leader in battle, in peaceful relations with other kings and in tribal assemblies. The ownership of property and the making of laws were not regal powers. Property was possessed by the family and the king's role was custodial. The law was the province of specially-trained law-men (*brithemain*, or the English term, "brehon") who acted as arbitrators between parties. They were responsible for transmitting and interpreting the law, among other things the intricate, socially-graded scales of fines (commonly calculated in cattle, as befitted a pastoral society). The Celtic kingdoms had genealogies and heroic tales preserved by poets (*filid*) and their tribal gods and goddesses were propitiated by priests (*druid*).

The Celtic king was a sacred and priestly figure. His coronation involved a ceremony in which the king, on behalf of the tribal god, was made the mate of the Earth goddess. The prince's "truth" (good fortune) was sustained by taboos in this essentially magical set of beliefs, just as the

14

ruler's descent was tied to a legendary line of predecessors, human and divine.

The physical size and features of the Celtic kingdoms must be estimated from sources such as the law tracts or the occasional foreign observer, for Celtic archaeological remains are relatively sparse. The kingdom might be "about a third of a modern county, and its fighting strength might be about 700 men."[1] In all likelihood, the king resided in a hillfort or fortified enclosure of a size appropriate to his standing. As the *Crith Gablach* , a law tract of the eighth century, put it:[2]

> What is the proper fortress for a king who is in constant residence at the head of his *tuath*? Seven score feet of full measure the size of his fortress in every direction. Seven feet its ditch; twelve feet its depth.... Thirty-seven feet his house; twelve bed-cubicles in a royal house.

These idealized measurements suggest a modest establishment, so far as we can trust their precise accuracy. Yet the individual *tuath* was not an independent entity. Each was subordinate to an overking (*ard rí*) who in his turn was beneath a king of overkings (*rí ruirech*). Between these several levels there were ties of tribute, alliance, marriage, or clientship. It is doubtful that the rule of an overking extended beyond the bounds of several modern counties.

As defined here, there were many tribes in the archipelago at the time the Romans arrived. The imperial invaders named dozens of tribal groups, each of which may have represented a high kingship, or federation of individual tribes.[3] In the area of the Roman occupation there was assimilation and some tribal autonomy. Elsewhere perhaps a hundred tribes were untouched in Ireland, a lesser number were unconquered in northern Britannia, and another group survived under garrison government in the west.

Celtic tribes did not stop fighting after the Roman conquest. Intermittent warfare continued, with the Romans and with each other. The newcomers brought new strategy, tactics and weapons--a new and efficient war culture-- but there was a standoff from the viewpoint of the whole archipelago (c. 100-

---

[1]M. O. Anderson, *Kings and Kingship in Early Scotland* (1973), p. 131, n. 56.

[2]Byrne, *Irish Kings and High-Kings*, p. 32.

[3]D. A. Binchy, *Celtic and Anglo-Saxon Kingship* (1968), especially on the Brigantes, pp. 13-14.

15

300 A.D.). From the third century, or the fourth at the latest, the tide of military affairs turned against the Romans. From the fourth to the seventh centuries there was a period of Celtic resurgence and expansion. Attacks on the Roman colony, followed by its dismantling and by Celtic migrations and new Celtic colonies, were all part of this period of uncoordinated movement. In the fifth century there were Irish raids which we know of through the life of St. Patrick. There were also major Irish migrations, from Ulster whence the Dal Riata established the kingdom which became the nucleus of Scotland; from the south whence a tribe called Deisi migrated to South Wales. These events coincide with the better-known Germanic tribal entry into the archipelago and in these actions Celtic peoples were playing an important formative role in shaping archipelago political divisions.

Romans

The Roman invasion of the archipelago was the most impressive and least typical episode of early colonization. The limited conquest made a lasting mark on the political geography of the archipelago. For four centuries, the occupied zone experienced a sometimes prosperous, usually civilized and always militarized mode of existence. The tribes outside Roman Britain encroached from the third century onward, adding pressure to the internal economic and political strains of the empire and the strain of invading continental barbarians. Concurrently, Christianity began to grow in the archipelago in the third and fourth centuries, to spread beyond the walls and other bounds of empire. This latest Roman institution lived on after the legions had gone and barbarians occupied the former province. The political legacy of Rome may be the dividing line created by occupation; but that line was overriden by the faith which Roman authorities originally opposed and eventually fostered.

The first Roman contact came with the expeditions of Julius Caesar in 55 and 54 B.C. The initial landing was nearly a disaster. Poor intelligence information put the Roman invaders ashore in an unsheltered location, their cavalry transports were held back by bad weather, and the same storm damaged the fleet in its open anchorage. Though his contacts with Celtic tribes were limited and barely successful, Caesar convinced the Senate that efforts should continue. The next year, he took five legions and 2,000 cavalry and landed in Kent. Marching inland after an unopposed landing, the Romans defeated the major tribes in the southeast. After two months of campaigning, Caesar took tribute and hostages and returned to his base in Gaul. These missions had been for reconnaissance, but they were not followed up due to rebellions in Gaul and pressing business in Rome. Caesar had demonstrated the practical possibility of invasion. For the Celts, his assault made some impact on contemporary political alignments, but its main long range significance was in the creation of alliances and client relations with Rome. By the middle of the next century, a more sustained attack was launched.

The basic strategic motive of the Romans was evidently to seize supplies and deny resources to Gallic rebels. The immediate occasion for Roman invasion was an appeal to the emperor by a client chief after he had been deposed. The invading force crossed in 43 A.D. and made a successful landing. Within months, Emperor Claudius came to lead the victorious army into the British capital of Camulodinum (Colchester). The four invading legions and their auxiliaries were reinforced and soon the Romans had occupied and controlled the southeastern corner of Britannia. In 51 A.D. a major campaign was launched to find and defeat Caradoc, one of the Celtic leaders who was at large in Wales. Overcoming stiff resistance, the Romans stormed the island of Anglesey, destroying the stronghold of the druids. Caradoc was surrendered to the Roman authorities but meanwhile a serious revolt had broken out in the eastern part of the colony. Queen Boudica of the Iceni led a rebellious tribal alliance on a series of destructive raids (Camulodinum, Londinium and Verulamium) which was abruptly and bloodily halted (60 A.D.).

After these early efforts to bring order, a new expansion phase (70-86 A.D.) moved the limit of Roman authority north into the Highlands and extended garrisons through Wales. Victory over the northern tribes at Mons Graupius (84) brought the completion of this phase and the furthest point of Roman conquest. There were more campaigns into the far north, but the limit of effective Roman occupation had been reached. In the second century, problems in other parts of the empire forced the withdrawal of forces. This would become a familiar theme; in fact, from the end of the first century, we can discern a shift toward a more defensive policy in the archipelago. Imperial commanders were more concerned with Roman politics, and soon, with barbarian aggression. The defensive policy embraced the elements of fortification, garrison deployment and systematic "romanization."

Roman fortification included the famous northern walls, the legionary fortresses and the walls of towns. The Roman army made fortified enclosures as a matter of course. There are even traces of overnight camp fortifications visible in some areas. But the Romans are remembered for their powerful and intimidating installations, stronger by far than the typical Celtic hillfort. The northern walls were the most striking example. The wall from Solway to the Tweed, begun in 122, was named after the Emperor Hadrian. It was overrun and restored at least five times. The Antonine Wall (from the Clyde to the Forth) was completed in 142, overrun within five years, and abandoned by about 163. There were probably different plans and different purposes for the walls at different periods. The overwhelming impression made by the walls is that they were to repel barbarian assault. The reality is more complex. Hadrian meant to divide and rule, by separating the Brigantes and the Selgovae. Later Emperors had different policies, perhaps the only consistent idea being that the walls were an admission that conquest had reached a limit, at least temporarily. Probably the last serious effort to carry the conquest to the extreme north was that of Septimius Severus, whose campaign was cut short by his death at York in 211.

Toward the end of the second century, the Roman towns, once considered safe, were being provided with earthworks, and the first half of the third century saw many towns building protective stone walls. Security was becoming a major concern throughout the empire. Another stage of the defensive policy came with the construction of the forts of the "Saxon Shore." These eventually stretched from the Wash to the Isle of Wight, on either side of the Channel. The Romans had long had to deal with pirates in the coastal waters; their *classis Britannia* was not a fleet of sufficient size to ward off interlopers, and fortified centers were settled upon as the best means to defend against Saxon pirates. Strategically, the forts resembled the walls: they were a means of regulating traffic, not preventing it. This was more clearly necessary when dealing with trading overseas, protecting merchants, craftsmen-- and tax collectors.

Garrisons were the corollary of fortification. In Roman Britain they consisted of professional soldiers, auxiliaries and support personel. Most legionaries in Britain had been in service elsewhere, some in distant parts of the empire. There have been conflicting estimates of their numbers, but there were probably in excess of 50,000 men. The number was always composed of regular and auxiliary forces; it might fluctuate dramatically during a political crisis in Rome; and it was always a very costly affair. It is not at all clear that income from taxes, customs or requisitions in Britannia was sufficient to meet the costs of the occupation. But it is evident that Roman authorities thought the cost was worth prolonged and strenuous efforts to hold the province.

The final key element in the holding strategy was "romanization." Within the occupied zone, the Celtic population was to be culturally assimilated. In his biography of Agricola, Tacitus made the widely-quoted comment that:[4]

> little by little, the Britons were seduced into alluring vices: arcades, baths and sumptuous banquets. In their simplicity they called such novelties 'civilization', when in reality they were part of their enslavement.

The sarcasm of Tacitus cannot change the fact that Britons were instructed in civilized Roman practices: languages, art, architecture, economic activity and administration were among them. The center for instruction was the town, the hallmark of Roman occupation. It might be one of the few *coloniae* settled by army veterans, or a *municipium* inhabited by natives with some limited rights of citizenship, or it could be a *civitates*, the urban center for a tribal community. The period from 80 to 130 A.D. was the great period for urbanization. The main elements of Roman town construction were water supply and sewers, paving and public buildings (baths, basilica, temple, amphitheatre) and private shops and homes. Town government was a part of the process of assimilation, in that residents had to bear responsibility as magistrates and councillors.

As an outpost of empire, the British province was remote but vital. As a stage in the development of the archipelago, Rome's colony meant revolutionary change in the Celtic cultural and political setting. The Roman strategy to cope with its neighbors and enemies had to be flexible in view of the topography and circumstances around its perimeter: the Irish Sea

---

[4]Cornelius Tacitus, *Life of Agricola,* as cited in H. H. Scullard, *Roman Britain: Outpost of the Empire* (1979), p. 47.

province was probably the most remote and untamed, the walls of the North were only periodically safe, the garrison of Wales was of doubtful effectiveness, and the Saxon Shore was an uncertain internal boundary. Each area was a product of regional geopolitics, and the sum of the parts was eventually a beleaguered outpost. The vast superiority of Roman technical skill was offset by the remoteness of Britain, the lack of effective sea power and relentless pressure on all sides from British and Irish barbarians.

In the first decades after the Claudian invasion, the area which became Wales was under heavy attack. Its terrain prevented it from being overrun in the way that the southeast had been. After the defeat of the druids in Anglesey, there was general pacification; concerted tribal operations were stunted, but only by a series of Roman fortresses and garrisons. The north was governed from Chester and a southern base was held at Caerleon, each with a number of connected forts in its region; the system was in place by 100 A.D.

The tribes to the north of the walls had several degrees of autonomy. Some like the Votadini were clients who allied with Rome, the profitable results being evident in the settlement discovered at Traprain Law in East Lothian. At the other extreme, the Caledonians were hostile to the Romans, and they allied with the Picts and other native enemies to create a permanent threat to the occupation forces.

A third part of the perimeter was the island hinterland, Hibernia, Man, the Hebrides, Orkneys and Shetland. Here there was very little political contact, though there was trade on a limited scale. Evidently the Roman authorities at one point contemplated an invasion of Ireland, perhaps on the same grounds as the original invasion of the archipelago, i.e. reducing enemy supplies and extending imperial power. However, there is no evidence of any campaigns and there is every reason to think that these island populations were quite secure in their remote maritime settings. Indeed, there was enough security, and mobility, so that we find substantial tribal migrations in the later years of the empire, through the Sea province and into parts of western Britannia. These are difficult to trace since archeological sources fail to offer clear distinctions between Iron Age Celts on the different shores of the Irish Sea--itself a hint of mobility.

The other part of the Roman perimeter was the "Saxon Shore." Here again was a different pattern of defense. Apparently the North Sea pirates had been successful in their operations along the east coasts of Britannia. By the third century, these sea-raiders were becoming more of a threat. The general level of barbarian raids was rising, and a decision to extend the forts along the Saxon Shore was made in the last quarter of the third century. In the year 276 alone, some 70 Gallic cities were victims of barbarian raids, and imperial control was severely threatened. The response included construction of heavy defensive works for many British towns, and similar construction even in Rome itself. The forts of the Saxon Shore were outwardly impressive signs of imperial power. At the same time, of course, they were only there because of the fear and frustration caused by the power of the seafaring enemy. The structures were costly to build and to maintain. Not only that, they also could become a political liability. That became clear in the revolt of the channel commander Carausius in the year 286. He had built up a powerful force and sharply reduced piracy; according to some accounts, he had taken over the pirates' role (and their booty). He was ordered arrested and executed as a rebel by the emperor Maximian. But Carausius declared himself emperor and managed for seven years to hold off the authority of Rome. His base at Boulogne fell in 293 and Carausius was assassinated. The episode showed that the British province was not a secure outpost of empire. It had become a potential source of grave insecurity. Indeed, as the fourth century began, there were signs on all parts of the Roman perimeter that political control was being lost. Defensive moves continued and became more desperate: more forts, tribal reinforcements (to replace withdrawn legions) and occasional political malaise at the center of the empire were the main elements of the crisis.

The weakening at the imperial center was manifested in military rivalry and ruthless measures to seize control. A military state readily created a series of generals with ambition to reach for the highest power. Magnentius was a general of British origin who made a bid for power in 350. He staged an 'election' by his soldiers and set out for the continent, taking a body of troops with him. This and later usurpations had the effect of weakening the British garrison, if only temporarily. Magnentius was defeated in 353, and those who had supported him were punished. Magnus Maximus, a Spanish soldier, repeated the revolt in 383. After victory on the continent he maintained his rule in the western empire for five years. A series of imperial 'elections' began in 406: Marcus who was murdered, Gratian who was

21

assassinated, and Constantine III who was executed by emperor Honorius in 411. In this period the usual army departure was paralleled by invasion from the continent and rebellion in the province itself. The once reliable colonial fortress had been converted into a seedbed of intrigue and instability.

There was another way in which central power had been weakened over a longer period. There was a tendency to split administrative control in the western empire, leading to the creation of regional power centers. A three-way power struggle late in the second century saw the governor, Clodius Albinus dividing imperial power with two colleagues (193-197). Later a "Gallic Empire" was created by the usurper Postumus in 259. The rebellion of Carausius in 286 had the same effect, and Magnus Maximus ruled over a western empire from 385 to 388. The formal division of the empire into East and West was recognized in 395, but this was an endorsement of old separatist tendencies in the face of mounting barbarian pressures. The Visigoths sacked Rome in 410. Meanwhile, major tribal wars and migrations cut across Gallic lines of communication in 407 and reached Spain in 409. The links with the archipelago were disrupted.

At the same time, barbarians were moving toward the archipelago itself, with its reduced Roman garrison and endemic internal struggles. The situation had been developing for at least half a century when in 410 the emperor told British civic authorities that they would have to look to their own defenses as there were no plans to send imperial troops.

The Britons were not defenseless. After all, many of the natives had seen service in the auxiliaries or militia. A fair number of legion veterans resided in the province, and certainly there were hired forces (and prospects of hiring more) from among the very tribes which were threatening Britannia. Since the third century, Saxons had been active in piracy, mercenary service, and probably some amount of settlement. We would misinterpret the Saxon Shore installations, or the special post of Count of the Saxon Shore (343) if we read these simply as signs of exclusive imperial defense. Still barbarian attacks continued. The most dangerous was the apparently joint assault by Picts, Scots, and Saxons in 367. This was followed by a serious rebellion in 368. In the aftermath there was reconstruction and more fortification. Attacks in the North resumed in 382 and in the west in 390. The barbarian general Stilicho was sent in to quell disorder in the late 390s, but the usurpers in the early fifth century effectively paralyzed Roman imperial control. In the distress of the government in Rome itself, power in Britannia reverted to its mixed native, colonial and mercenary population.

Before turning to a closer look at the next period of colonization, we need to examine the Christian entry into the archipelago, which may well have been the most significant development of the Roman period. Christianity apparently reached the archipelago in the second century, but our evidence is scanty until the fourth and fifth centuries. In part this is because of the ambiguous policy of the empire. Sporadic persecution of Christians had been in effect from the middle of the third century. In the fourth century there was endorsement of the church and a formal ban on paganism. However, conversion was slow, especially in a remote area like the archipelago, and under a loose religious policy, which for example, allowed the cult of emperor worship to continue through the fourth century.

We have two serious problems in trying to reconstruct Celtic religion. On one side, classical authors tried to make the priests and gods of the Celts fit into the religious framework of Mediterranean civilization. On the other side, Christian missionaries and later translators were often interested in denigrating (or assimilating) pagan practice. In light of these handicaps, and with inconclusive archeological evidence, the historian's task is formidable. It seems likely that Caesar exaggerated in describing a coherent druid system with its schools, ideology and structured organization. Also, there is not enough evidence to prove the Celtic belief in transmigration of souls assumed by the ancients. The same must be said for human and animal sacrifice, although here we do have a scattering of archeological support. Likewise, there is suggestive evidence for the existence of a cult of the head: in statuary, in grave finds, and in the slight evidence of the practice of head-hunting. One recent author has concluded that "when all the evidence is weighed up, the druids were probably little more than 'witch doctors' to a primitive and undoubtedly very ancient religion."[5]

Christian missionaries made contact with the outer zones of the archipelago about the time that they reached the Romanized areas. Tertullian commented (c. 200 A.D.) that there were "tribes of Gaul, also places in Britain which, though inaccessible to the Romans, have yielded to Christ."[6]

---

[5]Lloyd Laing, *Celtic Britain* (1979), p. 81.

[6]*Adversus Judaeos*, 7; see Hadden and Stubbs, *Councils and Ecclesiastical Documents relating to Great Britain and Ireland* (1869) v. 1, p. 3.

It seems clear that the new faith profited from the ending of persecution, but that it was hardly dependent upon the imperial government, and indeed exceeded that government's sphere of influence. During the fourth century we have the first reference to British bishops. They were recorded at the Councils of Arles (314), and Sardica (347) and at Rimini (359). In this period between myth and history, we can begin to identify some of the first great missionaries. Late in the fourth century, Dubricius (*Dyfrig*) was reportedly preaching in southeastern Wales where a number of later church dedications seem to attest to his memory. Likewise in the north, Ninian was reputed to have converted the southern Picts, and a monastery at Whithorn (Galloway) was a later tribute to that tradition. A British monk named Pelagius journeyed to Rome to study where he became the central figure in the famous controversy with Augustine over the heresy which bears his name. It is not known whether Pelagius returned to his homeland, and few memorials were likely to have been built to a heretic. But it was recorded that the Gaulish bishop, St. Germanus, visited Britain in 429 on a mission to preach against the Pelagian heresy. This and other missions showed an important link in the late Roman church, namely a tie between the surviving church in Gaul, and the missions in the archipelago.

Of course, the most renowned missionary work in the archipelago was that of St. Patrick. A Briton seized by Irish slave-traders, Patrick escaped, was educated and returned to Hibernia and worked at the conversion of the native population.

The Christians established a body of believers in many parts of the archipelago by the time that the last traces of secular Roman rule were slipping away. Ironically, the greatest legacy of Rome was its latest and least characteristic feature: a monotheistic, non-idolatrous and charitable faith.

Angles and Saxons

The appearance of Germanic settlers in the archipelago has always been interpreted as a momentous event. But nationalist English historians are too eager to find the source of their political and cultural identity in this period, and in the subsequent amalgamation under the Wessex dynasty. Thus, Sir

ANGLES AND SAXONS

PICTS

SCOTS

Iona

Dal Riada

Strathclyde

Rheged

Armagh

Bernicia

NORTHUMBRIA

Lindisfarne

Jarrow

Catterick

Deira

Whitby

Elmet

Lindsey

Gwynedd

Chester

Powys

Offa's Dyke

MERCIA

Magonsaete

EAST ANGLIA

Dyfed

Gwent

Hwicce

Dyrham

ESSEX

Canterbury

WESSEX

SUSSEX

KENT

Frank Stenton wrote that "It is not until the second half of the sixth century that an outline of continuous English history begins to appear," and that[7]

> the central interest...is the evolution of an effective monarchy, covering all England and, overriding all the differences of race and custom which separated the *various English peoples* from one another.

Most writers have similarly pushed "the English" into the sub-Roman period, which has complicated the definition and abbreviated the stages of the *adventus Saxonum*. When we view events from an archipelago perspective, it seems more accurate to describe a series of stages of development:

1-federated Germanic tribes, 360-430
2-British succession, early migration, 430-560
3-major Germanic migration, 550-650
4-early political consolidation, 650-750

The period around the last request for Roman troops was one of political chaos. We cannot fully appreciate it by concentrating on incoming Germans. We have to place that movement in its larger context. From about 360 there were frequent and major movements in Europe and into and around the archipelago. We can put together a rough outline of these moves. We have noted the attacks around the archipelago perimeter; in the wake of these there were migratory moves in and around the archipelago, followed by major migration and confrontation between migrant Saxons and native Celts.

There were ample reasons for mobility in the late fourth century. The restless continental tribal movements of the Franks, Vandals and Saxons were powerful agents. These peoples, and the tribes displaced by them, sought new lands and settlements. Several factors may have caused the moves: changes in sea level, climate variation and land exhaustion have been cited by scholars. Also we know that there had been earlier signs of this type of migratory exercise, as with the Goths in the north in the second century.

The empire had no means of containing such movement. When the conditions threatened to get out of control, it was common to employ frontier

---

[7]*Anglo-Saxon England*, (Oxford History of England, v. 2, 3rd edition, 1971), p. 8. Italics mine.

tribes in defense of the empire and apparently the same policy was tried in Britain. Some amount of native recruiting to militia units was probably used, and barbarian tribes were hired to police part of the frontier. There is not much concrete evidence of this policy in Britannia apart from some signs of Germanic settlements in the southeast and the Welsh tradition regarding the movement of Britons from the vicinity of Edinburgh to north Wales, under the leadership of Cunedda in the early fifth century, perhaps to stop Irish incursions in the latter area.

The fifth century was a time of sizeable movements, military and migratory, and the vacuum of power drew Britannia's neighbors into protracted political conflict. Roman "withdrawal" probably made a very small dent in the British population. Troop levels had already been lowered, and the last to leave in the early fifth century may not have had a noticeable effect. The resident population surely had the means of self-government and self-defense.

The Saxon tribes in federated status gained in terms of relative political power when Roman control declined. We cannot recreate the events completely, because our sources are severely limited, and what sources we do have allow enough leeway for historians to arrive at widely different scenarios. The generally agreed elements of the story are as follows. Roman direct control was given up by 410; the possibility of Roman reinforcement was real until c. 450; by that time the Saxon federates were beginning to rebel against British authority, and by the last years of the century, the Britons defeated the Saxons in a major battle. Nevertheless, the Saxons had firmly secured control of the southeast corner of Britain from which they would make their major colonization in the next century.

This phase of British rule was the time of the fabled "King Arthur." He was probably a historical person, a military leader of some stature, but his political status is shrouded in mystery. His mythical exploits have overshadowed the tiny amount of verifiable information. Arthur probably was the leader in the victory at Mt. "Badon" (495?) and he was killed in a battle in 515. Some Arthurian historians assert that he ruled the whole of Roman Britain; we can say that he was the last non-Germanic ruler for whom that claim could be made. Perhaps this position on the threshold of Saxon rule lent sentimental support to this legendary British ruler.

A generation after Arthur's death we find the only surviving "British" source for the sixth century, "The Ruin of Britain" by the monk Gildas, written about 550 A.D. Gildas does not mention Arthur by name, but then he refers to few individuals. His tract was more a sermon than a history. The analysis of this source has posed many problems for historians. The primary concern of Gildas was to condemn the petty politics and immoral behavior of British rulers. After a lurid description of Saxon invasion a century before he wrote, Gildas described the revival of British rule and its current decadence, and issued a prophetic warning of its demise.

The last phase of Saxon "advent" probably began after a disastrous plague in 549. Surviving town life would have been devastated, migrations may have been made necessary, with natives moving to more remote areas, and incoming continental peoples replacing them. In any event, the political sequel seems to be a distinct turn toward expanded Saxon occupation. Their first major victory over the Britons at Dyrham (557) secured the area around the Severn Valley. A generation later the great victory at Chester (616) marked the culmination of the immigrants' political expansion. The Britons were now concentrated in separated areas of the West, Cornwall, Wales and Cumbria.

With the seventh century, a new kind of colonial situation was emerging. The Saxons had come in a manner very different from that of the Romans: first as raiders or pirates, then as federated tribes, then as settlers and only after several generations becoming predominant political powers. Out of numerous conflicts there emerged a group of viable kingdoms, but the record of these years is dim. We have to begin with a review of the origins of the tribes, to which we may add a sketch of the institution of kingship in the sixth and seventh centuries, followed by a summary of the political affairs of the Saxons in the seventh and eighth centuries.

Because of our lack of written contemporary sources, the earliest account of tribal movements we can find is in the work of Bede, the monk of Jarrow, written in the early eighth century. He gathered his information from works like that of Gildas, from clerical annals, from traditions of Northumbrian kinsmen, and from more general folk memory. Bede described the continental homes of the Angles, Saxons and Jutes, and he pictured their migration as a wave of conquest. Indeed, archeology supports Bede's location of the home of the immigrants, but it seems that those tribes, in addition to Frisians and Franks, moved along the North Sea coast and into Britain over a rather long period. In the course of this movement, it is unrealistic to think that the migrants' tribal identity was unaffected.

Of course the tribes kept no written records, so their names, as recorded in Bede's work, were apt to be convenient forms of reference deriving from racial composition and (current) geographic location. "Angles," "Saxons" and "Jutes" were transformed into "Northumbrians," "Mercians" and "East Anglians." It may never be known how much change occurred beyond the nominal level. Bede was writing at a time of significant political change, and as one historian observed, "men were giving new names to new farms and villages or adopting old names of ancient towns and strongholds, and beyond these local names new ways were needed for describing larger areas." Bede's own people were "those races who live to the north of the river Humber" (*illae gentis quae ad boream Humbri fluminis inhabitant* = Northumbrians).[8] There is evidence that the old Celtic names clung to the area (Deira and Bernicia), and this helps to explain the laborious invention.

This kind of problem has been deftly sidestepped by most modern writers by simply referring to the newcomers as "English." It is highly unlikely that Bede would have used that name in the eighth century. His best-known work, *Historia Ecclesiastica Gentis Anglorum* is usually called the "History of the English Church" or "the Religious History of the English People." Yet a close examination of the title has convinced at least one scholar that it should be "Religious History of the Anglian Peoples" as it is the "narration of the earthly vicissitudes of the Christian church in Britain from the conversion of the Angles...up to the time of Bede."[9]

From another direction, a recent analysis of *gens anglorum* cites a description originally made by Pope Gregory and applied erroneously to all of the inhabitants of the island. This may have been a compelling authority, one which might explain how a Saxon king (Alfred) would assert his dominion over and announce his identity with "the English.'[10]

---

[8]Peter Hunter Blair, *Northumbria in the days of Bede* (1976), pp. 19, 21.

[9]Giosué Musca, *Il Venerabile Beda: storico dell'Alto Medievo* (1973) pp. 129-31. (My translation).

[10]Patrick Wormald, "Bede, the *Bretwaldas*, and the Origins of the *Gens Anglorum*," in Patrick Wormald, ed., *Ideal and Reality in Frankish and Anglo-Saxon Society* (1983).

The political identity of the English was evolving between the seventh and the tenth centuries. One way of appreciating the dimensions of this process is to look at the array of political structures in the Atlantic Archipelago. The new and old inhabitants of the archipelago were ruled by kings, and in many respects royal powers were similar, if derived from different backgrounds and circumstances. The native Celt, the Pict, the Romanized Briton, and the immigrant (Romanized?) Saxon may be compared *via* this major political institution. How were kings chosen; what powers did they have; what conventions governed their action?

The royal office may have been hereditary in some tribal traditions, but its "elective" character was more widespread, and its actual transfer was often effected by force. Law or custom might confine the eligibility to the male relatives of the king, but they could not prevent an irregular succession. That was guarded against by the Celts by choosing a "tanist," that is, the most eligible heir, and designating him as the future ruler. In some Saxon kingdoms, the office of king was actually shared, but joint rule need not reduce the rivalry at the time of succession.

The new king would be vested with his authority in some sort of ceremony, for instance a pagan ritual such as that mentioned already, or a form of public proclamation, or later, a clerical consecration. The king's name was then added to the regnal lists, or to a royal genealogy which traced the ruler's ancestors far into the human and divine past. That exercise added to the king's power, particularly when there were no rival sources of information, and in a society in which the royal power rested to a great degree on belief in the king's literal descent from the gods.

To what powers did these kings succeed? All held a paternal power with respect to their own people; they also exercised power in a public role toward the world outside the kingdom. The king's paternal function required him to maintain the beliefs, the laws, and the property of his tribe or kingdom. Every king bore a priestly identity, from the "Woden-sprung" Saxon, to the archaic Celt, to the anointed Christian ruler. Only the first of these actually functioned as a priest, but all had symbolic religious character. The kings also had an important role in law. They did not see themselves as makers of law, but as its custodians and enforcers. While the Celtic *brehon* arbitrated disputes free of royal control, the Saxon kings brought laws more directly under royal supervision, especially when clerical servants began to produce written codes of legal custom in the seventh century.

In most early realms, property belonged to the tribe, but there must have been numerous instances, as when neighbors were conquered, where the rights to property were not so clear. Also, where rules of inheritance had to be applied in complex cases, there might be an occasion for royal influence. With their mobility and their more turbulent political history, Saxon rulers exercised more direct control of property during their early ascendancy in the archipelago.

The public powers of kings were reflected in their military and diplomatic responsibilities to their people. We are apt to think of these leaders primarily in their martial poses; they of course were engaged in less hostile relations as well. In practice, most kings stood in a superior and/or inferior relation to some other ruler. This hierarchy, quite plain in the Celtic laws, was also a feature of Saxon kingship. It was a means of producing orderly political relations--at the very least to provide an alternative to war.

That same theme was evident in a number of the common early political conventions in use. One ruler might give hostages to another as surety for the fulfillment of an agreement. This went one step further with the practice of "fosterage," where a son was placed in the household of another to be raised and educated. Marriage was another more emphatic form of alliance. There were also ongoing ties between a ruler and a "client," either a lesser king or noblemen. Roman experience, barbarian practice and common sense produced a range of similar security measures, at the personal or the political level. The importance of these arrangements was the greater in view of the absence of a more modern idea of political identity and loyalty.

All of the foregoing were devices to avoid or reduce the need for fighting. Needless to say, battles were still fought. Indeed, the class devoted to warfare, royal and noble, was pre-eminent in these societies. The great deeds of real or imaginary heroes were everywhere extolled. It was of course in battle that kings were made and unmade most regularly. Victors became "over-kings" of the vanquished, and the most successful might aspire to the title of "high king." In Ireland this was the rank of the legendary kings of Tara, in England the title of "Bretwalda" ("Britain-ruler") was coined for this level of power. Before the ninth century these were transitory positions, producing some tribute, prestige and honors. There were certainly not settled

31

"high kings" in the earlier centuries, nor were there the institutions or other conditions which might have made such powers permanent.

The conventional political outline of the years after 600 traces rising Anglo-Saxon royal units (especially Northumbria, Mercia and Wessex) and shows them moving toward eventual English unification. Anticipating unity does not help us to understand the earlier centuries. A welter of lesser consolidations and continued petty internecine warfare characterized the seventh and eighth century archipelago. By the year 800, the numerous kingdoms of England and Scotland were sharply reduced, while Wales and Ireland were relatively unchanged. In every area, some kings had raised themselves to greater heights, but in only a few had they established lasting dynasties. The earliest reputed Irish high king was Niall ("of the Nine Hostages") in the fifth century, and the first Saxon ruler given such a title was Aelle of Sussex (480). Ceawlin of Wessex was mentioned by Bede as the ruler of the south in the 6th century. The first Christian "King of Tara" (Diarmit Mac Cerbaill) was noted in the Irish annals for 544, and the Pict king Bridei and the Welsh Maelgwyn of Gwynedd appeared in the same decade. The later years of the sixth century were the time of major Saxon advance, but we need to bear in mind that the Saxon kings, engaged as they were for several centuries in internal power struggles, were also involved in the politics of Scots, Picts, Welsh and Britons.

From the seventh century, historians often speak of a "heptarchy" in the Anglo-Saxon kingdoms. The term was coined in the 16th century and it gives a picture of misleading simplicity and stability. The kingdoms (Northumbria, Mercia, East Anglia, Kent, Essex, Sussex and Wessex) were the result of earlier constellations, some still loosely-connected. The Angle and Saxon heptarchy was paralleled in the neighboring areas by like formations of kingdoms, which showed some of the same signs of consolidation, but where of course there were separate stories of political development.

The early seventh century saw the emergence of Northumbria as the leading Anglo-Saxon political power. AEthelfrith of Bernicia, the first successful ruler of Northumbria, was victorious over invading Britons at Catterick in 600 and over the Scots at Degsaston in 603. Bede said that he "ravaged the Britons more successfully than any other Anglian ruler" and this was confirmed by his famous victory at Chester in 616. Later the same year, AEthelfrith was killed and his successor was an exiled nephew, Edwin.

32

He was reputed to have ruled over all of Britain (according to Bede) from 616 to 633. He was killed in battle by the leading Welsh prince Cadwallon of Gwynedd, whose ally was Penda, the king of Mercia. There followed a year of political turmoil in which Cadwallon killed the successors to both Bernicia and Deira, and was murdered in his turn by Oswald, son of King AEthelfrith. For a short time, the Northumbrian ascendancy was restored, but before the end of the seventh century, Mercia was becoming the predominant power.

The rise of Mercia began with King Penda. Power over surrounding lordships was growing in the later seventh century, and Hwicce, Magonsaete and Lindsey were brought into Mercian control. The great eighth century rulers, AEthelbald (716-56) and Offa (757-96) generally controlled the southern kingdoms, with occasional resistance from Kent and Wessex. During this period, the famous structure known as "Offa's Dyke" was built along the western frontier, either as a fortified line or boundary. It may be that assessments for this project were behind the famous listing of tributaries known as the "tribal hidage." We have an 11th century copy of this document, and we can only infer the state of affairs which it portrayed in the eighth century. It is likely that it reflected the true character of "ascendancy," that is, a complex and changing array of dependent kingdoms.

Southern coastal settlements (from the 490s, according to the *Anglo-Saxon Chronicle*) were the source of the Saxon kingdom of Wessex. Expansion inland was highlighted by Cynric's victory over the Britons at Salisbury (552). The battle of Dyrham (577) led to a Saxon base in the area of Gloucester, Cirencester and Bath. There were two groups of Saxons (Thames Valley and Wiltshire) which combined to form the core of the kingdom. Wessex was in the shadow of Mercian power until the eighth century. Then some expansion began, but only with the reign of King Egbert (802-839) was there a clearly ascendant power in the south.

In the course of alternating ascendancies we may lose track of other important developments going on at the same time. New instruments and more sophisticated methods of government began to appear in the seventh and eighth centuries. Charters for the grant of land, codes of customary laws, expanded coinage and taxation were all significant indicators of a shift away from simple tribal kingship toward what we might call territorial kingship. While the British and Celtic kings could draw strength from their traditions, they could also be tied down by them. Laws were inflexible, land was not ultimately theirs to control, the new religion created a system of authority which rivalled their own. Germanic kings, on the other hand, were less bound by their traditions as a consequence of their migration; they might capitalize on a situation where expanding territory offered opportunity to enhance their legal and economic position. The church's place in the Saxon setting was also more readily exploited by the crown, which was able to negotiate with missionaries rather than contend with entrenched familial-clerical powers.

The rivalry between the incoming warrior-kings and the resident rulers operated largely to the advantage of the immigrant; his mobility, flexibility and power were crucial. At the same time, we tend to repeat some old mistakes when we conjure up the image of Anglo-Saxons inexorably conquering the native tribes. First of all, Saxons (or other rulers) were not perpetually at war with their neighbors, and there were a number of other forms of important political contact, even with Picts, Scots and Britons. For instance, the sons of AEthelfrith went into exile in the North and one married a Pictish princess. Bishops from Dal Riata were brought into Northumbria and it appears that the son of a seventh century ruler there married an Irish princess of the Uí Néill. There were exiles and marriages of note in the relations between the British kingdoms of Elmet and Rheged and the Saxon Mercia and Kent.

The kings we have discussed were the leading members of a warrior class common to barbarian societies. They were descendants, at least in spirit, of the epic heroes whose portraits come down to us in transcribed Celtic and Saxon folklore: the godlike Chu Chulainn ("the hound of Ulster"), the warrior aristocrat Beowulf; or the romanticized (but historical) characters like Conn "of the hundred battles" or Cadwaladwr of Wales or Arthur "dux bellorum." If we discount these legendary sources as political evidence, we still must examine them carefully for social history. The prevailing myths tell us a great deal about the structure and the values of ancient society, even if the living replicas of legendary heroes spent more time managing estates than feasting in the hall with their companions. The warrior was also an important member of his kin-group, and his position would make him eligible to be a royal adviser. In other words, the heroic fighter had significant everyday functions in government.

34

The kin-group remained central to social and political life for centuries, well beyond the period we are discussing. Yet some early variation was probably significant. As a consequence of migration and growing royal initiative, Saxon society saw a relative decline in the political capacity of kinship, in its legal activity and its relation to property. The essential political consequence here was the beginning of sharper distinction between the powers of Celtic and Saxon kings. But variations went further in the respective societies.

Patterns of settlement, positions of social importance and methods of social control were all subject to many variations in the archipelago. Rural society prevailed, but the disappearance of Roman towns was not total. In the general rural pattern, there was a basic distinction between the pastoral (and mobile) and the agrarian (fixed) patterns. Unfortunately, our evidence does not draw precise lines between groups; Celts formerly were lumped in the pastoral group, but Irish evidence (e.g. pollen analysis), suggests a mixed agriculture in some places. Surely the pastoral mode was better for highland zones, intermediate areas might have both side by side; open plains would encourage crop cultivation--and each of these would be conducive to different patterns of settlement and local government.

The means of social control were kin or community-oriented. The latter became dominant in Saxon areas, though hostages, sureties, clients and blood-feuds were still common. The kin remained as a viable institution. The vill, the hundred, the shire, and their moots (courts) were communal forms found in most northern European societies, forms which developed later among the Celts and Britons. Local communities, when tied to legal institutions, formed a critical stage of political growth. They were the first step beyond the tribal, personal forms which all had shared at one time.

The final measure of the contrast developing between Celt and Saxon was in positions of leadership. The Celts gave great prestige to their "men of art" (*aés dána*). Poets, lawmen, historians, priest-magicians, were an enduring feature. The sixth century saw a compromise worked out between the Celtic intellectuals and the Christian church (attributed to the Convention of Druim Cett, 575). The "men of art" remained a vital part of Gaelic society for another thousand years. But in Saxon society, where the bardic and priestly functions were less well-established, clerics became the chief record-keepers, legal authorities and artists, as well as agents of spiritual authority.

35

This contrast meant more than a different role for men of religion, it meant an opportunity to create a more concentrated structure of royal power.

With regard to the general position of the Christian Church in the archipelago, the post-Roman period saw a flourishing "Celtic" church beside a pagan Saxon invasion (400-600); then a dual conversion from Celtic and Roman sources restored the Christian presence in (southern) Britannia (560-770); the net result was an apparently uniform faith in the culturally-divided communities, all of whom would soon be visited by the scourge of the viking (c. 800).

The post-Roman period had mixed significance for the archipelago Christian. We have only to compare the complaint of Gildas with the missionary work of his Irish contemporaries, such as St. Columba (d. 597), to show the different directions of development. The "age of saints" was populated by clerical heroes whose careers can only be partially reconstructed. The best known was St. Patrick, whose life and mission have been remembered in his *Confession*. We are not certain of the date of Patrick's mission, but after his consecration as a bishop, he returned to Ireland and began the process of conversion of the "Scots" (the traditional account puts his mission between 432 and 465). Patrick apparently was successful because he made efforts to accommodate the mission to the native culture. By the end of the century there was a strong and well-established church in Ireland. Meanwhile, the church which Gildas represented was struggling with heresy while the flourishing Irish monastic movement was gaining sufficient strength to begin sending missions abroad by the sixth century.

It was this external activity of Irish monasticism which made the first sixth-century converts in Britain. The famous monasteries at Iona (563) and Lindisfarne (634) were indicative of the activity. Of course such establishments had political parallels (the new kingdom of Dal Riata; the conversion of the Northumbrian rulers.) The process of conversion in the south began with the famous mission of Augustine in 597. King AEthelbert of Kent was converted with help from his Frankish Christian wife. Over the next century, other Saxon rulers were converted, though of course one conversion was not always enough, and in some places pagan traditions held on tenaciously.

The Celtic and Roman conversion processes met in Northumbria. Paulinus had been a bishop in the original Roman mission and had baptized King Edwin in 627, but he fled when that king was killed in 633. The new King Oswald had been in exile at Iona, and he brought the abbot with him to be his bishop. Aidan founded the monastery at Lindisfarne, and the Celtic mission in the north continued.

The conjunction of the missions generated some conflict. Historians seem confused about the nature of the struggle. Stenton said that "the strands of Irish and continental influence were interwoven in every kingdom and at every stage of the process by which England became Christian."[11] Following Bede's account, most historians put the resolution of the conflict at the Synod of Whitby in 664. King Oswy was confused by the calendar variation which caused his Kentish wife to observe Easter a week apart from the date he had derived from the clergy of Iona. The king was satisfied by the Synod that he should alter the calendar of his kingdom. This caused the exodus of some Irish clergy but it did not settle the Easter question or the disputes over church government. In fact, the Easter question, which was rooted in an old controversy, had been in the process of resolution for over a century. By about 630 the southern Irish had conformed to the Roman method, but the monks of Iona were not ready to change until 705, and the church in Wales held out until 768. Resolution of this problem was only one part of a much larger and longer process of accommodation. We may have read into this issue too much of a jurisdictional dispute. There were clear signs that the Celtic clergy recognized Roman pre-eminence early on.[12] Also, we can only begin to see conclusive evidence of Roman jurisdiction in most Celtic areas in the 11th or 12th centuries. The concentration of Bede and later historians on the divisive issue of Easter dating has obscured broader agreement and common achievements of the clergy in the archipelago. By the eighth century the signs of those achievements were everywhere: in missions, in learning, in church discipline and government.

The mission of the Christian had the dual purpose of a holy life and a life leading others to salvation. If the former took precedence, one sought the ascetic ideal; the prayer and self-denial which had characterized the original

---

[11]*Anglo-Saxon England*, p. 125.
[12]Kathleen Hughes, *The Church in Early Irish Society* (1967), p. 166.

monks of the eastern deserts was now emulated in the hermit-cells of the devout, scattered on the rocky shores and islands in the archipelago. On the other hand, the missionary whose vocation was to convert or instruct (St. Patrick for instance) necessarily mingled with and made adjustments to pagan society. Temples were reconstructed, charms and symbols were borrowed, feasts and holy days were reconciled, and the divinity of pagan kingship was integrated with Christian belief.

The role of the church as the center of learning was developed at different rates of speed. Schools and *scriptoria* were able to expand and evolve most impressively in sixth-century Ireland, and it was probably not until Bede's generation or later that some British establishments were able to equal the "Celtic" monastic centers. Students from Britain were not unusual in the Irish schools, and the itinerant Irish monks were widely-known in Britain and on the continent.

The matter of discipline and governance of the clergy was yet another plane for interaction. The Irish bishop had adapted to his environment and was a familial servant in his *tuath*, apt to be united with one or more neighbors in monastic federations (*paruchiae*) in the sixth and seventh centuries. This idiosyncratic organization developed before there was any serious reorganizing in the British church. When the great plague of 664 killed the Archbishop of Canterbury, Theodore of Tarsus was named to the post. He created a set of diocesan boundaries which were suited to the former Roman province and the current pagan kingdoms. In these dioceses, the bishop was a territorial administrator responsible to royal and papal authority.

In secular affairs the literate cleric was a potent new political figure. Clerical skills enabled him to write and collect the laws (dooms, tracts, or "saints' laws"). The clergy provided a diplomatic corps and hitherto unavailable means of communication, though how well this was used may be open to question. The successor to the throne was likely to demonstrate formal ties to the church by way of the coronation ceremony. Anointing of the ruler was at once a sign of divine sanction and a form of clerical security. There was unquestionably a new political configuration developing by the end of the eighth century.

The Celtic population of the archipelago was a varied assortment of pre-literate tribal communities, the product of centuries of movement to and from the European continent by several routes. The Roman entry was different.

The planned assault and coordinated occupation made a profound impression on Britannia. In simple terms, an inner, civilized zone and an outer, archaic periphery were created. When the Roman polity crumbled, the Christian order survived, mainly outside the Roman area. In the former province, successor tribal kingdoms had to be recolonized for the faith. The experience of the Roman zone produced a tougher political structure and a more centralized church; the social conservatism of the outer zone meant a stronger church amid less-developed political units. Germanic settlers colonized the bulk of former Roman territory, bringing strong kingship, warrior aristocrats, pagan beliefs, and heroic tradition. When converted, they displayed marked legal and administrative advantages, derived from their migratory and militant past.

This divided archipelago faced further episodes of external colonization, a violent and uncoordinated phase of viking expansion and more coherent assaults by the later Scandinavian raiders and their descendants. Invasions continued to overlay the earlier migrations and settlements in the archipelago, but the political consequences would soon become more durable.

SCANDINAVIAN
ASCENDANCY

SHETLAND

ORKNEY

HEBRIDES

Iona

Lindisfarne

Brunanburh NORTHUMBRIA

Jarrow

Inishmurray Lough Neagh

CUMBRIA

Inishboffin

Cuerdale York

Clontarf Lambey
Dublin

Gainsborough

DANELAW

Chester

Limerick

MERCIA

EAST ANGLIA

Thetford

Morganwg

Maldon

Bath

London

Thanet

WESSEX Southampton

Canterbury

Sandwich

CHAPTER 2

SCANDINAVIAN ASCENDANCY

> ...it is good to remember that the nations as
> we come to know them were not god-given
> inevitable entities. And it is good to reflect
> that the Scandinavians played a part, possibly
> a decisive part, in the making of England, of
> Scotland, of Ireland, and of Wales.
>
> (H. R. Loyn, *The Vikings
> in Britain*, 1977, p. 35)

The years 800-1100 are commonly labelled "Anglo-Saxon" in English history. Yet the central political fact, from the perspective of the Atlantic Archipelago, was omnipresent Scandinavian intervention--in raids, colonies of settlement, and forced political consolidations. This ascendancy has been obscured by Anglo-Saxon historians with the simple device of a caricature of the "viking." These illiterate heathens, whose brutality far surpassed their political intelligence, indulged in bloodthirsty and mindless savagery, or so it would appear. A more sober assessment would surely find that the outpouring of Norwegian, Danish and Swedish adventurers fell far short of the Roman imperial effort, but that it was quite as effective as, and geographically more extensive than, the *adventus Saxonum*. Ultimately, viking power did not become the basis for a durable empire, but it did prevail for several centuries in the archipelago. In spite of small numbers, fierce internal rivalries, divided command, and immature institutions, the Scandinavians exerted their authority over a large part of Europe and in every region of the Atlantic Archipelago.

Until recently the viking was cast in the role of a villain. He was beaten by heroic English kings, with occasional help from Irish or Scottish allies. The record of this villainy--and heroism--is found in the annals of the ninth century. These annals were probably commissioned by the royal heroes themselves and certainly written by clerics, some of whom were victims of the viking raids. We should not be surprised if these accounts are not impartial. For their part, the vikings left no written records, so their view of events can only be approached through the saga literature, based on oral accounts and transcribed in the 12th and 13th centuries. In short, the failed political exploits of the Scandinavians were doubly distorted by the nature of the historical record. This distortion serves the needs of modern Anglocentric historiography, but it does not help a fuller understanding of the political history of the archipelago. Needless to say, the modern historian may more safely ignore the colonial politics of the vikings than could the ninth-century Saxons or Celts.

Scandinavian migrations began long before the eighth century. The major population movements of the Cimbri, the Teutons and the Goths originated in the Baltic region in the first century A.D. Several hundred years later, the Germanic migration was swelled by tribes known as Angles and Gautoi. The latter may have been the Swedish tribe called "Geats" in the epic poem *Beowulf*. Some have equated them with the Jutes mentioned by Bede. Among these mobile populations, as might be expected, there were early signs of trading activity in the Baltic. Sites such as Birka in Sweden, Hedeby in Denmark, and Skiringsslar in Norway probably provided facilities for merchants by the eighth century. Through contacts with the Mediterranean and Central Europe, amber, furs, fish, hides and slaves were traded for gold, silver, jewels and wine. The sea-faring communities on the Baltic, the Atlantic and the North Sea were developing vessels of excellent design for this trade, and for collateral piracy. Among the well-preserved remains of ships of the period are the sturdy *knarr*, used as a cargo vessel, and the sleek, familiar *Gokstad* ship, evidently designed to carry personnel. We may doubt that this maneuverable, shallow-draft vessel was perfected with the object of raiding monasteries, but its utility to pirates operating in the islands, fjords and estuaries of Scandinavia is easy to believe.

The prevalence of piracy, or the trade on which it might prey, would offer a way around one of the most troublesome questions of viking history. Why did raids begin? Historians have been obliged to speculate about the numbers and the motives of raiders. If large numbers of raiding parties suddenly flooded the coastal waters of the archipelago, there must have been large and profound motivation: we have heard of land shortages, climatic changes and political oppression as general reasons. We could easily add to the ranks of eligible vikings an assortment of debtors, outlaws, and fortune-hunters. However, recent studies suggest that we have accepted vastly exaggerated numbers of vikings. If we reduce the numbers, we reduce the need for a cataclysmic explanation.

In addition to piracy, the object of colonial settlement was a central feature of the early viking era. From the first generation of attacks, there is some evidence that viking settlers were establishing communities in the northern parts of the archipelago. Of course these could serve as advance bases for raiders. In later years, decidedly commercial communities were established, especially in Ireland.

In the ninth century, with the second major phase of attacks, large-scale military operations began in several parts of the archipelago. The new operations were a departure from scattered, indiscriminate raiding of religious houses. Now the numbers of men were much larger, there were greater demands for booty and there was much more potential for colonial settlement. Thus there was a shift toward a more explicit political objective, even as the impact on the residents of the archipelago produced more serious political consolidation as a direct result of the assaults.

After a period of relative calm in the later tenth century, the most vigorous period of military-political attacks was unleashed. By this time there was evidence of coordinated action, of something like imperial design. Until the middle of the 11th century, there was a real possibility that the archipelago would be consolidated under a viking emperor. A Norse invasion in 1066 failed, and that turned out to be the last serious opportunity, because a viking descendant brought a politically powerful regime into the archipelago from Normandy.

The net effect of the Scandinavian ascendancy was to overlay the archipelago with northern culture and an immature empire. The hegemony was brief but vital in consolidating the Saxon kingdom, forcing modernization in Celtic Ireland, and planting longterm Scandinavian political outposts in a number of the lesser islands.

The Viking Era

The classic picture of the viking attack has been drawn from the reports of early raids at the end of the eighth century. In 793 the *Anglo-Saxon Chronicle* stated that:[1]

---

[1]Dorothy Whitelock, ed. *English Historical Documents*, v. 1 (2nd ed. 1979), p. 181.

In this year dire portents appeared over Northumbria and sorely frightened the people. They consisted of immense whirlwinds and flashes of lightning, and fiery dragons were seen flying in the air. A great famine immediately followed those signs, and a little after that in the same year, on 8 June, the ravages of heathen men miserably destroyed God's church on Lindisfarne with plunder and slaughter.

This disaster was to be repeated often in years to come. Its shock was evident in the comment by the Northumbrian scholar Alcuin, who was lucky enough to be at the court of Charlemagne at the time[2]

Lo, It is some 350 years that we and our forefathers have inhabited this lovely land and never before has such a terror appeared in Britain as we have now suffered from a pagan race, nor was it thought possible that such an inroad from the sea could be made.

In fact Alcuin did not do justice to his "forefathers" who included some pretty terrifying Saxon invaders. Still the intervening years had produced a settled population quite unprepared for this type of attack. Surely the monastic houses had not been fortified against such visitations.

The first raiders were probably from Norway. After striking several east coast targets (including Jarrow in 794), they moved into the Irish Sea. There they attacked Lambay (near Dublin), Iona, the Isle of Man and Morganwg (South Wales). In later years the raiders hit the west coast of Ireland, raiding Inishmurray and Inishbofin. Some sites received return visits, for example Iona was attacked again in 802 and 806.

The clerical reporters of these raids may have exaggerated their impact. Some writers even suggest that the raids were "an extension of normal Dark Age activity made possible and profitable by special circumstances."[3] This may be true, for research indicates that in Ireland, during the first generation of these assaults, there were 86 acts of violence against religious houses involving Irishmen, during a period when there were some 26 raids by "gentiles."[4] Perhaps the viking raid was more destructive, the losses in loot and slaves more severe, or the apprehension of the heathen enemy, readily cast as the scourge of God, evoked more fear.

---

[2]Letter to the King of Northumbria, 793; ibid., p. 842

[3]P.H. Sawyer, *The Age of Vikings* 2nd ed. (1978), p. 203.

[4]D. O'Corrain, *Ireland before the Normans* (1972), p. 83; see also Kathleen Hughes, *Early Christian Ireland* (1972), pp. 148-59.

The actual raiding process is lost to accurate historical reconstruction. These were small operations which could be conducted by a small band of pirates or adventurers. Those same individuals may have been colonial settlers elsewhere in the archipelago, and we shall probably never know which came first. Perhaps "the first raids in Britain were, in fact, a by-product of the Norse colonization of Orkney and Shetland which began in the second half of the eighth century."[5] Surely those settlements began with "raids," and thus we can best understand the two as concurrent features of the same colonial movement.

The random surprise attacks of the early years were scattered and few in number. Soon they were succeeded by more ambitious and more powerful expeditions. For England, there seems to have been a lull after only a few raids, until the appearance of Danish forces in the 830s. In Ireland there were recorded incidents in 807-812 and 821-824. What we find in the early, quintessential viking period is a scattering of small, deadly and uncoordinated raids. Their effect was lethal--but local.

The opening of the new phase of Danish raids coincided with the decline of the power of the Franks on the continent, a power which formerly restrained the Scandinavian seafarers and forced them under some degree of obedience to the Danish crown. With their continental restraint removed, the Danes began a generation of military and political expansion.

There were concurrent raids on England and Ireland in 835. As groups of attackers grew larger and more ambitious, the first instances of armies wintering in the archipelago were reported. A fleet in Lough Neagh stayed over in 840, another off Dublin in 841, and another at Thanet (Kent) in 850. These forces evidently had more political ambition than their raiding ancestors. Danish royal direction of an attack on Hamburg and Ragnar's seige of Paris in 845 were examples of maturing political objectives. This was true of the attacks around Dublin (850) and York (867). The centers of power were now targets, a sure sign of a colonial enterprise. For a full picture of this period and its vital political changes, we need to sketch Scandinavian, Saxon and Celtic politics in the ninth century.

---

[5]Sawyer, *Age of Vikings*, p. 206; F.T. Wainwright, *Northern Isles* (1962), pp. 117-162.

The ninth century was the period when dynastic powers took shape in Denmark, Norway and Sweden. The Danes united under Kings Sigfred and Godfred (790?-810), resisting Carolingian power and establishing unprecedented internal control. The Norwegian crown effectively merged several regional powers under Harold "Fairhair" after 885, and by the end of the century there was a resurgent royal power in Sweden. The details of these political changes are obscure, and their relation to viking activity was not always what we would expect. For instance it was Harold's victory over viking raids *on Norway* which brought his power to a peak in the last years of the century.

There are better indications of the political effects of viking attacks in the archipelago, but the experiences were not always well-recorded. The Picts were victims of viking aggression, and the Scot Kenneth MacAlpin was able to take the Pictish throne and unify Scotland (c. 850) with some help from Norse attacks on his enemy, but he probably also benefited from intermarriage between ruling families. The picture is a little clearer in the area of Wales. Here a formidable power was being developed by Rhodri Mawr, prince of Gwynedd. He was reputed to be the killer of Gorm the Dane in 855, while repelling one of the many raids on Anglesey. How far this contributed to his wider rule it is impossible to say, and after his death (with six sons to divide his inheritance), Welsh politics reverted to disunity. The trend reversed again in the tenth century with the help of alliances with Wessex, no doubt inspired in part by hostility between the viking (and native) rivals.

Viking leaders and their communities in Ireland were enmeshed in Irish politics. The wars of the period pitted native and viking forces against each other in every imaginable combination. Major Norse or Danish forces arrived in 840, 851, 852 and 853. One of the first effects was to give play to fierce rivalries between Norsemen and Danes; the invaders also added to forces enlisted in the feuds between Irish kings. By the 860s, the general pattern shifted to one of overseas moves from Ireland: attacks on Scotland as early as 866; secondary migration to Iceland (from about 870) and forced migration from Dublin to western Britain (880?-910). In other words, viking entry into Ireland added volatile elements to local politics, but the sequel was gradual assimilation with no durable political innovations. We hear of Ivar ("the Boneless") as "king of all the Norsemen in Ireland and Britain" but we have no evidence of institutions established by him. Probably Norse influence brought a mixed effect and did not force the evolution of 'high kingship' in Ireland. "It was rather the consequences of continued viking presence and the economic effects of the Norse towns that subtly changed Irish society in the 11th and 12th centuries and prepared the way for a new breed of kings." [6]

The most studied theatre of political change was in the south of England. There the major Danish invasion began in 865. The *Anglo-Saxon Chronicle* spoke of a "great army" whose engagements and settlements over the next decades constitute our best-recorded incident of political change in the ninth century. The Danish forces overpowered the Northumbrians, the Mercians and the East Anglians. Wessex alone withstood the attack, and around its government a slow and gradual realignment proceeded over the next century. The leaders of the emerging English political unit periodically gained allegiance from other parts of the archipelago. Thus through their own colonies and the impact on natives, the Danes brought significant political change, literally shaping the entity we call England.

The first and most active phase of the invasion was from 865 to 886. The *Chronicle*, probably drafted near the events and under Alfred's direction, left a detailed memorial. At first, the Danes had great military success. They began from a base in East Anglia, and under a multiple command they moved north toward York, where another base was secured. The army then turned south and conducted its first, inconclusive campaign in Wessex. Afterward it marched on the Mercians and defeated them. In 874 the army divided (for reasons we do not know) and one section went north and occupied York.

The remaining active force in the south attacked Wessex in 875 and again was held off. A second division in the army allowed part to occupy Mercia (877). When a third assault on Wessex was beaten in 878, Guthrum the Danish leader signed a treaty with King Alfred, accepting baptism as part of the agreement. The Danes then withdrew and settled in East Anglia. There were further attacks, some by the new settlers and others by Danes en route to the continent. Alfred's position was only secure when he occupied London in 886, assuring his control of southern England. Again he made a

---

[6]Byrne, *Irish Kings and High Kings*, p. 268.

treaty with Guthrum, though it meant neither the end of Danish aggression nor the Saxon effort at restoration.

We have an unusually clear picture of Alfred "the Great" (849-899) because he was the subject of an intimate biography by Asser, monk of St. David's (later Bishop of Sherborne). More than any other Saxon king, we know details of the king's military career, and his striking dedication to advancing the intellectual development of his people. What stands out in our context is that "Alfred was the first king in England who identified himself with the 'English,' irrespective of their local affiliations." His dealings with tribal rivals were apparently subordinated to a higher sense of obligation. "West Saxon kings of the 10th century were to accept Alfred's conception of royal duty; in so doing they made possible the creation of England.'[7] Surely the ruler had an important part in such a development; just as surely, there were external and impersonal factors involved.

In the period of Danish invasion there were two critical and complementary developments which contributed to the formation of the English polity. The establishment of the "Danelaw" and the consolidation of Wessex made distinct but connected contributions. These were followed by a "reconquest" in the tenth century which seemed to unite England under its now-centralized dynasty.

The "Danelaw" referred to that part of England conquered and colonized by the Danes in the ninth century, roughly the region northeast of a line from London to Chester. The area was under the rule of *jarls* and armies which had settled, chiefly around fortified boroughs (e.g. Leicester, Lincoln, Stamford, Nottingham, Derby). There was a great range of density, from the small numbers of colonial aristocracy in the southeast, to the heavy rural population in the midlands, to the mixed population of York, with Danes from this invasion plus Norse-Irish immigrants in the tenth century. The Danelaw was distinctive in that it literally provided for the observance of Danish legal customs, but the area did not attain a strong separate political identity. Its experience may be better understoood through a brief comparison with the Scandinavian colonies in Dublin and Normandy.

In the case of Dublin, there were several instances of eviction. Viking communities in Ireland took a very long time to be assimilated. In

---

[7]D.J.V. Fisher, *The Anglo-Saxon Age, c. 400-1042* (1973), pp. 225, 231.

Normandy, the Danish colonial aristocracy of the tenth century was soon transformed into a class of Frenchmen, but their political structure kept some of the ancestral features through an unusually centralized government under their Duke. In the Danelaw, two closely-related cultures had a more comfortable coexistence. The racial difference of Ireland and the political circumstance of Normandy were not duplicated. Danes in England might therefore assimilate as well as their cousins in France without developing the same political mechanism.

The early consolidation of Wessex can be dated to just before the Danish invasions, with the submission of Kent, Sussex, Surrey and Essex to King Egbert in 823. Yet this, like other tributary alignments, did not carry with it formal and institutional change, i.e. annexation. In 860 Aethelberht succeeded to the thrones of Kent and Wessex and later Alfred allied Wessex and Mercia by marriage. But the dominant factor in consolidation was war. The Danes defeated the only other powerful Saxon kingdoms, but they were unable to defeat Wessex. In the century after Alfred there was a series of accessions to the developing English power center. Each of these was temporary and breakable, but there were parallel additions to governmental structure (political, clerical, legal). These were the essence of the "reconquest" of the Danelaw--which was also the "conquest" of other parts of England.

These complex events are too quickly lumped together as the "unification" of England. There was indeed an erratic trend toward more centralized political control by the English ruler. Edward the Elder advanced the frontier of Wessex to the Humber, even as the Norse-Irish were invading in Lancaster. Then under Aethelstan there was a major victory over a coalition of Scots, Britons and Norse at Brunanburh (937). But shortly after that the Danish kingdom of York had a brief revival under Olaf, which was terminated when his successor Eric Bloodaxe, an exiled Norwegian prince, was killed as he fled from York in 954. By the third quarter of the century, Edgar of Wessex (957-75) had assumed a wide authority, and in 973 he received the submission of Kings of the Scots, the Islands, the Cumbrians and several Welsh princes, prior to an elaborate coronation ceremony at Bath. This point has been understandably taken as the formal date of origin of unified English royal authority, but the critical role of Norse and Danish invaders and rivals is also clear, especially in their absence during the 960s and 970s.

Yet that absence was mainly a product of political events in Scandinavia. A crisis in Denmark c. 920 brought Swedish and then German intervention and the formation of a new dynasty. The formidable founder, Harold "Bluetooth," conquered Norway and died in 985, a convert to Christianity. His son, Sweyn Forkbeard, and his grandson, Cnut "the Great", dominated the half-century 985-1035 in both Scandinavia and the archipelago. Norwegian power had been dislocated with the troubled succession after Harold "Fairhair" in 945. The several rivals for power over the next few decades had allies in the archipelago, and in the case of Eric "Bloodaxe" who ruled briefly in York, actual experience there. But by and large the Scandinavians were unable to assert significant force until an effective junction of Norse and Danish power was made after 980. The fully political, non-migratory assaults of the next two generations were well-organized and aimed at the wealth of England (under its fledgling Wessex leadership). When this colonial enterprise failed after 1040, it was owing to instability at home, not to weakness in the colony. The nearest thing to a "viking empire" was achieved between 980-1035.

Scandinavian Empire

There was a weak native central authority in the tenth century archipelago, reaching to most of what would now be called England. Whether this was Stenton's "effective monarchy, covering all England" may be doubted. The Scandinavian ascendancy had shaken many of the petty regimes of the archipelago, destroying some and consolidating others, and so a new pattern had to emerge. King Edgar told the Danes to make "as good laws as they can best decide on" in 962 --a century after the invasions and after the reputed "reconquest." This was a fair indication of true royal power, a model commonly assumed to apply to Irish kings, but one which held good across the archipelago. Indeed, the last quarter of the tenth century showed some vigorous local power concentrations, disrupted in almost every case by the most serious Scandinavian colonial campaign of all.

The political horizon of the archipelago was dotted with the sails of independent chieftains--vikings like the earls of Orkney, kings of Dublin,

York or Limerick and lords of Man. Some were their native rivals, Scottish *mormaers*, Irish kings, earls of Northumbria and princes of Gwynedd. Among the native rulers, the stronger were the kings of the English, the kings of Scots and Irish high-kings.

During the serious invasion of the southeast by the Danes, some related and unrelated events furthered political concentration, though not in any coherent fashion. As the later tenth century saw massive raids in the south, there were continued attacks in Ireland (Limerick and Dublin in particular) and there were raids by the Scots into northern England. There was no evidence of joint native resistance, while there were a number of coordinated viking efforts. The most ambitious of the latter was when a force from Orkney, Man and the islands joined the Dublin vikings at Clontarf in 1014. The viking force lost to the Irish high-king, Brian Boru, who was killed in the battle, but who lived on as a symbol of the high-kingship, which never did become a sustained political force.

There is some evidence that Sweyn was the mastermind of the united viking campaign in Ireland, but the major Scandinavian assaults were once again reserved for England (990-1016). The newly-forming English monarchy offered a bleak example of how a wealthy early medieval government might crumble under hostile attack. The great Danish invasions of the later tenth century were a remarkable sustained effort. Even if the numbers involved rarely exceeded a few thousand men, the continued and eventually successful campaigns were impressive. The destructive and profitable work bore the mark of the legendary "Jomsvikings," a band of fulltime military professionals. The saga literature portrayed them as something more than human, and historians long mistrusted the literary evidence. With the discovery of four fortresses in Denmark dating from the last half of the tenth century, the tradition has gained wider acceptance. Sweyn Forkbeard may have been the king responsible for building the fortresses at Trelleborg, Aggersborg, Fyrkat and Nonnebakken. The camps might have housed about 4,000 men and the assorted accessories for the kind of expeditions which were sent against the archipelago. The strategic location of the forts near major waterways was an additional feature insuring greater security for the Danish crown while large armed forces were dispatched on long missions.

When raids began along the south coast of England in 980, there were soon signs that this was no random viking adventure. Some of the early raiders used harbors on the Norman coast, which prompted an Anglo-Norman treaty (991) to deny havens to the enemy. In the same year, a great fleet reported to number 93 Norwegian and Danish ships appeared off the south coast. Olaf Tryggvasson and some Danish allies led attacks on Kent and East Anglia. These ventures culminated in the poetically-celebrated English defeat at Maldon, after which the treaty declared a truce, an alliance, and a tribute of 22,000 pounds of gold and silver. If this device temporarily suspended fighting (and whether or not the tribute was actually paid), the possibility of such profits was a strong attraction, and other fleets appeared in the next three years.

In 994 a serious threat came with the joint fleet of Olaf and Sweyn which sailed up the Thames to London. There it was turned back, but the invaders raided over a large area of the southeastern counties. Their campaign of destruction brought an English offer of truce and tribute. While the fleet was in Southampton, Olaf visited the English court, was converted and baptized, after which he left, vowing not to return. In fact, he went to Norway, won the crown there, and tried to convert the Norwegians (995-1000). However, this desertion was small relief for the English, who still had to deal with Sweyn.

The next invasion was in 997, and thereafter the Danes were on English soil almost every campaign season until their final victory 20 years later. The first visitation lasted three years and represented a shift to continuous campaigning reminiscent of 865. Now, however, there was no plan of settlement, only war, devastation and tribute. The first targets were the southern counties, and the army moved from Cornwall to Kent, living off the land and causing considerable destruction

In 1000, the army crossed to Normandy, but it returned in the following year to raid in Sussex and Devon. A truce was arranged in 1002 with a tribute of £124,000.

The English ruler during the Danish invasions was AEthelred "the Redeless" (weak counsel). The king had been implicated in the murder of his step-brother, King Edward. This and other unsavory allegations can be found in the chronicles, but even without them, any king who was unable to defend his people and was responsible for the hated "danegeld" in order to make tribute, could not expect better treatment by chroniclers.

In 1002 AEthelred turned again to Normandy for help. He married the Duke's sister, Emma, thereby restoring the alliance. The king evidently was emboldened by this, or else he was enraged by repeated humiliations from the Danes, for in November he ordered "all Danes" in England to be killed. According to the chronicler, "he had been told that they intended to kill him and his councillors, and afterwards to possess his kingdom." This pre-emptive strike was a major blunder (unless renewed Danish attacks had already broken the unstable truce). There were stories that Sweyn's sister, a hostage, was one of the victims, but regardless of her fate, any Danes (or Anglo-Danes) who hitherto wavered in their loyalty were now driven to support Sweyn.

From 1003 to 1005 Danish forces attacked in the same coastal areas as before, only moving further inland. Advance was checked at a major battle in East Anglia, and the fleet departed, to return in 1006, once again exacting a large tribute. After a short lull, the fleet and army reappeared in 1009 with the largest force to date. The English had tried to prepare a fleet, but it was put out of action by storm damage and treachery. The invaders moved up the Thames, but again London held. The army attacked and burned Oxford, withdrew to its ships and sailed to Ipswich, where it landed and won a major battle near Thetford. In 1011 a successful siege led to the fall of Canterbury and the capture of the Archbishop. A special ransom was added to the demand for tribute, and when the archbishop refused to allow it, he was tortured and killed.

In 1013 a renewed assault by the Danes bore clearer marks of an attempt on the throne. At all times, this had been a prospective prize, and the odds increased as English government failed to deal with the invaders. In this attack, the invasion force landed at Sandwich, moved to the Humber and there secured the allegiance of a large number of Danish Englishmen. After securing control over a large area, Sweyn launched an attack on London. Failing again, he marched through the west and back to his ships at Gainsborough, seeming to demonstrate his control of the countryside. Months later, London surrendered and by the end of the year, AEthelred joined his family in exile in Normandy.

The kingship of England was Sweyn's at last, but he did not live to exercise it for more than a few months, dying at Gainsborough in February 1014. His young son Cnut was promptly recognized as his successor by the Danish troops, but in the current state of affairs, that would hardly suffice. Cnut would have to win the crown for himself. When Sweyn died, members of the *witan* made an agreement with AEthelred for his return from Normandy upon promise of amnesty and reforms. Cnut was forced to leave, and in doing so he abandoned his Danish supporters in East Anglia. He also put ashore a group of mutilated hostages at Sandwich, and the Danish force in London exacted a tribute of £21,000 before leaving.

The Danes returned the next year, and the bitter campaign was highlighted by the great military efforts of the Saxon heir, Edmund "Ironside." During the year, Cnut converted to Christianity and old AEthelred died. Cnut defeated Edmund, but was ready to recognize him as king of Wessex. Edmund died in November 1016, and Cnut took the title to the whole of England.

Cnut's reign (1016-1035) brought a respite from exhausting raids--for the English. The king himself was soon off on a long series of expeditions to Norway (1019-1028), surely financed in part by his new subjects. At the beginning of this Danish reign, we need to pause to assess the political situation, in the viking world, the archipelago, and England.

When Sweyn Forkbeard died in 1014, his oldest son Harold became king of Denmark. Harold died without heirs in 1019. Cnut then assumed the Danish throne and turned his attention to securing the crown of Norway. There the situation was unstable. As the Danes were coming to power in England, Olaf Haroldsson (alias Olaf the Stout) asserted an ancestral claim and ruled Norway from 1016 to 1026. The king's Christianity alienated some of his subjects, who fought for Cnut. But a broad group of Swedes, Norwegians and Danish rebels fought against him. Cnut ousted his rival, who was killed in a battle in 1030, but who soon became a hero ("St. Olaf"). When Cnut died, he was succeeded by his rival's son, Magnus, who in turn later took power in Cnut's Denmark.

In these diffuse dynastic patterns it is futile to look for the makings of a North Sea Empire in the early 11th century, even if we believe there was such a plan behind the Danish campaigns. Surely there was a lust for power, and just as surely, if the joint rule of England, Denmark and Norway had endured, it might have created a new political orientation. But we must recognize that rulers of these distant provinces were only just beginning to assert strong control *within* their native realms, as the Wessex kings had been trying to do for much of the tenth century. By the 11th century other parts of the archipelago showed similar consolidating tendencies: from 1014, the leading prince in the northern isles was Thorfinn "the Mighty" a principal figure for half a century; about 1040, hegemony over the princes of Wales was established by Gruffydd ap Llywelyn; by 1052, King Diarmit in Ireland had expelled the last Norse king of Dublin; and from 1058, Malcolm Canmore ruled a durable central regime in Scotland.

It is true that the exercise of authority by Scandinavian rulers began to take on some imperial coloration in the 11th century, and there were several areas where Norse power would remain (Iceland, the northern islands, Man). However, the timing was poor, for two centuries of raiding had generated far more in the way of *defensive* political consolidation than any of the viking leaders could muster for the management of maritime empire. The power which Guthrum, Sweyn or Cnut wielded was that of armed violence; settled authority was not mastered soon enough to convert their dominions into a stable polity.

It remains to ask what the Scandinavian ascendancy meant to England, where the tenth century had seen the first stage of effective political union. The defense against the Danes had been a severe test for the new kingdom. It may be noteworthy that in 1016 the realm passed intact to its new ruler, which is to his credit and that of the existing regime. There had to be some perception of unity, moreover one which was shared by Englishman and Dane. As yet, "nation" could not be far from tribal federation, and its political meaning was anything but clear.

When Cnut was proclaimed king in 1016, he settled into a brief period of military rule followed by some moderate measures which allowed two decades of exhausted calm. He married the old king's widow, and Emma's dowry no doubt included an alliance with her brother, Richard of Normandy. The duke still had custody of Alfred and Edward, the sons of the late king.

At an assembly at Oxford in 1018, Cnut affirmed King Edgar's laws and took an oath from his subjects to support the legal settlement. It is likely that the "Laws of King Cnut" were drafted by Archbishop Wulfstan, and the text was plainly and purposely derivative.

The traditions of church, administration and local government were not seriously disrupted. The new king rewarded his followers, punished some troublesome opponents, and affixed heavy and persistent taxation on his kingdom. The danegeld had proven to be a source of great treasure, at least if we assume that the recorded tributes were actually paid. The total amount levied between 991 and 1018 was in excess of £230,000. A country which could afford this was certain to be taxed further.

That Cnut's rule was a success was awkwardly affirmed by the confusion after his death. Harthacnut was meant to come into all of his father's titles, but he was wary of leaving the Danish throne while Magnus of Norway looked on. Meanwhile, his illegitimate half-brother Harold Harefoot, was made regent in England (1036) and king the following year. Then Harthacnut reached an accord with Magnus (either would succeed if the other died without heirs). By the time Harthacnut reached England in 1040, Harold had died and the throne was vacant. The last heir of Cnut only lived for an unimpressive reign of two years. At his death in 1042, Edward, the son of AEthelred, was brought to the throne.

At this point, political fortune shifted away from Scandinavia proper, though plans and projects of invasion were revived several times. The balance of influence in the English succession, just like the power balance in the archipelago generally, was swinging away. Part of the reason was Scandinavian in-fighting, and that in part came from traditional regional hostilities; part of the recession was due to Christian influence and dampening of bloody vandalism; part was the result of increasing efficiency of English government.

After Cnut's death the Scandinavian Ascendancy went into decline. There were two main revival attempts before the end of the 11th century: the invasion of England by Harald Hardrada in 1066 and the island campaign of Magnus Bareleg in 1098. The first of these was a disastrous failure for Norway. The second event affirmed Norse suzerainty over the island colonies and may have helped that sector of ascendancy to last until the 13th century.

In our use of the word, "ascendancy" means a power to intervene and control political affairs. That it was intermittent simply places Scandinavian power in the same class with most of its medieval contemporaries. That it was effective in some degree, in spite of illiteracy and irreligion should make it even more notable. That it "disappeared" in the 11th century is superficially correct. We need to look beneath that surface and try to assess the ascendancy and its several contributions to life in the archipelago.

It will suffice to divide the ascendancy contributions in broad terms of settlement and government. These fit the types of evidence, all of it imperfect. From place-names, other language evidence and contemporary comments, we can reconstruct the outlines of Scandinavian settlements-- farms and trade centers. We know they existed but we can only guess their date of origin, their size and their relative significance. Even so, the penetration of the Scandinavian element was an extremely influential socio- political factor in the archipelago.

Linguists have demonstrated that there was an affinity between Old English and Old Norse, the spoken tongue of vikings across Scandinavia. This was possibly enough to make communication fairly easy and it may be the reason for substantial entry of words of Norse origin into modern English. On the other hand, the absence of written Norse meant that the immigrants would retain the language of their new church and government. Latin and Anglo-Saxon usage had to continue, and the Dane had little choice but to adapt.

The relationship was decidedly different in Celtic areas. There language differences were so substantial that no easy assimilation was possible. The Northern Isles became predominantly Norse in speech and custom, it being fairly easy to envelope a small native population. On the other hand, in Ireland a large and complex society could only be trimmed with foreign- language enclaves. The same was true along the coast of Wales, while in both a gradual process of interchange went on over a long period. In northwest England (Cumbria) there was another variation as Hiberno-Norse immigrants entered what was mainly a British area in the ninth and tenth centuries.

Unfortunately these areas of settlement preserved only a few scraps of the immigrant language in runes (carved stones), charters, and personal and place names. In the Danelaw we find better evidence of the migration of words--often of very ordinary use--into the common language, e.g. window, knife, husband, fellow, sister. This wordplay is ultimately frustrating to the historian, for there is no way to measure the impact of words and names to arrive at an index of Scandinavian influence. Perhaps it is just as well, as we may be looking for the wrong thing. Immigration meant some degree of assimilation on all sides--a hybrid culture can never be exactly analyzed, and it remains to be shown that such analysis can add very much to our understanding of political history.

The period brought very substantial changes ancillary to settlement, particularly in trade. Recent writers have emphasized the link between the trader and the pirate, and the viking has been plausibly represented as both. Logic would suggest that gold and silver inspired craftsmen and moneyers, ships sustained the movement of goods as well as men and treasure, and finally, if our chronicles are anywhere near truth, the raiding parties were only employed for something like two or three months out of the year. Even when we deduct for an exaggerated number of vessels engaged in raids, there would still be large numbers which could be used for purposes other than attacking monasteries. Recent excavations in both York and Dublin (in the 1970s) have given new evidence to support the image of the viking as a commercial colonial influence.

Coinage has provided excellent evidence for some phases of the ascendancy. Much of the vikings' loot was probably melted down, some may have been minted, but coins found in viking hoards usually have been of alien origin. Some early issues of coin have been found from the kingdom of York and from Dublin. Of course the treasure hoards display the wide range of sources. Some very large quantities have been found which can be associated with the Danegelds of the early 11th century. One of the most interesting hoards was the largest in the archipelago, found near Cuerdale, Lancashire. This was apparently buried in the period around the early expulsion from Dublin, either by migrating exiles or local merchants (c. 902). The large quantity of silver (88 pounds) makes it "four times larger than any other viking hoard from Britain or Scandinavia." [8] Among the articles in it are 7,000 silver Frankish coins. Here as in all such finds, we may have evidence of "safe-keeping," though burial seems the crudest possible method. There were evidently important consequences and complications for trade as a result of viking activity.

The questions relating to settlement also bear on government. Here again the archipelago displayed interesting and important variations. We see

---

[8] James Graham-Campbell and Dafydd Kidd, *The Vikings* (1980), p. 34.

a fascinating pattern of assimilation and separation during the Scandinavian ascendancy when we look at the outlines of government, at laws and at institutions.

To people of the early medieval archipelago, government was not an abstraction, it was the personal performance of the king, supported by powerful members of the kin or tribe, sometimes affirmed in the assembly of community members: the Saxon folk moot, the Scandinavian *thing*, or the Celtic *airecht*. We have to resist the temptation to see these as prototypes of legislative bodies. Such meetings were a practical necessity in an age of oral communication. The embodiment of the tribe or folk might serve a judicial function or provide ceremonial or political affirmation of the power of the leader. There were exceptional cases, such as the Norse community in Iceland from the late ninth century which was managed on the model of an autonomous republic (until its submission to Norse kings in the 13th century).

The original units of personal power had been very small. There was a differential rate of expansion of these units between Celt, Saxon and Scandinavian, one which we can probably never reconstruct fully. It seems clear that the viking period was one in which growth was being forced to accelerate in most areas. The kingship of Edward the Confessor (1042-66) was fortified by two centuries of Scandinavian pressure; the Irish high kingship, much slower to develop, was more of a reality by 1052 when the Norse king was expelled from Dublin; the more direct Scandinavian influence was seen in the Irish Sea area under a ruler like Thorfinn the Mighty, or Magnus Bareleg at the end of the 11th century. While the scope of government grew, it did not lose its personal nature, and it also adhered to broadly common legal features.

One reason that the Scandinavian Ascendancy has been relatively unnoticed is that its impact on the law and legal systems in the archipelago was ambiguous. The so-called "re-conquest" of the Danelaw is symptomatic. The Anglo-Saxon appeared to absorb successive assaults from Alfred to Cnut (and on to William)--while the law codes, the courts and the lawmen remained unshaken. Before we rush to worship the innate Saxon legal genius or reject the barbarians from the North, we must remember that basic legal principles were broadly similar in Celtic, Saxon and Scandinavian societies; lords everywhere had a vested interest in promoting and securing lawful behavior; and the most provocative innovator on the scene was the Christian Church--recording, learning, teaching, condemning. In all of the three basic modes of Scandinavian legal impact in the archipelago, there was little which upset these elements of continuity. Those modes of contact ranged from the importation of a full-fledged Norse system as in Shetland or Man, to the co-existence most evident in the Danelaw, where a third of England was governed by imported laws under domestic license; to Cnut's appropriation of the collected Anglo-Saxon laws, re-issued under Scandinavian authority.

The principles of early archipelago legal systems were less obvious to contemporaries than to historians; that is, we know of no examples of theoretical exposition; we have only the scattered codes (or fragments), plus charters, writs and some other instruments used in the legal process. Still it is possible to deduce the central ideas which were present in the laws and other documents. The first principle was that custom was the ultimate authority. This was reflected in various forms of 'ancestor-worship,' reverence for old practices. The idea of modern legislation was anathema. This helps to explain the wisdom (or necessity?) of Cnut's code of old Saxon laws.

The status of the individual was a second central feature of the laws: free and unfree, lord and client, and degrees of nobility were some of the gradations recognized in the laws. Aside from a welter of different proper names for various grades or ranks, the social orders were not very different-- and they were not affected in a serious or fundamental way during the ascendancy.

Intersecting the status scale was the line of identity and authority attached to the kin. Groups of kin remained in the center of all systems of law: vital issues such as inheritance and compensation were assessed in the context of kinship. The difference becoming noticeable between Ireland and Wessex, for instance, was due to more rapid penetration of lordship authority (at the expense of kin), that is, what we would call more "advanced" institutions of government.

A fourth principle common to all systems was some form of surety or sanction: oath-helpers or hostages were a personal guarantee for a personalized system of law. The Scandinavian immigrants did not alter this basic feature either.

Moving from principles to practice, laws were the tools of lordship, and the real revolution of the ascendancy period was the elevation of English royal lordship. All lords were concerned with lawful behavior; so far as the lord could assume authority or jurisdiction over an *area*, he might enhance his wealth, power and prestige. Often he had to do this at the expense of the kindred. The 'territorial imperative' was a critical step in legal evolution. It was also a step which was elementary in a *colonial* setting (either in the fashion of Shetland, or the Danelaw, or Cnut's Code). The king's laws were first promulgated for petty kingdoms and slowly broadened across England. The courts in which cases were heard were those of former folk or area jurisdiction (cantred, hundred, shire or wapentake). We cannot detect a 'national' system at this stage, but the process of expanding jurisdiction was clearly underway. The royal legal power received by Cnut was far greater than that of Offa or Egbert. Cnut had the additional advantage of being a conqueror whose domain was already heavily settled by kinsmen.

Cnut's aide in the law-drafting process was probably Archbishop Wulfstan. That prelate had drafted the laws of AEthelred, and he may have provided Cnut with the same service. This was but one of many examples of the Church's involvement; her contribution was more significant than that of any political force. The church brought literacy and learning to the legal process, and in so doing, fundamentally transformed it.

The most obvious contribution of the church was in the writing of laws. As early as the fifth or sixth century Irish canons were being transcribed; in the seventh and eighth century the Irish secular laws were committed to writing and at the same time, the earliest Anglo-Saxon dooms were being recorded. Most of these documents actually survive from later copies, made during a prolific period of documentary transcription in the 11th and 12th centuries. At that time, the earliest Norwegian laws (composed around 1100) were written, and copies were made of the ancient Icelandic Laws. Clerical scribes once again put historians in their debt. Very few written Scandinavian laws survive; some of them were altered; many more were either destroyed or not copied. What is pertinent here is that the conversion of the Scandinavians was much too late (c. 1000) to provide a good, contemporary body of legal writing to set alongside that of the Irish tracts, the Saxon dooms and the Welsh lawbooks.

The Scandinavian ascendancy did not end abruptly with the death of Cnut, nor immediately upon the deaths of his two successors. The Scandinavian rulers in this period actually seemed to become more conscious of their roles as imperial sovereigns, or at least they tried to hold and extend their influence in and around the archipelago.

King Magnus Olafsson succeeded Cnut on the Norwegian throne in 1035. By treaty with Harthacnut, Magnus took the Danish throne in 1042, and he was ready to assert his claim to the English throne with an invasion fleet when he died. Magnus was succeeded by his uncle, Harald Hardrada, who intended to force the claim to the English throne. He may have been involved with some raiding expeditions, but we know that Harald led a major invasion in 1066. He took an estimated 300 ships and 9,000 men and sailed along the east coast, entered the Humber estuary, and marched toward York. In his company were the earl of Orkney and the exiled brother of King Harold of England. The invaders took York, then withdrew a short distance from the city where they were encountered by the English forces and badly beaten at Stamford Bridge. Harald Hardrada was killed, and his son Olaf was allowed to leave, with only two dozen ships. This marked the last of the viking invasions of England. A fleet did land several years later during a rebellion in the North, but the attackers were bought off. Another fleet was prepared in 1085, and when the Danish king was murdered, that threat disappeared.

There were still further ventures in the Irish Sea area. The most notable was a series of expeditions led by Magnus Bareleg, King of Norway. In 1098 he killed the earl of Shrewsbury in a battle in Anglesey, setting back the Norman advance in North Wales. Magnus installed his son in power in the Orkneys, and he asserted his authority over the Isle of Man and the western isles. Magnus made a treaty with King Edgar of Scotland (1097-1107) settling the island realms for the time being. The expedition of Magnus in 1098 is the last occasion which we might reasonably link to the viking age, though in fact that pattern had been out of date since the tenth century. Since then, attacks were decidedly more professional and more political. "Monarchs had taken over the business of war" and had put vikings out of business by asserting the traditional prerogative of battlefield leadership.[9]

---

[9]Gwyn Jones, *A History of the Vikings* (1968), p. 392.

Thus the last century of expeditions was more purposeful, if not more successful.

The Saxon restoration in 1042 saw the son of AEthelred brought to the English throne. This was only remarkable if one thought that the Danish royal family had somehow secured permanent possession of the crown. And a glance at Scandinavian politics would correct that notion. The plain fact of three royal deaths within seven years meant that a dynastic shift was probable. By all standards of inheritance then current, Edward was the likely heir. He was fortunate to have been spared the fate of his brother Alfred, who came to England after Cnut's death, was captured, blinded, and died of his injuries. There were rumors that Earl Godwin of Wessex was responsible; in any case, Edward was brought over from Normandy, and kept in King Harthacnut's court. On the kings' death, Edward was quickly endorsed by the *witan*.

It was not at all clear to leading Saxon noblemen that Edward represented their restoration. Godwin was a leader of a sizeable faction which portrayed Edward as the tool of Norman advisers. Godwin and his sons held large territories, his daughter was married to Edward, and thus there was a potential claim to the throne. Godwin took it a little too far in 1051 when he mustered an army against Edward and was forced into exile. He returned in 1052, faced the charges against him and was reinstated. In the interval, it was rumored that Edward had been visited by the duke of Normandy and had made a promise of the royal succession--a promise which cast a shadow over Godwin's house. In 1053, Harold Godwinson became the leading earl in England on his father's death. In 1055, his brother Tostig was made earl of Northumbria, and the family's power grew. Harold helped to ward off an attack from a Norse-Welsh alliance in 1058, and in 1063 he led a successful invasion of Wales, defeating the most important Welsh prince, Gruffydd ap Llywelyn. Thus Harold had every reason (except heredity) to succeed the childless Edward when he died. At the bedside of the dying king, Harold was told that he should succeed. That directive was accepted by the *witan*, and Harold was consecrated at Westminster the following day (January 6, 1066).

The 30 years since the death of Cnut saw a marked shift of power within the archipelago. Where once there had been a potential Scandinavian empire, there were now signs of resurgent native powers. The Norse expulsion from

Ireland (1052) testified to the growing authority of the high-kings. The Welsh princes had made temporary effective alliances with Norsemen and there were some indications of potential for political unity. The Scots under Malcolm Canmore (1058-97) and the islanders under Thorfinn (d. 1064) were building effective power centers. There was necessarily a compensating loss of central (imperial) power, or the possibility for it. That fact has been obscured by the power and swiftness of the Norman entry in 1066. But as the viking era closed, the several sectors of the archipelago were showing signs of growing autonomy.

Even though a temporary Danish unity was brought to England in the 11th century, the chance for a full-fledged Scandinavian hegemony was severely limited by the political instability of the northern kingdoms. The power of the northern invaders came and went, leaving behind a fragmented political scene. Historians who regard "Anglo-Saxon England" as a steadily uniting entity from 450 to 1066 must imagine a certain continuity between Arthur, Alfred, AEthelred and Edward. This is only possible if we artificially focus on England and ignore the archipelago, for when we study the totality, we find a wide range of rulers sharing the experience of viking assault.

The new heathens and their converted descendants were buccaneers initially, like their Saxon forerunners. Both groups later settled, made social and political establishments, and were partly assimilated and partly segregated in archipelago society. One historian has described the viking impact as:[10]

> ...the significant Danish contribution to the making of the English people, and the infusion of Danish and Norwegian blood, thought and practice into the whole of the British Isles and much of the Western Europe. There was the important viking contribution to European trade, and the equally important religious, artistic, mercantile and institutional borrowings from Europe, which ensured the northward expansion of the bounds of Christian European civilisation. Finally, there was the clear demonstration that because of dissension at home, the superior resources of their neighbors, an inability to evolve an exportable political and social system, and above all a lack of manpower, no Scandinavian king in Viking times would achieve a durable empire held together by the North Sea and the Baltic , or even a purely Scandinavian hegemony.

---

[10]ibid., p. 13.

The 'exportable political and social system' which came after 1066 was a marked improvement on what the Norwegians took with them into Normandy in 911. It would supply a number of the deficiencies of earlier viking attempts to rule, indeed it would be the basis for a Norman hegemony.

NORMAN AND ANGEVIN

COLONISTS

ULSTER

Newcastle

LEINSTER

York
Fulford
Stamford
Bridge
Humber

Chester

Lincoln

Waterford

Aberdovey

Montgomery
Shrewsbury

Cambridge

Fishguard
St. David's

Haverfordwest

Hereford

Evesham

Woodstock

Pembroke

Canterbury

Damme

Bruges

Clarendon

Hastings
Lewes

FLANDERS

Bouvines

NORMANDY

BLOIS

BRITTANY

ANJOU
TOURAINE

POITOU Mirebeau

AQUITAINE

CHAPTER 3

NORMAN AND ANGEVIN COLONISTS

> ...from the time of the marriage of Emma, the sister of Duke Richard II, to Aethelred king of the English, the relationship began to take the form of an aristocratic penetration of England; and this, after Duke William's conquest of the kingdom, became an overwhelming aristocratic and ecclesiastical colonization. From England, colonization spread to Scotland and conquest and colonization into Wales; and overlordship was strengthened and even extended in northern France. In the early twelfth century there must have seemed to be no limit to the lands which the Norman kings and their barons might not dominate in one way or another.
>
> (John Le Patourel, *The Norman Empire*, 1976, p. 319)

The best-known colonial conquest in archipelago history occurred in 1066. There has been endless debate over the relative Saxon and Norman shares in the resulting English regime. Much less notice has been taken of the variable rates of Norman penetration in the archipelago. England was most quickly and completely subjugated and feudalized, but elsewhere the conquest was slow and ambiguous: delayed by a century in Ireland, imported by aristocrats into Scotland, and confined to garrisons in Wales. In the widest sense, the Norman impact was clear. The conquest shifted the archipelago out of the Scandinavian and into the French orbit, where the chief strategic orientation remained for the next four centuries.

We can only speak of a Norman "empire" in the 11th century sense of overlordship, not fixed imperial rule. Yet there were unmistakable marks of Norman and Angevin "colonies"--feudal tenures, ecclesiastical baronies, castle communities. Anglo-Norman landowners, clerics and merchants knew there was a new regime, as did the native inhabitants of the archipelago. It was visible in the mobile royal enterprise on both sides of the channel.

The Norman Conquest has been called the last successful foreign invasion of England. There may be some value in recognizing that a strong invader helped to stem the tide of further invasions. But 1066 was merely the beginning of the end, and its consequences were not as dramatically successful as the last invasion thesis suggests. Many further invasions were launched, at least half a dozen by Danes and Norwegians in the last third of the 11th century alone. Over the next four centuries, three English usurpers successfully invaded their realm, and others tried and failed, beginning with the sons of the Conqueror. Also, there were countless skirmishes and episodes in which the borders within the archipelago were violated with some regularity. It is correct that no more Cnuts or Williams came to colonize; but we must not mistake that as a sign that the colonial period was over.

The 12th and 13th centuries were the scene of remarkable political developments: in the 12th, the Norman inheritance collapsed, and after 20 years of anarchy the patrimony was reconstructed and expanded by Henry II. His aim was to rebuild a strong English monarchy as part of an ambitious cross-Channel federation. The English crown, with its federal connections, was to be strengthened by expanding legal and ecclesiastical authority and by extending power in the archipelago.

But as the 13th century began, King John, Henry's youngest son, met challenges in every quarter, and the Angevin federation started to fall apart. As it did, there were important political and constitutional changes inside English and archipelago government, changes which resulted in much stronger royal power in a constitution with a broadened base in the community. By the end of the 13th century, the political power in the Atlantic Archipelago was strong enough to resist outside interference. This allowed the dominant kingdom in the archipelago to try out its own imperial strategy.

Norman Hegemony

The Norman Conquest was a dramatic and decisive event. The new French regime changed the geopolitics of a large fraction of the archipelago. Yet the aggressive new feudal superiors had no plan of empire to match their efficient lordship. So the cross-channel government made problems as rapidly as it made progress. Failing to solve its central problem of royal succession, the Norman hegemony degenerated into civil war 70 years after William's great victory. However, the new orientation was strong enough to allow a great-grandson of the Conqueror to restore a French-based regime after two decades of fighting.

The Normans as a "race" have fascinated historians. The area which became Normandy was occupied by Norwegians in the tenth century. They intermarried with Frankish natives and were content to call themselves "French" by the 11th century. However, Norman writers cherished their special identity, as wide-ranging military exploits took their leaders as far as Sicily and Jerusalem. The growing Norman rivalry with the Capetian kings of France probably enhanced the Norman interest in the archipelago long before 1066. We have already noted the treaty between Duke Richard I and AEthelred (991), the marriage of the duke's daughter Emma to the Saxon king (1002) and the exile of that king and his sons, as well as the marriage of Emma to Cnut (1017). These connections fostered additional ties in personnel, in trade and in government. When Emma's son Edward the Confessor returned to England, he brought Norman royal advisers. The latter were the pretext for rebellion by Saxon earls in the 1050s, indicating some fear of outside influence. That influence, while noticeable, was certainly not as great as one of the Norman chroniclers thought: Dudo of St. Quentin said that the Norman duke[1]

> rules and governs the Bretons and the Normans, threatens and devastates the Flemish, wins over and allies with the Danes, the Lotharingians and even the Saxons. The English also are obediently subject to him, and the Scots and Irish are ruled under his protection.

It is not hard to discredit such statements, since they were written sometime during the reign of King Cnut. The interesting fact is that such excessive ambitions were welcome fare for the Norman dukes at an early date. William of Normandy was a most unlikely conqueror of anything when he came into his father's inheritance. It was the year of Cnut's death, William was eight years old and illegitimate. Royal and baronial neighbors expected to take advantage of the Norman heir, and it was not until 1047 that William's hold on his duchy was secure.

During the Godwin crisis (1051-2) it is possible that William visited England and was given some sign of royal favor regarding the succession-- these events seem to be best known among Norman chroniclers. By 1060,

---

[1]Cited in R.H.C. Davis, *The Normans and their Myth* (1976), p. 62.

William had more concrete assets: his father-in-law, the count of Flanders, became regent of the king of France; his arch-enemy, the count of Anjou died, triggering a civil war. William capitalized on the turmoil and took control of the county of Maine and the duchy of Brittany. Thus William was building a powerful position for himself. Few rivals would distract him from a campaign in the archipelago and he could expect to enlist a number of feudal and mercenary allies to join him in such an enterprise. A most unlikely ally was also credited to William by the chronicles. Harold of Wessex, Godwin's heir and Edward's most powerful subject, reportedly was forced ashore in Flanders, taken to William's court, and persuaded to swear his support for William's claim to the English throne. Whether or not this was true, when Harold witnessed the old king's death, he made sure of his own succession. Harold's coronation the next day was prompt, speed being dictated by several political circumstances: there was a living male heir (Edgar "the Atheling", grandson of Edmund Ironside); there was an outstanding claim on the throne by both the king of Norway and the king of Denmark; and there was a state of open rebellion by Harold's brother Tostig, who had been driven into exile (1065). Thus there were many pressures on the new king, even without the threat from Normandy.

In fact, invasions were hardly unknown to the archipelago in the years before the Norman enterprise. There had been a series of attacks over the two decades before 1066. Some were raids by earls who had been exiled (Godwin, 1051; AElfgar, 1055 and 1058; Tostig, 1065). Other attacks were more dangerous. A combined Welsh-Norse assault in 1058 was successful enough to provoke a major campaign under Harold in 1063 to break the Welsh threat. Meanwhile, Malcolm of Scotland had invaded the North in 1061, as he was to do several more times, attempting to extend his power over border regions in Northumbria. Tostig was leading raids with Flemish allies, on the Isle of Wight and the east coast, in early 1066. But the most serious threat in the north was the invasion in 1066 by Harald Hardrada.

King Harald of Norway invaded, with the support of Tostig, in early September. He defeated the forces of the northern earls at Fulford on September 20th. When the Norse king entered York, the leaders there surrendered and agreed to march south under his command. But Harold of England arrived near York on the 24th and attacked the invaders, defeating them at Stamford Bridge. The chronicles report heavy casualties and the deaths of the Norse king and Tostig. But what should have been a decisive victory for the English king was soon overshadowed by the news of a Norman landing in the South.

William's preparations had gone on most of the Summer, and Harold had mobilized his forces to oppose an assault. However, the long wait and the northern landing had forced the king to break up his defensive positions. Near the mouth of the Somme, William gathered his forces--waiting for some six weeks for a favorable breeze. There were about 7,000 men and 600 or more vessels, according to modern estimates. In his force, William had about 3,000 mounted knights, not strictly a "Norman" force, but a polyglot assembly of adventurers from many districts on the continent. William also carried a ring and banner from the pope. The crossing concluded with a successful landing in Sussex at the end of September.

Harold was in York when he learned of the invasion. He made a forced march of astonishing speed to London, where he called out the Sussex *fyrd* (militia) which joined his household troops, putting in the field a number close to that of the invaders, but far less powerful than the force Harold might have assembled given more time. The Saxons confronted the Norman force at Hastings on October 14th, and in an all-day battle the Normans heavily defeated the defenders, killing Harold and many other Saxon nobles. In the immediate aftermath, William had to secure his position. The conquest had just begun.

In November and December, William marched up the Thames and circled London, inflicting heavy damage. He succeeded in frightening the remaining leaders into submission, and on Christmas Day he assumed the English crown. To the casual observer that might seem the climax of the conquest, but William knew his power was barely effective within the bounds of the old Wessex kingdom to say nothing of the western and northern regions. Moreover, the new king still had to govern in his ancestral domain, to which he soon returned. William departed for Normandy in March 1067, leaving a select group of barons in charge and taking an important collection of hostages with him. He spent the rest of the year in Normandy, attending to the affairs of the duchy.

Government in the early Norman colonial period took over existing Anglo-Saxon machinery and used many of the old officials. Such a policy was reliable as long as there was a general acceptance of Norman colonial authority. Some minor rebellions in 1067 and 1068 indicated that the regime was not secure, and more serious trouble began in 1069. William's earl of Northumbria was killed and revolt flared up in Mercia and Wessex as a Danish fleet appeared in the Humber estuary. William defeated the Mercians, bribed the Danes to withdraw and recaptured the castle at York. Then during the winter of 1069-70, William directed a brutal campaign of destruction across Northumbria and into the northern parts of Mercia. The king's power was virtually unchallenged, and only a pathetic rebel group on the island of Ely held out. The Danes who were expected to aid them were again bought off by William, and the rebels dispersed. The crushing of the northern rebellion marked the end of the English conquest. A few later revolts did not materially affect the strong royal position, to which was soon added the establishment of the Welsh marcher lordships and a settlement with the king of Scots. By about 1075 it might be said that the enterprise begun a decade earlier was virtually complete. In the remaining twelve years of his reign William faced other rebellions, but no more serious resistance from his English subjects. After 1075, his task was largely one of settling the complex colony which he had created.

To put the Norman conquest and the subsequent colonial government in proper perspective, we have to trace the perimeter and then take a closer look at Norman government within its boundaries. The general policy of the Norman king seemed to be to fortify the boundaries of the old English state and to forego the costly and unprofitable business of conquering the archipelago completely. In Wales this policy was not hard to implement, since Harold of Wessex had already subdued Gruffydd ap Llywleyn (1063) and broken the general resistance of the Welsh. However, their scattered population and rugged terrain meant that no further subjection was realized. Instead William created several major border provinces. These "marcher lordships" were extensive and relatively wealthy landholdings, and the earls of Hereford (1067), Chester (1071) and Shrewsbury (1075) were chosen from William's close companions. A marcher lord was given quasi-regal power (justice and taxation) as his reward for providing border security. Of course an ambitious lord sought more than security in the expansion of his domain at the expense of the native princes. A careless lord would overstep his authority, as did the rebel earl of Hereford in 1075. He was imprisoned for life, and the earldom stood vacant; meanwhile a native prince (Rhys ap Tewdwr) became William's feudal representative in South Wales.

In 1066 Scotland had an independent kingdom which was a shaky coalition of four major political-cultural areas: the northwest and the islands were Norse and Irish; the southwest (Strathclyde and Cumbria) was British, Irish and Norse; the southeast (Lothian) was part of the old Anglian kingdom of Northumbria; and the heart of the kingdom was Scotia, or the land north of the Firth of Forth, a combination of Pictish and Irish settlement. In 1058 Malcolm III brought some unity to the kingdom. His father had ruled Cumbria, his first wife was the daughter of the Norse ruler of Orkney, and previously Malcolm had an alliance with the earl of (English) Northumbria. Malcolm himself was inclined to become an ally of Anglo-Saxon England: he spent years in exile at the court of Edward the Confessor; in 1067 the Scottish court received the exiled Edgar the Atheling, and in 1070 Malcolm married the Atheling's sister Margaret. That marriage produced six sons and brought the influence of a strong and devout English queen into Scottish affairs. Still, Malcolm's favorite pastime seemed to be the invasion of northern English lands, in the course of which he caused considerable damage and realized almost no political gain. During the years of William's conquest, when Malcolm might have capitalized on English disaffection, and when there was a steady stream of exiles coming from the south, Malcolm's policy showed little change. In 1072, William the Conqueror led an expedition into Scotland, and Malcolm prudently made himself William's vassal, gave his eldest son Duncan as a hostage to the Norman, and forced the Atheling to leave Scotland. This settlement, coupled with the earlier devastation of northern England, gave William a safe zone on his northern frontier, though after the conqueror's death, the pattern of Scottish invasion and English intervention resumed.

As is quite clear by this point, the Norman Conquest was far from complete when one sees it in the archipelago context. The exact dimensions were not designed by William, but were the product of his limited aims and native resistance. The areas unconquered were those in which William had no interest or those where he had no power. There is no evidence that William's aims were different from those of the Romans or the Danes, that is, he was attracted to the areas of the greatest or most easily seized wealth. He probably had good sources of intelligence due to the long Anglo-Norman connection. On the other hand, there was no reason for William to conquer Ireland or the outer islands, nor for him to be too concerned with total conquest in rugged Wales, remote Cornwall or Cumbria. These areas, whether marches or autonomous regions, might shelter his enemies. William had to be content with drawing clear and powerful boundaries. When he constructed the "New Castle" on the Tyne (1080) and when he made his expedition to St. David's (1081) he may have been marking the limits of the conquest, leaving further expansion for others. There was no need for him to conquer the whole archipelago.

A weighty factor in William's policy was that his prime concern was with the duchy of Normandy. The modern observer sees him as preeminently the king of England, but William saw English estates as a lucrative annexation to his Norman patrimony. Surely the new holding brought him the prestige of royalty and its attendant wealth. Yet it is unlikely that he regarded the new crown as fundamentally more important than his ducal title. In fact, the formulation may not have occurred to him: the Norman lands and lordships, augmented as they were in 1066-1072, were an extension of the original lordship, as were William's successive extensions on the Norman frontiers; and it was an extension which was presaged by the early 11th century Norman links and William's own presumed "right" to the English throne.

One puzzle of the Norman era is that a fully-developed "empire" did not appear. The colonies in the archipelago, however closely linked with Norman personnel, retained most of their autonomy even as they were thoroughly penetrated by colonizing of their land, church and trade. To understand the apparent failure, we have to look at the entry of feudalism, the church's political role, the development of the legal system, the growth of administration, and most of all, the matter of unstable royal succession.

In warfare, feudalism was one way to manage the integrated Norman strategy of mounted knights and fortified castles. It assured close personal ties between lords and the duke-king. William had thus a quick and effective means of paying for a standing army and providing for its supply. His network of castles was centrally-controlled and flexible. His army still had the customary *fyrd* and mercenary forces, made more formidable by the feudal core of mounted knights.

74

Politically, feudalism was secure at the top, but "open" at the bottom. It lent itself to multiplied lordships and overlapping of homage. For each vassal was apt to subdivide his property (and lordship) in order to provide for the necessary support to meet his obligations. Also, the feudal structure was a static form, around which the dynamic features of a changing society were in motion. Changing economic and political circumstances were bound to affect the essential framework. Finally, the feudal experience of the rest of the archipelago was unlike that of England. The only thorough application of the system was found in England, or so we are apt to deduce from sources such as the Domesday Book, compiled in 1086. In that year, William called all his English tenants "in chief" (his major vassals) to make oaths of homage to him as their supreme lord, but elsewhere the king did not have the same power (e.g. Cumbria, Gwynedd, Ireland) and only could impose a general lordship over the respective local rulers from time to time.

In other words, the king's feudal authority was significantly greater in southern England than in its remote parts or its neighboring provinces. Thus the conquest meant a notable increase in the differences between archipelago regions in terms of central political power. Moreover, the general setting prevented the feudal order from enjoying a long duration. As a leading authority has said: [2]

> Ironically, the conqueror's system of military tenures, seemingly a consummate expression of the feudal idea, was in fact compromised from the beginning by factors that would ultimately destroy it: a money economy, a strong [Saxon] monarchy with a long tradition of direct and general allegiance, a military situation [in the archipelago and Normandy] that favoured the use of mercenaries and a political condition [i.e. 'Norman empire'] in which Norman feudal vassals were often less dependable to the monarchy than native Englishmen.

The Norman Conquest came at a time of significant reform in the Christian Church. It is likely that some measure of change was in progress in the 11th century among both Norman and English clergy, if not Irish, Welsh or Scots. What is quite certain is that the conquest was followed by important reorganization and reform in England, and that change had major political implications.

---

[2] C. W. Hollister, *Military Organization of Norman England* (1965), p. 278.

Historians used to credit the Normans with a unique gift for ecclesiastical reform, but now emphasis is on new personnel and a new sense of royal power in the church. It took four years for William to remove Archbishop Stigand, through a properly-convened council under papal legates. The appointment of Stigand had been uncanonical, since he had usurped the place of the Norman bishop Robert of Jumièges. This was why the Norman expedition had been given papal sanction in 1066. Several other bishops were removed, and William was able to substantially change the hierarchy: it is not likely that his appointments as a whole were superior to those of the Anglo-Saxons, but his archbishop of Canterbury was an exceptional individual. Lanfranc was an Italian trained in law who became a Benedictine monk. He had been an abbot of one of William's monasteries prior to his consecration in 1070. Within two years a church council adopted his proposal establishing the supremacy of archbishop of Canterbury. He was given jurisdiction over the dioceses of England (south of Trent) and Wales, while the archbishop of York was made superior over northern English and Scottish dioceses. Although the latter provision never was fully implemented, there was a better definition of power within the church, and William's authoritarian policy was to be aided by the decision. There was more reorganization and relocation of bishops and cathedrals, the church was ordered to establish a separate system of courts and there was some integration of the hierarchy into William's feudal structure. In all, the church after the conquest was plainly a more organized and politicized body in England. In Scotland there is some testimony to a revived royal influence, partly through the piety of Queen Margaret (1070-1093). The Welsh and Irish churches evidently continued to function under the influence of local propertied families, as had been their tradition. In a sense this also meant a politicized church, though not a centralized one.

The task of governing the archipelago after the conquest made it wise to assess and restate the law. William apparently intended to maintain the bulk of Anglo-Saxon law and practice which he found in England, but we have no certain evidence of his attitude toward the Celtic legal systems. In general, his views were pragmatic. It was simpler to administer a familiar native code (with some addenda for French aristocrats) than to import a new structure for the whole society. And yet a novel structure was imported in the feudal tenures of the tenants in chief. Moreover, the operation of that system had a major role in the eventual development of the "common law." The Normans found an operating set of hundred and shire courts, where earls and sheriffs had presided over local affairs under rough royal supervision. The newcomers were anxious to preserve this type of system. Indeed, it was so valuable that some of the Norman lords treated the courts as their own property, and in the 12th century the crown was going to need a major campaign to recover judicial authority. This was one root of "common" law, the other was the traditional idea of the "king's peace," which antedated the conquest. The notion that crimes committed in the vicinity of the king were more serious was stated in early law codes; that idea was literally moved about by the itinerant form of early government (and much later by the itinerant royal justices). The concept of "the king's peace" was thus slowly enlarged to comprehend the king's dominions.

The king's administration, as we would call it, was handled by a small coterie of reliable officials and principal tenants. There were two facets to the core of government: the *curia regis,* or the formal body of the king's trusted advisers; and the royal household, or those close to the king who served him in the many capacities required (treasurer, chaplain, constable, chamberlain, etc.). The Norman kings and their predecessors followed an itinerant pattern of government. The king was apt to spend most of his time moving from one part of the realm to another: stopping periodically with some important tenant, keeping in touch with affairs in all parts of the realm, perhaps keeping order by a timely show of force, certainly hearing pleas and petitions before his "court." Given this itinerant method, and given the separate business of Norman, English, Breton and other communities, there had to be some innovation in Norman colonial government. As far as records indicate, or the creation of new officials suggests, the amount of change was slight. William and his sons used a deputy when they were not in residence (justiciar in England, *seneschal* in Normandy), but the creation of "imperial" treasurers, chamberlains, or episcopal sees was never contemplated (or so recorded).

The course of Anglo-Norman politics goes a long way toward explaining the constitutional void. At the core of the matter was the dispute over the royal succession. That was serious enough to cause periodic rupture of the "empire" and prevent the execution of any coherent imperial design. The conqueror himself governed his expanded domain much as he had constructed it in the first place. By travel and campaigns in the troubled

77

areas, he asserted his personal authority in his inimitable style. But William's heirs did not enjoy a peaceful succession. His eldest son Robert was rebelling at the time of the king's death, apparently because William refused to give him real control over some of his inheritance. The death-bed scene which several chroniclers describe fails to make the facts clear, and historians have conflicting ideas about traditional Norman succession practices. Whether the inheritance should have been intact or divided, we do not know; in fact it was divided, with Robert getting Normandy, William "Rufus" getting England, and the youngest, Henry, getting £5000. What is more, we know that none of the sons was satisfied, and they fought over the inheritance for the next 20 years. In 1100 Rufus died in a suspicious hunting accident and Henry seized the royal treasury and took the throne, making the unusual gesture of granting a coronation charter of assorted promises to his subjects.

Henry proceeded to restore the "empire" by defeating Robert in Normandy (Tinchebrai, 1106) and imprisoning him and disinheriting Robert's son. Henry held the crown and duchy jointly for 30 years. He advanced the consolidation of government in the archipelago, but he faced endemic border wars in Normandy until 1128. The reunion of the conqueror's dominions was significant, but the style of Norman "empire" was still an itinerant and personal one. Some early stages of judicial development and financial evolution (exchequer) were not turned toward combined rule, nor had they advanced very far before the major crisis at Henry's death, the "war of Norman succession." Henry had but one surviving legitimate son, and he died in 1120. The king forced his barons to support his daughter, Matilda (married later to Geoffrey of Anjou), but when Henry died in 1135, his nephew, Count Stephen of Blois, seized the royal treasury and had himself proclaimed King. Thus began the "interregnum" or the "anarchy"--a period of twenty years in which the rival claims to the throne were fought for indecisively. The Norman inheritance was emphatically shattered, and the pieces of the old patrimony would have to be reassembled by Matilda and Geoffrey's son, Henry of Anjou.

The warfare over the succession was not confined to the areas of Norman influence, for this breakdown had important side effects in other parts of the archipelago. King David of Scotland had invaded England as soon as the crisis began. He was rewarded with Stephen's recognition of

Scottish control over the northern counties, in exchange for the fealty of the Scottish heir, Prince Henry. Even when the Scots invaded again and were soundly beaten in 1138 at the "Battle of the Standard," the earlier concessions were not lost. Until Stephen died, the king of Scots enjoyed a long period of independence and influence in the North of England (which last was the basis for longstanding territorial claims on the part of Scottish successors). In Wales there was also a trend toward local independence, but one which was divided among a large number of native contenders. Overall, the interregnum saw a serious decline in Anglo-Norman royal influence.

In two decades of war and internal confusion, the feudal political system was badly crippled. The Norman "empire," such as it was, was completely dismembered. The count of Anjou seized Normandy; the king of Scotland seized three northern English counties; and Anglo-Norman barons pursued dangerously independent political courses. After 1145, there was little meaning in the term "Norman Empire," especially to the colonists who still influenced politics in the Atlantic Archipelago.

Angevin Federation

In the second half of the 12th century, Henry II acquired the lands and lordships of the Normans and added to them the Duchy of Aquitaine and the lordship of Ireland. This massive patrimony might have been governable, for Henry demonstrated remarkable capacities as a ruler. But historians were mistaken to label this as an "Angevin Empire." Contemporaries knew no such title, nor was one required in a world of feudal federations. The sons who were to be Henry's viceroys were even more restive than the sons of the conqueror, rebelling against their father and each other. What is more, only two sons outlived Henry, and the youngest managed to lose Normandy, Brittany, Anjou and Touraine (1202-06). Thereafter the crown's interests became naturally and visibly centered in the archipelago, where there was still some potential for federal development, at least until the crisis of John's reign (1212-15).

Henry was installed as duke of Normandy just before his 17th birthday in 1149. When his father died two years later, he became count of Anjou. The next year he married Eleanor of Aquitaine, lately separated from the king of France. The Angevin heir landed in England in 1153 to challenge his mother's rival Stephen of Blois. King Stephen tried unsuccessfully to bring Henry to a decisive battle, and when the king's son died in August, 1153, the pressure grew for a negotiated settlement. By November, parties had agreed to the Treaty of Winchester, whereby Henry was recognized as Stephen's heir, land holdings were to be restored to conditions c. 1135, and the "adulterine" castles (est. 1,200) built in the interim were to be destroyed. Stephen died a year later, and shortly Henry and Eleanor were crowned in Westminster Abbey. The Angevin dynasty would rule England for the next two and a half centuries; but the Angevin "empire" would not last half a century. We have to study Henry's manifold restoration, his plans for federation, and the forces and conditions which subverted his plans.

As he put it, Henry wanted to restore his power to its status in "the reign of King Henry my grandfather." In large measure, he met or exceeded that objective around the entire extent of the "empire." His achievement consisted of reasserting and extending his feudal lordships, amplifying royal legal power and asserting regal authority over the church hierarchy.

Henry attained the full ancestral rights to Normandy, the duchy now a more tightly-governed domain than it had been under his predecessors. His power in Anjou was similar, and his eventual control over Brittany was moving in the same direction. In Aquitaine, Henry's authority was limited. There the aristocrats, burghers and ecclesiastical lords maintained a large measure of autonomy. In the archipelago, Henry's kingdom of England was the power center, as was Normandy on the continent. Completing the urgent task of reducing unlicensed castles and expelling Flemish mercenaries, Henry set about a systematic review of his barons' terms of knight service. The results of this inquest were compiled in the Baronial Charters (*cartae baronum*) of 1166. The knights enfeoffed before 1135 and since were listed, indicating the service still owing to the crown. Thus Henry should have been in a good position to realize the full power of his feudal lordship. In addition, he saw to it that the old annual *hidage* (a tax based on size of holdings) was replaced by an irregular levy on incomes. Further, the king broadened the system of military assessment to the kingdom at large by his Assize of Arms (1181) which prescribed weapons and duties for men of all ranks.

The notable skill which Henry brought to governing was nowhere better illustrated than in his English legal reforms, which were vital to the origin of the common law. The courts of law (hundred and shire, baronial and ecclesiastical) had little royal supervision during the war of Norman succession. By temperament and by training, Henry was inclined to make improvements in legal administration. The royal exchequer was restored to its function as regular auditor of the sheriffs' accounts. Judges were sent to visit the shire courts (Assize of Clarendon, 1166). Special writs were devised to deal with disputes over property (petty assizes) and a process to prove the right of ownership in baronial courts was created (grand assize, 1179). The new procedures used juries to present criminals and to testify as to possession or ownership of property. Through these reforms, the crown established a popular and effective system of justice, and one with a fair amount of profit for the royal treasury.

The crown's influence in ecclesiastical courts was less easy to establish and the effort led to one of the great crises in Henry's reign. Church courts had enlarged their jurisdiction during the interregnum, and many cases heard in them were appealed to the papal curia without reference to the crown. Henry wanted to restore royal power in this sector too, and his appointment of Thomas Becket, a close companion and chancellor (1162) was meant to give the king a pliant accessory in this cause. However, the new primate showed a stubborn and independent character when confronted with the king's proposals (Constitutions of Clarendon, 1164). Henry called them "ancient customs" --the right of royal courts to decide in cases of clerical appointment (advowson), the right to hear all appeals, the right to sentence clerks found guilty of felony in the church courts, and other provisions. In the dispute which followed, Becket fled into exile. When the king ordered the coronation of his eldest son Henry in 1170, the archbishop of York officiated in Becket's absence. This affront to his rank was among the reasons why Becket returned to England late in the year. On his arrival he excommunicated those who had conducted the disputed ceremony. In December, a group of Henry's knights went to Canterbury and murdered the archbishop in his cathedral. The outrage forced the king to do penance (including a public whipping and provisions for new royal monastic foundations). Henry was forced to allow appeals to Rome, but otherwise he eventually secured the "ancient customs" in much the form that they had been proposed.

Henry's larger domains posed a greater and more complex political problem than any of his ancestors faced. One historian reminds us that he was "more of a Norman than an Englishman and as much an Angevin as either."[3] Others point out that the "empire" was "a great congeries ruled by French knights and French clergy who, though living under different lords, were linked together by innumerable ties of blood and marriage, education, ecclesiastical offices, homage and fealty."[4] The foremost biographer of Henry II has said that[5]

> The so-called 'Angevin Empire' was never in fact an empire: in Henry's developed conception it was a commonwealth of seven internally self-governing dominions, linked merely by dynastic ties and oath-takings: the inherited unit of England, Normandy and Anjou under [the king's] eldest son Henry, Aquitaine under Richard, Brittany under Geoffrey, Ireland under John, Welsh Wales (*pura Wallia*) under its native princes, Scotland under its native king and Toulouse under its hereditary count.

Such at least was the arrangement evolved by 1180. Was this or could it ever be a "federation?" Surely it could have been, within the terms of 12th century government. The king's patrimony made some of it a unity and his energy or activity could bring in the rest. Some of its lordships were feudal in the fullest sense, others were not. Yet the direction in which they would evolve under Henry's dominion was subject to current political events. Several of the highlights of the Angevin political story will illustrate the general problems of government which Henry and his federation faced.

In Wales, the Norman Conquest had imposed the divided regime of marcher lords and native rulers. The latter were periodically subdued by or affiliated to the English crown, but of course the interregnum severely disrupted these connections. Henry was eager to restore the ties. On one occasion he brought the Welsh princes and the king of Scotland to meet him (Woodstock, 1163). He tried to extract oaths of homage and fealty. The apparently innovative idea was resisted by the Welsh princes and a general rebellion followed. Henry collected a large army, including Scottish and

---

[3] Barrow, *Feudal Britain* , p. 163.

[4] H.G. Richardson and G.O. Sayles, *The Administration of Medieval Ireland, 1172-1377* (1963), p. 5.

[5] W.L. Warren, "The Interpretation of Twelfth-century Irish History," *Historical Studies* (Papers read before the Irish conference of Historians;), v. 7, ed. J.C. Beckett (1969), p. 16.

French contingents. When he marched into north Wales (1165), the enemy wisely avoided contact, and Henry had to withdraw. Hereafter, the royal policy mellowed, the king being content with looser forms of acknowledgment of his lordship. By 1177, the Welsh princes arrived at a settlement, confirming their allegiance to Henry. Even before this, the King had employed Welsh mercenaries (1168), and he had used Welsh support in putting down a rebellion in 1173. Henry had also given his endorsement to some Welsh involvement in Irish politics.

In that part of the archipelago, the high-kingship was coming to mean more than before, though a strong traditional element in Irish society still saw the king as but a part of a "triarchy" of military, religious and legal authorities. In one particular dispute, Dermot MacMurrough, king of Leinster, sought Henry's help in recovering his throne (1167). This unusual request was one which Henry could not at the moment oblige, but he authorized Dermot to recruit help in south Wales. A group of adventurers from assorted backgrounds (Welsh, Flemish and Norman) joined Dermot in his reconquest. A renegade noble, Richard de Clare (alias "Strongbow") took part in the expedition. For a year or two, a number of sorties by small but powerful invading parties seized portions of the southeast coast. When Dermot died in 1171, he bequeathed his title to Strongbow, although in Irish law the bequest was invalid. Henry had watched these events with growing concern, and he had ordered the conquerors to return and had sequestered Strongbow's estates in Wales. When these acts had no effect, Henry went to Ireland himself in October 1171. He captured coastal towns and forced the invaders to submit to him along with many native leaders. The natives took oaths of fealty, and the Anglo-Normans in Ireland were forced to acknowledge the king's feudal lordship.[6] This was not a conquest, nor was it the fulfillment of the curious papal bull "Laudabiliter" (1155) which called for English subjugation of the canonically unruly Irish. It might best be described as the establishment of an Angevin feudal "colony."

The Scottish throne stood in an altogether different posture. The Norman *rex Anglorum* had developed close personal and feudal ties, especially with King David (1124-53). The main issue between the crowns

---

[6]"Anglo-Norman" is a term with a tradition, but it is not accurate since the invaders were English, Welsh, Flemish and French.

was the disputed part of old Northumbria (the counties of Northumberland, Cumberland and Westmorland). David had been raised at the English court, and a number of Norman families had begun to migrate to Scotland in the middle of the 12th century, but when the anarchy occurred, the Scots tried to take advantage of the English crown's embarrassment.

David's grandson Malcolm took the throne at the age of 11 in 1153. The Scottish king was also the earl of Huntingdon, an English title which put him in a position similar to the English king's relation to the king of France. Malcolm and his brother William "the Lion" were no more obedient to their overlord than their English cousin was to his, and they eventually had to be subdued by force.

Henry did not elaborate a full-fledged plan of federation with an institutional and theoretical structure. The first indication of his plans came in 1169 at a conference with Louis VII at Montmirail. Henry made it clear that he planned to have Henry the Younger succeed him on the English throne (and in Normandy). A coronation in England was indeed held in 1170. Geoffrey was to become the duke of Brittany (where Henry had lately secured lordship). Richard was to be count of Poitou and duke of Aquitaine. During an illness in 1170, Henry drew up a will embodying these arrangements.

After his return from the Irish expedition, Henry was faced with a dispute within the family. In particular, Henry the Younger demanded grants of land to go with his titles, and his brothers Geoffrey and Richard joined him in seeking support from the French king. A council of French barons pledged to aid young Henry, and they were joined by the king of Scotland and a group of disaffected English earls. A series of conflicts in 1173-74 ended in victory for the English king. King William "the Lion" had invaded England and was captured. He and others were forced to make peace with Henry in the Treaty of Falaise (1175). William was especially humiliated, having to pay homage to Henry for his kingdom, and accepting English garrisons in five Scottish castles.

With his victory, Henry did not notably advance the stability of his federation. He did in fact pass more authority to his sons, but he could hardly satisfy their ambition in so doing. In 1177 he made his youngest (and landless) son John the "Lord of Ireland." By 1182, Henry was making another will, increasing the control given to his sons. Now there was a falling out between the young Henry and his brother Richard, which lay behind another family rebellion. The entire picture was shaken in 1183, when the "Young King" died, to be followed by Geoffrey in 1186. Such plans as Henry II had for a family federation--which plans were not marked for a long and happy career anyway--were forcibly altered into a compact inheritance. Richard was the natural heir, and John after him, of this "Commonwealth...of dynastic ties and oath-takings."

Was the Angevin federation then a total failure? Looking at the archipelago at the end of the Henry II's reign, reviewing what one author has called "the Lordship of the British Isles," we can see that the Angevin federation probably was everything that Henry expected it to be. We may expect him to have sought and created international and multinational institutions, however it would be anachronistic to do so. His image of government, and that of contemporaries, was bounded by tradition, by the sense of communal heritage. He was styled "King of the English," and "Duke of the Normans," that is, the peoples, not rigid areas, were units of lordship. And any overlord with sufficient power might become the prince of a given community. Surely the Norman and Angevin experiences proved that, just as they also proved that those communities might as easily be lost. The king of France in the 12th century was still dreaming of a Carolingian past; the king of England perhaps had Norman fantasies; neither had visions of the modern state, according to our evidence.

Therefore, we should not expect to find traces in the archipelago of some form of superstate. What we do find is the series of declarations of fealty, homage, or liege homage, by the king and barons of Scotland, the Welsh princes and marcher lords and the kings and high-kings of Ireland. It was the essence of such contractual loyalty that it could be renegotiated. The death of one party, the marriage of another, the intrigue of a third: all might lead to revision. Contractual relations did not simply run between the English crown and the several lordships: they might be found between other leaders and English or other vassals as well. Lordship was a political "marriage of convenience" unrestricted by modern constitutional inhibitions.

Of course any plan of Henry's reckoned on successful defense against the claims of the king of France. With the death of Louis in 1180, a new figure came on the scene in the person of Philip (later "Augustus"). His mission was to advance the frontiers of monarchic control by every means available; his resources were greater than those of his father, and his enemies were not as strong or determined as the young Henry of Anjou had been.

The successors of Henry II found strong opposition to the maintenance of the family federation. Richard I tried to distract the French king by undertaking a joint crusade (1190). But Philip returned after only a short time, while Richard was captured and held for ransom in Vienna. This enabled France to put pressure on both Normandy and Aquitaine, and even Prince John was dealing with Philip in anticipation of his own inheritance of the kingdom. But Richard was ransomed, returned, disciplined his brother, was recrowned (1194) and then went back to the struggle against Philip. When Richard died in 1199, he had spent only 6 months of his reign in England, though the government had apparently not suffered by his absence.

Within a few years of his accession, John lost Normandy and fell into a very serious domestic crisis and a feud with the Church. On the first point, John had a rival, his nephew Arthur of Brittany (son of Geoffrey). Arthur did homage to Philip of France and was in return regarded as the rightful Angevin heir. Philip declared John's holding of Normandy to be unlawful on grounds that the French king's permission had not been sought before John assumed control. John was forced to pay an enormous relief and give up some Norman lands. This did not satisfy Philip, who soon heard other charges against his vassal, and demanded John's appearance in court.

During subsequent fighting in Poitou, John went to the aid of Queen Eleanor, who was besieged in a castle at Mirebeau. Among the besiegers was Arthur of Brittany, who was captured along with a force of 200 knights. Exactly what ensued is uncertain, but Arthur died, allegedly at the hands of John. The story aroused a large segment of Brittany, and it undoubtedly weakened support for John elsewhere, although that was balanced by the fact that John had disposed of his only serious rival for the succession. What was of immediate importance was that John was forced to leave Normandy, and by 1204, most of its strong points were in Philip's hands.

With the loss of Normandy, a prolonged crisis began, one which reached a climax with Magna Carta in 1215. The story is normally told in three parts: John's struggle with Philip, the clash with Pope Innocent III and the alienation of the English baronage. To these we must add a fourth: John's brief campaign to dominate Scotland, Ireland and Wales.

The general outline of events was as follows: with the death of the archbishop of Canterbury in 1205, the king and pope argued over a replacement, leading to the king's excommunication in 1209. John meanwhile seized church revenues and continued his arbitrary (and effective) administration. Between 1209 and 1211 he made important extensions of power over Scotland, Ireland and Wales. Before this work could be completed, fearing papal deposition and French invasion, John made a series of dramatic moves. He accepted the pope's candidate as archbishop (1213); moreover he gave England and Ireland to the pope and received them back as a "fief" and promised an annual tribute. Then John surprised a French invasion fleet and began to prepare his own attack on Philip. In July 1214, John and his allies were defeated at the Battle of Bouvines. Returning without victory, John faced a deteriorating political situation. He began to maneuver and to make concessions; a charter of liberties for the church (Nov. 1214); a charter for London (May, 1215); and a charter for the barons (June). The latter was annulled by the pope and renounced by the king, and civil war broke out in late 1215. The next spring a French invasion of England gathered considerable support. But when John died in October, support ebbed from the invaders. Within a year the French withdrew, winning only a nominal tribute. The net result was that the English crown began to recover from a series of checks: French lordship, papal authority and baronial liberties were affirmed. Beyond those results, the king's dominions in the archipelago regained some autonomy.

Surveying the archipelago, we may be impressed with John's energy and determination. According to one historian: [7]

> John came very near to being one of the most successful kings of English history. His expeditions to Scotland (1209), Ireland 1210) and Wales (1211) gave him a mastery throughout the British Isles possessed by no English king before or since.

With regard to Scotland, John brought King William to what must have been a humiliating submission in 1209. At the beginning of his reign, John had seemed to promise the satisfaction of William's claim on the northern lands (Cumberland, Westmorland and Northumberland), and William had done homage to John at Lincoln in 1200. The next few years are difficult to

[7]Barrow, *Feudal Britain*, p. 201.

trace, but by 1206 the two were meeting again, and by 1209, a treaty called the Treaty of Norham--which no longer exists--was evidently negotiated (and renegotiated three years later). Its provisions can only be guessed, but they probably included a promise by John to make a grant of the lands in question to William's heir and to abandon a frontier fortress. In return, John received hostages, offers of dynastic marriage, and a large cash payment (an estimated 15,000 marks).

With his Scottish relations apparently settled, and with a number of hostages taken, John turned next to planning the subjection of his Irish lordship. Since the initial invasions some forty years before, the English adventurers had taken about half of the territory from the native rulers, but there was still a state of endemic warfare, if now more confused by the rival cultures present in the island. If John's first visit to Ireland in 1185 had only produced disorder, his contribution as king was the reverse. His essential policy was simple: build up royal power as a means to order and profit. He began the construction of Dublin Castle in 1204, he caused the further introduction and adoption of English law, and he took a number of measures to coerce the powerful men and families in Ireland. He appointed tough royal officers, took every occasion to revise charters, and took extraordinary measures against particular baronial enemies. For example, John de Courcy, a powerful leader in Ulster, was replaced. At the same time, King John sent some of his most powerful barons, William de Briouze and William the Marshal, earl of Pembroke, to manage great territories in Ireland. Both men had been hostile to John after his losses in France. The policy could have backfired, but for the timely and highly successful invasion which John led into Ireland in 1210. The king landed near Waterford in June. As he marched through Leinster and then the north, there was only light opposition. Marshal was astute enough to give him full support; Briouze was foolish enough to flee into exile. The bulk of the lesser English lords and a number of Gaelic chieftains paid homage to the king. John left after two months, having made a number of governmental improvements and having suffered no losses. In the coming years of crisis, his most loyal support would be from Ireland.

John's force left Dublin and made harbor at Fishguard in August 1210. The situation in Wales was not to be resolved as effectively as Scotland and Ireland. There was no royal figure here, though several native princes saw themselves as candidates for a crown. Against them were arrayed the entrenched positions of marcher lords (John had been one himself, by marriage to Isabel of Glamorgan, 1189-99). One of the more impressive of the princes during John's reign was Llywelyn ab Iorwerth of Gwynedd (later known as Llywelyn the Great). He had pledged fealty to John in 1201, and he married John's illegitimate daughter Joan in 1204. But Llywelyn had more compelling concerns closer to home. When the king had disciplined the powerful Briouze and Marshal families, he unsettled the power structure in south Wales, and this encouraged Llywelyn and others to act. In 1210 John ordered the earl of Chester to invade, and this expedition produced several new castles. In 1211, John himself led an expedition into the North in May, but had to retire when supplies ran out; he returned to battle in July, this time determined to win. Llywelyn surrendered land, an indemnity and thirty hostages.

The English king clearly saw his control of the archipelago as a vital preliminary to raising the force he would need for a successful campaign in France. That campaign was in John's mind the entire time. He had made an abortive attempt in 1205; he was making preparations again in 1212 and the next two years, until in fact he managed to launch an assault in 1214.

In 1212 a complicated set of events, for which we have insufficient documentation, saw disruption of the archipelago strategy and a new urgency added to the continental campaign. In June there were attacks on the new English castles in Wales, and John (then in Scotland helping William suppress an uprising) ordered his army to gather at Chester for a final crushing of the Welsh princes. The order was not to be executed.

According to the chronicles, John learned of a conspiracy "to drive him and his family from the kingdom and choose someone else as king in his place." It is likely that this "conspiracy" was tied to Philip's own preparation for his "Crusade" against the excommunicated English king. John's anger at the abrupt complications in his plans was displayed in grisly fashion when he ordered the hanging of 28 young Welsh hostages in Nottingham.

Philip's invasion was, like John's, a long-held plan. In 1205 there was some sign of such an enterprise, and again in 1209. Philip no doubt intrigued with some of John's barons on each occasion. Indeed, two barons fled in 1212 (Eustace de Vesci and Robert Fitzwalter) and their estates were then attacked and forfeited. They have been seen as ringleaders in the 'conspiracy', and they might have been Philip's agents. They were specifically guaranteed safety in John's later negotiations with the pope, something their role as ordinary conspirators would have hardly earned them.

In any case, the French invasion plan went ahead into the Spring of 1213. John was asked for help by the count of Flanders whose messengers probably informed the King of the massed invasion fleet. John sent 500 ships to raid the harbor of Damme (near Bruges). They discovered a French force estimated at 1700 vessels, of which about one-fourth were put out of action. The French counter-attacked on land, but the English force narrowly escaped, and Philip postponed his projected invasion.

Thus it seems likely that John's archipelago expansion was derailed by the alliance of France and the pope. John had quite brilliantly disarmed the Roman flank with his surrender, and he followed that up in May 1213 with his offer to make England and Ireland a fief of the Apostolic See. This was inexpensive in practical terms (an annual payment of 1000 marks) and highly profitable in diplomatic terms: now it was quite out of the question for Philip to crusade against the pope's vassal.

John chose in 1213 to press his advantage in the continental sphere, rather than to finish his internal empire. The significance of that choice is hard to weigh, for by this point the king had certainly exhausted the resources of many and the loyalty of most of his subjects in the archipelago. That he failed to conquer Wales may only have added slightly to the ranks of his opponents. Those numbers were dangerously large already, and John's only real hope of political salvation was a major military victory in France. John tried to mount an expedition in late 1213, but had to postpone it until the next year because many of his barons refused to obey the royal summons.

John left for Poitou in February 1214, where his campaign faltered, in large part because he had uncertain allies in the old family domain. His more reliable allies, Otto of Brunswick, the Holy Roman Emperor, and Count Ferrand of Flanders, were defeated by Philip at the Battle of Bouvines in July, thus ending the possibility of major victory. John returned to England in October.

The king's actions had failed to retrieve his losses in France. From the end of 1214 the crisis turned into a serious constitutional confrontation, one in which a pattern of reform was begun, a pattern with profound longterm political consequences.

Communities, Councils and Colonies

The theme of John's reign had been colonial failure. It began with his loss of Normandy, Brittany, Anjou and Touraine. When he failed to regain the French lordships, John sealed the loss of his vassals' loyalty. Meanwhile, he pledged his realms to Pope Innocent to avert a French attack, but then died in the course of a French invasion. A lesser colonial theme in John's reign was played out within the archipelago, where the king initiated and then aborted an effort to consolidate the dominions of the crown. In striking contrast, when John's son faced a civil war half a century later, although the English king was subservient to the papacy and often sought counsel from the king of France, there was little chance that the kingdom of Henry III would be similarly endangered. The reasons for this were complex, but they may be reduced to three essentials: the extension of political communities, the growth of royal councils and the recession of colonial influence. Each of these factors was evident in a variety of forms in the archipelago, and our discussion will only highlight the most prominent features. These illustrations will suggest what might be learned by examining a phenomenon once regarded as exclusively English, from the more revealing vantage point of the archipelago as a whole.[8]

Politics is the life of communities of men and women, be they tribal and traditional, or urban and progressive. The 13th century was a time when the forms of political life were changing. For the past century and a half the feudal order had overlaid the traditional community of vill and hundred, cantref and commote. The manor and the borough had come to dominate but were only beginning to acquire permanence through bestowal of charters, and thus the constitutional establishment of their "liberties." That process produced a sense of communal patrimony--at least for the better sort of inhabitant. But the charter represented yet another step in the line of political evolution: the recognition of a political community, in this case at the local level, with sufficient importance to demand and receive written authority from the crown to exercise its jurisdiction. This act would simultaneously

---

[8]Recent correctives to older, Anglocentric interpretations may be found in G.O. Sayles, *The King's Parliament of England* (1977), and M.T. Clanchy, *England and Its Rulers* (1983).

affirm the higher power of the crown, while it represented the political strength of a group of subjects, and channelled that strength in a productive direction. People in the 12th and 13th centuries had a number of notions of "community," including kin, region, manor, county, guild, town, and more vaguely the "community of the realm." The unformed idea began to assume several significant shapes at the turn of the century. A few examples may illustrate the kind of development which was taking place.

A commune being a sworn confederation had distinct conspiratorial character. It was often an object of fear and scorn, what Richard of Devizes, the 12th century chronicler called "a tumult of the people and a terror of the realm." Needless to say, a particular commune meant many different things to its members. The population of London had at least two experiences in the 12th century, in 1141 and again in 1191, when it formed communal organizations. After the later episode, London continued to have an elected government, the first such authority in the archipelago. To John, who had tried to use the situation to his own advantage while King Richard was out of the realm, the event was less propitious. As king, however, John tried to summon the "community of the realm" to the support of his French campaign in 1205. This did not materialize, but John once more encountered the concept in the crisis of 1215. In this case, the community was dictating the terms to the king.[9]

When he returned from France in 1214, John levied a scutage as was customary after an expedition, only the collection was very disappointing. Baronial resistance to the king was mounting steadily, and by the early Spring, a group of dissident barons presented John with a list of demands. He angrily rejected these, but John knew his position was not strong. In fact, he had been preparing the ground for concessions such as the barons sought, for John had already given a "Charter of Liberties" to the Church (November 1214). In May 1215, John granted a special charter to the City of London in hopes of retaining their allegiance, but his conciliatory moves were not convincing. The rebel barons marched on the capital, and by early

---

[9]An early discussion of the concept was Helen Cam, "The Theory and Practice of Representation in Medieval England," *History* I (1953) 11-26. G.W.S. Barrow explained the Scottish variation in *Robert Bruce and the Community of the Realm of Scotland* (1965), which he has expanded and updated in *Kingship and Unity: Scotland 1000-1306* (1981). The most comprehensive treatment is Susan Reynolds, *Kingdoms and Communities in Western Europe, 900-1300* (1984).

June the two sides were negotiating. The document which was adopted drew upon some earlier models such as the so-called coronation charter of Henry I (1100). Archbishop Langton was one of the main composers. The bulk of the charter dealt with feudal customs which John promised to observe carefully. In addition there were clauses dealing with the legal system, promising prompt and fair justice; clauses governing merchants' affairs, the regulation of royal forests, and other economic concerns; clauses concerning taxation, including the radical provision for the "common counsel of the realm" on particular forms of tax; and a security clause which created a Council of Twenty-five, chosen by the barons, to oversee the king's compliance with the charter. The sanction to be imposed by this council, if complaint was made and not remedied within 40 days was to declare war on the king!

The charter was an omnibus bill of indictment. The king plainly granted it in order to escape an immediate crisis. He probably had no intention of abiding by the charter, and he wrote to Pope Innocent asking to be absolved. The papal absolution was given, but it only left Rome in August, by which time the king was already preparing to do battle. All the same, the charter was distributed to all the sheriffs, some hostages were released under its terms, and the document became a matter of public record. John had been forced to give a list of promises. Many of the terms were simply statements of accepted custom, others were general and reasonable statements of principle. Yet the setting was in one sense revolutionary. A large majority of the baronage arrayed itself against the king and confronted him with demands. Surely both sides were uncomfortable with this visible rift, but its impression was indelible.

By the Fall of 1215, the king and the rebel barons were at war. The pope had ordered the rebels excommunicated in July, the archbishop had been suspended in September, and a special legate was dispatched to intervene with the French. By then, however, some advance units of French troops were arriving in England and Prince Louis landed in Kent in May, 1216. While he only had a flimsy title to John's throne, he temporarily attracted more support in the war. Most of the east and south fell into his hands, though John retained a few major castles there. John died while campaigning in Lincoln in October, leaving his nine-year old son Henry to succeed him.

Henry's minority was a blessing in disguise, for much of the hostility that existed had been directed at John himself, and an underage heir could not (yet) be assumed to be as evil as his father. Moreover, the regents who were picked to tend the young king were widely trusted. William the Marshal was named "rector;" the papal legate Guala, cardinal priest of St. Martin, represented the king's feudal lord; Peter des Roches, bishop of Winchester, was made Henry's guardian and tutor; Hubert de Burgh, made justiciar by John in 1215, also joined what was in effect a regency council. In November, this group issued an edited version of the charter in the king's name. This time, as a voluntary measure, and in the form of a coronation charter, the document made a more durable impression. The Council of Twenty-five was deleted, as were a number of other clauses. Now, however, it was the court faction who stood behind the charter and the rebels who were placed in opposition.

The French forces remained in a commanding position until 1217, but their reinforcements were disrupted and their ranks thinned somewhat by desertion. While Louis held London, his allies were routed in a battle at Lincoln, and peace negotiations were begun. The Treaty of Kingston (September 1217) has not been preserved, but evidently it restored the status quo and made promises of future loyalty. Louis also received a payment of 10,000 marks, payable by 1221. After the treaty, the "great" charter was re-issued, having been separated from the clauses on the royal forests, now known as "the Charter of the Forest." The political purpose of this re-issue was to confirm the promises made in wartime, to clarify some terms left incomplete in 1216, and to give further assurances to those who were coming over to the king's side at the end of hostilities. Undoubtedly, this third issue within little more than two years also served to emphasize the importance of the document. These confirmations or re-issues were to become a standard feature of medieval politics. There was plain political expedience at work, but each time the act acknowledged the crown's obligations to the community. That there were close to 40 re-issues also proves that the memory of the obligations was kept alive, and in every instance of re-issue there was an opportunity to make changes or additions. So, in the re-issue of 1225, we find that the people of the realm gave Henry III a fifteenth of their movable property "in return for the concession and gift of these liberties." Charters were becoming an important ingredient in the English medieval political scene.

The non-English parts of the archipelago were also influenced by the charter. There were many chapters dealing with feudal custom, and those barons who held of the king in the marches or in Scotland or Ireland were of course involved; any clergy who were subject to the archbishops of Canterbury and York were also party to the charters; merchants who came into London or other specified towns might be affected. In the only article dealing with Scotland (no. 59) John said [10]

> We will treat Alexander, King of the Scots, concerning the return of his sisters and hostages and his liberties and rights in the same manner in which we will act towards *our other barons of England,* unless it ought to be otherwise because of the charters we have from William his father, formerly King of the Scots; and this shall be determined by the judgement of his peers in our court.

The Welsh were granted a form of treaty, the hostages of the princes were restored, and those rulers were promised reinstatement "by the judgement of their peers" and according to laws in force in the area in question, i.e., either English, Welsh, or the "law of the march" (articles 56-58). The Scottish and Welsh sections were annulled along with the rest of the original, and the special clauses were not included in the reissues. On the other hand, Ireland was not mentioned in the original, but it was the subject of a copy which was approved in late 1216, and sent to Ireland in February 1217. Sometimes called Magna Carta Hiberniae, this was probably less significant in its actual content, since it was an edited imitation of the original. What was significant was the fact that it represented one of the earliest cases of direct transmittal of a legislative act from England to Ireland.

In all instances, the original charter was overtaken by events. Llywelyn lost no time in resuming hostilities at the head of a coalition of Welsh princes. They took control of much of South Wales, leaving King John in possession of only Pembroke and Haverfordwest by the end of 1215. In the following year, Llywelyn arranged a partition of territory, settled at a meeting at Aberdovey. Then he invaded the lands of Powys and secured his dominant position in Wales by the time of John's death. In 1218, Llywelyn concluded

---

[10]J.C. Holt, *Magna Carta* (1965), p. 333.

the Peace of Worcester, which recognised many of his conquests and gave him custody of several royal castles during the king's minority. For the next few years, under these terms, there was a period of stable control in Wales, until resurgent marcher lords disrupted Llywelyn's power in the 1220s.

Alexander II of Scotland probably had the most to gain from King John's embarrassment in 1215, and yet he was unable to capitalize on the situation. This was not for want of trying. Scottish forces moved across the border several times in the crisis period, even to go as far south as Cambridge where Alexander gave homage to Louis in 1216. However, the disputed territory in northern England slipped from his grasp. In December 1217, Alexander did homage to Henry III and awaited the visit of the papal legate to rule on the terms of the treaties of 1209 and 1212. Pandulph made visits to Norham (1219) and York (1220) and finally produced a settlement which dealt with marriage agreements for the sisters of the respective kings. There was no mention of the land question. Alexander's one great ally, the French prince, had made his peace and left; in order to lift the sentence of interdict and excommunication, Alexander had to accept the arbitration of the papal legate, who of course represented the feudal lord of the English crown. Therefore the Scots could expect little relief. Indeed, even the plan to conduct a full coronation ceremony was disallowed by the pope "since that king is said to be subject to the king of England."[11]

In Ireland, the aftermath of the charter's arrival was relatively calm. The power of William the Marshal, which had prevented Ireland from being a source of unrest in 1215, helped to maintain stability during the regency of Henry III. Neither of these conditions had a great deal to do with the charter, and politics in Anglo-Norman Ireland were much more a function of the relations of the magnates with each other and with the crown.

Such a formula seems indeed to have general application in the 13th century. However, to understand political development in this period, especially the changing role of councils, it will help us to look across the archipelago and try to place the principal actors in their proper settings. Baronial and aristocratic leaders shared similar if not identical values and goals: they were community leaders and their power rested on military prowess, property ownership, familial tradition and political status as

---

[11]A.A.M. Duncan, *Scotland: The Making of the Kingdom* (1975), p. 526.

advisers or confidants of princes. These terms applied equally to an earl of Fife, a lord of Meath, a baron of the Welsh March or of England. Also, when we refer to "barons" we may forget that the French feudal terminology covered many layers of old and respected rank. The blend was uneven in various parts of the archipelago, so that while the *mormaers* (high stewards) of Scotland might readily convert to "earls" by the 13th century, the Irish *rí* or the Welsh *brenin* were a good deal slower to alter their titles, and slower still to alter their beliefs about traditional power.

One idea which all areas and all aristocrats shared was that of a right or a duty to offer counsel to a ruler, to serve him on some form of council. The English royal court had become the most advanced and elaborate of these bodies in the archipelago. Its form had been emulated by the Scots, exported to Ireland, and imitated in marcher lordships in Wales and in the remoter principalities of England. The courts or councils of rulers were of several basic types: intimate groups of advisers, larger professional bodies, and still larger assemblies of the king's subjects ("peers"). All councils sat with the ruler to endorse and enforce royal decisions. The members would have been chosen by the (adult) ruler, the business was that which he referred to them, and the decisions were usually his to make. The councils which were normal in the 13th century were the "Great" councils of feudal nobility which would attend regular crown wearings of the English king; small councils which frequently sat to conduct routine business; and special "afforced" councils where those attending had been summoned for particular business. The name "parliament" was used by the 1230s in England to denote the meetings of one or another of these bodies.

The nature of royal councils was at the heart of the English constitutional debates of the 13th century. In the crudest and earliest stage of development, the radical Council of Twenty-five provided in the charter was supposed to be a method of controlling the enforcement of that document. That was rendered unnecessary, but the idea of conciliar control lingered on. Such control was of course accepted routinely in cases such as the regency of Henry III (1216-1227), though there were always debates over the place and power of regents. This sort of argument merged with more serious challenges to royal choices and royal conduct later in Henry's career.

The particular problem in Henry's choice of councillors was the selection of and dependence on "foreigners". He restored the power of Peter des Roches, his father's adviser, and with him, Peter des Rivaux and other "Poitevins." These men helped Henry in his "coup" in 1232, which ousted the longtime justiciar, Hubert de Burgh. The new advisers seemed ruthless and greedy, naturally to those who opposed them. The last straw was the policy which Henry endorsed of placing his son Edmund on the throne of Sicily. The cost of this crown was repayment of massive papal debts, and that outraged the king's vassals. The Sicilian plan has been ridiculed, though it might have made some sense as part of a larger dynastic scheme.[12] The point is irrelevant in that the English baronage decided it was impossible and intolerable. When the pope threatened to excommunicate Henry unless the agreement was fulfilled, he inspired a baronial response. At a council meeting in April 1258, seven dissident barons swore to band together to obtain reforms. When a parliament was summoned to Oxford in June, the "community of England" swore the same oath as the barons, "that each one of us and all of us together will help each other...saving faith to the king and the crown."[13] This vague and cautious oath was the prologue to forming a council chosen by representatives of the king and the barons, which council was given a set of instructions as to reforms. They included shire court collection of grievances, reform of administration, a Council of Fifteen to oversee the king's work, and a provision for parliaments three times a year. The pressure built up during the crisis carried over into further extensions of reform in what were called the Provisions of Westminster (1259), which called for protective measures for gentry and lesser folk against the baronage; a large number of specific legal reforms and administrative reforms were stipulated, most of them to protect against rapacious landlords.

The general direction of reform continued until 1261, by which time King Henry was able to reassert himself. He received papal absolution from his oath to support the Provisions of Oxford, and by the end of 1261, Henry had resumed much control of the administration. After a tense period of maneuvering, civil war broke out in 1264. At the Battle of Lewes, Prince Edward won his part of the field, but Simon de Montfort won the battle, and thereby gained control of the king for the next fifteen months. A provisional

---

[12]The larger "Savoyard" policy is explained in Clanchy, *England and its Rulers*, pp. 235-40.

[13]Harry Rothwell, ed., *English Historical Documents*, v. 3 (1975), p. 362.

regime was established under three "electors" and a Council of Nine. But by this time, support for the rebels was ebbing steadily, as the community generally lost sympathy with the innovative political measures and saw more plain signs of personal ambition among the king's enemies. In the late Summer of 1265, Simon's forces were attacked at Evesham and the leading rebel was killed. More than a year later, the last rebel stronghold fell.

The rebels were beaten, but of course their campaign left its mark in England and around the archipelago. The major consequences included Llywelyn's recognition as Prince of Wales in the Treaty of Montgomery (1267). The Provisions of Oxford were exported to Ireland, or to the Anglo-Norman community there, which helped to establish a tradition of holding parliaments in Ireland. The Scots had known such an occasion as a "colloquium" in the early 13th century, and they would only begin to borrow the English usage c. 1290. But Scotland had also found the 1250s to be a time of serious conciliar strife. In their case, one faction had kidnapped the young King Alexander in 1255. Both King Henry and Prince Llywelyn had at different times intervened, but when the king's abductor died in 1258, affairs began to return to normal. Ironically, Alexander had endured a humiliating form of control, but he was not treated to the kind of constitutional intervention practiced on Henry III.

While councils were exploited and political communities were expanded, the character of government was changing in all parts of the Atlantic Archipelago. There were significant changes in archipelago revenues in the 13th century, paralleled by alterations in the machinery for handling government money. A variety of impulses was behind the changes, including rising costs, especially military; political turbulence with consequent revenue decline; and shifting economic activity within the archipelago. The feudal sources which were slipping at the beginning of the century had nearly evaporated by its close in England (they remained a major source in Scotland until 1500). When this happened, the rising cost of government forced innovation--taxes on movable property, customs duties and levies on clerical income. While sources changed, so did the royal offices charged with accounting and management of funds. The ancient exchequer of England was copied in Scotland, implanted in Ireland and exported to Wales, or at least to Chester. As the oldest office of the bureaucracy, the procedure of the English exchequer had become cumbersome.

In the crisis of 1258, moreover, barons tried to control appointments to the body and to regulate its working. In other words, the exchequer looked to be a vulnerable point in government. The king always had some money handled more directly through his personal servants in the royal household. His chamber was the traditional personal treasury; in the 13th century his wardrobe (once a storehouse under the chamber) was used for expenditures. This office became much more active in finance in the second half of the century, receiving payments from sheriffs, making loans and disbursing funds to overseas military units. The exchequer remained in place for the purpose of auditing, and the wardrobe and chamber rendered accounts of their business. Control obviously lay closer to the crown and in a more convenient and flexible situation. Administrative exports were never as simple as contemporaries (or historians) expected. In the first place, the governments of Wales, Scotland and Ireland all had to deal with sharply-divided communities. Put loosely, each had a feudal (or feudalized) part and each had a native, Celtic, or "backward" part. This made a basic contrast. To be sure, England was far from a unitary state, and it had important subdivisions in some of the outlying palatine jurisdictions. Still they were analogous and subordinated to English royal power. The Scottish king was only beginning to supplant Norwegian power in the North and was dealing with a substantial Gaelic population in the rest of the kingdom, not yet neatly couched behind the "highland line." The "Prince of Wales," Llywelyn "the Last" (1246?-1282), could only claim authority--and that quite recent--over about two thirds of Welsh territory, the rest being under the power of marcher lords. Something similar was visible in Ireland in the mid-13th century. The lordship cherished by the English was divided into a number of major holdings. These were struck by an unusual number of succession failures, so that many were divided among female offspring, while one of the larger (the Ulster earldom) fell in to the crown (1242). Smaller holdings combined with less connections to magnate interests in Britain to produce a somewhat more peaceable and governable Ireland.

In addition to these internal divisions of an elementary kind all over the archipelago, traditions of government were vastly different from one part to another. The experience of Norman "conquest" was of varied strength and duration, and Angevin "federation" was even less impressive. Each area had a blend of inherited and imported customs and institutions. The Scottish crown had taken the most from the English example, as it was in the best position to do so. The Welsh marches were actual parts of the English regime, and the native rulers in the 13th century were joining the feudal structure. Although Anglo-Norman Ireland had the most direct imports, that area also had the most vigorous native rivals. While every area had signs of enduring native tradition, these signs were dim reminders of a bygone era. The reviving English royal power was beginning to assert itself in more and more aggressive fashion, *vis a vis* both the native regimes and the old continental colonial connections.

English political reform had less effect on the archipelago in the later 13th century than the shifts of political alignment relative to the European continent. When John came to the throne in 1199 it was but a century after the last great Norse invasion, and the northwestern part of Britain, the western islands and the Orkneys and Shetland were still part of the Norwegian patrimony, if a distant and independent part. Similarly, John inherited the cross-channel domains and it was in his reign that Normandy and Anjou were reoriented toward a consolidated French crown. Finally, Pope Innocent III was successful in bringing the English crown into another kind of colonial relation. In all of these cases, there were definite signs of recession during the reign of Edward I. The kings of Scotland had obtained cession of Norwegian rights in the Hebrides in the Treaty of Perth (1266). The surviving English lordship in Gascony evolved into a new kind of "French connection." The papal tie underwent slower but equally profound change, one symbol being the stoppage of John's annual tribute after 1289. Collectively these changes meant that the archipelago had more control over its own destiny. The causes of change were diffuse and widespread, but the change created an opportunity for the wealth and power of the English monarchy to be used in pursuit of political ambitions in its immediate vicinity.

The Norse parts of the area we know as Scotland had to be subdued if there was to be any progress in unifying that kingdom. The work began in the reign of Alexander II. In 1222 he had sailed along the coast and received the homage of the men of Argyll. In 1231, the marriage of Gilbert of Angus to the sister of the last Norse jarl of Orkney began a slow process of assimilation. In 1235, Alexander put down a revolt in Galloway, and evidently these successful moves induced further expansion. Negotiations were opened with the Norwegian court to acquire the outer isles. In 1249, Alexander set out with an expedition which he did not live to complete. The ensuing regency interrupted these efforts, but when Alexander III assumed his own rule, he resumed the policy of expansion. Diplomacy again failed, and there was some Scottish piracy unleashed which provoked a major Norwegian assault. A large fleet entered the Firth of Clyde in Sept. 1263. After some raiding, a severe storm disrupted the invaders' fleet, a confused engagement was fought, and the Norse king retreated to Orkney. Perhaps planning to regroup there, the king of Norway died in December. After prolonged negotiations, his successor gave over the rights to Man and the western isles to Alexander for 4,000 marks plus an annual tribute of 100 marks. This Treaty of Perth was settled in 1266. The Orkney and Shetland islands remained under the lordship of Norway for another two centuries, but in all other respects, Scottish unification took a major step toward completion; Norwegian colonial activity henceforth was in decline. This did not mean total severance, for Alexander's daughter Margaret married King Eric II of Norway in 1281; she died giving birth to another Margaret--the "Maid of Norway" who would be the last of the Canmore line.

French colonial links had been of the utmost importance to England--and Scotland--from the end of the 11th century. The loss of Normandy was a blow to this pattern--a blow from which there was no recovery, although such recovery was a major object of royal policy for some time. The French invasion of 1216 was an even greater sign of change. Although its extent was impressive, its duration was brief. There was no chance of another Norman Conquest, or even a renewed Angevin federation. For by this time the English baronage had acquired a keen sense of its own institutions and a growing sense of differences between their government and that of France. These tendencies would appear again and again in the troubled middle years of the century, particularly on occasions when the king chose loyal "Frenchmen" as his advisers. Another link to France which was of mixed impact was the personal relation between Henry III and Louis IX (St. Louis). In a number of diplomatic matters, Henry seemed to be under the tutelage of his French overlord. This had predictable repercussions at home when, for example, the Treaty of Paris confirmed the revised royal style without the title "Duke of the Normans." Again, when Henry put his disputes with the barons to the "arbitration" of Louis, the result was a rather short rebuff to the rebels. A further remaining link was of course the tie to Gascony (formerly part of Aquitaine). Here the English crown enjoyed a sort of colony of its own; a loosely-managed and valuable commercial link to the French crown, as well as a check to its pretensions toward unification. The English kept alive a patrimonial dream of ancestral French possessions, and so long as they did, the French cultivated England's archipelago neighbors, especially the Scots. However, the crucial separation from Normandy established a new geopolitical outline.

Papal authority had grown tremendously in the 12th and 13th centuries. This was colonial or imperial power, for it was, like contemporary secular powers, a matter of *lordship*. Papal lordship was essentially spiritual. That it became increasingly temporal in the 13th century could not alter its fundamental nature, but it did evoke more hostile responses. Spiritual lordship had been at the heart of papal authority, and it was elevated by successive reform movements and by the visible demonstration of the crusade. In the 13th century the structure of papal government grew (in the curia and in countries like England) to such an extent that it invariably competed with the temporal governments of the day. The practical business of paying for such rule, staffing so many positions, managing so many details, was overwhelming the operation while it was undermining the moral position of the papacy.

The papal fief in 1213 was plainly a royal evasion of the consequences of interdict and excommunication. King John adroitly won papal backing at a crucial time by what was a patent maneuver. The political authority latent in the feudal submission was what appealed to the pope. Perhaps it was vital to his policy; in the next reign, the visits of papal legates, nuncios and general involvement of Rome in English government reached an alltime high. Papal justice, taxation and administration were a pervasive theme in the archipelago, especially in England. Major treaties were negotiated by legates; major taxation programs were proposed, conducted and managed by curia officials; places in English churches were filled by Rome, pleas in English courts were removed to the curia. There was ample evidence that a theocratic colony was being created.

This dominion was to outlast the 13th century. Only the first signs of its rupture were evident under Edward I. He caused the annual tribute to be stopped after 1289; he imposed extraordinary taxes on the English clergy in 1294, which touched off a great crisis, both in papal relations and in the political framework of his own kingdom. Papal colonial "power" depended more than others on the goodwill of the colony. Edward was the second (and last) English king to go on crusade (1270-74), returning two years late for his own coronation. His devotion was rapidly undermined in the years ahead, and the goodwill built up by his father was quite quickly reduced in one generation.

The erosion of colonial ties was well underway by the last quarter of the century, while internal political development showed signs of an increased consciousness of community and an ability to use councils as a new kind of instrument of government. The latter were not to develop all around the archipelago, because the English crown took advantage of declining foreign influence to further increase its relative power. The Welsh lost their autonomy while the Scots went to great lengths to preserve theirs. Ireland would remain outside this pattern and actually regain cultural autonomy in the 14th century. These changes were the products of a new colonial policy, centered in London, which had at long last replaced the old influence of powers outside the archipelago.

PART TWO

ARCHIPELAGO NATIONS

The nation-building of the Atlantic Archipelago was peculiar and precocious: peculiar in that three national units in close proximity survived the long effort of England to incorporate them; precocious in that a partial Welsh annexation came as early as the 13th century; a form of parliamentary management came to Ireland at the end of the 15th century; and a royal union brought Scotland and England together at the start of the 17th century. Each of these events produced limited political union because they were ahead of their time, and the limited unions in turn allowed both English domination *and* continued non-English identity. The latter was indeed fostered by the absence of a new, alternative unified political entity.

Still, a collective order in the archipelago was created by the 18th century. The forces responsible were a combination of royal recovery in the 15th century, religious reform in the 16th and imperial expansion in the 17th. The kings of England and Scotland restored their treasuries and their dynasties, though the English were better endowed in the former, the Scots in the latter. Both nations had a major clerical overhaul, the English model being influential over more archipelago territory, the Scottish model being more ambitious. During these years, English *imperium* grew steadily: palatine power was in recession, exemplified by the termination of Welsh marcher lordships, extended power of royal councils and restriction of outlying authorities. Also there was military renovation: armies and fleets of the modern state began to appear, first in archipelago garrisons and outposts overseas. Only one ruler in the archipelago was in a position to develop these forces, but with Elizabeth there was insufficient money, with James insufficiently warlike policy. Both Cromwell and William III remedied those deficiencies after 1650. A third manifestation of the new direction was in physical expansion--conquest and plantation, within the archipelago and overseas.

And yet the 18th century archipelago was still composed of four national units. Multiple identities--and a shortage of imperial institutions--were produced by the same forces which made England pre-eminent. We have to look closely at the major stages and themes: the conflicts of patrimonial interests in the 15th century, and their reconciliation in the next; the burst of politico-religious upheaval in the protestant reformation, which transformed the political processes in the archipelago; and the international and "civil" warfare which opened the way to forced unification, under Oliver Cromwell and then under William III.

CHAPTER 4

PATRIMONY AND POLITICS

> In a turbulent world, the idea of inheritance
> was one which all accepted without question
> as part of the natural order....The most telling
> charge that could be brought against a tyrant
> was to say that he had thrust men out of their
> inheritances.
>
> (T.F.T.Plucknett,*The Legislation of
> Edward I*, 1947, p. 110)

When colonial influence declined in the archipelago at the end of the 13th century, native princes vied for pre-eminence. The several degrees of political power and the different systems in the archipelago had one thing in common. They shared a sense of patrimonial rights--both of individuals and communities. The inheritance was "a unit of political power and itself a creature of politics."[1]

The patrimony--inherited power in land, title or jurisdiction--was recognized in the 13th century, but it was regularized in the 14th. The conception of patrimonial *right* was extremely important in political, legal and constitutional terms until the 16th century. It was the matrix in which royal, aristocratic and communal interests, in all the different areas of the archipelago, were bound to interact. The central question was how royal, individual and communal patrimonial rights could be reconciled. The answer was complicated by the uneven operation of patronage (the creation or transfer of patrimony); the existence of dissimilar customs of inheritance; and the effects of international warfare.

The kings and barons whose struggles preoccupied older histories, were operating in a political maze, stumbling toward a more secure future while clinging to old, familiar patrimonial values. Our sketch will review four major aspects of political evolution in the period: the shaping of the inheritance of Edward I, with its manifold impact in the archipelago; the English obsession with the French crown; social change in the 14th century;

---

[1]G. A. Holmes, *The Estates of the Higher Nobility in Fourteenth Century England* (1957), p. 7.

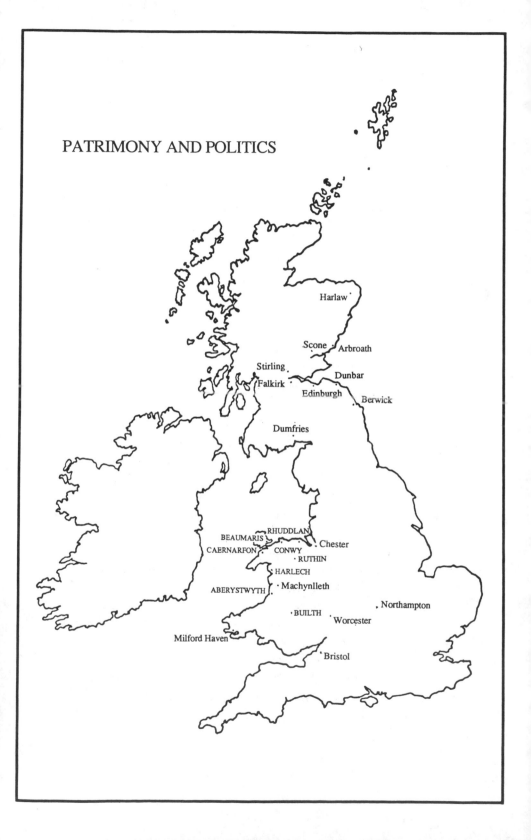

PATRIMONY AND POLITICS

and the "breakdown" of authority, the crisis in patrimonial politics which repeatedly erupted between 1377 and 1461. In all its forms, violent behavior by and toward Richard II, Owain Glyn Dwr and Henry VI was traceable to instability in the patrimonial political system. Military defeat, economic stress, and political jealousy did not produce fundamental change in concepts of individual or communal patrimony. Instead, the crisis discredited the old regime and prepared the way for stronger dynasties with sufficient power to reconcile the patrimonial rights of the crown, the individual and the community.

The Edwardian Inheritance

Edward I was a vigorous defender of his patrimony. Some of that energy came from his long and turbulent apprenticeship, especially the period of Earl Simon's rebellion. Edward's early acts as king were connected to a policy of recovery or confirmation of royal rights. That policy extended to the subjection of Welsh rebels (1277-82) and the management of the Scottish succession (1290-96). While paying for campaigns in Wales, Scotland and France, Edward overtaxed his subjects and precipitated political crises. His son's inheritance was marred by the residue of these ventures, and when Edward II failed in his father's wake, he was deposed and replaced by his own son, Edward III (1327). The lesson was that patrimony was never completely secure; inheritance had to be guarded, augmented and often upheld by force.

The individual, especially a ruler, inherited particular property and title ("lordship") within a larger context of an inherited body of social values. Edward I was a fascinating case. Henry III apparently named him after Edward the Confessor. The prince himself had a great interest in Arthurian legend, and we know Edward appreciated the value of regal symbols if only because he later ordered the seizure of Welsh and Scottish regalia. Prince Edward inhabited the realm of the chivalric knight, made the tournament a major pastime, and took up the banner of the crusader. In short, he was the model of a young man of his class and condition.

On the material level, Edward was vested with a growing list of lands and lordships. As an infant, he was made earl of Chester. At the age of ten he was titled duke of Gascony, and at fifteen he became lord of Ireland and

Wales. The appanage grant in 1254 gave Edward Ireland, Gascony, Oleron, the Channel Islands, plus other estates, but said these lands "may never be separated from the crown...but they should remain to the king of England forever." He received other territories on his marriage to Eleanor of Castile. Such creations for young princes were common enough as sources of income for a princely court. For the young Edward, these lordships were fraught with political problems which became painfully apparent in the deep crisis of his father's reign. Edward had to fight to hold his lordships, and to defend his father's royal prerogative. These two objectives seem compatible to us, but evidently Edward sometimes put his own inheritance ahead of the maintenance of royal power, even supporting Simon for a time (1259). As one writer commented, "his self-interest outweighed consistency."[2] But any landowner was liable to the same charge: in a political system where the power base of king and noblemen was in the land, the distribution of that commodity was bound to be a political act which divided loyalties.

During the crisis in England, Edward's lordship in Wales was effectively challenged by the native prince, Llywelyn ap Gruffydd. Rebels in North Wales in the 1250s were unchecked due to the troubles in England. In 1258, Llywelyn adopted the title "Prince of Wales" and that title was confirmed in the Treaty of Montgomery (1267) which ended the baronial rebellion. The princely title seemed to indicate reviving native political power, but such an idea was not accepted readily by the Welsh marcher lords, among them Prince Edward. Here was a direct challenge, not only to the crown, but more directly to English barons on the frontier.

The other major formative lordship experience was Edward's position as lord of Gascony. Here he had administrative power during his father's lifetime, while Henry held the title of duke of Aquitaine under the terms of the Treaty of Paris (1259). In this situation, Edward was the vassal of the king of France and the manager of a large and successful trading colony. These rights of lordship were every bit as valuable as rights in land, and Edward spent considerable time and energy in securing and exploiting his Gascon lordship. He resided there in 1254-5, 1260-63, 1273-4 and 1286-9. When not present, he deputized his authority to close relatives and trusted aides.

---

[2]Michael Prestwich, *The Three Edwards* (1980), p. 6.

The Gascon income was important to Edward, and the cost of defending it would become even more important.

Edward inherited the English crown while he was on crusade in 1272. Fortunately for him, the civil war had been concluded and its property and other settlements were well enough accepted so there was a relatively peaceful succession. Indeed, Edward delayed his return in order to settle affairs in Gascony. He arrived in England in August 1274. His first acts as a ruling monarch revealed a keen sense of patrimonial rights. In October Edward began a general inquest into rights and liberties in England and the Channel Islands. The sworn testimony of jurors in every hundred recalled the famous Domesday survey two centuries earlier, or the *Cartae baronum* of 1166. The immediate effect was the collection of a mass of testimony in the "Hundred Rolls." During the inquest, jurors frequently complained that they could not determine the basis for local jurisdiction. There followed extensive judicial inquiry, known by the opening words of the principal writ used, "*Quo warranto* "--by what warrant (is authority exercised)? Edward was pursuing a dual objective: he had a means to survey property and to test local authority. The result was in almost every case either a recovery of lost power or revenue or the establishment of new royal restraints. The practice of systematic inquest was continued. In March 1279 the crown created 25 panels of commissioners to study tenements and liberties throughout the kingdom; at the same time, a commission surveyed the performance of distraint of knighthood.

The major early statutes, which mark Edward's reign as one of great legal and constitutional importance, had serious consequences for patrimonial issues. Historians do not agree about what Edward was trying to do: one has called his work "a vast royal blackmail"; another said he aimed "to clarify or amend the common law"; and a third said "the king was merely seeking to do the best he could for the family of which he was the head, and failing that, for himself."[3] What seems certain is that Edward applied strong legal pressure across English and archipelago society to affirm royal patrimonial rights. In 1279 the Statute of Mortmain forbade alienation of land to the church, but in practice the prohibition could be waived by royal license. In

---

[3]Plucknett, *Legislation*, p. 45; F.M. Powicke, *Henry III and the Lord Edward* (1966), p. 379; K. B. MacFarlane, *The Nobility of Later Medieval England* (1973), p. 266.

the statute known as Westminster II, the first section demanded strict observance of conditions made in bequests (1285). In 1290, two important acts were passed. *Quo warranto* proceedings were culminated by a general law, and henceforth royal charters were the sole means of attesting jurisdiction. Even more important, the statute *quia emptores* abolished subinfeudation. When a fief was purchased, the new owner assumed the existing feudal obligations; no new lordships were to be created. Thus attrition would tend to concentrate lordship in the crown; meanwhile the law made land transfers easier. It should be added that these statutes were enforceable in England, and in other royal jurisdictions. Thus there was a chance of enforcement in the March of Wales and Anglo-Ireland but Scotland did not follow these laws in any region, nor did the native parts of Wales or Ireland.

In his lordships outside England, Edward I had a more challenging task in maintaining his authority. Wales was the first to receive Edward's attention. He had suffered substantial losses of territory to Llywelyn and as some of Edward's greatest English barons were also marcher lords, their support had to be carefully maintained. Llywelyn's title of "Prince of Wales" was an ominous sign of achievement; a modern version of several heroic Welsh figures who had united the nation (in fact or in myth). Unity was not durable at this time, and Edward benefited from the rivalry between Llywelyn and his brother Dafydd. The Prince refused to do homage to Edward (among other things he learned that the king had captured and imprisoned Eleanor de Montfort, his fiancée). In late 1276 a state of war existed. In the next year, Edward invaded, captured Anglesey and forced Llywelyn to submit. The Treaty of Conway gave Edward large pieces of territory and an indemnity of 50,000. Llywelyn did homage at Westminster for which he retained his title and a much shrunken domain, and he was allowed to marry Eleanor de Montfort. It seemed that this victory would settle Welsh affairs, but Dafydd launched a rebellion against the English in 1282. A number of royal castles were seized, and other Welsh leaders, including Llywelyn, were obliged to stand against the crown. This was a much more serious uprising than that of 1277, and Edward treated it accordingly. He brought in a large number of mercenaries and a fleet of 60 ships.

Edward's expenditure was twice that of the earlier campaign, but his strategy was similar, as he crossed the north coast, tried to take Anglesey, and meanwhile had other forces operating in the south and west. Llywelyn was killed in a surprise attack, and by April 1283 the last major Welsh fortress was taken and Dafydd was captured in June. In the wake of his victories, Edward accelerated and expanded the construction of massive castles which would now secure the lordship. This was followed by major constitutional change. Edward summoned the barons and representatives from English counties and towns to meet at Shrewsbury (Sept. 1283) to discuss the future of Wales. The following Spring Edward issued the Statute of Wales which embodied his conclusions on the subject. The preamble stated that [4]

> Divine providence, which is unerring in its dispositions, among other gifts of its dispensation with which it has deigned to honour us and our kingdom of England has now of its grace wholly and entirely converted the land of Wales previously subject to us by feudal right with its inhabitants into a dominion of our ownership, every obstacle being overcome, and has annexed and united it to the crown of the said kingdom as a constituent part of it.

To symbolize his new authority, Edward seized the crown of King Arthur and the cross of Neath; he created several new marcher lordships and had shires created in the former tribal lands. All Wales was subject to him, either directly or through marcher lords. In fact, Wales was not "entirely converted," but Edward installed new administrators and offices, and ordered the introduction of English writs into the legal process, while he explicitly kept the inheritance customs of the Welsh (partible inheritance). In 1301, Prince Edward (born in Caernarvon in 1284 and now the next in line to the throne) was created the first English "Prince of Wales." That title was created to affirm the patrimonial right of the heir to the English throne at the same time that it refuted (or annexed) the title of the native Welsh princes.

One of the most impressive and expensive facets of the Welsh conquest was Edward I's network of castles. The strategy was old, but Edward's designs and his investment were striking and novel. He may have drawn on experience in the near East, or in southern France where *bastides*, or fortified towns were a recent development. In any case, he employed a builder from that area to supervise the works. Some ten new and very formidable structures were built between 1276 and 1296, at a cost of about £100,000.

---

[4]*English Historical Documents*, v. 3, pp. 422-27.

Further construction by the marcher lords and renovation of older castles added to the garrison design meant to subdue the Welsh once and for all. The fortified towns adjoining the castles were populated by English colonists. The church hierarchy in Wales was visited, grievances and losses owing to the wars were put to an inquiry, and the administration of the church was brought more fully under the authority of the archbishop of Canterbury.

Rebellions did break out several times over the decade after the conquest. They serve to underline its strength in that they were all serious, and all were suppressed. In 1287 Rhys ap Maredudd rebelled while Edward was in Gascony. The revolt was quickly beaten. In 1290 a dispute between the earls of Hereford and Gloucester broke into fighting but this was put down. In 1294 a significant uprising (again while the English were mobilizing a Gascon campaign) was put down with some difficulty. In all cases, Welsh resistance was subdued. The reasons were clear enough. Now there was a more direct and more effective royal presence. Edward recruited Welsh soldiers on a number of occasions to fight in France or in Scotland, and his combination of direct rule and lordship over the march gave him unprecedented control.

Political turmoil in Scotland followed a dynastic failure and English intervention. Originally Edward I probably would have been content with the peace of the border and the prospect of eventual dynastic connections. There had been close and cordial relations between the two courts for about half a century and there was regular if vague recognition of Scottish homage to the English crown. Alexander III came to England in 1279 and did homage to Edward, though it is not clear whether this was in respect of lands held in England or in regard to Alexander's royal title. The course of diplomacy in the earlier 13th century suggested that the latter point was moot. Certainly Henry III had not been straining to enforce his lordship over the Scots.

The decade after 1279 saw a tragic series of events. Three Scottish royal children died between 1281 and 1284. Then Alexander III died accidentally in 1286. His only survivor was a three-year-old granddaughter, Margaret "the Maid of Norway." A council of Guardians governed during the regency and no immediate effort was made to bring the princess to Scotland. After King Edward returned from Gascony in 1289, negotiations between the English, Scots and Norwegians recognized the young queen and agreed that her future marriage would be subject to Edward's approval; in all probablity she would be the wife of the English heir. In 1290, Margaret was brought from Norway, but she died on the journey after reaching Orkney.

King Edward capitalized on the opportunity to arbitrate the rival claims to the Scottish throne. For whatever the Scots thought of the royal homage to England, there was general acceptance of the king's role as arbiter in the dispute. There were some 13 claims in all, but only two were serious candidates. The hereditary issue was around descent from a brother of King William (d. 1214). Robert Bruce was descended in the junior line; John Balliol was one generation further removed from the crown. King Edward was more concerned with the politics of the rivals. Bruce had been a landowner in Dumfriesshire and Durham. Balliol held lands in Northumberland and Durham and had few connections with Scotland. The candidates all submitted to Edward as their "superior lord" in 1291. Edward convened a special court which met to hear the claims in 1291-92. In November 1292, the judgment was given in favor of Balliol.

Edward apparently believed that he had not only chosen a king for Scotland, but one who would accept constitutional innovations. In any case, that was the import of Edward's attempt to hear appeals from Scottish courts. By so doing, he was exercising "direct lordship", in other words controverting the terms of the submission of 1291. Whether or not Balliol was a party to such action, Edward undermined the authority of his chosen Scottish leader. In 1294 the English king demanded King John's performance of military service in Gascony. A similar demand in Wales inspired revolt. In 1295 a Scottish parliament in Stirling renounced English authority, set up a governing council, and made an alliance with France. These acts brought an English invasion in 1296.

By July, Edward had received Balliol's surrender. He was taken in custody to England, where most of the Scottish records and regalia had preceded him. During his triumphal march through Scotland, Edward received homage from hundreds of noblemen, clergy and lesser landowners. He was sure by the end of 1296 that he had made an effective conquest. But the next year saw the uprising led by William Wallace, the son of a lesser landowner and an unlikely national hero. He and a small band of followers attacked English forces and gradually drew strength from the disaffected elements in Scotland. The rebels won a convincing victory at Stirling Bridge, but Wallace was beaten the next year at Falkirk. Thereafter he avoided major battles and held to guerilla tactics. The English launched major attacks in 1300 and 1301. Their most powerful assault was in 1303, and when Wallace was captured and executed two years later, the English again seemed to be in control.

In 1305 Edward produced a scheme for the government of Scotland which would have made it a dependent state with no more autonomy than Wales. He created an executive similar to that of Ireland (lieutenant, chancellor, chamberlain), a set of justiciars (four pairs of Scots and English) and a Scottish advisory council. Edward assured himself of control of the castles, especially in the south. Finally, the plan called for the elimination of traditional Scottish laws and the introduction of English law. There was hardly time for this ambitious colonial scheme to take effect before Robert Bruce led a new revolt against English rule, one which was to gain what can be described as Scottish independence.

Bruce was the grandson of the unsuccessful candidate for the kingship in 1290-92. The younger Bruce had been at odds for some years with the prominent Comyn family. Whatever Bruce's political plans were, he had to obtain the support or submission of that family and their allies. Bruce met John, "the Red Comyn" in a church at Dumfries in early 1306, and in the course of an argument, stabbed and killed him. The meeting may have been designed to plot a joint rebellion, but the aftermath required Bruce to go it alone. He was proclaimed "Robert I" at Scone in March, but within three months he had been beaten in battle and fled into hiding. From this inauspicious beginning, Bruce stubbornly began a comeback in 1307. He was helped by the death of his major antagonist, Edward I, and the succession of the less warlike Edward II. But Bruce had first to win a civil war (1307-09) to take the leadership of the Scots, and then he faced a long campaign against the English installations in Scotland (1309-14). The climax came as Bruce was about to take the last castle held by the English at Stirling. In June, 1314, Edward II brought a large force into Scotland. At a point on the Bannock Burn near Stirling, the two armies met and the Scots won a decisive victory. Edward fled to Dunbar and took ship for England. This event marks the conventional "independence" of Scotland. To be precise, Bannockburn was a rejection of English lordship, a rejection which would be tested repeatedly over the next few centuries. Edward's conquest was revoked, but his patrimony was not forgotten.

Edward I had been given the lordship of Ireland in 1254. It was specified in the grant that no land should be alienated from the crown. But Edward, who never visited this part of his inheritance, did alienate land, and in this and other ways he showed that his main interest in Ireland was as a revenue source, one which he would not hesitate to exploit. The constitutional position in Ireland was unlike Scotland or Wales. There were still numerous native Irish "kings", with no one clearly superior to the others. The area of Gaelic authority had been reduced to about one-fourth of Ireland by the expansion of the Anglo-Norman colony in the 13th century. In the latter, feudal lordships were loosely responsible to the English king's justiciar in Dublin. Anglo-Irish lords stood somewhere between the status of barons of the Welsh march and members of the Scottish nobility. Ireland's unique feature was its colonial government.

Both the "high kingship" and the Dublin regime were minor concerns to Edward I. Gaelic leaders were unable to unite behind a single ruler for any length of time. Thus when Brian O'Neill, king of Ulster, claimed the high kingship in 1258, his support was slight and he was defeated (and beheaded) in 1260. The native kingdoms also suffered from military inferiority which they were only beginning to offset by the employment of the mercenary "gallowglass": Norse-Gaelic warriors from the western isles who wore armor and fought with the Norse battle axe.

Edward's principal Irish concern was maintaining the revenue of his colonial regime. His officials tackled corruption in administration, which threatened the king's revenue. Shires were made more active units, counties and liberties sent members to early Irish parliaments and in 1284 there was a major inquiry into Irish administration. Thus there was surface evidence of reform or improvement, but beneath that surface, royal financial needs were beginning to sap the strength of the lordship.

Edward's lordship of Gascony made him a vassal of the king of France, a situation which was the reverse of Edward's relations to Welsh, Scottish and Irish princes. A vital difference here was that part of France was undeniably Edward's patrimony, and on the other hand, Edward's vassalage was clearly and irrefutably set out in the Treaty of Paris. Edward was not just sentimentally interested in his Gascon lordship. The annual revenues of the colony were about four times those of Ireland. In 1273 Edward instituted inquiries about titles and lands. In 1286 he negotiated further settlements

117

implied in the 1259 treaty, and he remained in Gascony for three years working out a system of administration.

When in 1293 a fierce naval battle between an Anglo-Gascon fleet and a Norman-Poitevin force led to serious disorder, including the sack of La Rochelle, Edward was ordered to answer for the damage in King Philip's court. Edmund of Lancaster went as the King's envoy, and was tricked into an agreement giving Philip the right to intervene in Gascony. In 1294, the lordship was seized, and Edward renounced his homage and began to raise an army. He was distracted on this occasion by rebellion in Wales, but over the next few years, larger forces and even larger revenues were diverted to Gascony. A truce was arranged in 1297, followed by a treaty in 1303, in which Gascony was returned to Edward. There was essentially no change in the basic position, but the ten years of hostilities had cost roughly twice what the routine revenues from Gascony might have brought in.

There is no doubt that Edward was a keen advocate of his lordship rights; he did not lack wit and energy in putting forward his legal case and using the instruments of royal power, even abusing them, in his cause; he was neither slow nor ineffective in his use of force to uphold the royal patrimony. What told against him was the cost of his collective ventures, in men, in money, and in morale. Of course units of fighting men had been moved about the archipelago for some time. Edward magnified the operations to something near the levels of William I but without obvious evidence of comparable need or the prospect of comparable gain. Because costs had risen sharply in the later 13th century, Edward was forced to be innovative. He exploited all possible sources of fighting men: feudal vassals, mercenaries, household retainers and aristocratic retinues. Some have referred to a "revolution" in military organization, but it is simpler to observe that Edward, like most contemporary rulers, took any expedient available when he had urgent need for military force, and that was rather often in the last decade of his reign.

It is too easy to fault Edward for excessive ambition. Ironically, his policies were too cautious in that he chose to assert "direct" lordship instead of devising a workable system of clientage. His Welsh and Scottish "solutions" show little imagination and less delegation. The royal policy was thereby tied in to English political development through the strain of governing the archipelago "conquests." This connection is quite clear in the major crisis of 1295. Edward wanted general assent to some heavy taxes to pay for his wars in Wales, Scotland and France. All the leading clergy, 48 nobles, representatives of the lower clergy, two knights from each shire and two burgesses from each of 110 cities and boroughs were summoned to the so-called Model Parliament in 1295. Far from a "model," this parliament had more members than any other in the middle ages. In some degree its pattern followed the parliament of Simon de Montfort in 1265. Edward chose a wide cross-section at this time in order to get more support for his tax: an eleventh from the barons, a seventh from the burgesses and a tenth from the clergy. And Edward had reason to expect some difficulty, as we can tell from the events which followed.

The grants of 1295 were not enough--either they were incompletely paid or collected, or the rising costs of castles in Wales and armies in Scotland and Gascony simply outran the royal estimates. One item definitely disrupted the calculations: Pope Boniface intervened with the clergy and directed them to withhold payment unless they had papal authorization. Edward's expenses would not wait. In 1297, Edward consulted with a few barons and declared new taxes. As he left for France, the king also ordered seizure of wool exports on promise of repayment and assessed a tax (with a threat of outlawry) on the clergy. These actions inspired baronial leaders to resist, to refuse payment, and to demand confirmation of Magna Carta plus some added clauses. The principal point here was that the king accepted the idea that no extraordinary taxation could be collected without the 'common consent of the realm.' So far that term was ill-defined, but it was plainly a concession to the broadest sense of patrimony. Obedience to this provision assured that parliaments or something like them would remain a part of the government.

It is hard to say what effect these events had in Scotland and Ireland. In the latter case, there had been a half a dozen meetings we can call parliaments before 1297. In that year and the three following there were three meetings: knights were added in 1297; burgesses in 1299, and both joined the barons in 1300. There was a more vigorous Irish justiciar who in all likelihood reflected Edward's policies in England. In Scotland, the year 1297 was of course one of rebellion and war. There had been four parliaments in the beginning of King John's reign (1293-94) but the political scene was in turmoil for the next two decades, obscuring further development.

The parliaments of the archipelago were plainly instruments of governmental convenience. They had slightly different functions in each area, and not all areas were equipped with these councils. The 13th century was a period of experimentation. That Edward settled on an enlarged English parliament was a product of his trial and error method. The experience of 1297 probably evoked bitter memories of the Oxford parliament forty years earlier. This king would not surrender power, but in order not to, and to maintain the revenues to carry on his wars, Edward accepted the principle of "common consent," one of the most potent of all political ideas.

Edward II failed to match his father's capacity as a ruler, and problems which had been barely manageable became overwhelming in the new reign (1307-1327). The young king's court favorites and his uncertain policies generated dangerous aristocratic opposition. The losses in Scotland plus invasion in Ireland appeared to forecast a major reaction to English expansion. The manifest failures of the king were briefly overshadowed by his counter-attack on aristocrats (1322-25) but the unrest grew and the king was overthrown and murdered in 1327.

At his coronation, Edward II had used a new phrase in his oath. He promised to observe "the rightful laws and customs which the community of the realm shall have chosen." In this case, Edward was not knowingly endorsing some advanced constitutional idea; in fact, he probably accepted this language to mollify some baronial reformers and to keep his current favorite at court. Piers Gaveston was a knight from Gascony who had won the king's affection, and who was created earl of Cornwall. Aristocrats distrusted the favorite, and in 1310 the king was forced to appoint 21 "ordainers." The following year he was made to accept their Ordinances-- revenue reforms, revised customs and judicial reform. The Ordinances did not become fully effective and once again baronial reform was awkward in implementation. Soon the animosity exploded again, and Gaveston was executed by several of the barons. Defeat in Scotland in 1314 intensified the mood of dissatisfaction, there were new purges and Thomas, Earl of Lancaster became the principal reform leader. New royal councils tried to implement the Ordinances while shifting court factions tried to manipulate the king. Hugh Despenser emerged as the new royal favorite and with accumulated gifts he built a great land base in south Wales. After Hugh was forced into exile, Edward attacked and defeated Lancaster. A number of the dissident group were executed and heavy fines and forfeitures accompanied the return of the favorites to court.

The downfall of Edward II seems natural in retrospect, but between 1322 and 1325 he had muzzled baronial resistance. Only renewed royal ineptitude saved the day. The Queen had been banished from court and dispossessed, but Edward unwisely elected to send her on a diplomatic mission to her brother, King Charles IV of France. Later, he allowed Prince Edward to join her to act as his representative and to do homage for Aquitaine. Meanwhile, Isabella had met the exiled Roger Mortimer, earl of March and former justiciar of Ireland. The two became lovers, and in 1326 they led an expedition which brought down Edward's government. The king fled to Wales, but he and Despenser were captured, the favorite was executed promptly, but the king had to abdicate in favor of his son Edward, before he was eliminated in a brutal murder.

While Edward II's English government was in such unstable condition, his lordship outside England was plainly losing all effectiveness, and no doubt making a large contribution to English instability. The Scottish king's brother Edward Bruce landed in Ulster in 1315 with a reported 6,000 men and he was soon joined by a number of Gaelic leaders and their men. Bruce's early campaigns brought victories in the northeast, and he assumed the high kingship in 1316. He returned to Scotland and convinced his brother to join him with reinforcements. The campaigning of 1317 was inconclusive, and Robert returned to Scotland. In 1318, Edward made another march out of Ulster, but was intercepted and killed.

Bruce originally enjoyed native support, but the effect of his foraging army, coinciding with three years of severe famine, made his continual campaigning intolerable. Fewer and fewer Gaelic chieftains saw him as a savior; more and more Anglo-Irish leaders were frightened by the evident instability of the lordship, and slowly came to its support. The invasion vividly demonstrated the weakness of the Irish polity, weakness owed in large measure to Edwardian policy. The exploitation of Ireland was a good illustration of the fragility of Edwardian patrimony.

That fragility was due in part to a conflict of laws. In a famous "Remonstrance" to the pope, Donald O'Neill king of Ulster wrote in 1317:[5]

---

[5]E. Curtis and R.B. McDowell, eds., *Irish Historical Documents* (1943), pp. 45-6.

as it is free to anyone to renounce his right and transfer it to another, all the right which is publicly known to pertain to us in the said kingdom as its true heirs we have given and granted to [Edward Bruce]...and in order that he may do therein judgment and justice and equity which through default of the prince [Edward II] have utterly failed therein, we have unanimously established and set him up as our king and lord in our kingdom aforesaid.

This "transfer" was alien to English usage; it had precedent in Gaelic practice, and it was one of the clearest cases of a direct confrontation of the two patrimonial systems. It was also prophetic in that the Gaelic revival of the 14th century would see more and more adoption of the *brehon* law by the Anglo-Irish, and less and less influence by the colonial legal system. In matters of inheritance there was a swing to the older system, among other things to avoid the troublesome matter of inheritance by female heirs. Irish kingship still was diffused and deficient. It lacked the property rights that other kingships had; it did not have the same military potential (witness the need for and the effect of introducing the "Gallowglass" or mercenary soldier in the 13th and 14th centuries).

The English were in serious difficulty in the north after Bannockburn. Raids over the border, the loss of Berwick (1318), and the secret negotiations with Lancaster (1322) were all signs of a condition verging on anarchy in the region. Edward's last march into Scotland (1322) was followed by a bold raid into Yorkshire by Robert I, in which Edward narrowly escaped the marauding Scots. A truce was agreed, but by 1327 there was another Scottish assault which led this time to a formal treaty (Edinburgh/Northhampton-1328). Edward III was the signatory, and the treaty recognized the title of Robert I, English claims were renounced, an alliance was made (saving the existing Scottish alliance with France), and dynastic marriages and tribute were prescribed. Thus Anglo-Scottish warfare seemed to be settled, albeit not on terms acceptable to the young English king. One of the provisions in 1328 was a promise that Edward would intercede in Rome on behalf of the King of Scotland. In fact, the excommunication of Robert and the sentence of interdict on Scotland were lifted in late 1328. Such papal punishment was of course a serious royal disability; since Bruce had murdered Comyn on consecrated ground and since he thereafter led a rebellion against his anointed lord, Bruce was clearly outside the grace of the church. In 1319-20, Pope John XXII summoned four Scottish bishops to the curia, and when they ignored his call, they too were excommunicated. The Scottish reply came in a letter, later known as "The Declaration of Arbroath" (named after the monastery at which it was adopted). From the "community of Scotland," the letter was signed by some 40 leading noblemen and royal officials. In its key section, the letter pledged loyalty to Robert Bruce:[6]

> The Divine Providence, the right of succession by the laws and customs of the kingdom (which we will defend till death) and the due and lawful consent and assent of all the people, made him our king and prince. To him we are obliged and resolved to adhere in all things, both upon account of his right and his own merit, as being the person who hath restored the people's safety in defence of their liberties. But after all, if this prince shall leave these principles he hath so nobly pursued, and consent that we or our kingdom be subjected to the king or people of England, we will immediately endeavour to expel him, as our enemy and as the subverter both of his own and our rights, and we will make another king who will defend our liberties. For so long as there shall but one hundred of us remain alive, we will never give consent to subject ourselves to the dominion of the English.

The divine, legal and popular elements of Bruce's inheritance were thus carefully distinguished. Naturally the last of these caught the attention of 19th century liberal writers as an early statement of popular sovereignty. In terms which the 14th century might better understand, the declaration was addressing the issues of patrimony ("rights" and "liberties") and the interaction of ruler and community in that regard. This was one sign of a rising consciousness of communal patrimony. The number of such incidents was increasing, though without any clear pattern. In rural areas, English shire courts were coming under the influence of landowners who would soon assume the form of the Commission of the Peace. Meanwhile, Robert I was creating a number of regalities, with hereditary local jurisdiction. The Scottish "royal burghs" were so constituted as a device to encourage colonization. In that special community of the church, the 14th century was a time of retracted Roman influence, but of continued foundation and endowment which also nourished patrimonial interests.

Edward I's patrimony was in lordships which encompassed the archipelago and a sizeable continental colony. Within his lordship there were innumerable individual and communal powers, each with their allegiance to

---

[6]Gordon Donaldson, ed., *Scottish Historical Documents* (1970), p. 57.

the lord king. In governing these communities and individuals, Edward had boldly pursued a process of incorporation which acknowledged the communities and powerful individuals, which collected them together (in various patterns). The king's dominions were made up of traditional groups which were just beginning to see themselves in terms of modern nationality. Most observers in the time of Edward or his son would probably concur with the chronicler who thus described one reason for civil war in 1322?[7]

> It was no wonder, for the great lords of England were not all of one nation, but were muddled up with other nations, some Britons, some Saxons, some Danes, some Picts, some French, some Normans, some Spaniards, some Romans, some Hainaulters, some Flemings, and some other assorted nations, the which did not accord well with the kind blood of England.

"Nations" were not yet perceived as territorial communities, but these enlarged tribes or families were coming together in larger and more durable political shape as the 14th century progressed. Edward I's policies had been an important stimulant for national development. An equally potent influence was going to come from the English crown's obsession with France.

The French Obsession

The "kind blood" of polyglot, localized England was heavily-laced with French influence in the 14th century. The recession of French power had not ended the use of the French language, or caused the loss of French cultural ties, or severance from French social customs. Thus the prolonged warfare with France was essential to an emerging English identity. The royal obsession which inspired the fighting grew out of three important royal patrimonial concerns: the real and remembered rights of the English in France; the novel claim (1328) of Edward III to inherit the French crown; and the persistent threat of French aggression against England or its dominions. The long and costly wars which were the product of the obsession had serious repercussions in domestic politics in the archipelago. The ancient links to France could not be forgotten. In the first place, one of them still existed in Gascony, and it had been recently reforged at very heavy cost. Edward I was acutely conscious of his father's treaty of 1259, which

---

[7]*Brut of the Princes*, v.1, p. 220; cited in Prestwich, *The Three Edwards*, p. 100.

eliminated the old patrimony, but which also provided for additions to English holdings in Gascony. More generally, the renunciation of rights, such as Henry III had made, did not produce sudden memory loss. In a culture which esteemed tradition and inheritance, old losses were not soon forgotten. Not only that, territorial connections were always subject to dynastic revision.

The most striking Anglo-French dynastic event actually came out of the Gascon settlement of 1303. Edward I arranged the marriage of Prince Edward to Isabella, the daughter of Philip IV. The wedding was in 1308, and their son Edward was born in 1312. Such a marriage would not ordinarily have had further consequences, but Isabella's three brothers all died without issue, between 1314 and 1328. Therefore the Capetian line came to an end and the junior (Valois) branch of the French royal family inherited, according to the Salic Law, which barred inheritance through females. By English practice, the son of Isabella stood to inherit before a collateral heir. Edward III was ambiguous in the assertion of his claim. It was made publicly in 1328, but not returned to with any energy until 1337. Some see this as a sign that Edward thought little of it; more than likely, Scottish affairs, English court conspiracy (Mortimer and Isabella were overthrown in 1330) and other business of the young king precluded the full-scale assertion of the claim in 1328.

The rather widespread fear of France in the early 14th century has received less attention than might be expected in standard English accounts. Military and diplomatic incidents preceded the outbreak of hostilities in 1337. We have already seen the crisis of 1293, involving the English king's feudal obligation, the Franco-Scottish alliance (1295) and the dynastic marriage between France and England (1303). French diplomatic ascendance was underlined by the "captivity" of the papal court, residing at Avignon in the south of France from 1309.

The French renewed the alliance with the Scots in 1326, promising aid in any warfare with England, a promise which was more often made than kept. This version of the Auld Alliance was acknowledged in 1328 in the Anglo-Scottish Treaty of Edinburgh/Northampton. If French aid was seldom realized in Scotland, the decade of the 1330s seemed to threaten a new militance. There is scattered documentary evidence of French plans to send large fleets into the waters of the archipelago in 1335 and 1336. There is evidence that Edward III was alerted and had ordered defensive measures.[8]

The French threat became a reality in May, 1337. King Philip VI ordered his officers to seize the ducal properties of his vassal King Edward. French troops overran Ponthieu, invaded the Channel Islands, and occupied Aquitaine. This was the first action of the "Hundred Years' War." It recalled any number of past confrontations between the kings of England and France, and it might possibly have been "settled" as those earlier disputes had been. The critical difference in this case was the introduction of Edward III's dynastic claim; it would be withdrawn and reasserted over the next century, and in the course of the struggle, dynastic or patrimonial ambition would take on some enlarged, "national" features.

It is easy to quibble with the name "Hundred Years War." The term was first used in the 19th century and it has endured because it conveys the sense of unusually prolonged hostility (1337-1453). It is a truism to observe that aims, tactics and strategy went through some significant changes in the course of the fighting. It is also fairly clear that the "England" and "France" which began the struggle were rather different from those two entities at the end. First we will concentrate on the military events as they impinged upon the Atlantic Archipelago. The next section will focus on the domestic political aspects of the fighting.

In outline, the warfare began with a period of English victories: destruction of the French fleet in 1340, and two very successful land campaigns with victories in northern and central France (Crécy, 1346 and Poitiers, 1356). At the close of this phase, the King of France was a captive of the English, and in the treaty of Bretigny (1360) King John was ransomed (£500,000) in exchange for Gascony, Poitou and other territory plus renunciation of the English dynastic claim.

The next half century saw significant French recovery from that low point: fighting resumed in 1369, and within a decade most of the lost lands had been retaken and the English only held several coastal enclaves (Calais, Bordeaux, Bayonne). Truces were made and broken over the next 30 years. A third phase began in 1415 with another stunning English victory

---

[8]H.J. Hewitt, "The Organization of War" and C.F. Richmond, "The War at Sea", both in Kenneth Fowler, ed. *The Hundred Years War* (1971), pp. 76, 96.

(Agincourt) and a campaign leading to the conclusion of the Treaty of Troyes (1420) which provided for the English king's succession to the French throne. Shortly thereafter, the tide shifted again. Henry V died (1422) just before his French legator, voiding the planned succession. The English nevertheless tried to implement the treaty, and Henry VI was actually crowned in Paris in 1430. However, another French recovery had begun, this time inspired by the heroics of Joan of Arc, a peasant girl of some mystical genius. A more mundane campaign of sieges and truces over the next 20 years (to 1453) ended with the expulsion of the English from all of their possessions except Calais.

The wars naturally involved the exploitation by English kings of all available resources in the archipelago--military, fiscal and diplomatic. However, the history of the archipelago since 1277 drew some indelible marks across this kind of plan. It was possible to draw upon the Welsh counties for archers and pikemen. How much this would weaken that frontier was problematic. It was much less wise to withdraw able fighting men from Northumberland or Durham or Cumberland, as the border continued to be vulnerable. The basic problem in the case of Ireland was the rundown of revenues. Edward I had made great demands on this fragile account, including a share of the cost of constructing the castles in Wales. While there was little more spent in that cause after 1330, the fiscal damage had already been done. Ireland's wealth, or that part which was within reach of the Anglo-Irish administration, was barely enough to meet the costs of that administration. After the Bruce invasion, the revenue was only a fraction of peak years under Edward I. Indeed, there were continued pleas for subsidy and the English crown mounted several costly expeditions (1361, 1394, 1399) to restore order in Ireland. Thus, the balance sheet for this corner of the archipelago showed a net loss.

The most serious problem of all, of course, was the Scottish opposition. Having an ally of France on the north flank, even one with slender resources, was extremely dangerous. Edward III was able to neutralize that threat. Ironically, his three invasions of Scotland (1333-1341) were successful, but his greatest advantage came when David II unwisely attacked in 1346 (in fulfillment of his obligation to France). The Scots were routed at the battle of Neville's Cross, and King David was taken prisoner. He was a captive for 11 years and had to agree to a ransom, most of which was paid. Actually,

127

the most serious aspect in English eyes was the potential for French invasion *via* Scotland. And the chief reason that one was not launched was the pressure of English attacks, at sea (Sluys, 1340) and on land (Crécy, 1346). The Scottish opposition shifted its character under the Lancastrians. There were fewer battles across the border and more Scots served abroad under the king of France, in fact the French royal bodyguard was a Scottish company, the *garde écossaise* (1445). Some serious internal political problems--regency, minority and aristocratic competition--brought a lull in Scottish operations to the south.

If any English king had ever contemplated mobilizing the archipelago, he would soon have found it impossible. The best he might expect would be coincidental calm in the outlying dominions. This not only would permit the use of most of his English forces in France, but it might be possible in such circumstances to recruit forces from Wales and Scotland. The actual military organization employed by the English king was irregular as it moved away from a classic feudal outline and older involuntary service. Even in the 13th century, the English king had begun to raise forces by a combination of feudal tenures, paid household retainers (bannerets), contractual (indentured) companies, and the private retinues of his great men. The conditions of the 14th century only magnified changes already in progress.

The principal English military operations in the war were the mounted raids (or *chevauchée*) which could strike at one of the major and accessible centers in northern France, usually avoiding major field engagements. Ironically, it was three such engagements which constituted the chief highlights of the war for England, though it is unlikely that they were sought, and it is generally agreed by students of warfare that the French tactical errors were responsible for the dramatic English victories of Crécy, Poitiers and Agincourt. Much more was expended and perhaps more was at stake in the less glamorous siege warfare which accompanied the other actions.

The equipment and supply of the invading army was costly and complex. There were clearly inadequate resources available to any king of England to pay for even a fraction of the cost of such a venture. The armies were allowed to forage and to requisition whatever food and supplies they could. This was not an unusual mode of operation, but obviously it ran into difficulty when an area was overrun repeatedly or when one army had adopted a "scorched earth" tactic to deprive the enemy of supplies.

In one other aspect, the war was costly. England had to try to develop diplomatic counterweights to France, and Flanders, Burgundy, or the Empire were each at one time or another enlisted in the English cause. But there was difficulty in constructing any sort of constant alliance. There was also difficulty in managing relations with the papacy, because of the Avignon situation and because of consequent anticlerical policies in England.

It may well be that the ultimate consequence of the wars was diplomatic. The English crown was removed from France (excepting Calais) after 1453. This harsh defining act was of great international significance for both nations. The fact that the English king continued to style himself "King of England, France and Ireland" until 1802 was never of practical significance after the 15th century. It was a curious echo of patrimonial claims, which by their nature died very slowly.

Society and Patrimony

From a modern perspective it is difficult to see subtle changes in the contours of patrimonial society. In the 14th and 15th centuries, England led the archipelago toward the establishment of a modern, post-feudal aristocracy. It looked and sounded like its feudal predecessor, but the peerage of 1460 was a very different thing from the baronage of two centuries earlier. Important legal changes in inheritance, the formal creation of peerage ranks, and more broadly, the conversion of a military aristocracy into a class with articulated political and economic interests formed the essence of this change. The chivalric code remained as a formal expression of the ethos, but it ceased to mirror life in the lists or on the battlefield.

The "rule" of primogeniture followed from the creation of the inheritable knights' fee. Before the practice became general, the fee was losing its value for military service. As we have seen, by the end of the 13th century, Edward I's legislation modified feudal inheritance. Yet the incentive to preserve the patrimony remained. Accidents of inheritance (death without heirs, minors, females and outright gift) could disrupt an estate; later in 14th century England, joint (husband/wife) tenures, trusts and restricted wardship were added variations on inheritance. "The crown's simple relationship to its tenants had been destroyed." Increased power over inheritance also meant increased freedom for the owner of estates "to defeat...the operations of

129

primogeniture, to buy lands for his younger sons, husbands for his daughters and masses for his soul."[9]

Such power of ownership was not evident where the English king's writ did not run in the archipelago. The patrimonial concept in the Gaelic, Norse and Welsh communities was much more conservative, as a few specific contrasts will show. On the basic nature of inheritance, the English king and magnates adhered to the principle of primogeniture (inheritance of the eldest male heir). Elsewhere in the archipelago, partible inheritance, often called gavelkind, held that the estate should be equally divided among male heirs. But there were numerous exceptions. In England, when there were only female heirs, they divided the inheritance. In some parts of England, it was common (as in Kent) for small, non-feudal properties to be divided. The jurisdiction which was part of the patrimony, the lordship, was frozen by Edward I in the statute *quia emptores*. But elsewhere, as in Scotland, no such law was introduced. There, in fact, Robert Bruce created new feudal baronies and local jurisdictions ("regalities") in the early 14th century.

The inheritance by custom and by feudal contract carried a number of duties and obligations with it. At all levels of society it was in the heir's interest to limit or reduce these duties. Thus, for holders of English manorial lands, copyhold tenure evolved from the 13th century. A tenant holding a copy of the manorial roll which prescribed his duties had a form of deed which the courts recognized, and which became a form of heritable property at a fixed rent. In the 15th century, the Scottish *feu-ferm* had limited dues, with a fixed annual feu-duty, which was secured by a lump sum payment for a feu charter. This began as a royal device (given to royal burghs in the 14th century, then to crown lands, and later in the 15th century to lands of others).[10] Such enhanced patrimonial rights, or modified tenures, were confined to the areas where they could be upheld in a strong central court. Otherwise, the power of custom and tradition was too strong for such innovation.

These contrasts in the patrimonial environment were paralleled by a complex network of royal patronage. In essence the original feudal bonds were a form of patron-client relation. These were replaced in the 14th century

---

[9]Holmes, *Estates of the Higher Nobility*, 55-57.
[10]Ranald Nicholson, *Scotland in the Later Middle Ages* (1974), p. 300.

by new contractual forms, often referred to as "bastard feudalism." That is, the crown contracted for military service on specified terms. At the same time, the crown still might reward its followers with titles and honors and estates, i.e. patronage. This practice, composed of the creation or transfer of patrimonial rights, was not new, but its exercise was behind some important innovation.

Most notably, it seems that the exercise of separate acts of patronage were responsible for the creation of the English peerage in the 14th century. The invention of ranks began in the reign of Edward III. At first, the ancient title of earl was the only distinction beside the generic baron. In 1337, Edward created his first son duke of Cornwall. In 1351, Henry of Lancaster was entitled duke, and the king's second son Lionel was made duke of Clarence in 1362. Somewhat later, under different political circumstances, Richard II made Robert de Vere marquis of Dublin (1385). The first baron created by royal letters patent was John Beauchamp (1387). These titles might be inherited, but the more radical feature of Richard's creations was that some were not attached to considerable estates. The noteworthy, later the defining characteristic of the peer of the realm was that he automatically received a summons to every parliament. Thus the peer was a permanent member of the royal council.

One of the more interesting byproducts of the creation of a peerage was the simultaneous appearance of a gentry class. That is, the peers were but a fraction (albeit the wealthiest or most influential layer) of a large landowning and fighting class. Those who remained untitled were still important figures in society and in the economic and military life of the community. The knights, esquires and gentlemen were recognized in the 14th and 15th centuries as the social and political leaders of the English counties. For instance, the office of justice of the peace was formally settled in statute in 1362, and this appointed local notable would meet quarterly with others of his class in a county court to hear and settle criminal cases and to perform other tasks in local government. The gentleman or the knight was bound by custom and interest into the same economic-social network as the landowning peer; oddly enough, the lesser country figure in the 14th century came to be part of the "commons" along with borough members of parliament--no doubt this was a byproduct of the current "invention" of hereditary titles, which set the peers apart. This division of the landed class was to have tremendous

131

political significance in the long term, preventing the formation of a solid and inflexible phalanx of the "country" interest. The division did not occur in Scotland, where there was a single chamber; in Ireland the Anglo-Gaelic division of landowners was paramount; in Wales the native gentry (*uchelwyr*) had no parliament to attend.

For our convenience we speak glibly of "aristocrats" and "nobility." But this upper class contained a variety of characters who experienced success and failure as individuals more than as members of a group. And that success depended as always on the security of one's patrimony. This principle was unchanged though all the vicissitudes of the 14th and 15th centuries. But if the patrimonial tradition remained, it did not have to be kept in fossilized form: the means of sustaining the estate, the ideals for which one would sacrifice the estate, and the competing values in society were all subject to variation. Thus in the apparently suicidal "wars" of Yorkists and Lancastrians, the partisans were as intent as ever on preserving what they held most dear. To help us to understand the contradictory politics of the 15th century, we have to review the economic and religious upheavals which shaped their environment.

The medieval economy has too often been stereotyped by the structures of manor and borough. An image of localized, restricted and immature activity dominates. And of course all of the proceeds (such as they were) went to mount and arm a feudal knight. But between 1300 and 1500 the "feudal" economy disappeared and was replaced by market agriculture and urban growth in England. Meanwhile, most of Wales, Scotland and Ireland changed slowly if at all. What to us is a "feudal" economy was, after 1500, only found in parts of the archipelago which were least affected by the classic feudal system! There were two broad types of economic change which operated in England in the 14th and 15th centuries: (1) common crises of war, famine and plague and (2) cumulative improvement of production and trade and economic structure. The first was shared by the archipelago by its very nature, the second was confined more narrowly to England and its immediate vicinity.

War in the economy is usually assumed to have had a purely negative effect. This cannot be proven, and it is dubious at best. For all the loss of property must be set against "war profits" from booty and ransom. The heavy expenditure on weapons, supplies, shipping and wages were all transfers of wealth, and were perhaps losses only in those cases where currency physically left the realm--indeed a large portion of the total, but certainly not all of it. There were also "indirect costs" in the form of increased taxation, corruption and their effects on the morale and hence the political structure of the archipelago.

Part of the negative impression came from the coincidence of war with other "common" catastrophic incidents--famine, plague and pestilence. There were major episodes of famine in 1315-16-17. These were not unusual in frequency or severity, but the dearth associated with warfare was now added to them. Even though no part of the archipelago suffered in the way that parts of France did, there were serious dislocations in a few places. Southern coastal areas were ravaged, the Scottish border was often described (on either side) in the bleakest terms, and Ireland during the Bruce invasion was devastated in a number of areas.

Surely the most frightening and depressing of calamities during the war years was the "Black Death". This surge of bubonic plague crossed France in 1347. It reached Southampton in 1348, and within a year outbreaks were reported in all parts of the archipelago. Cities and towns, or other concentrated populations were the most vulnerable. Fleas biting infected rats transmitted the disease to humans who suffered debilitating fevers and sores, and those infected usually died. There is no way to accurately measure the mortality, but it seems that upwards of 20% of the population died in the first plague--an incredible loss, but all too normal in a case of initial contact. Even more depressing perhaps were the return visits of the disease in 1361, 1369 and thereafter at irregular intervals until the 17th century. The first plague alone did immeasurably more damage than the wars of the two centuries, even in direct physical terms. When one adds the psychological impact, the loss was greater still. In social terms, the main impact of loss of life was in the lowest classes, and there a major decline in the labor force produced two opposing effects: increased presssure on wages and decreased demand for basic commodities. Because of the latter, price movements were unstable and generally downward; because of the shrinking labor force, wages were apt to rise, pushing prices back up. The English government, representing the confused and angry landlords, moved quickly to stabilize wage levels. In 1349 the Ordinance of Laborers ordered that the level of wages paid in 1347 (before the plague) be restored. In 1351 this was restated in a statute (either to give it more force, or because there was some fear of the royal power being exercised in this manner on a broad economic issue). In any case, the statute was not likely to have more power than the ordinance in actually controlling economic behavior. Considerable regulatory effort was made, using the justices of the peace as agents. Legislation and other measures were unsuccessful in defeating the plague's impact, because, among other things, the landlord conspired against wage controls, in order to compete in a shrinking labor market. Ironically, in an era of supposed economic controls and uniform levels, there was little evidence of such ideals in the 14th century economic structure. The English experience was not unique; Welsh and Irish reactions were pulled along in the same direction; Scottish response to the effect of the plague did not include such drastic measures, because as far as we can tell, the loss of life was much slighter. The density of population and the less developed economy were in this case a sort of protective barrier. In fact the plague had appeared much earlier in England, giving rise to the Scots calling it "the foul death of the English." Alas, their turn came, as it did again on the later visitations.

While the trauma of these events should certainly not be minimized, we need to remember that the general performance of societies in terms of production, distribution and exchange of goods and services has been influenced by a wide variety of historical developments. In the archipelago, in these two centuries, the course of alterations was very significant. The land was still the essential element, either in pastoral or agricultural production (livestock, crops, or mixed farming). The major variation between the 13th and 15th century was an increase in market production. This was always present, but it seems to have been accelerated by war's demands for movement of men and material, consequent expansion of shipping and general increase in levels of production. The early 13th century saw considerable expansion of agriculture known to English contemporaries as "high farming."

Manufactures and trade were a small sector of the economy in the early middle ages, and it was in the period we are studying that they made very substantial increases for the first time. Some of this too was war-related, most of it was simply the evolution of processes, helped or hindered by government. For instance, while England had become a major producer of raw wool in the 13th century, her access to Flemish manufacturing centers was disrupted and the crown pushed a policy of industrial development whereby England shifted to a major role in wool manufacture. Trade was also in its infancy. Until the late 13th century, Italian bankers and Baltic traders were prominent in "English" commerce. This economic dependence was challenged in several ways around 1300, and in the next two centuries there was irregular growth, toward a position of some trading power by the opening of the 16th century. In this instance, the English kings enjoyed a physical and political domination which they usually exploited to give them control over the archipelago's trade.

The later medieval period was one in which the political importance of the church was still great, even though it went through a recession in the 14th century. We have already noted how the papacy physically moved from Rome and resided at Avignon (1309-1377) and then suffered the trauma of schism when there were two (and briefly three) popes (1378-1418). There followed a short period in which leading churchmen proposed a constitutional reform of church government in the form of direction of affairs via church councils, a movement which failed, but which had serious consequences: the power of popes was restored in all its fulness (on paper) and exercised with jealous regard for prerogatives, while in the community at large, there was at least a vague awareness that this authority had been challenged. There are at least three aspects of the relations between the church and archipelago society which we must review to form some idea of the impact on contemporary politics: the church and its power over temporalities, the church and its relation to doctrine, and the church in its broad connections to emerging national units.

The pope retained, through the so-called captivity, his power to appoint men to benefices in all parts of the church. The English king challenged this right with the statutes of Provisors (1351, etc.), but elsewhere there was continued exercise of this capacity. While the English statutes applied to Wales, they did not apply in Scotland. In most specific cases of appointment, below the level of archbishop and bishop (12 in Scotland, 15 in England, 4 in Wales, 23 in Ireland) church livings were usually in the gift of great landowners. Indeed, the proprietary connection itself was varied in the archipelago. Where the Irish bishopric was still apt to be a family property, the English tended to a more cosmopolitan model. Of course the incomes were irregular because over time the several sees had acquired vastly different properties and values.

The papal curia in Avignon became a better-organized and well-equipped bureaucratic machine. It was ironic that when challenged by English royal policy ("praemunire" ordered all cases on appeal to go to the court of the archbishop of Canterbury, and no further without royal license), the curia had in fact become a much better legal institution than before--if one which probably cost more to use. The Scottish church had no such experience, for until the end of the 15th century there was no archbishop in Scotland and thus a more direct relationship with Rome. The church in Ireland had divided authority and the church in Wales was subject to Canterbury, but both usually conformed to the prevailing English position on canonical jurisdiction.

Older histories assumed without any substantial argument that problems of church governance were behind a growing looseness in matters of morals and doctrine. We might as well credit the prolonged and dismal record of war and plague with the sort of social disease which fostered first anticlerical and then heretical behavior. We must also guard against exaggerating the impact of this nonconformity, knowing as we do that the eventual storm of the 16th century reformation was on the horizon. For in fact the "horizon" of the 14th and 15th century saw no such thing. It saw instead the critical condition of an institution which was expected to be the hub of the universe, the guide for all political action and the moral arbiter for all men. For defense or preservation of that institution, John Wyclif criticized papal power, and he eventually opposed the doctrines which seemed to uphold that power. At the same time, pietistic and mystical believers were approaching the perceived weakness of the church from another, possibly more wholesome direction. Wyclif was an Oxford scholar and sometime royal official whose work began to attract notice in the 1370s. He was tried for heresy but protected by John of Gaunt, the duke of Lancaster, and thus escaped punishment, even when his doctrines were denounced. Wyclif taught that the church should not take property and that unworthy clerics were unable to administer valid sacraments, and he went on to question the nature of the eucharist and to advocate vernacular scripture. Some followers, known as "Lollards," carried his ideas to a wider audience, and there were some among the governing classes who were also adherents. But Wyclif himself was not a promoter, his "disciples" had no movement, and by 1403 there was severe legislation in

England against his ideas. After a series of burnings of unrepentent Lollards, the cause weakened and died or went underground. There were few traces of Lollardy in Wales, Scotland, or Ireland. In fact, the best evidence in Scotland comes from the arrest and trial of English Lollards.

One of the more interesting political features which appeared in church affairs in this period was the evident racial or national consciousness in areas of Celtic background. The main avenue of advancement for the Welsh gentry had been a career in the church. The bishops of Wales had frequently been natives. That avenue was blocked from the end of the 14th century (1 of 16 were Welsh, 1372-1400). English servants of the crown or of marcher lords garnered these and all the lesser but valuable posts. There were also ugly incidents at Oxford (where most Welsh students went for their education) including a serious riot in 1395. In Ireland, the famous Statutes of Kilkenny (1366) had ordered

> no Irish of the nations of the Irish be admitted to any cathedral or collegiate church by provision, collation, or presentation of any person whatsoever, or to any benefice of Holy Church amongst the English of that land.

Some licenses were issued to exempt in specific cases, but the law was confirmed in 1416 and the practice was continued. The opposite policy held in the Irish community, where it was rare for an Anglo-Irish candidate to be installed in a benefice. This practice extended to the mendicant orders and other monastic clergy. These provisions were graphic illustrations of a condition of patrimonial political conflict which was beginning to approach crisis proportions.

The Crisis of Patrimonial Politics

The tides of victory and defeat in France set the tempo for political crises in the archipelago, but the nature of their impact was determined by collisions of patrimonial rights in the several different regimes. It would strain credulity to impose a uniform pattern on all the acts of political violence, but the frequency and intensity of 15th century disputes represents something more than selfish aggrandizement. Kings, barons, clerics and communities all had patrimonial interests; the conflicts between them were especially open

137

and direct in the 15th century; the exhaustion from this level of strife produced a reaction in favor of more unified dynastic or national patrimony.

In navigating through the prolonged period of crisis, we can only select a few of the major events: the tyranny and deposition of Richard II, the rebellion and defeat of Owain Glyn Dwr, the traumatic succession to the Scottish crown, the enfeebling of the lordship of Ireland, and the violence of Jack Cade's rebellion. While such a selective sketch cannot support a full analysis of 15th century political development, it will point out the features in the archipelago which prompted that most romanticized of patrimonial battles, the "Wars of the Roses." These "wars" closed the crisis era quite emphatically and were more responsible than any other facet for the political trend toward what once was called "new monarchy." In our terms, the end of the 15th century was to see not a "new" royal power or recovered skill in the use of old power: what appeared was a new merger of royal, individual and communal patrimony.

Richard II, second son of the Black Prince and grandson of Edward III, came to the English throne in 1377 in difficult circumstances. The war was going badly, there had been French raids, the treasury was low and there was rising animosity to the old king's court favorites. Technically, the ten-year old monarch had no regent, but magnates like his uncle John of Gaunt and cousin Edmund Mortimer, earl of March, were the greatest English landowners and de facto councillors. There were also councils of magnates and of the larger community (parliament) from which the young king would receive ample advice.

The crown's financial weakness caused resort to highly unpopular poll taxes in Richard's early years. The collection of this tax sparked a rare popular revolt in 1381, when a group of peasants marched on London. They killed several high officials and dispersed when Richard promised them a pardon. The leaders of the rebellion were captured and executed; in modern revolutionary terms, the incident was a total failure. In terms of the 14th century "community of the realm," it was an ominous sign. That such an outburst went as far as it did "suggests that the nobility, the natural leaders of society in such an emergency, allowed the situation to get out of control."[11]

---

[11]Anthony Tuck, *Richard II and the English Nobility* (1974) p. 51.

In 1385, Richard assumed full power in his own right. He led an army into Scotland and subdued the enemy but alienated some of his noblemen. He argued with Gaunt over strategy and he made some reckless new creations: the dukes of Cambridge and Buckingham were elevated; Michael de la Pole was made earl of Suffolk, and the other main royal favorite, Robert de Vere was made marquis of Dublin, giving him the land and lordship of Ireland. Within a year, Richard changed the title to "duke of Ireland" and gave de Vere full palatine powers; this was academic, for de Vere never was likely to convert his formal title into real power. Instead, his and other elevations were more significant, were perhaps only intended to have weight, in the struggles within the royal court and between rival noble factions. Richard's creations provoked a reaction which culminated in the "Merciless Parliament" of 1388. A number of courtiers were "appealed," i.e. convicted by parliamentary denunciation. There were eight executions and a number of forfeitures, most of which were used to pay off the king's debts.

As before, the baronial efforts had little staying power, and Richard soon regained control. His foreign policies and domestic strategy were likely to lead to renewed problems. Richard wanted peace with France, and this he achieved with a series of truces, 1389-1396. He also sought security by isolating Scotland and increasing his own power on the border, even as he shored up dwindling royal power in Ireland. To that end, he led the first royal venture into Ireland since King John's reign, and with a force of about 5,000 men he was quite successful in temporarily reinforcing the Anglo-Irish community.

By 1397, Richard felt strong enough to launch a counter-attack on the "Lords Appellant" of 1388. The tyranny of Richard involved sweeping forfeitures, exile for several magnates, and execution for a few others. Richard employed a court of chivalry, which was not the proper royal venue for serious criminal charges. He exiled two of his leading opponents, the earl of Norfolk and Henry Bolingbroke, after a duel at Coventry (1398). When Henry's father, John of Gaunt, died in 1399, the king reversed earlier assurances and disinherited the heir and began to redistribute the Lancaster estates to his followers. This act struck at the fundamental idea of patrimony and so shocked the aristocracy that Richard fatally undermined his position.

Henry was in Paris when he heard of the king's action; without French support, he enlisted a small force and landed in eastern England in July,

1399. At the time, Richard was in Ireland, leading a second, smaller, and relatively ineffective expedition. The king's timing was incredibly poor; in his absence Henry found a rapid growth of support. Bolingbroke said he had only come to recover his estates, but the support accruing to him was taken as a sign that he should seize power. In any case, the rebel force headed for Bristol, as the king returned and went to Chester. Richard was taken into custody at Flint and on 29 September he confessed to a list of charges of misgovernment and was formally deposed "by the authority of the clergy and people". By February of the following year, Richard was dead.

Richard's reign posed basic questions about patrimony and patronage. The king or the community might exceed their limits; only a balance between them would produce "good governance." Surely many archipelago leaders identified with Lancaster's defense of his patrimony. But he too, in taking the crown, had disinherited the heir presumptive, Edmund Mortimer, earl of March (then eight years old). Therefore, many could justify their opposition to Henry's coup on the same basic grounds, and there was no shortage of rebellion in the early years of the new reign.

The most serious of the rebellions was the one which began in Wales in 1400. Evidently Owain Glyn Dŵr was initially defending private, patrimonial interests. He was involved in a dispute with lord Grey of Ruthin over land which both claimed and Grey had seized. Owain's complaint was ignored by the parliament in 1400, and in September, he and his followers took matters into their own hands. Glyn Dŵr was proclaimed "Prince of Wales" (he was descended from princes on both sides of his family). He led a force on raids of a number of boroughs, beginning in Ruthin. At the same time, revolt had flared in Anglesey, and the king, who was proceeding south from Scotland, made an effective march through North Wales. Instead of following up with negotiated settlement, Henry was content to approve a number of vindictive laws passed in parliament in 1401. Welshmen were excluded from borough offices, and from trials of Englishmen, from holding land or other property in English boroughs in Wales, or in the main boroughs or towns in the march or on the English border.

When these measures were added to the communal taxes which Henry had imposed in 1400 (normal at the time of his accession, but excessive in this case), Welsh communal patrimonial grievances were aggravated. While independent rebellion went on in Anglesey, Owain shifted his activity into

South Wales and he began to have more success. In 1402 there were successful raids on the march, in one of which Glyn Dŵr captured Edmund Mortimer, the uncle of the Earl of March, who became an ally and married one of Owain's daughters. Mortimer's brother-in-law was the younger Henry Percy ("Hotspur"), formerly Justice of Chester and North Wales, who had fought for Henry IV against the Scots but having fallen out with the King decided to join forces with Glyn Dŵr. The Northern rebels, like so many before them, said they were only opposing the king in order to defend their estates. Henry prevented a junction of his enemies by intercepting Hotspur at Shrewsbury (1403). The Percy heir was killed, and weeks later his father the earl of Northumberland surrendered. King Henry continued on to Hereford, then marched across Wales but returned to Hereford without engaging the enemy.

Owain's main strategic problem was the presence of major English coastal fortresses. He entered negotiations with the king of France which produced some effective raids on Caernarvon, Harlech and Aberystwyth. The success of these ventures emboldened the rebel leader to go a step further: he summoned a parliament to meet at Machynlleth; he formalized an alliance with France, and in 1405 he entered a scheme with Mortimer and Northumberland, in which England and Wales would be split three ways. In the so-called "Tripartite Indenture," Owain would have ruled all Wales plus the English border. But this scheme was never more than that. A French landing (Milford Haven, August 1405) and march toward Worcester did not produce the expected offer of negotiation from England. A rebellion in Yorkshire was beaten and the king used the occasion to seize Northumberland's castles and estates. The earl later joined Glyn Dŵr in Wales. In 1408 the earl died in Yorkshire and Owain's cause was weakened by the recapture of Aberystwyth. Harlech fell in 1409 and Glyn Dŵr's family were taken prisoner. After a final attack in 1410, the last Welsh Prince of Wales vanished. This remarkable rebellion was the longest and most impressive of any in the middle ages; that it ultimately failed was owing to Welsh geopolitics, French alliance and English patrimonial rivalry, in other words, the same factors which helped it in the first place. The remote and divided Welsh communities probably never had enough cohesion to go beyond effective but occasional guerilla warfare. The French had inadequate resources and small trust in Welsh power, though they may have dearly wished for their own "Calais" on the coast of Britain. The English patrimonial rivals, Mortimer, Northumberland and Henry of Lancaster, were certainly using Wales as a haven and Owain as a convenient ally or scapegoat. When Owain's usefulness to all these parties ended, the English Prince of Wales was able to scatter the rebel opposition. Post-rebellion Wales was nominally under the rule of harsh and repressive anti-Welsh laws. In some ways the government of the Principality gained autonomy and would regain its reputation as a haven for rebels by the 1450s. This development grew out of the fall in land revenues during and after the rebellion, which meant that most lords had little to exploit:[12]

> most marcher lords followed the crown's rapidly established practice of frequently allowing the annual Great Sessions or sessions in eyre in each lordship to be prematurely suspended--even completely terminated--in return for a substantial grant from the community.

The practice became a "habit difficult to break." Some 40 out of 52 general sessions in one county were so suspended. This was a case where direct contact between the individual and communal jurisdiction saw the recession of the former. It was not a novel or unique event, but part of a larger 15th century pattern of commutation.

At the time of Lancastrian succession the Scottish crown had its own kind of patrimonial embarrassment. The reign of Robert III (1390-1406) was marked by weakness of the sovereign and deputizing of power to royal dukes (Rothesay, who died mysteriously in 1402; Albany, who followed him and ruled until 1420). The titular successor, James I, was captured at sea and put into English custody where he remained for 18 years (1406-24). During this long period of regal incapacity, there was continuing patrimonial rivalry, but the role of the crown was insignificant. A famous dispute over the earldom of Ross broke into conflict in the Battle of Harlaw (1411). The duke of Albany and Donald MacDonald, lord of the Isles were the contenders; the battle was indecisive, and historians do not agree about its significance. Had the MacDonalds gained a clear victory, it might have been followed by a resurgent Gaelic movement which would have changed Scottish history. In fact the stalemate merely endorsed existing lowland political ascendancy. It

---

[12]R. A. Griffiths, "Wales and the Marches" in S. B. Chrimes, *et al. Fifteenth Century England* (1972), p. 153.

was such a divided and exhausted "community of the realm" to which James returned to take his throne in 1424.

The king was released after complex negotiations and after a sizeable ransom was promised (£40,000 in four years). The arrival of a capable and committed ruler brought real changes to Scottish politics. James had the Albany Stewarts tried and executed on various charges, and this was only the beginning of a series of forfeitures and land confiscations whereby the king soon tripled his income from crown lands. James was also responsible for a large amount of social legislation and legal change. In the process he held many councils and parliaments and laid the groundwork for institutions which matured in the next century (Convention of Estates,Court of Session, Convention of Royal Burghs). In general, James can be called "totalitarian" though it is an anachronism. Sir Robert Graham undoubtedly had some strong 15th century epithets for him; Graham had been banished and forfeited, and he became the leader of a gang which assaulted the king while he stayed at the Dominican friary in Perth. The king hid in the privy outlet while the chamber was searched, but he was found and murdered by Graham (1436).

The demise of James I tends to obscure his very real success in recovering royal patrimony. The death also produced another royal minority. James II was only six when his father died, but in his short reign the new king continued regal extension. He also attacked powerful families (the Livingstons) and the king literally destroyed his enemies, taking part in the murder of William, Earl of Douglas (1452). They disputed over a bond between Douglas and the earls of Crawford and Ross, which James felt derogated from his royal power (as it was surely meant to). The murder touched off a rebellion which in turn led to the complete submission of the Douglasses. The episode may be said to mark the full return of royal power, consolidation in Scottish politics and decline of unchecked aristocratic influence.

After Richard II's expeditions in 1394 and 1399, Ireland fell more and more into a tribalized, Gaelicized political pattern--one which was arguably more stable and more peaceful than periods of Anglo-Irish colonial ascendancy had been. Colonial Ireland was now seen by some English in mainly strategic terms. The famous pamphlet, *The Libell of Englyshe Polycye* (1432), called Ireland "a butres and a post under England". This reflected a more insular view of England as a nation, and the corollary was that Irish defence was a matter of (English) financial calculation.

King Henry sent his son Thomas as his lieutenant to Ireland, but there was no more sound financial support for him than for his predecessors. Lancastrian government became synonymous with regal poverty, and Irish accounts were left until last. In this sort of economic isolation, Irish affairs naturally tended to be dominated by Anglo-Irish lords and Gaelic chiefs, allied or otherwise. The 15th century saw erosion of the lordship's authority:[13]

> The law of the Saxon kings has often been broken; the Goill set no store by legal document; none of them obeying the king's law, each of them is an earl for himself.
> About Eire the principle of them all is respect for the strong man; fearful their greed; all respect for law is gone.

This condition was not confined to Ireland.

The government of Henry IV, his son and grandson was plagued with compound problems--war, finance, patronage and lawlessness. These connected strains overtaxed the patrimonial political system at several points, primarily in England and Wales where the English crown's jurisdiction was most significant. The problems were not unique, but their conjunction produced an explosive climax, beginning with Cade's Rebellion in 1450. Rebels called for Richard of York to come from Ireland to lead a baronial reform council; this was an odd sort of echo of the 13th century, and more important, an ominous portent of the move which would be made by the "Yorkists," producing the Wars of the Roses.

Historians once were gentle with the pathetic figure of Henry VI (1422-1461), perhaps because Henry VII tried so hard to have him canonized. When Henry V died, the nine-month old boy inherited the kingdoms of England and France, thanks to the Treaty of Troyes (1420). Henry VI was in fact crowned king in both countries, but his reign was to be remembered more for its *losses* in France. Henry and/or his councillors presided over a government marked by waste, corruption and debt, and there was an appearance of venality through easy pardons and lavish patronage. Reaction

---

[13]Tadhg Og O Higgins, cited in J.F. Lydon, *The Lordship of Ireland in the Middle Ages* (1972), p. 258.

was not merely a matter of faction. In 1449 parliament passed an act of resumption, which would have reclaimed estates given away since Henry's majority. Two stronger versions of the act were passed 1450. There was a sense that the royal patrimony had fallen prey to corrupt officials. In early 1450 two of them were murdered: Adam Moleyns, Keeper of the Privy Seal was lynched; the duke of Suffolk, the king's chief favorite, was executed.

In June, a mob led by a man calling himself "John Mortimer" (or "Jack Cade", or "John Amend-all") entered London from Kent. The rebels offered a petition to the king, telling him[14]

> his false council has lost his law, his merchandise is lost, his common people is destroyed, the sea is lost, France is lost, the king himself is so beset that he may not pay for his meat and drink, and he owes more than ever any king of England ought....

The rebels went on to urge the king to purge his councils and replace the guilty parties:

> to take about his noble person his true blood of his royal realm, that is to say, the high and mighty prince the Duke of York,... the mighty prince the Duke of Exeter, the Duke of Buckingham, the Duke of Norfolk, and his true earls and barons of this land, and he shall be the richest Christian king.

Cade's rebellion had about as much political significance as the revolt of 1381, if we look for direct consequences. But this time there was a clear and forceful statement by the rebels which explained their discontent. The king's councillors caused the waste of his patrimony. The cure was to be found in the "true earls and barons," who presumably would be able to restore the royal estate.

York did come from Ireland, but later in the Summer, long after the rebels had been dispersed and their leaders executed. The duke had to force his way into Henry's presence, because the duke of Somerset had become the chief royal confidant. York retired to his Welsh estates, and in 1452 he was tricked into meeting the king unarmed; Richard was obliged to swear allegiance in a public ceremony which "more or less imposed a suspended sentence of attainder upon him."[15]

---

[14]A.R. Myers ed., *English Historical Documents*, v.4 (1969), p. 267.

[15]J.R. Lander, *Conflict and Stability in Fifteenth Century England* (1969), p. 75.

In 1453 the English were finally and completely expelled from France. But Henry and his wife (Margaret of Anjou) ended a long period of tension by producing an heir to the throne (Prince Edward, born Dec. 12). These events might have turned things around for the dynasty, but Henry had already suffered a mental collapse in August. The royal patrimony now was literally incapacitated, the stage was set for the wars of the Yorkist succession.

The "Wars of the Roses" derive their name from the heraldic symbols for Lancaster (red) and York (white) which were evidently better known to Tudor publicists than the contemporary fighters. Similarly, the "wars" and the partisan alignments were better known to 19th century writers who coined the title for these escapades. Historians cannot agree on when the "wars" began (1452 or 1455) or when they ended (somewhere between 1471 and 1499). The battles were hardly part of a connected enterprise and there was only one period with something like a "campaign." What was most significant about the political struggles of the 1450s was the apparent degeneration of English royal power in a great duel between rival claimants to the royal patrimony.

Richard, duke of York, was the wealthiest subject of the king and was heir general to the throne. His father and his uncle had been implicated in treacherous activity against the Lancastrians earlier. At the age of 20, Richard inherited large estates in East Anglia and in Ireland and Wales. As a ranking member of the aristocracy, Richard served the crown in France (1436-1445) before he was made lord lieutenant of Ireland in 1447.

The position of the Yorkist heir was one which underlined the dangers of patrimonial politics. He had a potentially superior claim to the throne; if it were realized it might affect many other potential heirs by example. When a practical crisis of government came in 1453, he had to be included in the settlement, which was an awkward and brief protectorate. The Lords insisted that York not have titles such as "regent" or "governor," as they denoted too much authority. When Henry recovered in early 1455, York was removed from his position, and though he regained the protectorate for a few months in the next winter, there was an armed stand-off from 1455-1460.

When the second protectorate ended in January 1456, a long period of maneuvering between ill-formed factions began. This came to a head when Richard took the field against the king's forces in Wales (Ludford Bridge) but the duke's men refused to fight their king, and the Yorkist leaders scattered, Richard to Ireland, his son Edward and the earl of Warwick to Calais.

In a parliament later in the year Richard was charged with treason and attainted. This "Parliament of Devils" (as the Yorkists labelled it) gave Richard no choice but to advance his claim by force; at the same time, it may have recruited supporters for him:[16]

> Some may have felt that he was treated too harshly in 1459. One of the most deeply-rooted emotions of the age was its conviction of the near-sanctity of the inheritance.... They felt with a deep passion that not even treason should permanently extinguish the rights of an heir.

In Ireland, York tried to plan his return. The Earl of Warwick met with him and perhaps concerted plans for an attack. In 1460, the Yorkists landed from Calais, beat the Lancastrians and forced them to retreat northward. York left Ireland and proceeded to London without haste. He arrived in October. With a troop of armed men he went to the House of Lords, entered and placed his hand on the empty throne, no doubt expecting an acclamation. When none came, he angrily entered the royal apartments. His demonstration had failed to ignite support. His next step was a military operation.

Queen Margaret had left Scotland at the head of a "great army of Scots, Welsh and other strangers and Northmen."[17] At Wakefield in Yorkshire, Richard engaged the queen's army and was beaten and killed on December 30th. The Lancastrian army continued south and won an engagement at St. Albans February 18th. The chronicles say that the queen's victorious but unruly and dangerous forces were causing panic in London and that Margaret's magnanimity caused her to turn away to the North. Any number of other reasons might be more plausible, but in any case she was pursued by Edward, the new duke of York. The forces met at Towton, where Edward won a major victory in the largest engagement of the Wars of the Roses (March 29, 1461). Margaret once again went to Scotland, this time with a much larger group of aristocratic exiles.

---

[16]ibid., p. 87.

[17]The Auchinleck Chronicle, cited in Nicholson, *Scotland: The Later Middle Ages* , p. 400

Edward IV inherited his father's claim and Henry VI's title and estates. The crown prince Edward was disinherited and later killed in the battle of Tewkesbury (May 1471). As we shall see, this great conjunction of estates was one key--no doubt the most important one--to revival of English royal fortunes in the later 15th century. It was part of a development most pronounced in England, but begun earlier in Scotland, and imitated after a fashion by deputies or marcher lords in Ireland and Wales.

The crisis of the mid-15th century had brutally juxtaposed the patrimonial claims of individuals, communities and crown. Some priority or order was demanded, and in the later 15th century, royal patrimony finally did prevail. Thus it became possible to erect strong dynastic royal power, stronger than at any earlier time.

The early signs of change were visible in Scotland with James I and II. England saw the same effect first with Edward IV. The variations of communal and individual patrimony were similar in Ireland and Wales, without the focus of royal central authority. The nature of an inherited power was basically the same as it had been in the 13th century. That power still drew the greatest respect and obedience. But the 15th century had witnessed a dangerous decline in the operating efficiency of mechanisms of respect (law, patronage, routine governance). In the process of restoration, there were bound to be adjustments in the relative strength of patrimonial rights.

CHAPTER 5

RELIGION AND NATIONALITY

> Wonder it is, that amongest so many pregnant wittes as the Ile of Greate Britany hath produced, so many godlie and zealous preachers as England did sometime norishe, and amongest so many learned, and men of grave judgement, as this day by Jesabel are exiled, none is found so stowte of courage, so faithfull to God, nor loving to thair native countrie, that they dare admonishe the inhabitants of that Ile, how abominable before God is the Empire or Rule of a wicked woman, yea, of a trateiresse and bastard; and what may a people or nation, left destitute of a lawfull head, do by the authoritie of Goddes Worde in electing and apponting common rulers and magistrates.
>
> (John Knox, *The First Blast of the Trumpet Against the Monstrous Regiment of Women*, 1558, preface, p. 1)

Royal patrimony was extended and the executive power in England, Scotland and Ireland was made more formidable in the later 15th century. At the same time, reform impulses in the church appeared. But religious reformation in the archipelago was going to have powerful political causes and was going to fundamentally reshape political ideas and behavior.

The basis for major political change was the royal recovery of 1460-1520. The fortified royal patrimony, the reactivated royal councils and consolidated royal power were the main cures for the disorders of the 15th century body politic. Revived royal authority had to cope with novel conditions in the period 1520-1560. The consequences can be seen in several revolutions in government. The first and best known was Henry VIII's break with papal authority and assertion of royal supremacy over the church in England (1534). The aftermath of Henry's action saw reformed administration in England, and constitutional reform in Wales (1536-43) and

RELIGION AND NATIONALITY

Aberdeen

Montrose
Perth
St. Andrews

Edinburgh

Flodden

ULSTER

Solway Moss

Yellow Ford

OFFALY PALE

LEIX

Towton

MUNSTER

Bosworth

Cambridge

Kinsale

Oxford

Pembroke

London

Ireland (1534-1542). Dynastic diplomacy nearly accomplished an Anglo-Scottish union (1543), but instead there was a bitter war, long regencies and deepening religious conflict in the northern kingdom. Across the archipelago, these political conditions helped to insure the continuation of religious minorities. The Scottish Reformation (1559-60), screened by English power, was possibly the most profound of the mid-century revolutions in government.

Rival faiths in Europe prompted continuing costly mobilization in the 16th century. One key dimension affecting the archipelago was the increasing use of English intervention (in the Netherlands, France, and Spain) to keep continental powers off balance. Whether this was cost-effective may be debated endlessly; conversely, the defeat of the only major invasion attempt, the Spanish Armada, was clearly a significant event for archipelago history. Sectarian conspiracies and invasion threats continued to promote fears for English security until the end of the century. Security was also the main impulse behind the Elizabethan campaign in Ireland. Within the archipelago, the incipient unity of 1540 had been overtaken by English aggression: the crosscurrents produced by Henrician fortifications, Marian plantations and Elizabethan garrisons. These militant features were expensive symbols of apparent amalgamation, symbols which paradoxically inspired sectarian and national resistance.

While religion was reformed, the political behavior of the communities in the archipelago was revolutionized. Fundamental ideas of authority were debated and radical reformulations were circulated (the "Godly Magistrate" and the "Christian Commonwealth"). Religious uniformity was deemed vital to political survival and thus it was legislated and sometimes brutally enforced. This had the predictable effect of encouraging organized opposition: plots, bonds, associations, and illicit congregations. A collateral result was the increasing identification and organization of national units. Each major element--England, Scotland and Ireland--perceived the other two as hated enemies: heretic Anglicans, rabid Scots presbyters, or subversive Irish papists. It was irrelevant to the stereotypes that each political unit had its sizeable religious minorities. But that fact was essential in preventing complete dismemberment in the archipelago, and in preserving the loose political federation which James VI inherited in 1603.

Royal Recovery

Inheritance had always required reinforcement, by guile, by law, by force of arms. In the later 15th century, the pace and scope of that reinforcement were dramatically increased in the case of the royal heirs in Scotland and England. Stronger governments were the inevitable result; it was not inevitable who would inherit those governments.

Edward IV's great victory at Towton (March, 1461) was certainly the largest battle of the "Wars of the Roses" and it was decisive. Still, Edward's rule was not secure, and he faced serious challenges for another decade. He built up his support among the English peerage, using both pardons and new creations. He relied on regional leaders such as Warwick in the North, Lord Stanley in Cheshire and William Herbert in Wales, while he looked for allies in Scotland and Ireland against the Lancastrians. Edward made extensive use of royal progresses and legal processes to give visible strength to his rule. There continued to be serious threats. The Irish parliament told him in 1474 that there were enemies[1]

> dayly conspiren to subdue al thys land to the obeysaunce of the King of Scottes havyng in their mynd the grete conquest that Bruse some tyme seuer to the kyng of Scottes made in the same land, whos malycyous entent to resist is inpossible to the kynges subgettes of the said land, which ben but pety nombre in comparyson of the grete multitude of here Iryssh ennemys Englysh reblez and Scottes.

However much exaggeration was here, there was warfare on the Northern border (1463), rebellion in Wales (1464) and the French showed willingness to capitalize on these disputes as it suited them. Edward sought and made a truce with France (1463) as the beginning to rebuilding English security. He was not sure of his own position until 1471. A brief uprising had dislodged Edward in the previous year, the earl of Warwick having allied with Margaret of Anjou and replaced Henry VI, now severely ill, on the throne. Edward returned in 1471, defeated the rebels, and after the Lancastrian Prince Edward died in battle, the old king was murdered in the Tower. Warwick

---

[1]Cited in A.J. Otway-Ruthven, *A History of Medieval Ireland* 2nd ed. (1980), p. 396.

had been killed in battle as well, and henceforth Edward's rule was firmly established.

In the second half of Edward's reign (1471-1483) there were increasing signs of royal recovery, in England, the archipelago and Europe. The level of political violence was still high, but the longevity of central rulers had begun to increase. The 1480s saw the last period of high-level brutality: the probable murders of Edward's sons by their uncle Richard III (1483); that king's defeat and death at the hands of Henry VII (1485); and a rebellion which led to the death of James III and the succession of his son (1488). Each of these acts of regal homicide decisively altered the succession: did they signify continued deterioration of political morality, or did they mark a ruthless will to intervene and "stabilize" politics? Our answer may incline toward the latter view, for Henry VII and James IV governed with energy and effect, managing their recovered prerogative with skill and without tyranny. Perhaps their achievement ought to be measured by the fact that most of their successors in the 16th century came to power without violence, even though the age itself was every bit as bloody as its predecessor.

Henry's rule was threatened by pretenders. Because we know they were impersonators, we tend to take them too lightly. Henry himself, with but a feeble claim to the throne, with a small force of perhaps 5,000 men, and with apathy rampant in the English aristocracy, was able to defeat Richard III in 1485. So even if the threats to Henry seem small to us, he could never treat them that way. Lambert Simnel (claiming to be the nephew of the late Yorkist kings) and Perkin Warbeck (imitation son of Edward IV) were able to muster support from Yorkists and other malcontents in Ireland, Wales and Scotland. Henry was quick to mobilize his strength, mainly English, and ward off the threats. Both pretenders were captured and imprisoned, Warbeck being executed in 1499. Henry also stabilized his relations within the archipelago as these threats were being met. In a traditional manner, his eldest son Arthur was made Prince of Wales, and given a council to govern the principality. In a novel effort, Henry sent one of his knights, Edward Poynings, to Ireland in 1494, where he settled the political situation briefly, and left the lasting mark of "Poynings' Law"--an Irish statute which required English permission for sessions and prior approval of Irish legislation by the English council. With Scotland, Henry negotiated truces (1491, 1497) and then the marriage of his daughter Margaret to James IV (1503). For all his efforts, Henry could not control the archipelago. In spite of Poynings, the king was obliged to maintain the Earl of Kildare, most powerful of the Anglo-Irish lords, as the royal deputy; Wales could not be effectively governed, except perhaps for the major towns; meanwhile, Scotland's king was busily enhancing his own central authority, capitalizing on the royal marriage between his father and a Danish princess (to increase Scottish authority over Orkney and Shetland) and expanding the crown's power over the western islands (1493-1507). Thus royal authority was being recovered or restored on several fronts. The pattern of internal crisis and instability had been changed.

Initially the means for royal recovery were found in resumption of royal patrimony. We have seen how this had begun in the 1450s, with acts of parliament in England and with royal action in Scotland. By further forfeitures and attainders (and the lucrative reversals of some of the latter), as well as by fortuitous inheritance or deliberate aggression, the English and Scottish crowns greatly extended their landholdings in the second half of the 15th century.

Edward IV added the royal Lancastrian holdings to his massive Cambridge, York and March estates. His enemies also forfeited estates in Wales and Ireland. On a smaller scale in Scotland, acts of resumption brought lands to that crown in 1455 and 1458, while later political crises continued to add to the patrimony. In England, Edward gained the massive Neville estates after Warwick's treachery (1471); in Scotland, James III forfeited the lands of the Boyds (1469), the Earl of Ross (1476) and the duke of Albany (1483). The widespread recovery of crown lands received general support on the assumption that it would render the crown solvent and less likely to resort to taxation.

The stabilizing of royal finance took more concrete shape in England. Efficient lords had always insisted on careful estate management; the period saw adaptation of some of these methods to crown lands. The English exchequer, antiquated and inefficient, was supplanted as central financial office, by the royal chamber. The treasurer of the chamber had from time to time handled the king's accounts, especially military campaigns, and now his function was made more permanent. In addition, the treasurer's accounts were subjected to audit by a Court of General Surveyors, a committee of the king's council which became something of a "crown land office."[2] Effective control over crown lands was greatly improved as were royal revenues. In England there was a near doubling of the income; in Scotland, there was a clear change from the land being a minor to a major source of income.

The recovery and management of royal estates was one illustration of the potential of royal conciliar machinery. The key to the crisis of the 15th century had been weakness at the center of conciliar government. A firm hand, clear goals and cooperative aristocrats would make the system work again. We have seen in the cases of Henry III, Edward II, Richard II and Henry VI how the council was a focus for political hostility. This was a kind of testimony to its strength and importance. The council was the agent of the royal prerogative. As such it was the heart of government: war, peace, justice, fiscal and other policy were its business. If a king controlled his council and used it with skill, he would succeed.

Edward IV resumed a practice of frequent meetings with his council, often sitting in its judicial role on cases of unruly aristocrats. Through the 'afforced' council in parliament, there were laws enacted against private liveries and the abuse of courts of law. By the reign of Henry VII, special sittings of the council in the "Starred Chamber" were employing the power of the crown effectively in reinforcing the judicial system - so effectively that there was a negative reaction, and the "Court of Star Chamber" was only rehabilitated and made a court of law in Henry VIII's reign.

There was another important dimension to the English king's council. Regional extensions were created which were designed to increase the authority of the crown at the expense of marcher lords. Where the early 15th century saw the earls of Northumberland and Westmorland as Wardens of the Marches, there was a Council of the North created by the end of the century. Richard duke of Gloucester was Lieutenant of the North (1482) before he became king. His council remained in his stead (1484) and although its powers declined toward the end of the century, they were revived around 1525. In Wales, the traditional title Prince of Wales was bestowed on Edward (1471) and later Arthur (1489), each assisted by a Council of Wales and the Marches which had jurisdiction including the border counties of England. These councils did not have palatine jurisdiction; they were *ad hoc*

---

[2]B. P. Wolffe, *The Crown Lands 1461-1536* (1970) p. 49.

creations of the king's council, without territorial bases, though the major local figures would be in their membership.

In Ireland, the king's council was the descendant of the Angevin original. It assisted the king's lieutenant or deputy or justiciar. The latter title was given to Kildare in 1470 and he was strong enough to prevent a new lieutenant, Lord Grey, from assuming power in 1478-9. Kildare had enough power to nominate members to the council, to support Simnel and Warbeck and only be admonished for his treason. For in the Irish situation, there was only one surviving powerful aristocrat, and after Poynings' mission, Henry VII had to resort to using Kildare again as his agent.

Conciliar power was also demonstrated through the work of the parliaments. These enlarged sessions of the king's council had been used often in the 15th century, and now their reduced frequency and altered shape signified greater royal effectiveness. During Henry VI's reign there had been sessions in England lasting on average about seven weeks per year; this was reduced by Edward IV to about three and by Henry to about one week by the end of his reign. Those parliaments which did meet were less apt to engage in aggressive measures when the resumption of lands was followed by royal fiscal autonomy.

In Scotland, taxing power had never grown as it had in England, and increased royal land revenues were relatively more useful in royal recovery. The crown experimented with smaller councils of lords, commissions of estates and committees delegated to do parliamentary business. Generally these offered welcome relief from the demands of attendance at parliament.

The Irish parliament declared its legislative autonomy in 1460, in the midst of the English dynastic crisis:[3]

> Whereas the land of Ireland is, and at all times has been corporate of itself by the ancient laws and customs used in the same, freed of the burden of any special law of the realm of England save only such laws as by the Lords spiritual and temporal and the commons of the said land had been in Great Council or Parliament there held, admitted, accepted, affirmed, and proclaimed according to sundry ancient statutes thereof made.

At the time of this statement there was a genuine uncertainty about the place of English laws in Ireland, but since the position of the Anglo-Irish

---

[3]*Irish Historical Documents*, p. 74.

community was receding, it would not be able to uphold the brave claims of autonomy; the formula in Poynings' Law would be more apt for a colonial minority government. With their varied circumstances, the parliaments of the archipelago were still vehicles of "common consent," yet at the close of the 15th century, their members, powers and procedures had come under closer royal supervision.

The resumption of lands and conciliar power were augmented by several kinds of royal consolidation. In the administration of justice, exercise of military power and symbolism of royal office, there were further signs of royal recovery. In most accounts of the 15th century a dominant theme is "lawlessness." The subject is problematic, because we have no statistics and must rely on impressionistic views of contemporaries. Some of these test our credulity:[4]

> There is no country in the world where there are so many thieves and robbers as in England: insomuch that few venture to go alone in the country excepting in the middle of the day, and fewer still in towns at night, and least of all in London.

Thus wrote the Venetian ambassador in 1497. It would be easy to find equivalent remarks for the other parts of the archipelago, and easier still to find unflattering comparisons between Wales, Scotland or Ireland and England. The problem of translating these into meaningful evidence is almost insurmountable, and not merely for the 15th century. If we cannot construct crime rates, we can cite evidence of increased concern for the administration of justice; numerous acts, proclamations and other measures were designed to reduce crime. New courts were created, old judicial circuits were activated, and there were some novel efforts to centralize and standardize the law.

The king's power rested on armed might, both in international and domestic affairs. The century certainly showed how the unchecked use of force could disrupt politics. Much has been said about "private" armies, but there were in fact few examples of that in the strict sense. Ordinarily an aristocrat would raise a force which would serve in his "livery" and under contract to the crown, for there was no standing army. Military provision, regulation and fortification were not centralized or standardized, but the 15th

---

[4]J.R. Lander, *Government and Community, England 1450-1509* (1980), p. 365.

century saw steps in that direction. The English laws against liveries (without license); Scottish efforts to limit bonds of maintenance and "manrent" (contract service); Irish attempts to deal with "coign and livery" (customary rights to quarter and requisition) were among these measures. In general there was growing reaction to the abuses of these practices. Liveried retainers remained and were used in 16th century, but their regulation however, was more effective.

Fortifications, ordnance and naval forces in the 15th century were another sign of impending military revolution. Gunpowder and artillery, on land and sea, were powerful but expensive new weapons. Individual leaders, regardless of their patrimonial wealth, would be hard put to raise a private train of artillery or a fleet of ships. Indeed, the "armies" which were engaged in the "Wars of the Roses" were small groups whose combat might better be classed as skirmishes. The same was true of most Scottish and Irish operations. Not only were there limits in size and resources, but in the late 15th century, the chivalric code was still used; there were usually talks before a battle, even if there were few words later.

The image of royal power was deliberately cultivated by the "Renaissance" prince, as it had been by intelligent medieval sovereigns. Dignity and display were inseparable features of effective power. The court of "His Royal Highness" Henry VIII was made more ornate. The image of the sovereign was fortified externally by the developing practice of diplomacy; crowned heads made impressive progresses through their kingdoms; pageant, public ceremony and the physical attributes of monarchy were carefully exploited. Thus in all parts of the archipelago, in the late 15th century, the residual powers of royalty--land resumption, control of councils, justice and military and ceremonial affairs--were turned toward more central, stablilized rule by Edward IV, James IV and Henry VII.

The first Tudor was for long the model of this "new" monarchy to historians. In our context, he was also notable for the introduction of a Welsh element into the royal dynasty. This was an ambiguous but important development. Born in Pembroke Castle, raised in Wales, and in exile, Henry's Welshness was neither racial nor territorial. His invading army, his royal court, his general policies, were none of them notably "Welsh." But his choice of the red dragon of Cadwaladr for his battle standard, the naming of his eldest son (Arthur) and a few legislative acts showed that he was aware of

158

and wanted to use his "homeland" for its political benefit. Henry's position outside the warring dynastic factions probably helped him establish stability, but most important was his good fortune to rule at a time of improving trade, declining incentives to civil war and favorable diplomatic conditions. Next to these, the real significance of Henry Tudor's Welsh heritage seems slight indeed, but it was certainly one element of his particular effort to reestablish royal power.

In the period of royal recovery there were signs of important changes in the church. Increased royal power over appointments and revenues was common, but so also were strains of religious reform on different levels. In a traditional manner, the Observant movement rejuvenated religious orders in Ireland in the late 15th century; the popular Lollard heretics were reviving in England at the same time, and christian humanists led by Erasmus were widely influential in intellectual circles. While sweeping allegations of corruption and decay in church life were false, the current level of abuses was accompanied by a rising level of anticlerical criticism. Accelerating reform in the church was apt to become a powerful force in governmental change.

Revolutions in Government

The reconstructed regal powers in the archipelago were drawn into complex European international disputes at the end of the 15th century. As diplomatic crises intersected with Martin Luther's theology and Henry VIII's divorce, profound political forces were imposed upon papal authority and upon the archipelago constitution. Henry VIII's assumption of supreme power in church and state began a constitutional chain reaction. The supremacy required new instruments of government and new criminal penalties; it simultaneously spotlighted the archaic constitutional condition of the principality of Wales and the lordship of Ireland, among the dependencies attached to the English crown.

Closer to the surface of politics, the royal supremacy also put a premium on the "defence of the realm" against rebellion and counter-reformation. This became a dominant theme for the rest of the century. In the hectic middle decades, defense was highlighted by fleets and fortresses, Anglo-Scottish war, and the first Irish plantation. The defenses of successive English rulers were of course invoked in the name of radically different religious settlements (1547-1558). This variety made England's position unstable, in spite of her predominant power. That in turn preserved diversity in the archipelago, but part of its price was escalating politico-religious hostility.

International relations on the continent went through a dramatic change at the close of the 15th century. Papal authority was challenged by the consolidating continental powers of France and Spain. Meanwhile, anticlerical movements grew throughout western Europe, as Italian politics increasingly absorbed papal attention.

The successive victories of France over England in the 15th century helped the growth of the central power on the old Capetian foundation. In 1492, Brittany (with its strong ties to the West of England and to Wales) was annexed by France and the act was ratified by the Treaty of Etaples with Henry VII. The English (British) tie to the continent was now concentrated in the tiny outpost of Calais. In the same period, the Spanish monarchy rose to greatness. The marriage of Ferdinand of Aragon and Isabella of Castile linked two lesser crowns and formed the base for a great imperial state. At the same time, that state was beginning to acquire its vast overseas empire, and soon it would be tied by marital diplomacy with the burgeoning Hapsburg power. The Holy Roman Emperor in the 16th century seemed to be about to regain the prestige and power of that ancient title; of course the rising star of France made a formidable obstacle.

These newly-magnified European powers took leading positions in a diplomatic arena managed by the international agency of the papal curia. Since the 13th century the papacy had considered itself superior to mere royal power, and that superiority was demonstrated most regularly through diplomatic channels. Perhaps the most dramatic instance was in 1494 when Alexander VI drew the line to separate Spanish and Portuguese colonial spheres in the Treaty of Tordesillas. Paradoxically, in the later 15th century the Roman pontiff had also become more and more involved in the politics of Italian city-states, to the point that the pope was easily mistaken for yet another petty prince, while he represented the authority of Rome at the head of the universal church.

In 1494, both France and Spain were drawn into Italian wars, and in the next thirty years, through one league after another, and one war or intrigue after another, there was a running battle with Rome. This meant a serious

160

drain on papal revenue, strenuous (if not scrupulous) measures to recoup that expense, and a general decline of Roman moral authority. In a sense, the climax of this process was symbolized by the sack of Rome by imperial army troops in 1527.

There were several periods and ways in which the archipelago was tied in with this deteriorating diplomacy. Henry VII showed considerable skill in allying himself with either of the great powers and playing for advantage. He was only drawn into a military display on one occasion. He otherwise secured a favorable marriage alliance from Spain and fair terms in commercial negotiations with the Netherlands.

Yet England was in an inferior position in relation to its great continental rivals. France could play upon its "auld alliance" with the Scots; Spain could exact a heavy price for a marriage alliance; the pope had extensive influence at the English court. With the reign of Henry VIII (1509-47) this picture began to change. The king himself was determined to make alterations, and he found a capable instrument in one of the royal chaplains, Thomas Wolsey.

Wolsey had been appointed by the old king in 1507, and by the time he finished a decade of royal service, he was a major international figure. His power base in England was a conventional blend of an unusual number of clerical and secular positions. Wolsey was made bishop of Lincoln (1514) and then cardinal and lord chancellor (1515). His accumulation of offices and livings showed both his power and his greed. Wolsey also aimed at a diplomatic career which would magnify the power of England. His first success was a treaty with France (1514) which broke down almost immediately when the French king died and was replaced by the young and aggressive Francis I. Wosley's next feat was an anti-Turkish treaty of "universal peace" in 1518, the Treaty of London. This broke down when the Spanish heir became the Holy Roman Emperor (Charles V-1519). Wolsey's self-advancement was not much more successful: he was a candidate for the papacy but never had a real hope of winning. He gained the office of legate *a latere* in 1524, meaning that he was as powerful as the archbishop of Canterbury (though that office could not be his, because William Warham outlived him).

Wolsey's diplomatic efforts could not change the fact that England was not very significant in the great rivalry on the continent. Costly and unproductive campaigns (or negotiations) commonly ended when the great powers made peace without consulting England. This diplomatic inferiority might be masked sometimes; or a willful sovereign like Henry VIII might wishfully project an unrealistic role for England in world affairs. The illusions were disspelled when the king sought a vital dynastic decision--the pope's dispensation for annulment of Henry's marriage to Catherine of Aragon.

The marriages of royalty were always political. That they were also governed by canonical rules meant that they invariably engaged the church courts in vital dynastic issues. The pressure in such cases was often irresistible: if a marriage within the prohibited degrees or a contested dissolution became politically necessary, there were ways to accomplish the desired end. This type of compromise of religious law was what Henry VIII expected to obtain, but powerful political forces were arrayed against him. His wife's nephew, Charles V, had assumed political control of Rome. Imperial pressure was exerted on Pope Clement VII to delay and frustrate the English king's desires for a new marriage. Those desires were partly emotional but primarily political. Henry and Catherine had no male children and only one surviving daughter. The king was determined to have a male heir and thus secure a stable succession to the crown. Henry's powerful Cardinal should have been able to obtain the annulment and when he failed to do so, he lost the royal favor and was deprived of his power (1529-30).

During the several years' campaign for the royal divorce, there were necessarily shifting and hardening attitudes toward the clergy. From 1529 these appeared in vivid detail. The parliament summoned in 1529 was allowed (or encouraged) to pass laws against certain clerical malpractices. The next year a new adviser, Thomas Cromwell, promoted a policy of royal pressure which culminated in an act declaring the royal supremacy over the church.

At first, Henry was probably emulating some of his predecessors, who had found it expedient on many earlier occasions to make statutes against the "pretended power" of the pope to "provide" an individual to a benefice, or to hear and determine causes in Rome on appeal from England ("praemunire"). In canon law both of these were eminently "legal" actions. In domestic politics, there were times when violators drew strong criticism (the early years in Avignon, the years of the Lollard heresy, the later years of the 15th century). Then it was safe and shrewd for the crown to appear to be protecting the rights of patrons or litigants--and it sometimes promised revenue to the crown through the sale of licenses to evade the law.

It was this sort of general background, and not some kind of "protestant" atmosphere, which lay behind the election and early work of the so-called "Reformation Parliament" in 1529. Some evidence can be shown for the survival of Lollard beliefs. There were cells of reform doctrine in Cambridge and around some of the seaport towns. It is also accurate to connect the spread of heretical teaching with the advent of mechanical printing and the growth of literacy in the general population of laymen. But even if all of these conditions were demonstrable on a much larger scale than was the case, that would not put Lollards or Lutherans in the royal council. Henry VIII and his minister Thomas Cromwell had very practical reasons for the legislation which was enacted in those years. The king was being frustrated in his diplomatic efforts to arrange a royal divorce, and in that crisis he was driven to secure his power over the clergy in England, first as an affirmation of his authority and then as a move toward constitutional reform.

Specific acts were generated in the context of escalating confrontations. In October 1529, Wolsey was indicted for violation of praemunire. He was accused of exercising a foreign jurisdiction to the derogation of the king's power. In December of 1530 Henry caused similar charges to be brought against the whole English clergy. In 1531 the clerical Convocations purchased an expensive royal pardon (£118,000) and recognized Henry as "singular protector, only and supreme lord, and as far as the law of Christ allows even supreme head." The qualified supremacy was a major step for the king. Still more significant was the Commons' petition to the king to reform the church courts in 1532. Henry forced the Convocations to recognize him as the supreme authority over their canons, thus confirming the royal supremacy.

With this internal affirmation of his power, Henry moved toward unilateral settlement of the divorce. In 1533 the case was brought to a conclusion: Henry secretly married a pregnant Anne Boleyn in January, and Thomas Cranmer was made the new archbishop after Warham's death. In March, an Act in Restraint of Appeals made it possible to conclude legal proceedings in the court of the archbishop. In May, Cranmer gave Henry his divorce, in June Anne was crowned and in September she gave Henry his child--princess Elizabeth. That month, Henry's excommunication was put into effect.

The royal divorce was the trigger for establishment of the royal supremacy. The idea of supremacy was not new, but its manifold constitutional repercussions were revolutionary. Henry VIII was evidently instructed in the sources and precedents for a doctrine of supremacy in 1530. The crown claimed an immunity from papal jurisdiction and a status described as "imperial":[5]

> By divers sundry old authentic histories and chronicles it is manifestly declared and expressed that this realm of England is an Empire, and so hath been accepted in the world, governed by one supreme head and king having the dignity and royal estate of the imperial crown of the same, unto whom a body politic, compact of all sorts and degrees of people divided in terms and by names of Spirituality and Temporality, be bounden and owe to bear next to God a natural and humble obedience.

The word "empire" has been a puzzle for historians. Some read it as rule without a superior (a power ascending in the polity); others see a power exercised by deputy (descending from a divine source, after the manner of the emperor Constantine, i.e. Caesaropapal authority). Attributes of both were present, the statute being drafted vaguely enough to comprehend any interpretation which might lend force to the fact and antiquity to the idea. And while the word "empire" did not mean what we now associate with imperialism, the effect of Henry's supremacy was going to be profound in all the king's dominions.[6]

In England, the supremacy was bound to produce change in government at the highest level: the royal governance was carried into discipline, revenues and organization of the church, but it was not possible to set aside "church" from government as if it were a department. Therefore the changes had repercussions which amounted to a general "revolution in government."[7] The revolution consisted of reorganized councils, rejuvenated judiciary, local

---

[5]24 Henry VIII c.12. On Henry's tutelage see G.R. Elton, *Reform and Reformation* (1977), p. 135.

[6]See J. J. Scarisbrick, *Henry VIII* (1968) pp. 357, 504-10.

[7]G. R. Elton's book of that name (1953) radically refocused attention on the secular aspect of reformation where most work has remained since.

government reform and conversion throughout toward a more professional mode of operation.

Revenue regulation began as early as 1532 with the first (or conditional) Act of Annates. The payments to Rome of the first year's revenues by a new bishop were temporarily withheld, with a clause in the act allowing its suspension by the crown. As Henry's policy options dwindled in 1533, a second act made the provisions definite. Other laws affecting "Peter's Pence" (annual parochial tributes, modest in total amount), the retention of eccelesiastical court revenues via restraint of appeals, and later the "augmentations" via monasteries, all channelled clerical revenues to the crown. The total value of church revenue was less than Henry had hoped, and the general impact of change was more than the king had bargained for.

There was no practical alternative to royal confiscation, yet the policy made a strong negative impression on the community. The political impact was particularly apparent when the government moved to dissolve the monasteries. A dissolution was a property condemnation with a transfer of resident clergy to other locations. Some small and scattered dissolutions had been conducted by Wolsey, the proceeds going to endow his new colleges. In 1535 a much more ambitious policy went into effect. Cromwell created a commission to visit monastic houses, inquire into their management and their accounts, and report to the crown. In 1536 it was decided to dissolve about one-fourth of the 800 houses, on grounds of small size, inadequate administration, plus allegations of scandal. Three years later, the axe fell on the remaining houses. The dissolution then proceeded to tiny chantries or chapels in 1547. The whole policy had a dual goal: to remove the houses which stood in special relationship to the Pope, outside the secular hierarchy; and to appropriate their revenues to the crown. Part of the crown's reward for this policy was an act of open rebellion in the North, the "pilgrimage of Grace" in 1536. There were multiple causes behind this uprising; rebels professed constant loyalty to the king, but opposition to his monastic policy. There was not much difficulty putting down the rebels. But the potency of religion in politics was plain to see.

By the time of the Pilgrimage, Henry and Cromwell had to face a set of deeper political issues prompted by the break with Rome. First, the nature of royal supremacy had to be defined, and uniformity in the new Church of

England had to be enforced. In the course of these acts, the rest of English (and archipelago) government was being reshaped.

Royal supremacy was declared in the Act of 1534, and a further Act of Succession required oaths from all royal officials. This logical sequel to the earlier separations from Rome required universal public acknowledgement of the constitutional revolution, an utterly unprecedented act. And since it was of a revolutionary character, there were some conservative and principled men who refused to take the oath and lost their lives (Thomas More and John Fisher, executed in 1535).

The supreme head of the church was bound to put forward the forms and articles of faith for his subjects. In the particular situation of the Henrician reformation, however, there was no true doctrinal *origin* and hence no clear path to reform in that sense. In its place, there was a dangerous track through different religious positions, all fortified by statutory penalties. There was to be uniformity--and statutory penalties were severe. But in order to conform, one had to be very alert! In a real sense, the faith was placed in a framework of current secular political decisions.

Scholars have debated at great length whether the Tudor parliament was a tool or an emerging legislative body. In fact it was both. No Tudor sovereign was intimidated by a parliament, but every successful ruler attended to parliamentary management. It is undeniable that the "Reformation Parliament" (1529-1536) was used by Henry VIII, and it is equally true that the course of those events left a clear impression that parliament was a competent council for the king in his role as supreme head.

Perhaps Cromwell had initially coached Henry on the idea of royal supremacy; certainly the king's secretary was busily engaged in working out the implications of the constitutional revolution. A modern state was being fashioned from medieval materials. One preliminary task was to reduce the "outliers," those separate and quasi-independent areas of Wales and Ireland, and garrisons like Calais. Cromwell's sudden fall in 1540 interrupted the process, but we can see signs of its early stages.

Once or twice, Henry had toyed with a reform of the medieval lordship of Ireland. His father's emergency action with Poynings' mission set an expensive example. In 1520, the earl of Surrey's expedition was a similar inconclusive effort to rein in the Anglo-Irish feudatories. This was the basic early Tudor problem--how to absorb all descendants of Anglo-Norman invasion into the English lordship? There was no answer unless it also included the Irishry, those Gaelic or Gaelicized landowners who now controlled a majority of Irish territory. Apparently some efforts to control the Pale were set in motion as early as 1533 and they triggered an Anglo-Irish revolt which ran intermittently from 1535 to 1540. In the latter year, a new policy of assimilation was tried, called "surrender and regrant," whereby the Anglo-Irish and Gaelic subjects made over their lands to the king and received them back on feudal terms, with a promise of primogeniture. This plan tried at one stroke to reform the landholding customs of the native lords. The following year, in a lavish ceremony, the Irish Parliament voted to declare Henry "King of Ireland." The change from his former title of "Lord" was not merely cosmetic--it was a major constitutional step, creating dual monarchy rather than a mere appendage.

The efforts to transform Gaelic lordship were interrupted in 1543, mainly due to the cost of the policy of "surrender and regrant." Thereafter, the assimilating policy was allowed to stagnate. The English role reverted to a customary colonial pattern, with the added pressure of royal supremacy and reformed religion. Under those conditions, it was not long before there were stirrings of nationalist opposition.

In Wales there was a simpler political problem: the Principality was easier to govern than the Pale, for there was nothing quite like the March in Ireland. Moreover, the long period of nominal royal rule (from 1284) had not faced the sort of resurgent native power that Ireland had offered. In the 15th century, there had been a special English royal council to deal with Welsh and border problems. This did not mean, as the Tudor preambles suggest, that Wales and the Marches were on the brink of anarchy. On the contrary, there were more serious problems of disorder in Scotland and Ireland. What the exaggeration meant was that the Tudor government was justifying its introduction of English law. The first of the "Acts of Union" (1536) showed this deception by ignoring the distinction between march and principality,[8] and applying the sweeping reform of English shires, court system and parliamentary representation to the whole of Wales; and giving the king the authority to suspend or interrupt the operation of the law. There

---

[8] 27 Henry VIII c. 26. P. R. Roberts "The Union with England and the Identity of 'Anglican' Wales," Royal Historical Society, *Transactions*, 5th series, v. 22 (1972).

was surprisingly little opposition to this measure, or to the introduction of the religious reforms. Wales had no separate legislative tradition, but rather it had two dependent executive structures, the March and the Principality, which by this time were rather easily incorporated.

Similarly, the crown was exerting its authority over the small outposts such as Calais. A royal commission was sent there in 1535, and shortly a complex reform act was passed. One of its notable features was the sending of two burgesses to parliament from Calais. The garrison was plagued with problems of organization and supply and poor command. The reform of its constitution did not alter the strength or liability of the garrison, rather it was another by-product of the central constitutional change. So too was the omnibus Act on Liberties and Franchises of 1536.[9] This law was meant to reform palatine jurisdictions so that "for the first time, the whole realm, without qualification, became subject to government from Westminster."[10] In fact, the areas were not transformed nor had they been immune from control before. What the central government was doing was flexing its constitutional muscle. It would be called upon in the next few years to flex its stronger military muscles.

In 1538 a truce was arranged between France and Spain and this seemed to create a serious threat of invasion. For a year or two, major preparations were made to meet this threat. In 1539 we find Cromwell making a note to present[11]

> a device in the parliament for the fortification of the realm, as well of the frontiers as otherwise. A device for defence of the realm in time of invasion, and for every man to contribute...

Cromwell listed about 28 locations in his memo, and many key points along the coast were fortified with new or rebuilt installations in Henry's major building program of 1539-40.

The coastal fortresses were indicative of the direction of affairs in the coming decades. There was not much time for the new regime to solidify Henry's supremacy in the constitution. Foreign wars and internal rebellions

---

[9] 27 Henry VIII c. 24 "An Act for recontinuing certain liberties and franchises heretofore taken from the crown."

[10] G.R. Elton, *England Under the Tudors* 2nd ed. (1974), 176.

[11] *Letters & Papers of the Reign of Henry VIII*, v.14, part I, no. 655.

were to keep up the tempo, and counterforce was required to anticipate serious military threats.

It was odd that the most active military effort in the 1540s came between England and Scotland. Mainly this was the result of Scotland's awkward position as a potential military ally of France and a potential dynastic ally of England. After yet another embarrassing defeat (Solway Moss, 1542) the Scottish crown passed to the infant princess Mary, and she was the target of an English marital alliance (Treaty of Greenwich, 1543). This agreement pointed to numerous obstacles on both sides to impending Anglo-Scottish union, and it was never ratified. Escalating disputes between the countries were followed by a series of English invasions, which only succeeded in driving the Scots to closer relations with France, including the marriage of Mary to the Dauphin.

The middle decades of the century have attracted much attention in the context of the fate of the Henrician reformation in England: protestant reform under Edward (1547-53), catholic reaction under Mary (1553-58) and a return to Henry's compromise under Elizabeth (1558). How did the 'revolutions in government' fare in this period? The central point was that royal supremacy was maintained despite swings in orthodoxy. For instance, even Mary Tudor accepted the affirmation of the royal title for Ireland; indeed, there was more active English administration on the old colonial model, and experimentation with the first 'plantation' (1550-58) in the counties of Leix and Offaly. The union with Wales (concluded in 1543) was continued without variation. The relation to Scotland and its regency government was even peaceful.

Looking more closely at politics in England in the 40s and 50s, we see a rising level of religious and political violence. The repeated public challenges to orthodoxy, while producing discreet reactions from many, also produced virulent strains of opposition, and an unmeasured amount of public sympathy for partisan positions--be they the martyrs of Mary or the recusants under Elizabeth.

There were several specific and serious outbreaks of popular rebellion, some with plain ties to the religious issue. In Cornwall, in 1549 there was a protest against the introduction of the Book of Common Prayer--a formulary of set services in English replacing old, familiar, and regionally-varied Latin service books (of course without references to Roman authority). This outbreak, and an economic insurrection in Norfolk, were put down, but each cost support for the Lord Protector, the duke of Somerset. Soon he was overthrown by a less scrupulous John Dudley, later duke of Northumberland. Though once a leader of conservative reaction, Dudley imposed a more radical prayer book in 1552 because of his speculative interest in clerical property. This latter-day "overmighty subject" caused the dying king Edward to change his will to leave the crown to Northumberland's daughter-in-law. Yet the coup against Mary Tudor failed.

Mary's accession was welcomed but her widely-known plans for a Spanish marriage were feared. This was the main reason for the rebellion which marked her early months. Wyatt's Rebellion (January 1554) was in fact the most serious revolt against Tudor rule, as it came close to taking control of London. The leaders were captured and executed, and Princess Elizabeth, whose interest in the succession seemed to be behind the revolt, was kept under guard for some time after.

The reign of Mary displayed several features of the growing integration of religion and politics. First, she was forced against her will to use the royal supremacy to revise the religious constitution. And in so doing, she was not able to restore the entire pre-Reformation structure. Notably, she was unable to return all the confiscated church property--that is, she could not do so without the risk of massive resistance. Therefore, while the mass could be restored, and unorthodox clergy (about 800) could be deprived, and the papal power could be acknowledged, there were definite political limitations. In a broader sense, politics undermined the Marian reaction. For the Spanish alliance did cause England to join in war against France in 1557. This war cost a large amount, and it only produced the loss of Calais. That symbolic failure combined with the persecution of several hundred protestant martyrs to demolish popular support for the regime--but Mary's failure to live or to produce an heir was her ultimate defeat.

Elizabeth thus did not have to face a strong popular catholic opposition. Philip of Spain hoped to woo her, the pope was persuaded not to excommunicate her at once, and she played a careful game of concealing her true beliefs. She did put in place a compromise settlement in 1559. She was the "Supreme Governor" of the church; her new prayer book was a blend of 1549 and 1552; and her clergy were mostly reformers but not rigorously screened as such. This "via media" had the advantage of not completely

170

alienating one extreme or the other. It had the disadvantage of not pacifying either. The climate was not one conducive to pacification: the last half of the century was to be an age of religious war.

Gordon Donaldson has called the Scottish Reformation the "Revolution against France and Rome." This neatly captures the combined diplomatic and doctrinal impulses, into both of which the English poked easily and often. In European diplomacy, Scotland came very close to becoming a French province (1550-59) partly out of her search for refuge from English invasion. Ironically, it was invasion by Elizabeth of England which led to the negotiation of the Treaty of Edinburgh (1560) and mutual withdrawal of French and English troops from Scotland. The treaty was in the name of the Scots' "old freedom and liberties," and nothing was said about the current religious situation. That was in flux since serious revolution began in 1559. Before then, some amount of reform activity had been tolerated. In the 1540s there were some isolated incidents like adoption of vernacular scriptures in 1543, the murder of Cardinal Beaton in 1546 and the adoption of assorted reforms in church councils in 1549 and 1552. John Knox had preached in a beseiged St. Andrews after the Beaton murder, and for his troubles he was sentenced to the French galleys. He later spent time in exile and returned to Scotland in 1559. Serious agitation began in Perth in May, one of Knox's sermons being followed by rioting and looting. Since early that year some notices had appeared on the doors of friaries, later called "Beggars' Summonses," instructing friars to vacate and make room for the poor and disabled. The Regent Mary of Guise moved to head off the crisis with unaccustomed firmness, for as of April 1559, in the Treaty of Cateau-Cambresis (between Spain and France) she had been strengthened, and she no longer felt the need to temporize with the reformers. But her introduction of additional French troops seems to have convinced both Scottish reformers and English leaders that defensive action was necessary. Negotiation was followed by entry of English troops; a large number of Scottish nobles opposed Mary of Guise and she was formally declared "removed" as regent in October 1559; she died in June 1560, even as the envoys were completing their treaty negotiations.

The Scottish clergy had been debating since May on the terms of what was called the "Book of Reformation"--a set of religious guidelines which probably constituted the "Book of Discipline" adopted in January 1561.

Meanwhile, in the Summer of 1560 a parliament met (without royal summons) and adopted a Confession of Faith and denounced papal authority and the celebration of the mass. There was no general reorganization of the Scottish church at this stage. In December 1560, Francis II died, and his 18-year old widow, who still had a claim to the English throne, would now be returning to rule Scotland.

The "revolution" had been conducted with the support of groups from all levels of Scottish society: nobles who were anxious to preserve their property in the church, clergy who were eager to promote reforms, burgh leaders who sought freedom from French control, plus a popular element with some prolonged exposure to ideas of reform. That is not to say that reformation was unopposed or that it was uniform in its aims. Still, with the emphasis on local congregational authority and a relatively open structure, the main impression is one of a popular movement.

The "revolutions in government" were profoundly important to the archipelago. England's royal supremacy led to easy Welsh annexation; a new assimilating policy nearly coopted Gaelic Irish aristocrats; a potential Scottish alliance was in sight in 1543 and achieved in 1560. Even so, these changes were overtaken by old antagonisms and new religious hostilities, and the wars of the later 16th century affirmed the political, cultural and religious disunity of the archipelago.

Religion and Warfare

The religious warfare of the later 16th century was the main force behind growing national identity in Europe and in the archipelago. There were three distinct modes in which that process can be seen: in English intervention on the continent, in the defense against invasion (especially the Spanish Armada) and in internal warfare in the archipelago, notably the Elizabethan conquest of Ireland. Collectively these crises promoted a garrison state which might have come to fruition under Elizabeth, had it not run into economic obstacles. All the same, the incomplete measures of militance added to the growth of multiple nationalist sentiments. With the loss of Calais, the old English tie with the continent was severed. For five centuries there had been some piece of continental ground among the dominions of the English king. Within a short time, Englishmen had a new type of link to the continent. Queen

Elizabeth fostered or directed an expanding series of military interventions in France, Spain and the Netherlands: some as aid missions, some as tactical harrassment, and later some more substantial invasions. These military measures all aimed to discomfit the enemy, France or Spain. They did not have as their objective the establishment of a base or a colony, or the reclamation of patrimonial estates. Instead, they were temporary missions at royal command to attack military targets and/or achieve diplomatic objectives.

English intervention went through several distinct stages, corresponding to the temperature of the religious conflict. At the beginning of her reign, Elizabeth was cautious in the use of power. The Huguenot community at La Rochelle was under attack, and there was strong sentiment to aid the rebels. A force was sent, but only as a private venture; in 1562, by the secret Treaty of Richmond, Elizabeth endorsed aid for the Huguenots and a detachment tried to assist the community at Le Havre.

During the 1560s the climate worsened on several sides: the Council of Trent concluded in 1563 and gave considerable impetus to the forces of counter-Reformation; the internal political pressures in England exploded in 1569 in the Northern Rebellion, an outburst like that of the Pilgrimage of Grace in which discontented conservative opinion lashed out at the government, without a coherent strategy. In this case, Mary of Scotland had become a captive ward of Elizabeth, and as the next in line of succession (and a Roman Catholic) she was the inevitable focal point for plotters. Whether or not the Northerners hoped to depose the queen, the opportunity was obvious, and the reaction to rebellion was swift and lethal. The rebels were dispersed, their leaders (Earls of Westmorland and Northumberland) chased into Scotland. Northumberland was turned over and was executed. In 1570, the papal bull, *Regnans in excelsis*, denounced Elizabeth as a heretic and placed all of her Roman Catholic subjects automatically in a state of rebellion against her; in one sense, this was a valuable tool for the queen. She could and did proceed against her Catholic enemies as enemies of the state (a process lending direct support to the 'nationalizing' of politics). Also, the papal bull forced recognition of the English outcast position which had been minimized by Elizabeth and deliberately evaded by Philip II for diplomatic purposes. Henceforth there would be much more direct confrontation.

The Dutch had rebelled against Spanish rule in 1567, and in 1572 the English sent a mission under Humphrey Gilbert--which force consisted of

173

volunteer companies. At the time, Elizabeth was dealing with what seemed a more serious threat in the Ridolfi Plot (1571). That scheme was engineered by an Italian merchant, with support from the duke of Norfolk and intent to involve Queen Mary. The plan was exposed and the main figures punished; this was one of a series of plots, real or invented. The seriousness was real enough at the time; and by 1580 there was very considerable tension. In fact, it is probable that the trigger for the next phase of English overseas activity was the assassination of William of Orange in 1584. The murder of the protestant leader was seen as a proof that it might happen in England; a general Bond of Association to protect or avenge the queen was circulating, and this was approved by Parliament in 1585 for all loyal subjects. More to the point, in 1585, Elizabeth endorsed the first major, official military expedition to the continent. The earl of Leicester led 6,000 troops in what was to be the start of a long series of expeditions. The next few years were critical, for Philip II was collecting forces and finances for his great armada, and the friends and foes of Elizabeth were converging on the figure of Mary of Scotland. Her execution in 1587 (for plotting the overthrow of Elizabeth) and the attack by the Spanish Armada in 1588 were the climactic points of the religious war, from the viewpoint of English royal succession. Equally important, in the wider view of war for English national aims, the years 1589-1603 were a period of continuous operations on the continent, heavy commitments to Ireland, and sporadic naval operations to distant targets. Aggressive and expensive English strategy were well-established features in the first three decades of Elizabeth's reign.

Perhaps the best-known military event for 16th century England, and the one with the most obvious religious overtones, was the Spanish Armada, the "armada catolica" designed to invade England in 1588. Its whole story is complex, its motivation was much more than religious, and it (like many great events) has been disconnected from its context almost to the point of distortion owing to the excessive attention it has received. For this was part of a series of events which saw English attacks on Spanish treasure fleets, then Philip's decision (1585) to prepare a major assault, then harrassing English raids on Spanish ports, then the dramatic conviction and execution of Mary (1587). In the postlude to the great assault, an English "armada" made an unsuccessful foray in 1589, and a series of later Spanish versions sailed in the 1590s. In short, the great Armada was the major episode in a long

Anglo-Spanish war (1585-1603). Englishmen at the time were elated with their triumph but they could not be certain that the victory would be the decisive event in the war.

In April 1587, Francis Drake led a daring raid on Spanish bases, particularly Cadiz, where he disrupted much of the preparation and destroyed a large amount of stores and about 30 ships; he was able to seize a treasure ship in the Azores *en route* home and thus even turn a profit on the expedition. The "Enterprise of England" was delayed for a year, which was long enough for Santa Cruz, Philip's leading admiral, to die and be replaced by a less-experienced general, the duke of Medina Sidonia.

When the Armada did finally set out for the archipelago, it consisted of 130 ships carrying 27,000 men. The cost to Philip had been tremendous, his treasury having to borrow heavily to finance the voyage. The English fleet was on station in the Channel. Admiral Howard toyed with a plan to intercept the Armada, but the queen insisted that they be near at hand. After a running battle up the channel, the great fleet anchored off Calais and that night the English launched a group of fire-ships which scattered the main Spanish force. The next day, in a confused action known as the battle of Gravelines, a number of Spanish ships were destroyed and the rest of the fleet sailed into the North Sea. It had failed to make its planned rendezvous with the duke of Parma and invasion of England was prevented. The remaining voyage around the archipelago and back to Spain was as costly as all of the action against the English. Some 60 ships returned safely; and Philip began to prepare for another armada.

Spain was at this time the leading colonial power in the world. Her great possessions, her sources of mineral wealth and her powerful fleets to operate the enterprise made her a formidable enemy. There is plenty of romance and ample bravery in the accounts of the English sailors who challenged this imperial force. In terms of numbers, the 16th century English navy was poor. Even a mission like Drake's to Cadiz was made on a joint-stock subscription--the government could not pay for it! While an adequate defense could be mustered in home waters, even against a mighty armada, it was quite another story to prepare, launch and sustain a royal navy. We are at the very beginning of English overseas activity in the 16th century. As we will see later (chapter 7), a creditable operation would be in place by the late

17th century, and it would be passing Spain *en route* to first place among European powers.

The English enjoyed tales of Spanish victims of shipwreck on the rocky coasts of western Ireland, meeting what they were sure was a gruesome fate at the hands of native cannibals. Contemporary English estimates of the Irish were unflattering in the extreme, and this was either an excuse or a balm to the English conscience as they undertook the conquest of Ireland. After Henry's flirtation with "surrender and regrant," the next two reigns saw reversion to English seizure and domination. While English accounts suggested that the Gaelic chief could not make the adjustment to the concept of primogeniture, leading to the rebellions of the later 16th century, in fact there is very little evidence of genuine English effort to bring cultural change in moderate fashion. By the reign of Mary, there was the first "plantation", i.e. confiscated land given to settlers who were to establish a new community (Leix, Offaly). Further, the first major rebellion, in Ulster, occurred where there were sure to be conflicts between ancient Gaelic interests (vested in the O'Neill family) and rival titles under the English crown (e.g. the earl of Ulster in the 14th century).

But there were other complications. An illegitimate son of Conn O'Neill had accepted Henry VIII as "King of Ireland" and made the required feudal oaths, took the title earl of Tyrone and gave up the ancestral name. The legitimate heir, Shane O'Neill, violently rejected this settlement, and he led a revolt which began in 1559. This was the first of several major uprisings in Elizabethan Ireland. Undoubtedly the queen would have preferred to avoid war there--especially if she had known that it would cost her over £1 million before the end of the reign. Yet this was far from the picture in these early stages. O'Neill was beaten rather cheaply by a coalition of Irish opponents and settlers from the western isles (1567).

Two years later, more serious rebellion broke out in Munster. This had been subdued by 1572, though here as in Ulster, the English authorities did not follow victory with a stiff policy of retribution. Former leaders of the revolt joined in 1579 when a small invading force landed with papal and Spanish support; a 600-man Spanish contingent came in 1580, but was surrounded and wiped out by the English. Fighting dragged on until 1583, when the government resumed the experiment first tried under Mary, namely the plantation of loyal colonists in lands taken from the defeated parties. In

Munster the plans and preparations were far more ambitious than earlier, but not much more successful.

Meanwhile the lines were being drawn for a new war in the North. Hugh O'Neill persuaded his cousin to stand aside so that the title "O'Neill" would pass to him. He made a pact with the other powerful Ulster family, led by Hugh Roe O'Donnell. The threat of the English encroaching on Gaelic society was epitomized by the building of a number of garrisons in Ulster. In 1595, fighting began on a major scale and O'Neill won an important victory in the Battle of the Yellow Ford (1598). This ignited widespread native support and brought on open rebellion in other provinces. The government in London was shocked into fullscale expenditure; a force of nearly 20,000 came over under the earl of Essex in 1599. Essex failed to follow his orders and was unable to make good use of his resources. Charles Blount, Lord Mountjoy, took command after Essex was recalled. A program of gradual expansion, construction of garrisons and reduction of the supplies available to the enemy was begun. In 1601, the last hope of the Irish hinged on a Spanish expedition which landed in the south at Kinsale. The 4,000 troops were the largest outside (non-English) force ever to land, but they were not enough. They were easily besieged by the English, the Irish leaders marched south but were beaten off before they could make a junction. The Spaniards surrendered and were allowed to leave. O'Neill retreated to Ulster and had to surrender in 1603--less than a week after Elizabeth had died. Hugh was allowed to retain the earldom of Tyrone, his religion was untouched, but it was plain to him and to other participants that the Tudor conquest was now complete. The Gaelic social system was breaking down; language and religion would remain a reservoir of the old culture, but the law, the traditions and the political aspirations of native Ireland were doomed.

To support her military ventures, Elizabeth had to mobilize English resources. The manpower, money and material needed were difficult to obtain, to organize and to deliver in a timely fashion. With the help of able councillors, Elizabeth revitalized her militia and military organization. The lord lieutenant (and deputy lieutenant) of each county became royal military aides; supply of ammunition was centered in an Ordnance Office, and other tasks were streamlined. These were signs of a developing garrison government for use in the archipelago and overseas. The intensity and the resolution of several decades of religious warfare had produced this trend, and the only thing likely to bring it to a halt was the cold shock of fiscal exhaustion. The Elizabethan era has always been noted for military exploits-- seen for the most part in the glamor of Drake's raiding or bold naval assaults on Spanish treasure fleets. The humdrum maintenance of fortresses and garrisons has attracted little attention. There was little in the way of Elizabethan military legislation, but there were growing numbers of writers on military subjects, there were increasing military employments at home and abroad and there was expanding scope for a professional military.

A Tudor garrison was not like its predecessors. One of the first innovations was evident in Henry VIII's fortress construction of the 1530s: instead of licensing the local governments to construct fortifications, the new installations were royal posts, designed to house units of a royal army, later to have civil-military royal governors. By this time we are beyond any revival of marches or palatine powers. The instructions from the Privy Council to these new governors give no hint of autonomy; their place was not hereditary, they were professional fighting men whose posts were political and military rewards; their method of appointment promised the queen loyal and efficient service. To be sure,Elizabeth had a sizeable contingent of aristocratic leaders. Not all were as ineffective or disloyal as Leicester and Essex, but the new style of royal governor had far more talent and reliability on average. In recent years the theory has been advanced that there was a sort of "revolution in government" in this sphere: [12]

> Every provincial capital, major seaport, and royal colony in Britain, Ireland and America [between 1570 and 1680] was affected by the transformation of medieval military captaincies into modern governorships. Captains became governors as they acquired civil duties.

Yet captains and garrisons were familiar enough, and they had certainly had their share (and more) of judicial and political authority. The Tudor experience seemed to promise a major shift toward central control, and the use of the garrison and its captain was aimed toward an increase of royal authority. As we shall see, the colonial application was an important natural development from this source, even though resources were never sufficient to produce a Spanish-style colonial administration.

---

[12]S. S. Webb, *The Governors-General* (1979), 138.

The systematic application of governors and garrisons might have meant closely integrated government. But the archipelago after the 16th century religious wars was politically divided as those wars were among the causes of continuing national identification.

Religion, Politics and Nationality

The religious controversy of the 16th century affected political theory and political behavior and institutions. In general the intended effects were conservative while the accidental results were sometimes radical.

Henry VIII had not intended to promote discussion of his sovereignty when he claimed "plenary, whole and entire power, pre-eminence, authority, prerogative and jurisdiction." Yet his supremacy strictly speaking was in secular jurisdiction (*potestas jurisdictionsis*). The spiritual authority (*potestas ordinis*) remained with the bishops. This division of power helped to open a problem of definition which took many generations to resolve. At the first, discussion of the polity and its nature was properly conservative and unadventurous. The humanist tradition (Thomas More, *Utopia*, 1516) was dominant. The notion of "commonwealth" (normally meaning general welfare, later taken more often to mean the whole community) was not radical. Thomas Starkey saw more capacity for civil reform than most (*Exhortation to the people instructing them to unity and obedience*, 1536). Thomas Smith was typical in his discussion of the types of political organization and the duty of obedience (*De republica anglorum*, 1565).

Continued religious reform in the later 16th century prompted less restrained or more ambitious discussion of political power. The most audacious writers were not English but Scottish. John Knox aimed his *First Blast of the Trumpet Against the Monstrous Regiment of Women* (1558) at Mary Tudor and Mary of Guise. "Knox was unwilling to countenance Elizabeth unless she would acknowledge that she was queen by a special dispensation of God and not by any law of man."[13] By implication the royal supremacy was denied, and a "godly prince" was one who conformed to the reformer's ideas. Authority was God's, it would be found wherever He chose to locate it, and reformers would be the first to know where that was.

---

[13]Gordon Donaldson, *Scotland: James V-VII* (1965), p. 92.

The scholar and reformer George Buchanan introduced arguments from historical precedent. Scottish kings had long been accountable by means of deposition, he wrote, and at least a dozen had been killed for their misgovernment.[14] This grim history was not used to advocate a republic, but in 1567 the coronation oath was revised to "maintain and defend...the true religion" and bishops and ministers took an oath calling the king "supreme governor of this realm, as well in things temporal as in the conservation and purgation of religion."[15]

Reform in Scotland had a long period of development without direction from a sovereign (1561-1585). This fact helps to explain the ascendancy of someone like Andrew Melville. After study and teaching in France and Geneva, Melville became principal of the college of Glasgow in 1574. Though not ordained, he sat as "doctor" in the General Assembly, and his teaching of future ministers exerted wide influence. His basic idea was parity among ministers, and the separation of the "two kingdoms" of church and state. Under this scheme the church would be the dominant partner, and though Melville's order was not formally adopted, the later history of the kirk and politics in Scotland was preoccupied with his model. What this development meant for the nature of royal power was obscured by the eventual migration of the Scottish king. What it evoked from King James before his departure was one of the clearest statements on behalf of royal absolutism.[16] The simple truth was that reformation appeared to place divine authority in the reformed kirk, the head of which should be the 'godly prince.' That formula encouraged response in the form of the doctrine of royal absolutism.

In practical politics, the effect of reformation was to promote and legitimize partisan activity. The work of conspirators was not new; its sanction had never been so open. More constructive forms of political expression were also equipped with partisan features. Meanwhile, political leaders had to use their power to prescribe uniform faith and worship. That prescription (with persecution) insured continued opposition even as it outlawed catholic, presbyterian or episcopal worship.

---

[14]*De jure regni apud Scotos* (1579).

[15]Donaldson, *Scotland*,146.

[16]*Trew Law of Free Monarchies* (1598)

The very idea of legislated uniformity was a novelty in the 16th century. Previously the heretic was a lonely outcast. That it was now necessary to legislate the orthodox belief and form of worship was an admission of serious division within the community. Not only that, the process of enforcement which flowed from these acts would become the major element in maintaining religious dissent. Persecution gave martyrs to the cause--and the cause was a potential political platform, i.e. a continuing, formed, defensible base for political action.

The acts of governments in the name of uniformity had a frightening appearance to the 19th century liberal (though we can easily find worse in our own time). We ought to remember their novelty and the lack of experience in enforcement as we criticize them. After all, obedience had been the norm, toleration of deviance had not. If the "supreme head" declared the proper form of dress, liturgy, or sacramental order, that should have been sufficient. That it was not was a measure of reformed commitment; that they were disobeyed surely came as a great shock to rulers.

What did governments do to achieve uniformity? The main means were through legislative acts, appointments of ministers, and judicial proceedings against offenders--i.e., the use of all the machinery of government. Patterns were quite different, however. In England and Wales there was a centralized pattern, with clear royal power in the church itself; in Scotland, the crown and church were engaging in a duel to achieve control until the end of the century; in Ireland, the "church" was in fact two bodies, the traditional Roman and the imported Anglican. Therefore, use of laws, officials and justice were not identical. Needless to say, the nature and degree of "uniformity" was hardly the same. One fact was shared. The process of enforcing uniformity always and everywhere rebounded into the political sphere.

Uniform worship was legislated in England and Wales for the first time in 1549. The act was aimed at enforcing the use of the first "Book of Common Prayer"--an order for services of worship which was novel in being written in English, but more so in being a collected set of service orders, and being anti-papal in tone. Henry VIII had published miscellaneous articles and injunctions, with particular penalties for those who disobeyed. The difference between this and a general act of uniformity may have been invisible to the judicial victims in both cases. However, from 1549, to 1552,

181

to 1559 there were periodic legislative declarations of the requirements for a loyal subject in the area of religion. Two observations seem appropriate. These acts had to confuse the subject wishing to conform, and they had to convince the loyal and the disloyal alike that matters of faith belonged in the domain of secular law. This was not true, but it was an understandable error. For the lawmakers were being called upon to state the *penalties* and provide the judicial power to enforce the creeds, not to enact the creeds themselves. The line was a clear one to the royal councillor, but less so to the puritan reformer. One major consequence was that during Elizabethan doctrinal controversies, theological opposition began to show signs of partisan argument, opposing the royal will in parliament--hitherto an unthinkable development.

In Scotland uniformity was oriented to the Confession of 1560 and was upheld by the courts of the kirk: session, presbytery, synod, and General Assembly. There were anomalies and a number of survivals from the old church. What was distinctive was the fact that the instrumentality of this Calvinist church was the local congregation. Further, the reformed kirk was not directly endowed with the old church's property, and there was indecision about adopting its old episcopal authority. Therefore, a strong structure of uniformity was created which tended to use more outwardly egalitarian forms.

In Ireland, legislative action was dictated by the English parliament, and the early laws on reformation were transported from the English statute book. The lower clergy in the Irish parliament were opposed to the new laws, and for their pains they were henceforth excluded from membership in parliament. When further reforms were introduced into Ireland, they had no natural base in a native reform party, and indeed they encountered opposition which was magnified by Jesuit missionaries after 1542. In fact, the Edwardian reforms were introduced by royal prerogative--no parliamentary endorsement or synod of clergy was used. Mary's rule brought a welcome reversal, however brief, and then in 1560 an Irish parliament was convened long enough to adopt parallel laws of supremacy and uniformity to those enacted by the English after Elizabeth's accession. Enforcement of uniformity in Ireland was impossible, for there was little more disposition to accept the new settlement in the Pale than there was elsewhere. This evocation of religious identity went a great distance to revise the basic political condition of

182

Ireland and to produce a new national identity and opposition to English rule. That identity was sufficiently developed before the Reformation, but the added fact of persecuting religion meant that the policy of conquest followed by the Tudors, emerging clearly under Elizabeth, would work against religious uniformity.

In an age of state churches, dissent was a form of political expression. There were variations in dissent, but all had political content. The early opponents of official policy were for the most part disorganized individuals. The scholars and merchants who were among the earliest adherents of continental ideas had little political influence. On the side of Rome there was at least more *perceived* potential, and later there were a number of conspiracies, real or imaginary, aimed at the overthrow of royal heretics. These too were by nature limited in number if sensational in character. More significant was the public form of organized dissent or criticism which appeared in the latter part of the 16th century.

Puritans and sectaries were sometimes startling in their open resistance to establishment. Religious threats and political action were forcing new and bolder forms of behavior. We have already seen the remarkable experience in Scotland where reformers opposed the royal power successfully until Mary was expelled and then controlled the regency of her son while a protestant settlement was achieved. In England there were other forms of organized political expression. In the crisis of the 1580s, when the catholic states of Europe seemed about to assault the English, and when the religious fighting in the Low Countries even brought the assassination of the Prince of Orange, the movement to form "Bonds of Association" received wary endorsement from the government, for indeed this counter-conspiratorial organizing was a novel and ominous kind of activity.

When the threat from Spain was beaten, royal policy turned on the outspoken reformers, and Archbishop Whitgift cracked down on printed works and unauthorized worship. Elizabeth had already been challenged in parliament by repeated puritan attempts to continue reform through lawmaking. By the 1590s the government felt able to bring pressure on these opponents. There was perhaps no genuine puritan "party" in a modern sense of the term, but a committed group of radical members was able to push forward measures which the queen did not want--questions of vestments, the prayer book, then issues of "free speech" and privilege. This sort of open opposition, firmly squelched though it was by the queen and her ministers, was a sign of the effect of religious debate--the issue for instance in the case of Archbishop Grindal's dismissal over "prophesyings". In spite of strenuous efforts, it seemed that the unleashing of reform could not be reversed.

The potent force of religious reform also could be seen in the shape of political institutions in the 16th century. Those bodies which were engaged in the reform were themselves altered by it, willingly or otherwise. In England and Wales the parliamentary council was probably given its single most important boost toward modern legislative competence by its participation in religious reform measures. In Scotland, the kirk was provided with its own legislature, the General Assembly, which rivalled the parliament in governing importance. In Ireland, the adoption of English legislation had no very positive effect for parliament, and subsequent military intervention, garrisons and plantations put a hostile face on the reformation.

In spite of careful drafting and meticulous management, the legislative experience of the Reformation Parliament had to create a sense of competence. Whether or not Henry VIII was sincere in saying that "we at no time stand so highly in our estate royal as in the time of parliament," behind the words lay an indispensable partnership, surmounted at first by the royal supremacy. The crown needed parliamentary approval for criminal penalties which would enforce the reformation statutes. So long as the king proceeded via established courts and judicial processes, the role of parliament was vital. Thus even though the laws were drafted for them, debates were normally perfunctory and votes were usually favorable, members of parliament attained much greater stature as a result of the reformation. Although Prayer Books, Articles of Religion and Injunctions were not made into statutes, the instruments of uniformity often were, thereby assuring parliament of a more permanent place in the constitution. It is entirely possible that such a place would have been assured by other means, because the threat from the forces of the counter-Reformation meant heavy military expenditure. The involvement in Elizabeth's subversive efforts in France and the Netherlands and the defence against the Armada were expensive. That cost was compounded by the inflation of the 16th century. Henry VIII, in spite of successful fleecing of the church's revenues and properties, left the crown poorer than when he arrived. His heirs continued to sell off crown lands--

even as they augmented the political power of the crown. As a result of her need for financial assistance, Elizabeth summoned fairly frequent parliaments. We can see in her reign the beginning of a pattern which became dominant in the next century--namely, the withholding of financial support until the crown conceded a point on policy. The occasions were provided by the wars of religion, the queen's taunters were often the bold members of advanced religious views.

The General Assembly in Scotland was an unusual constitutional development. As Gordon Donaldson described it:[17]

> The assembly may have been in practice nothing more than a development from the 'great council of the realm,' consisting of protestant lords and their associates, which acted as the provisional government in 1559-61....Slightly differently regarded, the assembly was a council of the realm strengthened by the addition of some clerical members....the assembly was plainly the 'godly magistracy,' or perhaps the 'godly estates,' the substitute for the 'godly prince' whom the Scots did not have.

This rival parliament changed its character and came to be dominated by a clerical oligarchy. For a time, until James could assert himself in the 1580s, there was a kind of party battle between this clerical faction and a more secular faction (sometimes the regent, usually the parliament). James was hoping to form a compound system (a *via media*) so when in the 1590s the presbyterian faction was given *de facto* recognition, the episcopal order was not abolished. Beginning in 1596, James systematically took more control over the meetings of the General Assemblies, by the simple device of shifting their place of meeting and hence obtaining more conservative attendance (e.g. at Montrose or Aberdeen). He was so successful that by 1610 a General Assembly followed his suggestion in adopting the restoration of episcopacy. Along the way, James played the assemblies and parliaments off against one another, and in 1606 parliament passed an act acknowledging the king's power to legislate for the church.

However it was used or abused, the assembly did remain part of the kirk structure, but it did not meet between 1618-38 and 1653-90. In other words, its main career came after the eventual establishment of Presbyterianism. Still the idea of such a body gave the kirk a unique political character.

---

[17]*The Scottish Reformation* (1960), p. 143.

The institutional effects of religion in Irish politics were more brutal, but they were masked by the dual systems which had operated before the 16th century. While the Pale was reformed along English lines, Gaelic Ireland was being suppressed. Its institutions had never had the shape and strength of the English, though their effectiveness was attested to by the Gaelic revival of the 14th-16th centuries. But Irish kingship, the Gaelic bards, brehons and their laws and customs were assaulted by English royal intervention: Henry's "surrender and regrant" and Elizabeth's policy of conquest. Historians have agreed that the policies were rooted in a strategic motive, i.e. that Ireland represented an open flank for the counter-reformation. But this cannot be well-argued until the 1580s or 90s as a realistic policy consideration, and much of the Irish alteration had already been attempted by then. It is better to put the policy in an archipelago perspective: from Henry VII's time, the "problem" of Ireland was one of finding an affordable means of providing domestic security. The two options seemed to be Anglo-Irish management (e.g. Kildare) or English colonial rule. Once the reformation was exported to Ireland, the first option lost its natural strength, because the Anglo-Irish were conservative landowners, not protestant reformers. Thus the crown returned to military governors (Skeffington, St. Leger, Sussex, Sidney, Essex, Mountjoy) and when the native population was proven to be disloyal, from the 1550s there were expanding experiments in planting colonies of loyal, later protestant, settlers to pacify and to build a loyalist community. At the same time, the native culture was attacked by outlawing gaelic customs, and in 1605 declaring their laws invalid. Strictly speaking this was not a result of religious opposition; English v. Gaelic hostility could and did appear among co-religionists. But the added emotion and tension of sectarian hostility made the issues culminate more quickly and decisively. By the end of the century, it is likely that the Anglo-Irish saw the war in Ulster as a fight to save their church, while O'Neill and others saw it as a fight to save their culture.

Thus religious divisions were made a more vital part of political life in the later 16th century. They strengthened old national identities and forestalled archipelago integration. But it is well to remember that every area had a mixture of Anglican, Presbyterian and Catholic elements, and the heaviest concentrations of the first were in England and Wales, the second in Scotland, the third in Ireland.

As Elizabeth's regime conquered Ireland and the Anglo-Irish administration spread over a larger nominal area, it was not able to overcome the Irish catholic majority--and in some respects, Anglo-Irishmen found sources of identification with the natives and against the English. A very different process went on in Wales, where the provision of a Welsh-language Bible seemed to foster autonomy in that lately-annexed territory. When James VI of Scotland succeeded Elizabeth on the English throne, he brought a personal union which "solved" the old issue of the Border, but James could not fuse the two nations, mainly because of their dissimilar national churches.

There were other signs of national consolidation in the years after 1560. In the Orkneys, the Hebrides and in some of the English palatine jurisdictions there was evidence of less particularism and more "central" rule. Garrison government in the archipelago (and in the colonies) could have been the base for a "British" union and national regime, but there never was sufficient planning or funding to complete a garrison system, even in Ireland. Had this been done, there is no certainty that religious hostility might not have undermined the incipient united regime.

We cannot hope to reconstruct the demographic outlines of sects and their geographic distribution. But it is important to keep in mind that every area was divided, and the minority in any one area would draw at least moral support from the fact that in a neighboring nation there was a sympathetic majority. This was a major force in attenuating moves to absorb one group or another and to preserve varied identities. The Anglican population of England and Wales probably gave some encouragement to a minority in Scotland which had little power, and a minority in Ireland which had most political power. The Catholic population in most areas was generally in rural districts, and it was especially strong in northern and western England, in west Wales, and in the Scottish Highlands. Outside of Dublin and other ports, plus some north-eastern counties, most parts of Ireland were heavily catholic. The main center of Presbyterianism was in Scotland with radical protestant elements representing an affiliated group. This classification poses serious problems, for in Elizabethan England, for instance, there is evidence that a major part of the clergy were puritan, i.e. they were Anglican in name, they held benefices in that church and professed loyalty to its Supreme Governor, but they were in favor of a further reform toward a presbyterian

187

model. One other type of protestant group should be mentioned--namely, the settlers "planted" in Ireland. The only group of any significant size was in Ulster. There were smaller groups in Munster and Leix and Offaly--and then much larger ones after the Cromwellian invasion in 1649. If their collective numbers were small, their peculiar position lent them a disproportionate political significance.

It is probable that the internal mixture in each sector of the archipelago was a positive factor in sustaining the several national identities. Hostile factions and foreign enemies deserve much of the credit for viable national sentiments. The presence of catholic plotters in Northumberland, of Jesuit missionaries in Galloway and presbyterian sympathizers in Cambridge University were each influential in this manner.

There might be public and official efforts to enhance national identity. One such project was the publication of the Welsh Bible. The New Testament, together with the Prayer Book, were first published in Welsh in 1567, and the whole Bible in 1588. The importance of this was twofold: the religious texts preserved the native language, and that language was now the idiom of religion. In the 16th century, the bardic tradition was faltering, medieval models were out of favor in literary circles and the gentrification of Wales was likely to proceed under strong anglicizing influence. As the influence of the printing press was just being felt, the timing of the Welsh language Bible was critical. On the other side, reformers were able to associate the revivalist, primitivist aspects of protestantism with patriotic Welsh ideas--the ancient British (Celtic) church, and the ancient prophetic tradition. Wales was unique in gaining this linguistic advantage; no other Celtic community (in the 16th century) enjoyed this nation-building asset.

The Scottish kirk had powerful national potential, offset by major inhibiting conditions. From the banding of the Lords of the Congregation in the 1550s to the National Covenant of 1638, a tradition of a community of believers making public affirmation of their faith and solidarity was powerfully demonstrated. In their communal and national kirk structure there was an effective disciplinary machine. However, there were serious weaknesses in the Scottishness of the kirk. The non-English speaking parts of Scotland were not readily incorporated in the reformed church, and the wearer of the Scottish crown became the Supreme Head of the Church in

England. These anomalies would force the kirk to struggle for its national identity for most of the 17th century.

In Ireland, the national development was retarded in two ways. The Anglo-Norman invasion produced dual political systems, and the reformation introduced the religious dualism which forced the Gaelic system to be dismantled. That apparatus itself, however, had not offered a basis for unification, but rather had fostered localism and separatism--the perpetuation of the "nations" of old families and regions. With these twin disabilities, Ireland could only absorb the successive colonies and constitutions imported through the Pale, until in the 19th century the Catholic church provided a rallying point for a native national movement.

English national development was greatly enhanced by the creation of the "Church of England." Although structure was not outwardly altered, successive changes in orthodoxy and emphatic policies of uniformity were effective instruments to mold a national institution. Historians usually place emphasis on the sects and their resistance to the establishment. The romantic and the revolutionary appeal of this approach is obvious; it should not mask the plain truth that by and large, through Star Chamber and High Commission, through statutes and wars, a durable allegiance was forged. That was accompanied by a broader and more centralized political structure than at any earlier period. Also, the politique *via media* of Elizabeth suggests that somehow there was less concern for religion on the part of the queen and her ministers of state. This is incorrect, for their concern was to defuse both extremes, (or pit them against one another), so as to build a stronger settlement on moderate lines. To handle religious protest as far as possible as a form of treason does not turn out to be less concerned, but rather to be more efficient.

The shape of the nations of the archipelago was a matter for princes and barons in the years before 1500. Religious changes over the next few generations had the general effect of opening, and complicating, all political processes. Religious belief was the most likely avenue along which the politically immature communities would move toward more outspoken and less deferential postures. Ideas of order and hierarchy were not overthrown, but the higher order of divine governance--invoked by a widening circle of ministers--was a formidable political solvent. Powerful "supreme heads" might channel it, but wars of religion and politics of uniformity broke down the old restraints. The two innovations also sustained the nations of the archipelago, especially as they moved into 17th century conflicts, inside and outside the partially-fortified "unitary state."

CHAPTER 6

WARS AND UNIFICATION

> I have observed that a treaty of union has
> never been mentioned by the English, but
> with a design to amuse us when they
> apprehended any danger from our nation.
> And when their apprehensions were blown
> over, they have always shown they had no
> such intention.
>
> (Andrew Fletcher of Saltoun,
> *Conversation Concerning Right
> Regulation of Governments,* 1704)

The wars of the 17th century--civil, foreign and imperial--drove the archipelago into the hands of an English oligarchy, one whose power lasted until the 19th century. During the wars, there were several attempts to organize the archipelago into a coherent political unit. All efforts at union were frustrated, whether they were made by King James or Oliver Cromwell or King William.[1] This century of war was not to be the basis of a unified nation, at least not in the sense of the later "integral" nations of Europe. Instead, it was clear by the beginning of the 18th century that an imperial archipelago had been formed by the forcible incorporation of England's immediate neighbors. The acquisition of extensive overseas colonies was a vital imperial corollary, and it is discussed in the next chapter. This imperial form of unification meant that older national identities would be preserved in two ways: by the assertion of English superiority and by the absence of an assimilating policy at the center. The resulting regime was a loose dynastic federation, and an advanced political machine for 18th century Europe. It had resolved the major issues of the 16th and 17th centuries, i.e. royal absolutism, established religion, economic stress and an enlarged political nation. Those issues were at the center of the crises of the 17th century, and each one played a part in shaping the form of unification which evolved in the archipelago.

---

[1] The sovereign after 1603 wore three crowns, figuratively speaking. Thus James VI of Scotland became James I of England (and Ireland). William III of England would have been William II of Scotland, while presently Elizabeth II is, to the Scottish Nationalist at least, Elizabeth I. For simplicity, the English numerals will be used.

WARS AND UNIFICATION

The Course of Unification

The process of unification covered a century and a half. Since our approach to archipelago politics is unconventional, it follows that the common periods offer less useful divisions here. In order to comprehend the unification problem, we need an overview of political events from the union of crowns in 1603 through the union of parliaments (English and Scottish) in 1707, to the defeat of Jacobite rebellions and the statutory subjection of Ireland in the first half of the 18th century. Only with these accomplishments can we begin to speak of continuous unified political control of the archipelago.

King James came to the English throne at an opportune time. He presided over victory in Ireland and made peace with Spain in 1604. By linking the thrones of England and Scotland in his own person, James had an unequalled opportunity for constitutional reform. But what would he propose? Evidently James had no idea of a complete archipelago federation, but he did put considerable effort into a formal union of "Great Britain." Surely James thought his plan of an incorporating act to combine parliaments, laws and churches was conservative and natural. His subjects thought otherwise, and a good number of them obstructed his plan. Although a treaty of union was negotiated in 1604, it was never ratified. All the same, a de facto union did come into being in the person and prerogative of the ruler.

In Ireland, James succeeded with some measures of greater assimilation, but he did not attempt any act of incorporation. The defeat of the rebel Ulster earls in 1603 still left them in possession of Irish land and English titles. They had little hope for the survival of their culture and way of life, and in 1607 Tyrone and Tyrconnel fled to the continent with a large number of followers. This move exposed them to charges of treason and opened their estates to confiscation. The estates comprised over 3 million acres which became the base for the Ulster plantation. The plan called for a major migration of English and Scottish families to settle and pacify an area which was historically the most rebellious part of Ireland. By the 1620s some 3,700 families had settled, but in most places the settlers were outnumbered by the Irish. The plantation could not create the sort of loyal colony which James wanted, but it was quite enough to alienate native owners. One special feature in Ulster was the addition to an existing Scottish Presbyterian minority already present. This group was not apt to be easily governed by the Anglican Irish establishment.

King James was faced with serious problems in English government. At the root of the difficulty was a gaping contrast between the precocious liberalism appearing in English politics and the renaissance style of the new king, whose peremptory and authoritarian mode served him well in Scotland and Ireland, but caused him no end of trouble in England. James's early and acrimonious debates with parliament were remarkable. He had withstood far more dangerous opposition in his youth in Scotland, but there his opponent had used force instead of the English concoction of law and pseudo-history. Indeed, not many Englishmen had ventured such opposition to the crown in earlier times, and those who did could expect rough treatment. Therefore, it is wrong to blame James for failing to "manage" the House of Commons, when such a task was inconceivable to him, and when it was yet to be an established part of the English system. We can see with hindsight that the reign of Elizabeth produced escalating disputes over money, religion and foreign affairs. And we can see how each of these matured into debates between privilege and prerogative. James summoned four English parliaments for a total of nine sessions; relations were difficult with all of them, and by the end of the reign, there was a serious accumulation of friction.

Charles I pursued the same basic royal policy as his father, yet he seemed to behave in a more arbitrary and authoritarian manner. The king's agents (Archbishop William Laud and the earl of Strafford) became lightning rods of discontent as the king governed for 11 years without a parliament, only to find himself facing a domestic uprising and desperately in need of tax revenues. Rebellion in Scotland, Ireland and England culminated in what may be called the "War of the Three Kingdoms." This "English Civil War" was a three-act archipelago tragedy: the early, connected rebellions in Scotland, Ireland and England (1638-42); two periods of multiple civil wars (1642-46 and 1648); and the English conquest of Ireland and Scotland led by Oliver Cromwell (1649-52). Cromwell's paradoxical contribution was a violent assertion of English power which effectively *preserved* Scottish and Irish national identity. Meanwhile, Cromwell began the systematic English pursuit of imperial glory, which would serve so well as a counterweight to separatism in the archipelago.

The royal restoration in 1660 was a common effort between the kingdoms. The restored government had to reconcile parties to the recent combat and to wrestle with problems of ancient conflict. The difference in the 1660s was that after the former governors were restored there was a different appearance to political dissent in the afterglow of regicide and republic. These perspectives tempered disagreements over the governing of England, the archipelago and the empire--but more crises were to come before there was a settlement.

The most profound political alteration of the 17th century occurred in what was later called the "Glorious Revolution." William of Orange, nephew of King James II, joined a plot to overthrow his uncle. He led an Anglo-Dutch invasion of southwest England in November 1688, and after most of James's officers deserted him, the king fled to France. The coup was followed by an agreement ("Bill of Rights") to stipulate limits on the exercise of the (English) royal prerogative, and to guarantee a Protestant (English) succession--in other words, a major constitutional revolution. Historians have concentrated on the English constitutional issues, so they have underestimated a vital corollary, William's securing of the archipelago as a strategic buffer against Louis XIV. This was William's price for "rescuing" the English and their liberties. The Scots had not invited him, and they were not thrilled with another power altering their royal succession. The Irish provided large numbers to fight *for* James II. So in the years 1689-91 William had to establish, by conquest, a military union in order to secure his base for the French wars (1689-1711). This task was threatened by French invasion; it was completed by the forced subjection of the Irish Catholics and the cooperation of the Scots.

When it was clear that William would die childless, and the only Protestant in line was his sister-in-law Anne, the Act of Settlement (1701) provided that the throne should revert to the line of James I's daughter who had been married to a German prince. This would place the House of Hanover on the English throne and avoid the reversion to the Stuart Catholic line. The act was a radical constitutional innovation, presaged by the terms of 1689. This also was a step which highlighted the Scottish legislative inferiority. An English parliament had presumed once again to alter the Scottish succession without consulting the Scots, and it rediscovered the one way to alienate all parties in Scotland at once.

Over the next five years, a series of legislative challenges were thrown from each side of the border. These were finally resolved by a treaty of union. English and Scottish commissioners met and drafted a set of articles, ratified by the respective parliaments. On May 1, 1707, both parliaments were replaced by the parliament of Great Britain, in some sense merely an extension of the English body. It was ironic that the union was nearly a reversal of the plan of a century earlier: James had tried to unite churches and laws, but this was not attempted in 1707. The parliamentary union was an objective surrendered quickly in 1604. Only the economic union was an object in both cases, and in 1707 it was more vital than ever for Scotland.

There was, and still is, bitter recrimination over the Act of Union and what some considered its virtual surrender to English supremacy. It was still better than the settlement imposed on Ireland at the end of the 17th century. King William's victory in 1691 allowed the establishment of a harsh Protestant "ascendancy" with legal suppression of Roman Catholics under a system of penal laws. The constitutional place of the Irish colonial aristocracy was however, inferior. Their colonial government, like others developing in several parts of the world, was to be managed by a distant, alien political caste, not much more familiar to the Irish Anglican than to his Catholic neighbor.

The dynastic coup of 1688 and the Act of Settlement had proscribed the Stuart (or any Catholic) line, while the Treaty of 1707 removed the possibility of a separate Scottish succession. What was not removed was the court in exile, which posed the intermittent threat of French-supported invasion linked to internal rebellion. This "Jacobite" threat was real, and it could channel a multitude of discontents. In the event, it was a failure. Its greatest political consequence was the negative fact that it offered an exclusionary principle to English Whigs (barring "Tories" from public office).

The finale for the Jacobite cause was an important event in the formation of the united government of Great Britain. When "Bonnie Prince Charlie" led an assault in 1745, his defeat was followed by an Anglo-Scottish occupation of the Highland zone, punishment of the supporters of the prince and a major effort to overhaul Highland customs and institutions. Private jurisdictions and clan anomalies were removed, theoretically making possible more uniform government of Scotland. This stage was both a victory of lowland over highland Scots, and a stage in Anglo-Scottish amalgamation. Its significance has been obscured by the fact that the next few generations saw both the "Scottish Enlightenment" and the northern version of industrial revolution. Scottish union with England might seem closer than ever once the Jacobite threat was gone. The end of dynastic rivalry was followed by the merger of the Scottish and English political patronage machines, a truer path to political union in the 18th century. Political unification was thus a prolonged and only partially completed process, the phases of which we need to examine more carefully.

Regal Union

The reign of Elizabeth presented James with some opportunity and some difficulty. Conquest of Ireland and victory in the long war with Spain brought greater English political security. The expense of these ventures, in direct financial and indirect political costs, were deferred payments which came due in the 17th century. But James undoubtedly felt in 1603 that he had inherited a viable and powerful empire. The new king had some appreciation of the labor involved in political consolidation. His own hard work after assuming personal rule in Scotland surely reinforced his ideas about royal authority, and we need to review his apprenticeship and rule in Scotland to understand his approach to the government of the enlarged kingdom.

When the 13-month old prince was recognized as king in 1567, he was of course under the control of regents. They were involved in bitter factional disputes for the next 20 years, one faction adhering to his mother's cause until her execution in 1587. Shifts of power among rival groups and occasional seizure of the king's person rendered government unstable. That instabilty was reflected in many of James's later acts and policies. He despised faction and sought reconciliation--on his own royal terms of course. For the last two decades of Elizabeth's reign, there was no certainty as to her successor. When Mary was executed, James seemed to be the only obvious choice. Even before that event, Elizabeth gave indirect recognition of James's title: in a treaty of July 1586, it was agreed that she would do nothing to the derogation of his title without provocation; she would provide a subsidy for him; and both countries would provide aid to one another in the event of an invasion.[2] For her part, Elizabeth was loath to designate an heir formally and thus create a rival court. For James, the period was one of frustrating uncertainty, which on one occasion brought him close to reckless intrigue. He was marginally involved with the plot of the earl of Essex, but James was also in close contact with William Cecil, the queen's secretary and the earl's great enemy.

In governing Scotland, by 1596 James had subdued the last recalcitrant Catholic earls in the North. He then reduced Presbyterian power by controlling meetings of the General Assembly and by increasing the power of bishops. James also asserted his authority in remote parts of the kingdom: he married Anne of Denmark (1589) and increased control over the Orkneys and Shetland; he curbed violence and extended the zone of royal authority in the North and the West. As James was intriguing with Essex, he was also publishing his thoughts on kingship: *The Trew Law of Free Monarchies* (1598) and *Basilikon Doron* (1599). These were conventional statements of divine right kingship, an old notion refurbished in the 16th century to bolster royal power against papal authority, aristocratic anarchy, or Calvinist theocracy. The king received his authority from God, with no intervening human agency, and thus he was not bound by laws or precedents, preachers or parliaments. Tudor sovereigns generally believed this, but they did not write tracts on the subject. The position of the English crown was indeed carefully and deliberately compromised by the Tudors, while James was busily building royal power on an old, traditional model in Scotland. He had been quite successful, but when he transferred his rule to England, there was apt to be a collision of basic ideas of royal power.

The unicameral parliament of Scotland was very different from its southern counterpart. The Scottish Parliament was under royal control, especially through a Committee of Articles, a kind of steering committee evolved in the 16th century as a device to do parliamentary business. The Scottish courts of law, and the law administered in them were unlike the English. Proceedings were not based on common law writs, and all business was under loose supervision of the crown. On the other hand, local law enforcement was chiefly a matter of baronial jurisdiction, although James had made a point of trying to reduce local independence.

---

[2]*Calendar of State Papers, Scotland*, v. 1, p. 529.

There was relatively little friction evident in 1603. The accession went smoothly, and general reactions of the English public and politicians were favorable. In part, this was owing to the high expectations which diverse factions held of the new reign. Catholics expected tolerance from Mary's son; Puritans expected reformation because of James's education and training in the kirk. But James was his own man with his own brand of via media who would soon alienate both extremes.

The first open rupture came at the Hampton Court Conference when James sat in session with the English bishops and heard arguments from puritan clergy on the correct form of church government. He used the opportunity to lecture them, making it clear that the office of bishop would remain, as indeed he had already shown by his policy in Scotland. The Scottish bishops would be strengthened further under James's influence, the office being eventually acknowledged by the General Assembly in 1610.

In his work toward formalizing the union, James encountered more opposition. Even before his commissioners met on the issue in October 1604, James issued a proclamation declaring that his royal title henceforth should be "King of Great Britain, France and Ireland, Defender of the Faith, etc." James also ordered the minting of a 20 shilling gold piece, the "unite." In early 1606 he ordered the use of a union flag (the cross of St. George over the cross of St. Andrew, an unhappy symbol to his Scottish subjects). By this point, the recommendations of the union commissioners had bogged down in the English parliament, and in 1607 the formal union effort was dropped.

As the plan for formal union was stalled and then defeated, James still conducted the government of his several realms, and in certain ways the union was an administrative fait accompli. By not recognizing this and providing regulation for it, parliament had only insured a continuous supply of friction. James appointed the key officials in each realm, he prepared legislation, raised taxes and other revenues, and he stood behind (or above) the courts of law. In specific areas such as the administration of the border (now the "middle shires") and the question of common citizenship (the case of the "post-nati")[3] the de facto union was affirmed.

---

[3] In Calvin's Case (1608) it was held that those born in Scotland after the king's accession in 1603 were also natural subjects of the king of England.

With respect to Ireland, union was on a different model. Indeed, the fact that the word "union" is seldom used in this context is revealing. The assumed regal power of Henry VIII was ratified by later Tudor conquest and plantation. Yet an anomaly remained. Was Ireland a kingdom or a colony? James said the Irish were his "free, natural and immediate subjects."[4] This they may have been, but they were governed by an imported set of institutions, neither free, natural nor immediate.

The Stuart succession could not produce a truly united regime either by law or in practice. The task facing James was difficult enough: having finally secured his position in Scotland through endless crises, he was to relearn his craft in London, under the carping criticism of foreign lawyers and politicians. Looking more closely at the manifold challenges to James's government--religious tensions, economic strains and political disputes--it is easy to see how the English and the archipelago context both required extraordinary royal skill or luck to avoid trouble.

The *via media* in religion was seen by Elizabeth (as far as we can penetrate her personal ideas) as a tactic or expedient. James saw it as a route to reconciliation. He envisioned a reunion of the churches which was at least a serious miscalculation. Extreme opposition was drawn from both sides, moderation could not mute sectarian hostility, and government resorted to dual persecution, thus annulling the moral advantage of a *via media*.

In 1604-05 James first scolded the Puritans at Hampton Court and he ordered stricter enforcement of the recusancy laws against Catholics. Anger at the latter was part of the background to the infamous Gunpowder Plot. It was discovered in November 1605 that a group of conspirators had planted a cache of powder in the cellar below the House of Lords, hoping to blow up the king and parliament. Informants exposed the plot and its mere existence caused a tremendous shock and seemed to verify the worst fears and fantasies of Protestants.

To the more radical Scottish and English Calvinists it appeared that the Anglican establishment was linked to conservative, if not papal, theology and liturgy. James continued to apply pressure to the kirk, which had been formally Presbyterian since 1592. The Scottish bishops were in the process

---

[4]Proclamation of March 11, 1605, cited in G.A. Hayes-McCoy "The Completion of the Tudor Conquest" in T.W. Moody *et al., Early Modern Ireland (New History of Ireland,* v. 3, 1976), p. 137.

of regaining power. After the king's move to London, the trend continued. By 1612, the bishops were well in place, and in 1618 James forced the adoption of the "Five Articles of Perth." Kneeling at communion, the traditional Christian calendar, private communion and baptisms, and confirmation were restored despite the opposition of the General Assembly. Few ministers suffered as a result of enforcement, indeed the ominous aftermath of the action was incomplete enforcement. James next moved to adopt a revised liturgy, which was composed by 1620, but which was not issued.

In Ireland, the Old English (Catholics) and their native co-religionists were drawing together in fear of continued Protestant persecution. The Ulster plantation was a source of anxiety, even to those in other parts of the nation. Royal policy was a source of confusion to many. Anti-Catholic laws were on the books, but were irregularly enforced. All parties in Ireland had looked to the new king as a deliverer, but he did not reduce the insecurity of his subjects, especially with large scale plantation. Catholics in Ireland now were liable to loss of lands which intensified their fears.

Against the background of frightened religious factions, Charles I assumed power with a policy of more vigorous Anglicanism. His object was an unremitting conformity, what might be called center extremism. The policy was manifested in the work of Archbishop William Laud (1632-45) and Thomas Wentworth, Earl of Strafford, President of the Council of the North and Lord Lieutenant of Ireland. The predictable result was to drive enemies into desperate acts of opposition. In England, the Court of High Commission had been created in the later 16th century to discipline clergy who strayed from the policy of the Supreme Governor. In the 17th century, this prerogative court was unleashed on religious critics of all social classes. Harsh punishments were meted out to the outspoken Puritan. Meanwhile, the Old English in Ireland, whose position vis a vis the crown was still an anomaly, were promised the relief of the "Graces," a set of measures to define and relax the legal position of these potentially loyal subjects (1628). Charles granted these acts in exchange for a large appropriation (£120,000), and then he held back on the promised legal changes. In Scotland, Charles approved the Act of Revocation (1633) which would have restored lands taken from the church in the 16th century, and he thereby alienated a large body of landowners. In these and other ways, the king and his servants were straining legal powers with the aim of strengthening the fiscal position of the crown.

The 17th century had a background of economic tension which helped to explain these problems. Massive inflation from the previous century created an unstable economic environment, one which was novel and frightening to many. Landed estates were not the secure base they had been in the past. Dissolution, confiscation, title searching, enclosure, all had direct impact on owners. As the crown felt the pinch of inflated costs against fixed sources of income, it encouraged or tolerated restrictive and abrasive economic practices, in both public policy and the private enterprise of courtiers. Production, labor and exchange were all invaded by inefficient regulation and arbitrary patronage.

One area where historians have concentrated their quest to explain the social origins of the revolution is in the impact of all these changes on members of the gentry. Since most leaders of society (rebel or royalist) came from this group, presumably an analysis of their fortunes would reveal underlying causal factors. For the class as a whole, this analysis proves daunting and inconclusive. And that is only considering England. The gentlemen of Wales, Ireland and Scotland (and their cousins who held property in more than one area) had the same problems. Every aspiring owner sought to improve estates and productivity. If while so occupied, he encountered a government which threatened his title, challenged his tenure or infringed on his operations, he would be less apt to support that regime. In Scotland, the Commissions on Kirk Land (1617, 1621) and in Ireland the Commission on Defective Titles (1635) probably weakened the natural loyalties of some landowners.

The general economic conditions in the early 17th century were not poor. There was considerable prosperity and improvement. One or two trade slumps seriously damaged the cloth trade (affecting England in particular), but overall conditions were not deteriorating. All the same, economic tension was a major problem. In its nature, the effect of inflation was uneven and would be more severe in major trading centers than in rural, pastoral areas. The economic instability increased the demand for regulation and patronage, which in turn magnified the political sensitivity of economic interests. The issue of chartered monopolies was only the most obvious and extreme kind of royal economic interference. There were about 700 of these in 1621, with an annual revenue of £100,000. For each happy monopolist there were probably a dozen dissatisfied merchants or speculators.

Economic tension, particularly on matters of trade, fed directly into the widening current of political debate. In its most striking forms, debate occurred on issues of war and peace, taxation and finance, and liberties of the subject. In the reign of James these debates were sometimes sharp, but the essential fact was that peace was kept and with it some prosperity. In his first four years, Charles I contrived to bring awkward alliances, unsuccessful wars, economic turmoil and a constitutional confrontation.

The proper role of government in foreign trade was becoming a question of great importance as the volume of traffic grew. Monopoly trading companies, tariffs, customs and port regulations, and colonial ventures were all significant matters of policy. Each was vitally affected by foreign policy decisions. The king correctly insisted that such decisions historically were his to make. Now, however, foreigners were divided into religious camps. Whatever choice was made in foreign affairs would engender intensified opposition, part based on economic interests and part on religious affiliation.

The fact of opposition to royal policy was something of a novelty in the early 17th century. There had always been the opportunity for royal councillors to offer conflicting advice; now there was growing discussion of public affairs *in public* and in parliament, notably in the English House of Commons. The impact of this sort of handling of government business was plain in King James's case. He once said of parliament [5]

> I am surprised that my ancestors should ever have permitted such an institution to come into existence. I am a stranger, and found it here when I arrived so that I am obliged to put up with what I cannot get rid of.

James revealed both displeasure and dismay, for compared to the Scottish and Irish parliaments, this one was impossible to overawe. His son Charles was of a different temper and did not feel "obliged to put up with" parliamentary opposition. In 1629, Charles pointedly "got rid of " the English parliament and began to govern without it. This rupture followed an escalating series of disputes. In 1625, the first session under Charles refused to vote the traditional lifetime grant of customs for more than one year, as a protest

---

[5] Letter to Ambassador Sarmiento (1614); cited in D.M. Loades, *Politics and the Nation* (1974), p. 331.

against the royal policy of impositions (arbitrary duties). Charles rejected this action and collected duties as his by royal prerogative. In the next session, money was sought for military campaigns, and when it was denied, parliament was dissolved. As the opposition clamored for war with Spain, the duke of Buckingham organized an expedition to Cadiz which was a failure. When Charles's second parliament met in 1626, the Commons refused to grant supply until their grievances were heard. The battle lines were drawn. Charles said "Parliaments are altogether in my power for their calling, sitting and dissolution." In reply, Commons members often referred to the "ancient, constant and undoubted right" to petition grievances to the sovereign. As tempers mounted, impeachment proceedings were begun against Buckingham, at which Charles dissolved parliament and ordered the imposition of a forced loan. The king's power to do this was upheld by pliant judges who convicted non-payers in the "Five Knights' Case" (1628).

The nation was now at war with France, Buckingham took charge of another unsuccessful expedition, this one to La Rochelle (1627) to relieve French Protestants. It was beaten off, and failure appeared to be the result of poor leadership, corruption and mismanagement. The next session of parliament passed a bill which dealt with the liberties of the subject, which Charles refused to hear. Commons then drafted the Petition of Right (no taxation without parliamentary approval; no imprisonment without cause; no billeting of troops; no martial law without approval of parliament). Charles assented to the petition, arguing that it created no new rights and only confirmed existing ones.

The political temperature rose sharply after Buckingham was assassinated by a disgruntled member of the La Rochelle expedition (1628). In the next session, parliamentary debate became more strident and in March, 1629, Charles ordered the Commons dissolved. On this occasion, as the Speaker of the House tried to rise to dismiss the members, three of their number held him in his seat, while three resolutions were read and passed, which denounced "papist" influences in court and government and defined any who advised certain policies as "betrayers of the liberties of England." The wayward M.P.s were imprisoned and Charles resolved to govern without parliament.

Technically the king was correct that royal government could proceed legally without parliamentary approval. Whether it could continue to operate without parliamentary finance was yet to be shown. The two main determinants of the answer were efficient collection of revenue and careful limitation of expenditure. On paper, the sources were sufficient. Crown lands (rentals, escheats, forfeitures) produced large regular revenue which could be expanded by various recovery processes (title search, resumption, confiscation). Customs and tariffs were important regular sources, as were the incomes of royal courts of law (King's Bench, Common Pleas, Chancery). To these were added some older, revived sources, generally "feudal" in nature, such as fines for "distraint of knighthood." One of the most significant sources, which nearly turned the tide for the crown, was the discovery of "Ship Money"--an old method of assessment for emergency supply of ships and crews. This produced about £750,000 revenue between 1634-38. Collection reached a peak of about £200,000 in 1636, after which the receipts fell off sharply. Current revenues, augmented as they were, very nearly enabled the crown to govern without any general taxation.

The other side of the ledger was not so promising. Long years of court corruption could not be banished overnight. The English court consumed about 40% of all revenues and its cost was extremely difficult to reduce. Major savings were made in foreign affairs. Peace was made with France and Spain in 1629, and the most important economy possible was thus in place.

On several occasions in the 1630s, the government shied away from military action. It was surprised, however, by military action from an unexpected quarter: revolt in Scotland put an army on the border and forced the king of England and Scotland to war. The Scottish uprising was brought on by the king's religious policy. That was a continuation of James's restoration and of the otherwise successful Arminian reaction led by Charles and his dedicated archbishop of Canterbury, William Laud. After his first visit to Scotland, and his ornate coronation in Holyrood Abbey (1633), Charles began to alter the kirk, first by directing changes in ministers' costume. In 1634, Charles ordered the composition of a new prayer book (putting aside the draft made in 1618) and new canons (1636). The new book was to be introduced in the Summer of 1637. Scottish bishops had been in charge of its drafting and it was not simply a touched-up version of the English prayer book. Nevertheless, its introduction was unwelcome and its general appearance was that of an alien intrusion, chiefly because the king chose to direct the use of it by royal proclamation alone.

There was a violent, perhaps organized, reception for the new prayer book. Rioting in St. Giles (Edinburgh) and elsewhere was followed by petitions and the formation of an ad hoc group of protestors, "The Tables". In February, 1638, the Scottish National Covenant was drafted. The document was circulated and signed by thousands of Scots. It contained a long recitation of religious legislation and authority, which clearly showed the king's duty to oppose "popery." The document professed the utmost loyalty to the king in that task but the covenant also obliged adherents to defend the reformed religion "against all sorts of persons whatsoever." That ambiguous phrase would authorize opposition to the king. Charles was forced to suspend the book and the canons. The first General Assembly in 20 years was summoned to Glasgow in November, and it proved to be a calamity for the crown. The assembly renounced the book, the canons and the articles of Perth and it deposed the Scottish bishops. The body was moving in a clearly revolutionary direction; both sides took steps to gather armed force. Charles attempted an assault in March 1639, but he failed to advance beyond Berwick, and there he made a truce in July. He promised to come to Scotland for sessions of parliament and a General Assembly, but he returned to London instead. What became known as the "first Bishops' War" was lost; Charles's conciliar rule was fast coming to an end.

Radical Unions

Between 1640 and 1660 there was a remarkable challenge to royal authority, commonly called the "English Revolution," or "English Civil War." The name does not do justice to the events. King Charles was badgered by self-righteous Scots, harrassed by an obstreperous English parliament, and startled by a vicious Catholic rebellion in Ulster. Most of his dominions were getting out of control, their political classes falling out along various lines of regional, personal and religious loyalty. The warfare of the 40s and 50s involved most of the archipelago, and it should be called the "War of the Three Kingdoms." In the course of the fighting, there were efforts to unite the kingdoms in several directions, all of which came to grief over the many divisions which existed. Historiography has misled us in

206

another way: the polar view of king vs. parliament fails to comprehend the true political diversity. There were at least four factions in Ireland, three in Scotland and three or more in England at any given time. This chaotic state should have been used to advantage by Charles, who remained the only legitimate recognized sovereign. The multiplicity of factions at least slowed down the king's defeat, and continued division in the 1650s was a major reason for the royal restoration in 1660. But Charles did not effectively exploit the disunity of his enemies, and instead he served as the primary force holding them together.

When he returned from the north in 1639, Charles brought Wentworth over from Ireland to concert the strategy for royalist recovery. Wentworth urged the summoning of parliaments to reassert the king's authority and begin his counterattack. The Irish parliament, under Wentworth's sure hand, voted £150,000 for the king in his emergency (March 1640). The English parliament was not so easily managed. When it met in April there were prompt demands for the hearing of grievances. Three weeks later, the members were on their way home, with nothing accomplished. In June, meeting without royal summons, the Scottish parliament passed a triennial act (providing that it should meet at least once every three years). The Scots were still on a war footing, and the king's plans had gone ahead for another confrontation. In August, the covenanters' army crossed the border, occupied Durham and Northumberland and demanded a daily ransom of £850 to pay its expenses for as long as it took to make a treaty. This second "Bishop's War" forced the recalling of the English parliament to raise the necessary funds; and this time the king would have to listen to their grievances.

Because they distrusted the king, leading opposition members of the Commons quickly moved to impeach the most feared royal advisers, Wentworth (now Earl of Strafford) and Laud. Both were arrested and imprisoned in the Tower. The process against Strafford was the main theme of the first six months of the "Long Parliament." He was not impeachable, and his attackers turned to the legislative trial by attainder. After considerable agonizing, the king gave his assent and Strafford was executed on May 12, 1641. Strafford's death was followed by a spate of reforming laws, the abolition of prerogative courts, the restriction of royal powers to raise money, and a provision against dissolving parliament without the consent of both houses.

In August 1641, the king went to Scotland to conclude the treaty which would bring the withdrawal of the Scottish army from England. Charles could have reasonably expected to find support among the Scots and the northern English for his position. But he failed to take advantage of splits and personal rivalries in Scottish court circles which might have given him the core of a royalist party there. In October, while the king was still in Edinburgh, a violent rebellion broke out in Ulster. Catholic rebels attacked and killed a large number of Protestant settlers. The enormity of the event was exaggerated as the reports flooded into Britain. A military response was clearly needed; but having just settled the Scottish incursion, and having taken out one key minister, it proved impossible to reach a deliberate decision on such a sensitive question. Would the king use a large armed force to quell Ulster Catholics--or London Puritans? Many of the king's former opponents argued that he must be trusted, as king. A major rift in the English parliament appeared by the end of 1641. Radical opinion wanted parliamentary controls on military appointments, and a militia bill in December called for removal of royal control over appointing lords lieutenant. The king was enraged by this encroachment on his traditional powers. In January 1642, he led a detachment of troops to the Commons and tried to arrest five leaders of the radicals. They had been warned and fled to safety. Thus the episode only raised the revolutionary temperature. Maneuvers continued for the next few months: the controversial militia bill was issued (without royal assent) as an "ordinance" by the Commons; both sides vied for control of the arsenal at Hull; by June both sides were producing position papers; in August, the king made the traditional act of raising the royal standard, near Nottingham, his formal declaration of war on his rebellious subjects.

The course of events leading to hostilities was a continuous process, no one event being a final cause. Yet it is arguable that the Ulster rebellion was chiefly responsible for the formation of the rival parties in England at the end of 1641; certainly it deserves close investigation. Wentworth's administration in Ireland had been tough and fiscally productive. But he made advances in royal power at the expense of abusing the rights of Old English landowners and Ulster Presbyterians. In the crisis of 1638-39 Wentworth made plans to raise an army to aid the king. This force was not ready soon enough to be sent to Scotland, and in 1639 it was disbanded. Some of the officers were among the Irish military men who conspired to lead a rebellion in 1641. Their plan was to seize Dublin Castle and to raise the rest of the country. The Dublin plan was exposed and aborted at the last moment, and the rebellion was only initiated on a large scale in Ulster. A considerable number of Catholics attacked their landlords, and there was widespread death and destruction. The insurgents probably did not plan to annihilate the settlers, but an estimated 4,000 were killed, with a further 8,000 related deaths. A like number of Catholics were killed in reprisals at later times. These are only rough guesses, for there were no accurate figures, indeed, the atmosphere of panic generated wild estimates of numbers, which at the time were quite influential. Assaults, arson and looting were disorganized but that did little to lessen their impact. Counterattacks were demanded by loyalist Protestants throughout the archipelago. By January 1642 the English parliament was trying to raise "adventurers" companies to strike at the rebels, but this project was caught up in the wave of hostility between crown and parliament. The Scots meanwhile had a ready armed force, for which the English parliament raised funds, and in April General Robert Munro landed in Ulster. The rebels were reinforced when Owen Roe O'Neill, one of the best-known Irish soldiers, landed in Donegal. By Summer, the revolt was spreading through most of Ireland.

In May and June representatives of the Catholic clergy and laity met in Kilkenny. They adopted a declaration asserting the justice of the rebel cause, framed an oath of association and set up a general council and four provincial councils. This confederacy swore its allegiance to King Charles, to parliament, to "the fundamental laws of Ireland" and to the Roman Catholic faith. In a general way, the confederacy was like the Scottish covenant--a league to resist outside pressure which threatened the dominant faith. In the case of Ireland, however, the association was the product of a long period of violence, not the means of marshalling a national army *prior* to any violent acts. By the time the confederacy called its first assembly in late 1642, fighting had broken out in England.

Actually a state of war had existed for about three years in the archipelago before there was any fighting between armies of Englishmen. The king only began campaigning in earnest when events in the archipelago were clearly beyond his control. During six years of rebellion in England, a kaleidoscope of factions spilled over the archipelago. No coherent royalist or rebel alignment remained in place for long, and although negotiations were a constant feature between the national elements, no international alliance was very durable.

In the first year of his campaign Charles had and lost his best opportunities. The initial battle at Edgehill (October 1642) was followed up too slowly, and royalist forces were held off outside London (at Turnham Green). Retiring to camp at Oxford, Charles laid out a multiple assault for 1643. He hoped to attack on three fronts: the East, the Midlands and the West. Some early success in Yorkshire, at Hull and at Bristol was wasted when the siege of Gloucester was lifted and a subsequent battle at Newbury failed to give Charles what could have been his decisive victory. Even before this stalemate, both sides were looking beyond England for reinforcement.

In the same month as Newbury, the English parliament endorsed the "Solemn League and Covenant." This militant Protestant union promised a Scottish force of 20,000 men. In return it held out the promise of a general Presbyterian settlement, while guaranteeing the Scottish kirk's future as it was recently reformed. There were already Scottish observers attending the Westminster Assembly which was trying to design a new church structure for England, and the terms of the League also called for a "Committee of Both Kingdoms" to oversee the joint operations of the alliance.

While the rebels thus attempted to form an effective alliance, Charles had been seeking Irish support through his loyal commander, the duke of Ormonde. The military situation in Ireland was anything but clear; there were at least three groups of rebels: O'Neill in Ulster, Preston in Leinster, and the clerical leaders of the Confederates. There were as many factions among the loyalists: Ormonde was at the head of the Protestants of the Pale; Robert Munro had come as the liberator of the Ulster Protestants; and Lord Inchiquin in Munster was in command of the parliament forces. In 1643, Ormonde managed to arrange a truce (alias "cessation") which allowed him to send some troops to Charles, but the number was not great, and the body of men was held in North Wales and was of little use to the king in the 1643 campaign.

In early 1644, a Scottish army of 20,000 crossed the border into England. This was the third invasion in six years but the first of real magnitude. This attack had the immediate effect of drawing royalist strength

210

away from any sort of repetition of the previous year's campaign. A few victories by the parliament forces in the south were followed by the first decisive battle, fought at Marston Moor, near York, on July 2, 1644. The combination of the Scottish infantry and Cromwell's cavalry were the main ingredients of success, though Cromwell himself saw "a great favour from the Lord." Be that as it may, the rebels were unable to capitalize on this victory. A month later, the Marquis of Montrose entered Scotland and joined a small Irish contingent to begin the most daring and dramatic campaign of the year. He defeated the main force of covenanters by means of long and elusive marches through the Highlands, interrupted by surprise attacks. This effort went on independently, while Charles himself was not so fortunate. His main force was defeated near Oxford, at Naseby in June 1645.

The king himself was still at large. He was becoming more desperate, as indicated by the "Treaty of Glamorgan," a text of which was captured after Naseby. In this, Charles had agreed to grant toleration to Irish Catholics, on condition that an Irish army be sent to his assistance. Charles knew that the prospects of such aid were slim, and so when the treaty was made public, he had no difficulty in repudiating it. In May of 1646, with no relief in sight, Charles surrendered to the Scottish forces at Newark in Nottingham. As this meant the end of the war, the Scots planned to return home (once part of their agreed stipend was paid) and they had little wish to bring an unemployed king in their baggage. Thus Charles was turned over to parliament in early 1647.

At this stage the radical direction of the rebellion became fixed. The English "New Model" army formed in 1645 was the main symbol and strength of radicalism, and it was after the army's victory and its exertions in the political realm that radical English politics began to replace the traditional royal focus in archipelago political life. The English parliament tried to disband its army without paying arrears, the soldiers refused to accept the alternatives offered: to be sent home without pay, or to be sent to Ireland for further service! Cromwell and other leaders in early 1647 formed an Army Council and in a meeting at Newmarket a "Solemn Engagement" was made not to disband until the demands of the army were met. Meanwhile, a cavalry troop took the king into custody and the army moved toward London.

In August the army took over the capital. A famous series of debates was held near the city (in Putney) in October, in which the Levellers, the

211

more extreme democratic faction, debated constitutional plans with the officers, representing the property owners. The debates were inconclusive, but they were highly significant as the first instance of full-scale political discussion in the revolution--some would say, the real beginning of a revolutionary movement. Without clarification of the main issues, extreme elements in the army became mutinous. The escape of Charles in November 1647 probably was vital in keeping order among his enemies. The king entered negotiations with moderates in parliament (English) and with supporters from Scotland (while he was in Carisbrooke Castle, Isle of Wight). The Scots made an "Engagement" with Charles in December, promising to aid his restoration in return for a three-year trial period of Presbyterianism in England, and some commercial privileges for the Scots. There was wide support for the Engagement in Scotland (and a deepening gulf between "Engagers" and "covenanters"). It was not until the next summer that a Scottish army came to put the agreement into effect, and in the meantime, there were uprisings in several areas of the south (Kent and Pembroke, especially). After putting down rebels in Wales, Cromwell led his troops northward, and the English met the invading Scots near Preston, Lancashire and defeated them soundly.

The moderates in parliament wanted to go ahead with the restoration of the king, but the army was now certain of his unreliability and determined to put him on trial. In December 1648, an army detachment under Colonel Thomas Pride prevented members from entering the House of Commons unless they were army supporters. Only about 70 were allowed to sit, and this was the origin of the "Rump" parliament.

A similar purge was going on in Scotland, after Cromwell entered Edinburgh in October and demanded that the supporters of the Engagement be barred from public office. General John Lambert remained in Scotland to oversee the work of that "rump," which in January 1649 passed an "act of Classes" which divided the enemies of the state into four groups. Large numbers were thereby excluded and the preponderance in Scottish government shifted toward the clergy.

The epitome of radicalism was of course the trial and execution of the king. In one sense it was unavoidable when the English army superseded its parliament; in a larger view, it was irresistible because of the record of mistrust compiled by the king; surely the "verdict" in the "case" was

212

inevitable as soon as the extraordinary "High Court of Justice" was created in January 1649.

The execution of Charles I was an English affair. No Scottish or Irish participation was sought on the court: the English army and the English "Rump" were disposing of their political nemesis without any outside assistance. Indeed, the army saw from an early point the necessity of asserting control of the archipelago. Cromwell told the General Council of Officers on March 23, 1649: [6]

> The quarrel is brought to this state, that we can hardly return unto that tyranny that formerly we were under the yoke of, which through the mercy of God hath been lately broken, but we must at the same time be subject to the kingdom of Scotland or the kingdom of Ireland, for the bringing in of the king. Now that should awaken all Englishmen, who perhaps are willing enough he should have come in upon an accomodation, but not he must come from Ireland or Scotland.

But there was to be no "accommodation," and both Scotland and Ireland were to be visited by General Cromwell in the next two years. In the interim, the monarchy, the House of Lords and the established church were abolished in England. The revolutionary Council of State (composed of generals and leaders of the Rump) became the executive in the new "Commonwealth of England." In 1649, this revolutionary government began the remodelling of the institutions of the archipelago, while the military power of the army subdued Ireland and Scotland.

Cromwell landed in Ireland in August 1649 with a force of 12,000 men. There were already two parliamentary armies in action (Michael Jones in Dublin, George Monk in Ulster), and a significant victory had been won just days before Cromwell's arrival (Ormond's defeat at Rathmines, August 1). In fact, the Cromwellian campaign was more on the order of a crusade than an essential strategic move. First there was the obvious incentive to avenge the massacre of 1641; then there was the spirit of "just compensation" embodied in the Act for Adventurers--which of course was being multiplied by the service of Cromwell's soldiers. Within a month of his arrival, Cromwell led an assault on Drogheda, north of Dublin, where the garrison was put to the sword. Cromwell's well-known excuse was that this was "a righteous judgement of God upon these barbarous wretches who have

---

[6]W.C. Abbott, *Letters and Speeches of Oliver Cromwell* (1937), v.2, pp. 38-9.

imbrued their hands with so much innocent blood." He overlooked the fact that Drogheda had been in the hands of the Dublin government until a few weeks before his attack!

Cromwell's next moves were to the south (Wexford, New Ross, Waterford) and by winter he had control of a strip of coastline from Derry to Kinsale. Early in 1650 he pushed inland, taking Kilkenny in March. By May, Cromwell was recalled to deal with the invasion of Scotland, but all that remained was a long, "mopping-up" operation. During the summer of 1650, the Irish Catholic royalists seemed to lose even the moral support of Charles II, as in August he endorsed the Kirk of Scotland in the Dunfermline declaration.

The new king had automatically succeeded his father on the Scottish throne (and was recognized by Scots as king of England as well). In the North, Charles seemed to have his best hope of restoration, yet that hope was slim in 1649. The "Engagers" who had supported the late king were proscribed. The kirk party was divided in its stance toward the crown. They faced an insoluble dilemma: to preserve their kirk required some form of English accommodation for security; but close ties with a king, or a parliament, or a general, compromised their security. English radicalism now had cut the traditional bond; its "commonwealth" forced a new crisis of politics, and most urgently, a new threat of English invasion.

It was May, 1650 before a preliminary treaty was arranged between Charles II and the Scots. While these discussions went on the marquis of Montrose had invaded (with Charles's approval) and was captured and executed by Scottish authorities. In late June, the new king landed, having signed the covenant and denounced his father's treaty with Ireland. The agreement between Charles and the Scots was ratified on July 4, 1650.

Preparations to fight the English were begun in June, and by July, Cromwell was on the border with a force of 16,000. The southeast was deserted and stripped of food and supplies. After a period of marches and maneuvers, Cromwell found himself penned in near Dunbar. The untrained Scots army, weakened by purges under the kirk's leadership, made a number of tactical errors and the English, though outnumbered, were able to inflict a major defeat on them (September 3, 1650).

The government fled to Stirling and purges of the king's household and the army continued. The king himself was involved in an abortive coup, and

214

the Scots displayed remarkable disunity. Cromwell took control of Edinburgh; in the west an army of radical Scots (the Western Association) was more frightened of an Anglican king than an Independent general; after a brief encounter with Cromwell's cavalry, the Western Association dissolved.

In 1651, after nine months of inactivity, generously supported by Scottish infighting, Cromwell outwitted his enemies and made an attack on Perth, cutting off reinforcement from the royalist north. The remaining forces in Stirling chose not to await a siege, and they marched into northwest England, along a route left (carefully) unguarded by Cromwell. Charles entered England with a force of 13,000 and he was overtaken and defeated at Worcester (September 1651). The king fled to France, and Cromwell's forces occupied Stirling. While it would be some time before the control of the Commonwealth was complete, the main operations were at an end. The "War of the Three Kingdoms" was over, and what remained now was to form a new government.

While Cromwell was securing control of Ireland and Scotland, or denying control to Charles II, the English Commonwealth was being organized. With abolition of monarchy and nobility, the republic had no clear constitutional framework to put in place of the old institution; furthermore, the new order was destined to operate in a sea of ideological turbulence which would preclude establishment of settled government.

In 1649 the chief elements represented in the Council of State were the Army and the Rump. Both were self-interested, self-perpetuating oligarchies. Their respective assets were the raw power of armed might and the remnants of legitimate constitutional authority. Both had elements of the propertied classes in them, both were hostile to all forms of religious establishment. Otherwise, they had no program and harbored growing hostility to one another.

In 1653, Cromwell forced the dissolution of the Rump, which he feared would make itself a perpetual body. He summoned an assembly of "Independents," a Nominated Parliament, nicknamed the Parliament of the Saints or the "Barebones Parliament"--after a London preacher in their number, "Praise-God" Barbon. In this assembly, there were six Welsh members, five Scots and six Irish. All of course were hand-picked, and in composition this body was more like a modern party congress or convention. When they met, they took on the characteristics of a parliament, and they began to make reforms and to attempt, in good parliamentary fashion, to control the process of revenue-collection. By the end of 1653 this body was also brought to an end. In early 1654, the Instrument of Government, a new constitution, was promulgated for a new order, known as the "Protectorate."

Oliver Cromwell was made Lord Protector for life. His executive power was enhanced, and a new council was created to assist him. The parliament was reformed. A narrower franchise, redistributed seats and reduced power over the executive were main features. A standing army was written into the constitution, as was substantial religious toleration. But the first parliament of this regime, even though well-screened, balked at many provisions and tried to amend the constitution. It sat for only four months (with token membership from all areas of the archipelago) before the protector dissolved it in January 1655. The next 18 months were a period of martial law, known as the "Rule of the Major-Generals". England and Wales were divided into 11 military districts, each one under the supervision of a general. Scotland and Ireland were already under various degrees of military occupation, so this period saw the largest measure of uniform government during the interregnum. The regime was not noted for severe repression. Martial law was imposed in response to royalist uprisings, which in 1653-54 had become more dangerous. The Major Generals probably had more duties as civil governors than as military policemen, but still the army paid heavily in political support.

In 1657 another constitutional change proposed a crown for Cromwell. The Humble Petition and Advice, an army document, signalled a number of features of apparent restoration: an upper house of parliament was to be created, there was to be greater authority in parliament, and the proposed crown--which Oliver refused--showed that constitutional innovation had been exhausted. The political climate was returning to the status quo c. 1640. The narrow-based regime was losing support, and after Cromwell's death in 1658 it was bound to change. For a little over a year, amid successive political crises, the royal restoration was prepared.

The revolutionary period did produce something more than political instability in England and military occupation of the archipelago. There were important innovations in government, some of which were carried over after the restoration. Destruction of castles, shifts of administration "out of court," the use of committee-management at many levels, security of tenure for

216

judges, and considerable elevation of status for the "Member" of the House of Commons--these were the most obvious signs of a substantial constitutional evolution. On the other hand, in the archipelago context, the civil war and English revolution produced the contrary effects of hasty schemes for closer union, and eventual strengthening of national, anti-union forces. There were several types of efforts: Anglo-Scottish alliance (1640-47); commonwealth unions (1649-59) and miscellaneous military combinations. The latter may be easily treated. In a number of cases there were expedient alliances and operations without longterm significance. Munro's long operation in Ulster (1642-48); the MacDonalds' campaigning with Montrose (1644-5); or Charles I's efforts to use Ormonde and the Irish, all were without positive political significance for union.

In the effort to preserve their kirk, the Scots sought a particular form of union. They wanted a Presbyterian system throughout the archipelago, although at first they were more sanguine (in the Covenant) of preserving their unique "reformed religion." The English were never likely to make the reforms desired by the Scots: Anglicans would not give up bishops; Independents would not accept a General Assembly. Only when the English were desperate for military help (1643-44) was there a real hope of swaying them. After Naseby, Charles was obviously losing the war and the Scots were losing their leverage. Ironically, in the Westminster Assembly, where a small group of Scots met with a large body of English clergy to discuss the church settlement, an agreed form of worship and a confession were adopted. Although these were less than the Scots had hoped for, their government did accept them; the English for their part did not.

The Solemn League and Covenant (August-September, 1643) laid the foundation for an alliance, the military terms being worked out in November. In January 1644 the Scots entered England and three commissioners went to London to participate in the Committee of Both Kingdoms. The body should have been an allied command, but its powers were generally superseded by the authority of the English parliament and its committees.

The Cromwellian union seemed to have the most potential for success. Physical domination was the foundation for a federal regime (1651-59), but it was caught up in the multiple tensions of the period. The measures to bring real incorporation were few, and the colonial attitude of the English military governors was sufficient to abort the growth of a larger national unit. Much more time and much less distraction was needed to draw political support away from the obvious royal alternative. In October 1651 commissioners for Scotland were appointed by the English Commonwealth, and the announcement was made that henceforth the two nations were to be one commonwealth. In January 1652, the commissioners directed the Scottish shires and burghs to elect representatives to agree to the union. In April the Scots were told to send 21 deputies to London to affirm the terms of union. The Scottish parliament was abolished (1651) and so was the General Assembly (1654). While Scots were present in the several "union" parliaments (1653-5, 1654-21, 1656-30) the final approval of union was delayed until 1657. Meanwhile military occupation continued and the members chosen were usually government nominees.

Although Scottish "union" meant denial of kirk authority and carried with it a continued military occupation, there were trading advantages and there was broad acceptance of the basic idea. In Ireland, the imposed military rule was a far more brutal affair. Again the major initial decisions were made in England. When Cromwell left Ireland in 1650, Henry Ireton was made army commander and lord deputy. In October, four Commissioners of Parliament were named. In the last days of the Rump, the Irish were given 30 members of parliament. Representation was maintained in later parliaments, but again the individuals selected were loyal supporters of the regime. The Irish occupation was in the hands of more radical protestant elements (Baptist, Independent), until a moderate shift in the late 50s.

In Ireland, there was a special problem because of the previous commitments of land grants to those who fought for the rebel side. The "Adventurers" of 1642, the soldiers of Cromwell and others were covered by the Act for Settling Ireland in August 1652. By this, an estimated 80,000 rebels, plus Jesuits and murderers of civilians were proscribed; the estates of enemies of parliament were forfeited as a base for the grants owing to supporters. Probably much more land had been promised than was available; but first there had to be surveys of land to determine the settlement. There were three surveys eventually made, in 1653, 1654 and 1655-59.

Large numbers were relocated: some transported to the colonies, several thousand Catholic owners evicted, and about 12,000 soldiers were settled on new estates, in addition to those who bought or leased confiscated land from "adventurers". This tremendous social change was paralleled by religious persecution: none of the main sects was safe in the eyes of the Commonwealth, the Catholics being only the most dangerous.

The Lord Lieutenancy remained, only with increased powers; Irish colonial status was affirmed, while a token number of representatives went to the union parliament. Thus the effect on Ireland was great, but it was not a major constitutional alteration. Instead of joining a union, Ireland was seeing rejuvenation of old ties and tougher administration.

With Wales, there was even less impact. While still electing M.P.s and briefly coming under the administration of a Major General, the principal innovation for Wales was the creation of "Committees for the Propagation of the Gospel" in the north and the south. Their functions were to police the clergy, and they had powers of removal plus authority to oversee funds from sequestered livings and forfeited royalist estates. The Committees only lasted until 1653, after which time Wales was included in an undifferentiated protectorial administration.

What did the varied "union" measures mean? In all cases, they were involuntary, minority-sponsored, even dictatorial. In few cases were they able to demonstrate significant advances in government. The sole exception might be the effectiveness of a military regime--though it appears that the army (and the rule of the Major-Generals) were excellent testimony for contemporaries *against* armed power in politics.

In the matter of religion, there was official toleration which guaranteed perpetuation of the divisions already present, however much real toleration there may have been. In economic terms, the union meant further English enrichment at the expense of others. In foreign policy, there was no room for the special interest of others or the hereditary alliances of non-English parts of the archipelago. All were shackled to the new, activist colonial policy of the protectorate.

The Cromwellian "Union" was not realized in any effective central agency or any joint committee of the commissioners (aside from the Council of State). There was no major role for the parliamentary delegations. The one institution which probably had meaningful "union" features was the army; the one reason for a "union" was for Cromwell to deny any of these areas to the supporters of his archenemy, the king.

Restoration and Revolution

After Cromwell died in September 1658, the republican regime fell apart. Within 18 months the restoration of the king was underway. This turn of events was ironically aided by the rivalry between the army and the Rump. At first, rival generals tried to assert their influence once Richard Cromwell had demonstrated his ineffectiveness as the new Protector. Then the Rump reconvened and tried to disband the army. In October 1659, General Lambert dissolved the Rump by force. By this time, many leaders were in touch with Charles. The decisive move came from George Monk, who was commanding the forces in Scotland. He marched into England at the end of 1659 and made his way slowly toward London. Once installed in the capital, having neutralized the several factions, Monk declared his support for the king. The Rump was recalled and fortified by the members removed at Pride's Purge. This body then dissolved itself after calling for new elections. In March, a Convention Parliament was elected and made the formal invitation to Charles to return to his kingdom.

The king entered his capital in May 1660, amid scenes of rejoicing and relief. Charles dated his reign from January 30, 1649. He had been crowned in Scotland (at Scone) in January 1651; he was formally recognized in Dublin in May, 1660; the royal title was proclaimed in London in the same month. The return to power did not mean a total rejection of the recent past, nor would such a policy have always been in the king's best interest. However, the restoration did require a full review of constitutional and legal matters, a review which occupied several years and which showed that many of the old problems had been restored, but restored in a new political context where they would have to be solved. The old problems were: limits on prerogative, religious uniformity, and the questions of authority in finance, religion and foreign affairs. The new context was one in which the spectre of revolution would force moderation; where the oligarchy of property would be more openly acknowledged, and where the triumph of the common law (in England) and businesslike government (vs. the rule of courtiers) could be conceded.

The physical restoration of the king was the easiest step in a very complex process which extended across the archipelago and dragged out over a generation. The beginning was made easier by not involving the king's

Scottish and Irish subjects (though the former had been the first to recognize him). Charles II was first faced with the reconstruction of royal government. He would naturally rely on the household, the court, the council and parliament, and the whole range of traditional royal officials. Every aspect of this job was lined with touchy decisions on personnel and precedents; the collective result was a restored monarchy in three kingdoms, with most of the traditional posts, filled by royalists and rebels, operating under limited conditions of modernization.

Closest to the king were those in his household, the royal court and the privy council. He was in complete control of these positions, but their relative place in government had changed since 1640. There was no hope of governing through this inner circle alone, but it still occupied the place closest to the king and retained paramount influence. The courtiers would never again be what they were under Charles I, and the king had to have able and talented men in more exposed official positions. The restoration meant that the making of policy was put in the hands of loyal supporters of the crown. Ormonde was returned to his position as Lord Lieutenant of Ireland. Edward Hyde (Earl of Clarendon) was the key minister in England. In general the restoration was not vindictive. Some punishment was owed to the king's enemies, and there were 13 death sentences and prison terms for a number of others. The generally fair and tolerant turnover assisted the smooth reconstruction of government and it was remarkable given the amount of violence, to persons and property, which had occurred between 1640 and 1660.

The restoration was naturally of vital importance to the peerage (English, Scottish and Irish). As a class they were an integral part of the monarchic socio-political order. The temporal and spiritual peers were reinstated, but there was a paradox in that the corporate embodiments (Houses of Lords, Convocation) were weaker than in 1640. The aristocracy as a whole was far stronger. Peers, gentry and wealthy merchants--the propertied wealth of the kingdoms--were strong in their local communities and in collective form in parliaments. The English House of Commons in particular became a dominant force in politics. It did so because it continued to assert financial control, it doggedly insisted on religious uniformity and it resisted whatever measures seemed to impede the common law and the "liberties of the subject" (code words for the power of private property). In other words, the tradition of parliamentary opposition was continued. This was most evident in England, for with the Irish parliament, Poynings' Law was in effect, and in Scotland, the Lords of the Articles were still a potent tool of management. The English council was able to draft and manage business, but the fate of the king' principal ministers (Clarendon, Danby) would show that there was now an emerging capacity for peaceful resistance to executive power.

The business of government went far beyond the confines of the legislative bodies. The law, the military and the growing official class were important components. They each continued to be managed in separate compartments for England, Scotland and Ireland. The law saw the greatest continuity between the interregnum and the restoration era. The interests of stability required upholding the legal judgments of the interregnum. The decision not to restore the prerogative courts (Star Chamber, High Commission, Court of Wards) was part of this continuity. The crown did regain power over judicial tenure, and there were increased property requirements for English jurors. These and other modifications were made by the new regime, but the essential power of the common law courts in England, Wales and Ireland was affirmed. In Scotland, the Court of Session was restored and senators from the College of Justice formed the High Court of Justiciary for criminal cases in 1670, following a precedent which dated from the 1620s.

The army was perhaps the most interesting survival. For at the Restoration there were assorted armed forces in being, most of them in impoverished condition. The best units were those led by George Monk, and they were purged of republicans, thus making the early months of restoration relatively safe. But this and other units were disbanded by the end of 1660. King Charles then began reconstruction of a royal army, the first standing army in peacetime in the history of the archipelago. The new army was modest in size and neutral in politics.

One of the elements not retained in the new government was the primitive union of the kingdoms. This issue did surface briefly in the formation of trade policy. In 1660, a Navigation Act renewed one of the innovative features of the protectorate--namely central state intervention in commerce. The act of 1660 hurt Scottish trade, the Anglo-Dutch War (1665) being one consequence. In 1667, the king asked both parliaments to appoint commissioners. Their talks began in January 1668 and went on for two years, with no success. The king did urge the Scottish council and parliament to move in this direction, but negotiations apparently were stalled by conflicting economic interests. On the one hand, this showed the crown fostering union discussions, but it also showed a lack of urgency in the matter.

The major issue of restoration for property owners was the recovery of land titles. Most royalists had made sacrifices and expected to regain their old property. In cases of confiscation (which affected crown and church lands primarily) there was to be full restitution. But where lands had been sold during the troubles, the buyers were usually confirmed in their holdings. In the latter instance, the former owners still had recourse to the law, to private acts of parliament or to litigation, and some royalists regained land in this way. Overall there was great discontent among the king's supporters. As one of them said, the settlement "made the enemies of the constitution the masters, in effect, of the booty of three nations."[7] The three nations were in fact quite dissimilar, and so was the "booty." For England and Wales, the Act of Indemnity and Oblivion (1660) set down the distinction between confiscation and sale; no general provision was made for the return of confiscated private estates. In Scotland, there was an earlier Act of Indemnity in 1651, passed in a time of crisis when the king was desperately seeking support. In 1660, there was no further act. In Ireland the issue and the action were different. Here the great losses of land were those of Catholics and the possibility of restoration was made more remote by the extent of promised land payments. As Ormonde said "there must be new discoveries...for the old (Ireland) will not serve to satisfy these engagements."[8] The surveys of the 1650s were complete, the armies of claimants were ready. In 1661 a Protestant parliament was elected, and in two Acts (Settlement-1662; Explanation-1665) the land was redistributed. The Cromwellian claimants did have to surrender one-third of their holdings, plus land which had been confiscated but undistributed. This created a fund for claims of restoration, and a scramble ensued in which few claimants were satisfied. There was no hope of a solution, only of some degree of mollification. The several land problems showed that there had been a significant amount of turnover and

---

[7] R. Lestrange, cited in Christopher Hill, *Century of Revolution* (1961), 201.
[8] Cited in J.C. Beckett, *A Short History of Ireland,* 5th ed. (1973), p. 83.

that it was undesirable or impossible for the restored monarch to do much about it.

On another level, the produce of the land (as a tax source) had been fundamentally changed by the wars and most of that change was preserved. As feudal dues, forced loans, subsidies and tax farmers disappeared, they were replaced by the land tax, supplemented by excise taxes on tobacco, alcohol and luxuries. Other features of landholding, forms of tenure, cultivation, manorial and pastoral organization, were less affected. In sum, the place of landed property was still one of premier importance in the society and economy of the archipelago, but restored landowners would no longer enjoy the same kind of seniority they once had.

The religious settlements generally showed a reassertion of royal political control over the churches, a recognition of plural religions and confused and vacillating government policy toward those religious groups which were not in political power. In England and Wales, the so-called "Clarendon Code" acknowledged dissent but made its practice difficult. Dissenters were barred from political activity, though the crown periodically waived the penalties for such activity by the means of declarations of indulgence. The "Code" was a series of separate statutes: a Corporation Act (1661); an Act of Uniformity (1662); the Conventicle Act (1664); and the Five-Mile Act (1665). These prevented dissenters from serving in local corporations, mandated Anglican worship, and restricted the places of worship and the movement of dissenting ministers. Together they added somewhat to the number of 2,000 clergy expelled from positions at the restoration. Since the king had promised "liberty to tender consciences," in the Declaration of Breda in 1660, and since he could gain political advantage from appearing to keep his word--he issued a declaration in December 1662 that he intended to seek legislative support for power to dispense with penal laws. In Scotland, the Act Recissory (1661) repealed all laws back to 1633 and actually restored the kirk to the position it held in the early 17th century. Presbyteries were not removed, but bishops were returned. About 270 parochial clergy (nearly the same percentage as in England) were removed, fines were levied to enforce the worship in the state church (1663), and the army was used to collect fines in some cases. Here again, an indulgence was used by the crown for political advantage (1669). In Ireland, the Catholic population was given informal toleration by Charles, while the Protestant community restored the Church of Ireland and a significant body in the north upheld a restored Presbyterian structure. There was an attempt from the Catholic side in the 1660s for a compromise. In 1660 a "Remonstrance" was debated, which aimed at reconciling the Roman faith with royalism. This was opposed by the papal curia and by the stricter members of the Irish hierarchy. Meanwhile, a significant number of the lesser clergy in Ireland were openly practicing their faith. Within the setting of de facto toleration, enough intolerance survived to fuel renewed escalation of hostility.

At first there were scattered minor incidents highlighted by Blood's Plot in Ireland (1663) and the Covenanting movement in Scotland in 1666. These merely proved that pockets of disaffection remained; neither uprising showed signs of growing into another national enterprise. In the 1670s there were more serious events. Charles II made the secret Treaty of Dover with Louis XIV in which he planned a Catholic restoration, either out of conviction or in order to gain a French subsidy; in either event, the royal judgment was questionable. In Scotland, the early 70s saw mixed conciliation and coercion of religious dissidents. Royal declarations of indulgence (1669, 1672) gave a number of ministers who had been "outed" a chance to return. Unlicensed ministers and their congregations were subject to fines (1670), and the death penalty awaited preachers at field conventicles which had sometimes been used as a cover for drilling with arms. In 1672, baptism by approved ministers was made compulsory; ministers illegally ordained could be imprisoned or banished. The later 70s saw increasing tension, and when an armed force dubbed the "Highland Host" was quartered in the southwest to collect fines, tension reached the breaking point. In March 1679, a group of fanatics murdered Archbishop Sharp; rebellion spread through the Galloway region and a force of insurgents briefly took Glasgow. They were defeated by Charles's illegitimate son, the duke of Monmouth. He fashioned a moderate settlement, but he was replaced by James, Duke of York, who was himself at the center of a serious crisis in England.

In 1678 one Titus Oates, a seminary dropout, told the authorities of a plot by Jesuits to kill King Charles and place his brother James on the throne. James was a Roman Catholic, his faith having become public knowledge in 1673. At that time, the Test Act required office holders to receive Anglican communion, and James resigned as Lord High Admiral. But the Oates tale was sheer invention. It gained credibility when the London magistrate to whom Oates had given his deposition was found murdered. The tale became more plausible when incriminating correspondence was found in the belongings of the duke's secretary. The affair was compounded when there were revelations about the French negotiations, and impeachment proceedings were brought against Lord Danby. The king decided at this point to dissolve parliament.

New elections brought a less co-operative parliament and a more dangerous issue. A bill was introduced to exclude James from the royal succession. Charles terminated the parliament, and twice more there were elections, exclusion measures, and royal resistance. In the last of these in 1681, parliament met in Oxford, the old royalist headquarters, and some of the opposition members came in arms. After Charles dissolved this parliament, he did not summon another.

The king's opponents had been dubbed "Whigs"--an unflattering reference to radical Scottish Protestants. The earl of Shaftesbury and some aristocratic and radical allies had actively organized political opposition during the "popish plot", and rudiments of "party" were evident in the "Green Ribbon Club" in London and in pamphleteering and organized action in the House of Commons. The Whig view of limited monarchy and anti-popery was ranged against the "Tory" doctrine of non-resistance to the anointed sovereign ("Tory" was also a pejorative term, referring to Catholic Irish highwaymen). The Whigs were utterly discredited when a plot was uncovered in 1683 in which the king was to be assassinated at the Rye House en route from the races at Newmarket. This helped to reinforce a strong tide of sentiment in favor of James. When he did succeed his brother in 1685, there were abortive rebellions: by the duke of Monmouth in Dorset and the earl of Argyll in Renfrew. Both of these were crushed and their leaders were executed.

Thus the monarchy had weathered a major crisis, and when James was crowned in 1685 he found a great display of support. His control of parliaments was unprecedented, his votes of money were ample and the royal policy of revising borough charters promised to create a permanently subservient English House of Commons. Yet within four years, James was in exile in France, trying to plan the recovery of his throne. This sudden reversal was the product of a royal revolution and a popular counter-revolution, both of which involved most of the archipelago.

James believed that the impressive support given him at his accession, combined with the Tory doctrine of non-resistance, opened the way for his plan of a Roman Catholic restoration. At his age of 53 he probably felt that he had to act quickly; what he failed to appreciate was the revolutionary nature of what he intended, or at least the appearance of subverting the established order which he would give. The king's policies generally involved the violation of statutes and common law principles. Only a small segment of the population of England, Wales and Scotland would be likely to approve the acts; his only major source of popular support would be in Ireland.

We do not know, nor did James, how many Roman Catholics or Catholic sympathizers there were. We do know that it was a minority divided between moderates and radicals, the latter seeking rapid change. James clearly sided with the radicals. Roman Catholic generals and admirals, a Jesuit privy councillor, a Catholic lord privy seal and secretary of state (Sunderland) were brought into his service. He created a new "Court of Commissioners for Ecclesiastical Causes"--a revival of the Court of High Commission which had been abolished in 1641. He continued the review of borough charters and the charters of colleges, using the renewal process as a way of replacing members with Catholics. By his Declaration of Indulgence in 1687, James proposed to relax the penal laws. A standing army was demanded in the wake of Monmouth's Rebellion, and it was augmented with several thousand troops from Ireland. James also appointed Catholics to government posts in Scotland, and extended his indulgence to suspension of penal laws, although in that case the measure was of much greater significance to Presbyterians.

The king's acts were even more congenial to the majority in Ireland. There he chose the notorious figure Colonel Richard Talbot to serve him. Talbot had been the agent-general in London for Roman Catholic land claims. He was created earl of Tyrconnell and Lieutenant General. He was to implement a policy of recruitment of Catholics to official posts, but at first a Protestant viceroy, the second earl of Clarendon, was installed to reassure the Anglo-Irish community. By 1687, Tyrconnell was made the Lord Deputy; a Catholic-dominated parliament was elected in 1689, and by then James was in Ireland himself, trying to win back his throne.

When three regiments of Irish troops were called to England in October 1688, James probably lost his last elements of popular support. In the preceding months, dramatic events shook English and archipelago politics. In April the king had issued his second Declaration of Indulgence, ordering it to be read from the pulpits of all the churches. As the declaration was a waiver of the Test Act and uniformity of religion, seven Anglican bishops petitioned the king to reconsider his edict. James made the serious error of arresting them on a charge of seditious libel. The king was thereby in the position of assaulting the clergy over whom he was Supreme Head. The act was as inflammatory as it was unnecessary. The bishops were acquitted by a London jury in June.

When the bishops' trial was about to begin, the royal court announced that the Queen, Mary of Modena, had given birth to a son (June 10, 1688). The king's age (56) gave rise to nasty rumors about the baby's origin, but the cold fact was that now there would be a Roman Catholic successor. Before this, James's daughters, Mary and Anne, both raised as Protestants, were in line to succeed. Seven leading English politicians (Whigs and Tories) wrote secretly to William of Orange (Mary's husband) and offered to support him if he would invade England to "preserve their liberties." By September, William had decided to go ahead with the invasion. By October James was convinced that this was happening, and it was at this point that he brought in his Irish troops. At the same time, James cancelled writs for a new election, and he tried to soften opposition by dissolving his ecclesiastical commissioners and restoring some borough charters.

William's decision was not a rash one. He had been involved to a degree in English politics, certainly since his marriage to Princess Mary (1677). William employed officers from the archipelago in his service, and he maintained political agents in London to dispense propaganda and to provide him with intelligence. William's decision was based upon the assurance that Louis XIV was involved elsewhere, and that the superior forces which James had (on paper) were in fact unreliable. By English accounts the "Glorious Revolution" was over in a matter of months. In the archipelago context, it lasted several years (1688-1691). At two points it was seriously threatened by French attacks on England (1690, 1692) as well as active French campaigning in Ireland (1690). The English who invited William may have been mainly concerned about what he would do for their

228

country; William certainly saw the operation in an archipelago and a European framework.

On November 1, 1688, William made his move. Dutch ships sailed through the Channel to a landing in southwest England (Torbay). William correctly judged that the location he chose would allow him more time to assess the impact of his arrival and the response of the English and their king. James was irresolute and his protestant officers began to desert him. James decided to summon a parliament, dismiss Roman Catholics and declare an amnesty. He sent a mission to William, asking him to leave, claiming that the king's measures had satisfied the original objectives of the invasion. William continued to march toward London, and James fled to France in December. When William and Mary were recognized as joint sovereigns by a convention parliament, and when they accepted the terms of a "declaration of rights," the constitutional battle of the 17th century was concluded.

The Declaration (later Bill) of Rights presented a list of limits on the exercise of the royal prerogative. The new sovereigns should not suspend or dispense with laws, set up prerogative courts, raise taxes or keep an army without the consent of parliament. They should not interfere in elections, and they should insure that those elections would be regularly held. These were general proscriptions; in the next few months and years more precise statutes worked out details in critical areas. For instance, in the Spring of 1689, a Mutiny Act provided military justice powers ("for the safety of the kingdom"). A Toleration Act suspended the operation of penal laws against Dissenters who took oaths of allegiance to the regime. In 1694 a Triennial Act mandated elections at least every third year; by now sessions were being held every year due to government financial necessity, but this act guaranteed regular and intense electoral activity.

Traditional older accounts portray these and other acts as making up a liberalizing revolution; parliament was seen as becoming more powerful, controlling the army, the religious policy and the financial process. This view needs substantial modification. It has been emphasized in many recent accounts that the crown had vast reserves of power, while the oligarchs who benefitted from the Glorious Revolution were themselves not democrats. Our account suggests an added reminder: William was the new governor of *three* kingdoms, and the only consistent view he had of them was as military assets or liabilities.

James brought troops into England from Scotland and Ireland, but he had not used them in battle. In fact it was a mutiny by Scottish troops (Ipswich) which was the trigger for William's Mutiny Act. William had to cope with the military of the three kingdoms, their varied political institutions and the several sets of circumstances. After William reached London he called for a Scottish Convention of Estates to meet in Edinburgh. Shortly after that body gathered, supporters of King James withdrew. The remainder passed the "Claim of Right", similar to the English Bill of Rights, except that it spoke of the "forfeit" of the crown by James and it stipulated the establishment of Presbyterian church government. Thus the Scottish version implied a greater reduction of royal power. At the time, the implication might have seemed irrelevant, for there was a large and mobilizing Jacobite faction (especially in the North) plus widespread disruption and anger among 650 ejected ministers. In spite of this potential, only a small uprising marred the Scottish scene in 1689. William had more cause for alarm in Ireland.

King James landed in Kinsale in March 1689 and gathered a loyal Catholic army. He marched to Ulster and laid siege to Londonderry. After a short time in this operation, James left to meet the parliament which was assembling in Dublin in May. That body was predominantly Catholic, being elected on revised borough charters. The "Patriot Parliament" conducted a social and political revolution, even defying Poynings' Law and disallowing appeals to the English House of Lords. Endowments were taken from the Church of Ireland, "liberty of conscience" was granted, and the land settlement was overthrown. The Acts of 1662-65 were repealed and the estates of 2,000 Protestant landlords were ordered confiscated. Most of these measures were understandable, but in the circumstances they were unlikely to help the king regain his throne. In any event, James was going to succeed or fail on the battlefield. In April or May he may have missed an opportunity to join forces with loyalists in the Scottish Highlands; then in late July the siege at Londonderry was lifted and the Protestants counterattacked at Enniskillen. Two weeks later, one of William's trusted generals, the duke of Schomberg, landed in Belfast and soon captured Carrickfergus (severing any possible link with Scotland). Schomberg tried to advance toward Dundalk but was held up by sickness and supply problems.

King William himself did not arrive in Ireland until June 1690, when he reached Belfast with 15,000 men. The French had already sent 7,000 men to reinforce James's army in March, but Louis XIV had demanded that an equal number of Irish troops be sent in exchange. The Jacobites marched toward Dundalk to intercept the "English" force (William's army was composed of elements of English, Dutch, German, Danish and Huguenot soldiers). The Jacobite army was outnumbered about 36,000 to 25,000. The major engagement, the Battle of the Boyne (July 12, 1690) resulted in defeat for James, though his escape to France three days later was in unseemly haste. His armies held out in the West of Ireland until the Fall of 1691, but James's cause was in disarray. When William failed to wage a conclusive battle by August 1690, he too left Ireland. Major campaigning resumed in 1691, and the Jacobites were forced to surrender at Limerick in October. The military terms of the treaty allowed the French to return to France (with any Irish who wished to accompany them). On the civil side, toleration for Catholics was promised (on the model of the reign of Charles II) and security of estates was also promised, subject of course to parliamentary ratification. But ratification was slow to come, and when it did (in 1697), it was in a very different form than promised at Limerick.

The last military element of William's establishment in the archipelago was the elimination of the Jacobite threat in the Scottish Highlands. There was only a brief offensive there under John Graham, Viscount Dundee. The Jacobite leaders suffered from divided counsels and lack of support from James (in Ireland). Meanwhile, William's supporters moved ahead. Gen. Hugh Mackay built Fort William at Inverlochy as a base for controlling the Highlands. The chiefs were ordered to take oaths of allegiance to William and Mary, and were given until January 1, 1692. MacDonald of Glencoe came in a week late, blaming his delay on bad weather. The government took the occasion to make an example, but chose an unfortunate method: a Campbell regiment was hosted by the MacDonalds: the hosts (or 38 of their number) were massacred by the guests. The official terrorism brought formal submission of the clans. It also fed a continuing hostility to authority which at times would fortify the lingering Jacobite cause.

The Glorious Revolution, to give it its English name, has to be seen in the perspective in which William of Orange saw it. In a daring amphibious raid, he captured the throne, the territory and the resources of a former enemy, at a critical point in his life-long struggle with France. The Anglo-Dutch federation was not destined to become a constitutional entity, but it was

231

a military fact of the first importance. The English had been transferred out of French alliance; the costly Anglo-Dutch maritime hostility had been ended; and lastly, the threat of further Anglo-Dutch wars had been removed. While the Dutch had "won" most of the earlier fighting with England, the cost had been high and the commercial competition had not been reduced. Navigation Acts, borrowed ship designs, growing English trade, improving technology and commercial reforms (national bank, national debt, company law and treasury policy) promised to sustain the English growth. William was not going to retard this, but he would be able to gain a brief respite for the Dutch from competition, and he would ally these expanding assets to his own political objectives. In fact, it may be that William's forced union gave England a vital advantage in the re-export trade, the key sector of Dutch success in the 17th century. Also, the colonial sector of Dutch and English activity was affected by the events of 1688 (see Chapter 7).

There is no question that the "Glorious Revolution" was a political event of the first magnitude. It meant a great deal more than its English interpreters have customarily allowed.

Parliamentary Union and Dynastic Rebellion

For some time, 1689 was seen as a watershed for "parliamentary sovereignty." Arbitrary and absolute power of the crown was curtailed by bipartisan defense of the Anglican church and the Protestant succession. This interpretation never enjoyed complete support in the Atlantic Archipelago. There were those who supported the losing cause and those who had never been blessed with "English" liberties. Some recent authors have noted that the new regime represented "that very English beast, the king in Parliament," and that "for the Divine Right of Kings was substituted the absolute, uncontrolled sovereignty of the...King, Lords and Commons."[9] Not only have conventional views failed to see that Scotland and Ireland were unlike England in the impact of the revolution, but the three together present still another picture. The Scottish revolution did create (or claim) contractual monarchy and did result in a Presbyterian settlement. These were compatible

---

[9]Bruce Lenman, *The Jacobite Risings in Britain, 1689-1746* (1980), p.33; Lawrence Stone "The Results of the English Revolution of the Seventeenth Century," in *Three British Revolutions*, ed. J. G. A. Pocock (1980), p. 90.

with oligarchy and thus were readily amalgamated in the *British* polity created in 1707. The Irish *counter*-revolution overthrew the brief Catholic regime and replaced it with a Protestant Ascendancy which ruled Ireland for the next two centuries. The collective picture was one in which an imperial English archipelago was engaged in major war with France for 25 years. This war required unprecedented mobilization and corresponding pressure for unified rule in the archipelago. The 17th century battles over prerogative and prelacy were superseded by the ships and soldiers of King William's Wars; only the occasional diversion for the Jacobite uprisings sustained the old themes. And when we look closely at those affairs, they expose the military foundations of the imperial archipelago and the decline of dynastic politics. To get a better picture of the archipelago at the turn of the century, we need to look at the reconstituted Irish ascendancy, and to retrace the formation of the Anglo-Scottish Union and then review the Jacobite rebellions, especially as they affected the evolution of the imperial archipelago.

The brief ascendancy of the Catholic Irish ended when James was defeated. Just how quickly and fully that ascendancy would be reversed was the subject of angry debate. The pillars of the new regime would be (1) an amended version of the Treaty of Limerick (2) a structure of penal laws to suppress Catholics and (3) a revival of Ireland's colonial constitution. The civil clauses of Limerick had promised a degree of religious toleration and some land for Catholics. William himself was interested in a moderate policy and the end of violence in Ireland. But Protestant opinion was generally hostile to toleration or land restoration. The Catholic population had owned nearly 60% of land in Ireland in 1641. By 1703 that share had fallen to about 14%, and it fell to 5% by 1780. This decline reflected the political weakness of the Irish majority, and that weakness was maintained by the structure of penal laws which was erected from the 1690s onward.

The English parliament enacted a requirement for oaths of allegiance from Irish office-holders which effectively excluded Catholics from public office. The next few decades witnessed a growing body of law directed against "papists." These laws were not expected to root out the religion or to convert the Irish to Anglicanism. The penal laws were meant to deprive the Irish Catholic population of any political capacity, and they naturally began with the emasculation of the landowning class. Land could not be bought or sold, bequeathed or inherited without onerous penalties. Beyond the ban on office- holding, Catholics were not allowed to enter the army, to study law, or to have any form of advanced education (in Ireland or on the continent). The right to vote was denied in 1727. The atmosphere of the period encouraged restrictive laws which ranged well beyond the Catholic community. Thus the Dissenters were also excluded from office, there were strict regulations of trade and industry, and other laws affected the Irish at large.

The Protestant Irish ascendancy was the product of the continued colonial garrison constitution. There was some patriotic criticism from the Protestant side, but the essential English domination was strengthened between 1690 and 1750. The elements were still the same: a joint crown, a lord lieutenant, judges and officials chosen by the English executive, and a House of Lords and House of Commons whose measures must first be cleared by the English Privy Council. What was new at the end of the 17th century was a tendency for the English parliament to act unilaterally on Irish issues. Sometimes this aroused no objection, as in 1691 with the law on oaths and declarations of allegiance. But the pattern continued, from the Wool Act of 1699, to the Declaratory Act of 1719. In 1698 the famous pamphlet by William Molyneux noted and deplored the trend.[10] The patriot answer was to employ borrowed "English" tactics in financial legislation, but only small concessions were won, not any fundamental change. At this juncture, even the patriot Protestants thought that an incorporating union might offer a better constitutional remedy (Molyneux himself said an imperial legislature was a device "we should be willing enough to embrace, but this is an happiness we can hardly hope for.")[11] Evidently enough M.P.s did hope for this, and in 1703 the Irish Commons petitioned Queen Anne for "a more firm and strict union." In their view, this would provide more direct and responsive legislation and representation. While Ireland was not considered eligible for this, Scotland was on the brink of union in the new century, though she got there through an unusual sequence of events.

The Scottish constitution had seen the most radical alteration in 1689, either because remoteness or lack of interest or inexperience of William's

---

[10]William Molyneux, *The case of Ireland's being bound by acts of parliament in England stated* (1698).

[11]ibid., pp. 97-8; See J.G. Simms, in *Irish Parliamentary Tradition* Brian Farrell, ed.,(1973) pp. 134-6.

advisers allowed a set of major changes to take place. The Lords of the Articles were eliminated, depriving the crown of an effective executive committee and experienced parliamentary managers. A royal commissioner from London was to handle the business of a session for the king. Powers of privy councillors were reduced and the General Assembly was restored. The Convention of Estates which met in Edinburgh took on a more radical hue especially after its Jacobite members seceded. Perhaps King William disregarded this, perhaps his view of Scotland was as a remote frontier with slender potential for taxation or recruiting, or with enough of an opposition to keep both sides distracted. The king's policy toward Scotland was careless at best, and this may help to account for the shabby affair at Glencoe. Yet William did not revise his priorities; he ignored the provision in the Claim of Right for regular elections, and he kept the initial convention parliament throughout the rest of his reign. Part of the background for Scottish affairs was the sorry economic state of the country, at a time when William would have gladly had more assets to exploit for his military policy. The 1690s were a time of extreme hardship. The years 1695-99 saw the last episode of general famine in Scotland. Poverty was paralleled by dependence on English trade and trade policy, a fact made embarrassingly plain in the Darien episode (see below, p. 250) and a fact which seemed to make a trading union with England an absolute necessity.

In the early years of the new century, the hostility between the nations produced some unnerving legislation. In 1703 an Act Anent Peace and War asserted the right of the Scottish legislature to consent to a declaration of war or to terms of peace. In 1704, the Act of Security claimed the right of the Scottish parliament to participate in the nomination of a successor to Queen Anne, implying the possibility of a separate succession from that of England. The English countered the latter with the Alien Act of 1705 wherein the succession of the House of Hanover was made mandatory; negotiations for union were suggested, the English threatening to declare Scots aliens and to ban their export of cattle, coal and linen to England.

Thus did the final stage of union discussion begin in an atmosphere of hostility. There had been some discussion of union in 1689; there was more in 1702. The talk was not serious until the dramatic measures of 1703-5 drew the alternatives in stark and simple outline. There was still a Stuart pretender in exile, there was still a French enemy on land and sea, and any serious dynastic crisis between England and Scotland would play into their hands.

The main concerns in the union negotiations were the royal succession, the established religion, parliament, the legal system, the administration and the economy. The Scots accepted the Act of Settlement which established the Hanoverian succession. The religious settlement was excluded from discussion, assuring the separate existence of churches, (further provided by act of the new parliament in 1708). The Parliament of Great Britain was created by the junction of Scottish and English bodies; there was no change whatsoever in the English membership, the Scottish parliament was replaced by 45 members of Commons and 16 representative peers (chosen by the total of 154). The legal systems were to be reconciled in public law, while in private cases, Scots law was to be preserved. Administration was by and large retained in separate organizations with little amalgamation, though later generations would make further changes. The economy was the most difficult area to settle. Scottish revenue was about 1/36 the size of the English, and the collection of the smaller amount was less rigorous and its accounting far more difficult to unravel. The English also had a far larger indebtedness which produced a tax obligation distasteful to the Scots. In trade, the English were loath to allow open access to colonial and other markets, while the Scots had at least as much cause for alarm if they could not find protection against English imports. The debt issue was settled by promising two installments of compensation, called "Equivalents", the first an amount of £400,000 sterling, then a later rebate on future Scottish revenue. On a lesser level, there were a number of other issues with regard to currency and weights and measures.

The Commissioners agreed to the Articles of Union in 1706, and they were then presented to both parliaments for ratification. The Scots finished the process in January, 1707, allegedly after a wave of bribes was absorbed. The agreement went into effect in May. The Anglo-Scottish union completed the process first seriously attempted by King James in 1604-07. But the end result was quite different from the earliest version. The form of actual union (incorporated parliaments, separate church and law) was almost the reverse of the Jacobean plan; it was a product of political conditions in the early 18th century, particularly the dynastic and military necessity of the time, and not simply the end of an inevitable process.

The Jacobite threat was an important feature of English and archipelago politics from 1689 to 1746. Externally, it was part of the French threat. Internally, it offered a focal point for political opposition; it was the enduring symbol of legitimacy and conservative monarchism; it was an occasional point of common effort against the imperial English power. Yet the Jacobite issue was far from dominant. To begin with, dynastic politics had declining importance in the archipelago, owing to the constitutional changes of 1689, the economic revolutions of the next generation, and the generally remote situations of the Jacobites themselves (Highlanders, Irish Catholics, Welsh and English squires).

The Jacobite rebellions (1690, 1708, 1715, 1745) were not serious threats to government stability, but this we know from hindsight. By an interesting paradox, contemporary politicians tended to magnify the "menace" and thus obtain a tighter grip on office, and more support for their policies. In England, this had a general effect of building and perpetuating a Whig oligarchy through the first half of the 18th century.

So far as there was ever a serious threat, it would have required a strong French invasion force to make it effective. The best chance of French invasion was in 1690-92. Another good-sized expedition sailed in 1708 but did not land. The later uprisings in 1715 and 1745 were deprived of substantial outside help. It is plain to us that the junction of domestic rebellion and outside aid never occurred in the right proportions; that of course does not prove that it could not have occurred, and incidents from the end of the 18th century would suggest that the possibilities were real enough.

When Queen Anne died (1714) the succession was at its most vulnerable point. George, the Elector of Hanover, was to take the crown, according to statute. Only a few months before, the Scots in parliament had voted in favor of ending the union (they were upset over the extension of the malt tax to Scotland, in apparent violation of the Act of Union). As George prepared to take his throne, Jacobite plotters prepared to oppose him. The earl of Mar raised about 10 to 12,000 men in Scotland without telling the Pretender, James III. Mar was easily beaten, as were rebels in northeast England. The government took these events seriously. The Riot Act (1715) was a product of frequent rioting in the cause, and its provisions gave more authority to the local justices. The Septennial Act (1716) showed fear of the results of electioneering in the aftermath of rebellion, and a seven-year interval between parliamentary contests was plainly meant to dampen the fires of electoral battle.

The Jacobite cause was punished severely in 1715-16, and had it not been for sympathetic juries, a large number might have been executed. The last chapter for the Jacobites came in 1745, though their fate was sealed a year earlier. A French assault in strength had been planned for 1744, but it was never launched. The next year, the French could not mount the campaign, but the pretender's son, Prince Charles Edward, took two ships, one of which landed in Scotland. The prince gathered a small force and marched into northwest England. His appearance failed to arouse the expected response. Irish and Welsh turnout was especially disappointing. Charles was forced to retreat to the North. His force made a stand at Culloden in April 1746. There a Scottish and English army led by the duke of Cumberland heavily defeated the Jacobites. The rebel soldiers were hunted down and the area of the Highlands was brought under tight military control. The victory was a small one in military terms, but it was doubly significant in British politics. First, it spelled the end of the Jacobite threat, for now there was no public response as there had been 30 years earlier. The Stuarts no longer represented a real and acceptable alternative. Second, the victory in the Highlands provided the government--both Lowland Scots and English-- with the opportunity to invade Highland society and accelerate assimilation. Laws were passed to terminate hereditary jurisdictions, to put confiscated estates into the control of a commission, and to end the power of the clans by altering feudal law and by outlawing the tartan and the bearing of arms by Highlanders. There were also public works including schools and roads, aimed at more positive social reform.

Within a decade, some of the exiled Highland leaders were returning, and soon some of the provisions of the settlement were being relaxed. This was no cultural annihilation, rather there was a determined effort to stamp out potential disorder and bring a more unified Scotland and Britain, at the expense of the erstwhile Jacobites.

At the opening of the 18th century there was an effective union in the archipelago, and in a superficial way, that union was the product of the wars of the 17th century. At times there had been deliberate schemes for union--by King James, by the Scottish Covenanters, by Oliver Cromwell, or by King William. But the stages of closer amalgamation had little to do with planning.

The single most potent fact was the inheritance of James VI. The next most effective element was the power of sectarian conflict. The last and crowning element was the international crisis of the late 17th century--the threat of France and the hope of empire. The collected factors were the ingredients of archipelago union, but because of their varied and volatile sources, the internal nature of the archipelago was no more settled than that of the blossoming colonial regime.

PART THREE

IMPERIAL ARCHIPELAGO

The political history of the Atlantic Archipelago in the modern era has been shaped by its situation in the British Empire. Though the last rites have been held for the empire, its obituary is still being written. Indeed, historians are making significant improvements in the analysis of the imperial experience, from its origins in the 16th century through its complex evolution in tandem with the home islands down to the 20th century.

The emerging unitary state of the Tudor period was unready or unable to produce a Spanish-style empire. Still there were many forms of control available, most of them used by the crown in its multiple efforts overseas: privateers and planters, charters and monopolies were to a degree ad hoc creations, but some drew on the example of earlier exercise of the prerogative in the archipelago.

The union which we saw taking shape in the 17th and 18th centuries was certainly no well-designed, compact constitutional federation. Instead, it was a series of compromises designed to maintain a working system of rule, whether it was for James's union of crowns, Cromwell's rebel Commonwealth, William's Anglo-Dutch military machine, or George II's Hanoverian dynasty. The dynastic era had been a time of experimental unions in which low levels of local integration were essayed within a framework of oligarchic central control. This combination prevented the construction, even the consideration, of elaborate imperial institutions. It was easy, after all, to govern colonial appendages in the way that marches and palatine counties had been, though contemporaries might have noticed that those models were themselves no longer operating in the 17th century. The royal council was as fertile as usual in creating and sustaining new groups of servants to oversee the growing function of colonial administration, but there were too many and complex innovations in the business; the task of imperial government had soon outgrown the agencies to which it was assigned.

The era of dynastic politics came to an end in the 18th century, being ushered out by a changing society, growing in size and wealth and shifting in distribution. These changes challenged all the political verities, and the process was intensified by ties between empire and archipelago. Foremost was the inherited common allegiance to the English crown, which provided the continuity and central focus for both archipelago and empire. Even though the royal prerogative was challenged at intervals, and even though its exercise in all the dominions was arbitrary at one time or another, it was unthinkable to overthrow it, until the imperial crisis of the third quarter of the 18th century. When American rebellion erupted, it had significant influence on colonial and domestic politics, even though they were soon engulfed by collateral revolutions, demographic, industrial and political. These gave the last years of the 18th century a special intensity, and they insured that archipelago and imperial ties, in terms of population, production and politics, would form the basis of 19th century development.

That century opened with formal parliamentary unification of the archipelago. The process of union and the history of this operation have received little attention from historians, yet those events offer a useful settting for the major political discussions and decisions in the 19th century. The union is also a vehicle for the continuation of the later empire/archipelago theme. The United Kingdom was only slowly and partially united, largely due to the difficulty of settling the place of Ireland within the union. Debates on this issue have obscured others of equal importance, and they distract us from the consequent rise in Welsh and Scottish nationalism and the more ardent displays of "unionism" in the later 19th century. At the same time, and with co-ordinate causes, the empire's government was called into question. Dominion autonomy, imperial federation and colonial nationalism were among the responses to the embarrassing discovery that the Queen-Empress had very skimpy constitutional clothes!

More serious by far was the slow recognition from the later years of Victoria's reign that the empire was being overtaken by foreign competitors. The economic advantages enjoyed until 1870 were no longer there in 1890. The political-military mission of the empire was now in question, and the archipelago connection itself had become a liability. Irish nationalists, industrial unions and irate women all attended the inaugural of the "age of democracy." The rowdy event was a distraction to the political leadership, but more important, it provided incentive to domestic and imperial populations outside "the pale of the constitution." More emphatic was the impact of war. The cost in lives, in treasure and in international position were more than the empire could bear. By 1945 there was no chance of retaining an empire, and the Commonwealth conversion, begun much earlier, and accelerated in the 1920s, was resumed in haste. In the archipelago, efforts were made to return politics to normal in 1918 and 1945, but "normal" kept changing. Political and social democracy were the major concern, and only after the withdrawal from empire did archipelago separation reappear. When it did, it was emphatically dealt with, by the Army in Ulster, and by referenda in Scotland and Wales.

As an "imperial sunset" fell on the remarkable British global enterprise, historians were struggling to interpret the empire which began in a series of awkward acquisitions in a world of declining great powers in Iberia and the Netherlands in the 16th and 17th centuries.

CHAPTER 7

ARCHIPELAGO AND EMPIRE

> The loyalty to the crown of English settlers
> was not matched by any comparable
> institutional framework; a well-informed
> observer on the continent of Europe might
> reasonably have expected the execution of
> Charles I would lead to the disintegration of
> his empire overseas...
>
> (T.O. Lloyd, *The British
> Empire*, 1984, p. 29)

The English crown enjoyed a pivotal position in archipelago amalgamation and in overseas expansion. This combined central authority was paradoxically responsible for the early success and the later decline of empire. No Roman or Spanish institutions grew up. No mighty legions, no treasure fleets, no army of administrators were settled in this empire. The historians of the 19th century believed there had been an "expansion of England," but they were wrong. There had been an impressive dispatch of privateers, merchants, planters, sailors and soldiers from the archipelago. The network which they created was a remarkable commercial phenomenon: a means of transmitting goods, money, men and ideas, to and from the archipelago, to all corners of the globe. The empire was a symbol of great power, even though within itself, the power was more symbolic than real.

At the peak of the "old empire" in the 18th century, severe crises in several sectors coincided with a major English domestic political transition (1748-1784). In America, the crown was openly challenged and beaten; in Ireland, the Protestant elite demanded and got a form of political autonomy; in India, the political role of the East India Company was extended and its relation with the British government reformed. In each case, political connections between the archipelago and the empire were critical, and each event highlighted weaknesses in imperial government.

The political crises of the 1770s were soon overtaken by more profound changes which drove domestic political evolution in new directions. The revolution in France evoked a reactionary response in the archipelago; rapid

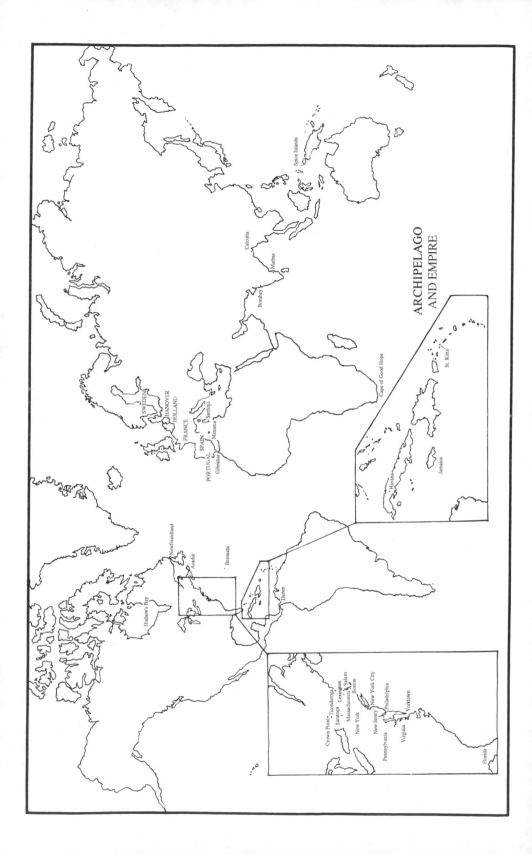

ARCHIPELAGO
AND EMPIRE

Spice Islands

Calcutta

Madras

Bombay

Cape of Good Hope

SWEDEN
HANOVER
HOLLAND
FRANCE
PORTUGAL SPAIN
Gibraltar Minorca
Sardinia

St. Kitts

Havana

Jamaica

Newfoundland
Acadia

Bermuda

Hudson's Bay

Darien

Crown Point
Ticonderoga
Saratoga Lexington
Massachusetts Salem
Boston
New York
New Jersey New York City
Pennsylvania Philadelphia
Virginia Yorktown

Florida

industrial development brought sharp changes in economic patterns for many areas; unprecedented population growth altered the face and form of society. Together, these components of social change prepared the way for political reform in the context of a massive new economic concentration. The archipelago and empire were partners in this transformation which spanned the 18th and 19th centuries and produced a great trading and industrial empire destined to be much wealthier than the projects of mercantilists ever imagined.

Imperial Polity

The empire grew out of a swirl of royal and private ventures in the early modern period. The men and measures involved were simultaneously working for the sovereign of the archipelago and the ruler of its overseas bases, factories and settlements. The experience was not a replication of palatine government, continental garrisons or Irish plantations, but those forms and experiences were surely part of the conceptual world of Elizabethans.

The English crown acquired an array of interests and a number of possessions, from India to Virginia, from Bermuda to the Spice Islands. The crown's control was as diversified as the conquests in its name. Growth of the navy and private captains, merchant companies and royal charters, the settlement or plantation of colonists, were the joint products of private entrepreneurs and official sanction or supervision. The variety of efforts and the remoteness of their locations assured that royal authority was used and abused by autonomous colonial agents. Having not begun empire as a systematic central enterprise, it could never be completely coordinated afterward.

The archipelago experience was an important ingredient in this constitutional recipe. The navy and its auxiliaries were mobilized to defend against counter-Reformation, especially the Armada. But those ships and crews were thereafter available for raiding and plundering--and exploring. The merchant company used legal and financial instruments developed over the years by staples, ports, guilds and towns as forms of royal protection. Those who settled colonies followed patterns of planting which were not too far from those of 13th century Wales, 15th century Scotland and 17th century

Ireland. Now the motives and circumstances were different, but the exercise of royal authority was unchanged. However, plantation at such great distance did affect the exercise of power.

English colonial efforts in the early 17th century were not in a dependent position in the same way that those of continental countries were. The English crown could not afford it any other way. Indeed, the government which could not send aid to the king of Bohemia in 1618, which sent poorly-equipped expeditions to the continent in the 1620s, and which could not afford to evict the Scots in 1640, was in no position to erect and run a worldwide imperial administration. The first English regime which came near that capacity was that of the Commonwealth.

The English military establishment of the 1650s was the most powerful and best-financed that the archipelago had yet produced. Oliver Cromwell initiated a policy of government-sponsored imperialism, one with a definite military and an occasional missionary character. There had been acts in support of merchants before, but the new direction of the 1650s lay in its more obvious character as a *national* endeavor. Nowhere was this more apparent than in the evolution of the Navy. From 1649 to 1651 the Navy List had increased from 39 to 80 vessels; by the time of the Restoration, 207 new vessels were added to the fleet. There was a nice irony here, as much of the cost was met from sale of sequestered royalist estates, a lucrative version of the Ship Money policy of Charles I. There was an apt contrast, too, in the substitution of a national trade monopoly for the personal, court-distributed type. The Commonwealth taught that it would be a far easier task to raise general revenues and general interest in the cause of the new imperial policy.

Regicide and republic put England (and its archipelago dependencies) in an embarrassed position in Europe. The cost of civil war, followed by the Cromwellian conquest, brought economic instability into partnership with diplomatic isolation. These hazards dictated Cromwell's strategy. Trade, religion and political survival welded an unusually coherent and well-financed policy. Serious depression (1648-1651) threatened to become terminal if the Dutch exercised their power to interdict English trade in the Baltic and with the continent. An English diplomatic mission in 1651 discussed a defensive alliance and a union against subversion; the Dutch rejected political ties and pushed for a commercial treaty; the English mission returned and the military government widened its ban on non-English vessels which had been imposed in the colonies in 1650.

The Navigation Act of 1651 said that colonial imports to the "Commonwealth of England, or into Ireland, or any other lands, islands, plantations or territories to this Commonwealth belonging" were only allowed in English ships. Colonial goods which had been re-exported were not admissible. Goods from Europe were allowed only in English vessels or those of the originating nation. It was clear that the act was aimed primarily at the Dutch trading power. More militant action followed in 1652, when incidents in the Channel sparked the outbreak of an Anglo-Dutch war. In that conflict, about 1,400 Dutch vessels were seized and that country's commerce was badly shaken. In 1654, Cromwell negotiated a mild treaty with the enemy, probably because he saw a more dangerous threat looming in the deteriorating relations with Spain. English policy was even more aggressive toward the Catholic imperial power, both in the Mediterranean and in the West Indies. Cromwell advanced what was called the "Western Design" to take advantage of an apparent decline in Spanish power in the Indies. In 1655 there were heavy English losses in an attempt to capture Santo Domingo, but success in taking the then unimportant island of Jamaica.

Charles II maintained the essentials of Cromwellian imperial policy: a military force and militant trade laws. The tiny standing army in its three establishments (English, Scottish and Irish) gave the crown a military capacity which transformed the polity. The pay, the governance and the disposition of these troops were all subject to parliamentary discussion. That was a small price for the reinforcement given to the restored monarchy. Charles also adopted the mercantilist legislation of the Commonwealth. There was a series of Navigation Acts (1660-63) to foster English trade and shipping on the same lines as the act of 1651. Enhancing national wealth and power through legal, commercial and military efforts was a policy pursued by most governments, so "mercantilism" may be viewed as nothing radical. Yet the path to these objectives was always full of twists, the routes chosen by absolute monarchs, by communities in the archipelago or by interests in the empire (planters, merchants, governors) were sure to diverge, offering opportunities for political dispute.

The dominant theme of the early restoration period was that of Anglo-Dutch naval and commercial warfare. Charles's advisers expected the Dutch to be beaten easily, as in the 1650s. But the English were trounced in the Second Dutch War (1665-67) and came off poorly in the Third (1672-74). The main action in both occurred in the Channel and the North Sea, but the strategic significance was worldwide. Both powers were pursuing imperial opportunities which were created by Spain's decline and which were threatened by rising French overseas activity.

The enforcement of the navigation acts against the Dutch was a major source of friction, but piracy and privateering were just as important. The English miscalculated badly in starting the war in 1665; without funds, they had to send the fleet to anchorage in early 1667 and begin negotiating. While talks went on at Breda, the Dutch sailed up the Medway and attacked the main English fleet (June 1667), towing away the royal flagship. This humiliation, on top of domestic disasters (plague in 1665 and the Great Fire of London in 1666), forced a quick settlement. The Treaty of Breda was surprisingly favorable from an English point of view. The English joined a "Triple Alliance" (1668) with Holland and Sweden, to oppose French expansion in the Low Countries, but this was a short-lived and deceptive tie. Charles was already negotiating secretly with France, promising war on the Dutch and Catholic restoration at home, in exchange for monetary and military aid from Louis XIV.

The commitment to France was "inseparably connected" to "the establishment of royal absolutism throughout the British Isles."[1] The priority accorded this political objective preceded the systematic development of a comprehensive imperial regime. Indeed, the Stuarts may have believed that such control would naturally flow from their military, naval, financial and religious policies. However, success of their absolutist policy rested on prior assurance of the crown's power, and this was not forthcoming. In the Third Dutch War (1672-74), the English defeat exposed the weakness of the regime, while it alienated Scotland's principal trading partner and invited an infestation of privateers around Irish ports.

In the early 1680s a more aggressive royal policy toward the empire developed. The Stuarts exploited the political reaction to the exclusion crisis and made the first (and last) attempt to erect a Spanish-style imperial regime. The new commission to the Jamaica governor in 1681 has been called "the

[1] J. R. Jones, *Britain and the World, 1649-1815* (1980) p. 97.

Constitution of 1681."[2] Both it and the new year's grant to Virginia put these governments on a new footing; legislative powers and executive authority were abridged in favor of increased crown control. In 1683 the Board of Ordnance was reconstituted, its Master General having overall charge of fortification and coastal defence; the actual forces at the Stuarts' disposal were small (the establishments amounted to 8,800 in England, 7,500 in Ireland and 2,000 in Scotland in 1685) and their greatest threat was probably to the towns in which they were billeted.[3]

The Stuarts nevertheless pursued a policy of constitutional revision which helped to promote rebellion. It was within the royal prerogative to seek revision of charters (which were the foundation of most corporate or communal powers). The process of revision was always complicated and the Stuarts tended to push the resolution too fast. In the mid-80s many felt this pressure, none perhaps more forcefully than the Massachusetts colony. The General Court there had long resisted London's authority, and by 1683 the royal government was starting to exert its power. The Massachusetts charter was annulled in 1684, and the duke of York was quoted as saying he wanted "to reduce all properties and independent government to an immediate dependence upon the crown."[4] The crown replaced the old charter with a new order--the "Dominion of New England." A new governor was sent to the colony, which was enlarged by 1688 to include New York and New Jersey. The main innovations of the Dominion were the enlarged area of executive authority and the absence of a legislature. Presumably there would have been further constitutional changes along these lines, but the collapse of James's government in England was quickly followed by colonial revolutions and the restoration of former charters.

In 1688 there was also a diplomatic revolution. Anglo-Dutch hostility was replaced by war between France and England in 1689-97 and 1702-13. These wars had important consequences for the colonies, the archipelago and England. The revolutionary period was critical for the archipelago, since the Anglo-Dutch alliance prompted French invasion plans and attempts. William's easy English victory was a blow to Louis XIV, who had expected

---

[2]Webb, *The Governors-General*, pp. 447-55.

[3]John Childs, *The Army, James II and the Glorious Revolution* (1980), pp. 1-2.

[4]R. R. Johnson, *Adjustment to Empire: The New England Colonies, 1675-1715* (1981), p. 53.

a costly and bloody campaign which would distract his enemy. Instead, the French were called upon to send aid to James in Ireland (1689-91). When that failed, a French fleet with twelve battalions (24,000 men) sailed in 1692 to invade, but it was intercepted off Barfleur and La Hogue and beaten. Some other invasion plans were also thwarted, and Louis was in effect outflanked.

Meanwhile, the war caused severe economic stress in the archipelago. Heavy military expenses meant heavy taxation, returning to the war levels of mid-century. There was sufficient pressure to force some basic financial reforms, including the establishment of a national debt and the founding of the national banks of England and Scotland (1694-95). These institutional reforms were a means of raising still more money to support government expenditure. The loans raised, and the lenders behind them, created what came to be called the "monied interest", a vital and powerful new force in politics. Most of the liquid capital was from commerce and industry, and it competed for political influence with older landed wealth. Increased numbers of government posts (customs, treasury, navy), created a fund of patronage which supported the operation of the political structure.

There were many ramifications from this central reorganizing impulse. For the archipelago, there was friction over the place of Scotland and Ireland in the trading empire in the later 1690s. In 1695, William Paterson, one of the founding figures in the national banks, helped to organize "A Company of Scotland trading to Africa and the Indies." The object was to raise funds in Scotland (and England and Europe) to support a competing trading company which would return a share of the commercial gains to the Scots. The effort was bound to infringe on Spanish claims, and as William III was trying to win Spain's neutrality, he was determined to thwart the enterprise. English interests combined to stop fund-raising there and in Europe, but the Scots went ahead. Some £150,000 was subscribed, by some estimates about 20% of Scotland's net worth! The Company tried to establish a colony on the Central American isthmus, but it met with Spanish hostility and American and English indifference, and it was a failure. The Darien incident was not isolated. There was more direct and equally selfish English policy affecting Irish economic life. The Wool Act of 1699 was meant to ban export of Irish woollens. It may have been unenforceable and its general economic consequences may have been mild. However, such acts showed a desire and capacity for English control of archipelago economic life.

Similarly, late 17th century imperial administration was designed to exert more control. The Trade and Navigation Act of 1696 was meant to settle colonial administration on a better footing, to conform the laws of England and the colonies and to improve regulations. Enforcement of navigation laws was to be supervised by the Commissioners of Customs, with the help of new Vice-Admiralty courts. The Committee of the Privy Council for Trade and Plantations (the "Board of Trade") followed a series of advisory bodies which were used in the Restoration period. It seemed to be a promising vehicle for "a disciplined imperial executive, capable of combining the various and disparate instruments of empire into a single, unified authority."[5] But the Board was without ultimate power over governors or other colonial officials; indeed, the Privy Council at this point was being superseded by the smaller inner "cabinet council."

While this effort at constitutional reform was mounted, there were continuing political skirmishes over colonial powers: efforts to recall colonial charters (1697-1702) and parliamentary review of the constitution of chartered companies were among these incidents. For instance, the charter of the East India Company was scrutinized, and in 1698 it was directed to merge with a recent rival under a new charter. The old company bought out the new and regained control by 1702. Another charter revision and "united" company were created in 1709; the profitable chartered monopoly was always tempting to political leaders, so its career was bound to be entangled with domestic politics.

War with France resumed in 1702. William had planned for this war, but he died just before it began. "Queen Anne's War" saw the first major victory for the British Empire, a victory which firmly established imperial power in the archipelago, Europe and the world. The immediate cause of fighting was a French threat to assume the Spanish throne. In both colonial and European politics such a merger might have been fatal to English ambition. The French move was blocked and English power was used to outflank its rival, especially in the Mediterranean. By alliance with Portugal (1703), the capture of Gibraltar (1704) and the occupation of Sardinia and

---

[5]G. S. Graham, *Concise History of the British Empire* (1971), p. 56.

Minorca, the British gained a strategic advantage in Europe while also winning a series of colonial victories.

Meanwhile in the archipelago, English control was solidified when the Scottish parliament agreed to join the new parliament of Great Britain. The primary impulse for union was the war with France. The Scots were admitted on an equal basis to imperial trade (and customs and navigation laws). This would be a vital source of economic improvement for Scotland, which had suffered severe hardship in the 1690s. By combining the commercial interests of England and Scotland, the domestic political picture was simplified, but certainly the enlarged polity would not find it any easier to govern its rapidly growing empire.

In the main theatre of the war, the continental threat was serious, and the British made a major contribution to meet it. A large army was sent under John Churchill, earl (later duke) of Marlborough. With his force of Dutch, German, English and Scottish troops, Marlborough won a brilliant string of victories, yet the war was far from an unqualified success. Tory opponents played upon the usual discontents created by such an expensive policy. The Tory (or "Country") view favored naval campaigns as opposed to large armies, in the belief that prizes and colonial conquests were a form of profit which rendered colonial wars far less expensive. However true this may have been, the cost of campaigning was a burden which helped the anti-war faction into power. Peace talks began in 1711.

The Treaty of Utrecht was concluded between Great Britain and France in 1713, and it marked the arrival of Britain's power at the front rank in Europe and the world. The main provisions, in the European context, were that the thrones of Spain and France were never to be united, and that Louis XIV recognized the Protestant succession in England, thereby renouncing the Jacobite pretender. In colonial terms, Britain retained Gibraltar and Minorca and Spain granted the "asiento" (a 30-year contract for supplying slaves to Spanish America). In addition, France ceded Hudson's Bay, Acadia and Newfoundland and the island of St. Kitts. This was the largest combination of imperial gains yet seen by an English or British government. Just as important, the treaty was followed by a quarter of a century without a major war between the great powers.

The period from 1715 to 1760 has been called the "Whig Ascendancy." Because of Jacobite rebellion, and the association of Tories with the rebels, there was generally single-party rule under the first two Hanoverian kings, George I (1714-27) and George II (1727-60). Instead of party rivalry, factions among the Whigs contested for patronage and office. The victors like Robert Walpole or the duke of Newcastle used patronage and restrictive legislation to build a stable foundation for oligarchic rule. The same devices were used to govern the archipelago and the empire.

Patronage in the early 18th century grew dramatically with the expansion of government, both wartime necessity and economic expansion causing the growth. Since there was still a system of appointed office-holders, this gave great power to the ministers of the crown. Indeed, in the early years (1700-15) there was a campaign to restrict "placemen" i.e., those who sat in the House of Commons by virtue of some kind of royal or ministerial influence. The campaign created some restrictions, notably that members appointed to hold office would have to stand for re-election. However, the attempted reforms neither reduced nor altered the essential condition. And ministers had patronage links to Scotland and Ireland as well. The Campbells (the duke of Argyll and earl of Islay) dispensed ministerial favors and were expected to produce dutiful Scottish M.P.s. In Ireland the affairs of government were delegated to "undertakers," social and political leaders of the ascendancy who "undertook" to maintain stable and quiet rule in the Irish parliament.

If patronage was the benevolent form of political management, repression was its darker side. The Protestant oligarchy, it should be noted, could not establish a full-scale system of state repression. There was, in place of such a regime, an assortment of restrictive measures which at least affirmed the ruling class and gave it the means to apply legal penalties to its enemies (political and social). The famous Riot Act of 1715 empowered a justice of the peace to declare an assembly illegal, thus making those in attendance guilty of a felony. In 1716, a new electoral law extended the life of a British parliament from three to seven years. Both of these acts were inspired in part by the Jacobite revolt of 1715; both acts were aimed at the main channels of public influence on politics: rioting and electioneering. The results of elections were of course most significantly influenced by patrons or purchase; costs rose steadily in the early 18th century and reinforced the control of oligarchy by making contests too expensive and thus reducing the numbers of contested seats.

Beside political participation, oligarchs buttressed their power in other ways. The Whigs tried to limit the creation of new peers in 1719 (but failed). In the same year, the British parliament passed a Declaratory Act which claimed uncontested power to legislate for Ireland. In 1725, General George Wade was sent as Commander-in-Chief to the Highlands where he built forts and roads to begin to subjugate the area and reduce its potential as a Jacobite stronghold. Another dimension of control was in the creation of military forces--raising regiments, impressing sailors and administering military discipline. But for the most part the oligarchy used legislation and the courts to enforce its political and social control, either in response to rioting or in defence of property.

The stable political order in the archipelago did owe some of its capacity to "English liberty." That inherited concept of the power of property versus royal authority (or "despotism") was something possessed by property and its owners, not by society in general. The resulting stability of the early 18th century thus could not be exported to the colonies, for there the oligarchy was new. More open ownership and a looser political environment tended to redefine "liberty."

The imperial crisis of the mid-century occurred as the fabric of society was being altered by a mixture of potent developments, demographic, cultural and economic. The archipelago society of the early 18th century was far from static, and movement to and from colonial communities would have prevented any such unlikely development. Whatever social stability we may find was subject to several major qualifications: this was a mobile society, undergoing what came to be called a "great awakening," with "improving" landlords, entrepreneurs and a collection of self-styled "patriots." The combination of these features produced a political scene of some vitality.

The most obvious sign of mobility in the 17th and 18th centuries was in the migration from the archipelago to the mainland American colonies and to the West Indies. The first "wave" of migration was in the 1620s and 30s, when perhaps 30,000 went to the mainland and 40,000 to the Caribbean and Atlantic islands. After a tapering off in the middle decades, movement resumed, now oriented definitely to the mainland. There the population reached about 250,000 by 1700 and by 1750 it was well over 1 million. In the early migrations there were large numbers of indentured servants, transported convicts and slaves. The latter category had the most rapid growth in the 18th century. By 1775 about 20% of the colonial population was black. As for the archipelago's role in this migratory phenomenon, no area of origin was excluded, persons of moderate wealth were always able to make their way in the colonies, and while data is scarce, it seems true that transportees were mostly Irish, mid-Atlantic shopkeepers were mostly Scottish, and there were large, communal settlements of Welsh migrants (eastern Pennsylvania) and "Scotch-Irish" (western Virginia). Yet these were only islands in a sea of settlement. It will never be possible to compile an account of the movement of all archipelago emigrants for the 18th century.

The cultural impact of the colonial experience was also immeasurable. Probably the increase in religious toleration was assisted by the physical distances, movement and variety induced by the empire. We can see in one episode how religious stimuli were transmitted. The "great awakening" was a term coined in the American colonies to describe the powerful impact of a revivalist movement, centered in Connecticut and inspired by the work of Jonathan Edwards. The phrase also suited the contemporaries George Whitefield and John Wesley, who built the Methodist movement, travelling widely in the archipelago and the empire to spread the gospel. Among those they influenced were some of the best- known Welsh figures in the 18th century: Daniel Rowland, Howell Harris and Griffith Jones. The latter was known for his work in creating a network of itinerant school teachers (1731-61) which made pioneering efforts in rural Wales.

In Scotland, where the convenanting tradition had made popular religious assemblies suspect, the kirk had experienced a secession of ministers in 1733, but not one based upon theology. When Whitefield preached in Scotland, he was opposed by Seceders, but he seems to have contributed to the impressive revival in Lanarkshire in 1742 ("the Cambuslang Wark"). Ireland, on the other hand, was relatively immune from such enthusiasm due to the combined effect of persecution and apathy.

The most striking 18th century intellectual event was the "Scottish Enlightenment." The Scots had a strong educational tradition and well-developed universities. The educated classes had been as close to current and traditional intellectual influences as any other part of the archipelago. From the second quarter of the 18th century, an eminent group of thinkers and teachers produced a brilliant body of work which historians describe collectively as the "Scottish Enlightenment." By the beginning of the 19th century, this phenomenon was fading. It was indeed a unique, perhaps an accidental event. The authors involved were not trying to be Scottish, but built upon classical tradition and recast principles and hypotheses for modern use. One speculative explanation for the high concentration of intellectual power was the diversion of energy from Calvinist debate and the neutering of Scottish politics.

Whatever its cause, the Scottish Enlightenment was a remarkable conjunction of philosophical, historical and scientific work. Some of the leading figures of the first generation were the philosophers Francis Hutcheson and David Hume, William Adam and his architect sons, and Joseph Black the chemistry pioneer.

Whatever else we say about it, the "Scottish Enlightenment" was anything but "typical" of archipelago intellectual life in the early 18th century. In fact, there were several signs of cultural revival only developed fully in the second half of the century. Individuals and societies devoted great energy to work in native cultural sources; alas some of it was spurious, but all of it was significant. That is, as indices of national (or ethnic?) identity, the poems of an Ossian (James MacPherson's creation) or the bardic verse of Iolo Morganwg (alias Edward Williams) were of more current political significance than literary value.

Groups such as the Gwyneddigion (1771), a gathering of London-Welsh, or the Scots in their St. Andrew's societies, were signs of growing consciousness of separate and valued traditions. In this activity there was a good deal of sentimentality; many of the active members were expatriate Scots or Welsh or Irish -- people unlikely to trade London society for rustic charms.

In the opposite direction, there was a surge in "tourism" in the archipelago. The Highlands and islands and North Wales became popular places to visit, though the traffic is hard to measure; also the romantic indulgence of writing and publishing one's "travels" produced more evidence for this period. Travel as a byproduct of the empire led to more natural (if not easy) commuting over the world's oceans, and as a corollary perhaps it promoted more movement within the archipelago.

The first half of the century saw another phenomenon which was the product of the empire, and which tied together some of the current social and political developments. The great fortunes in tobacco (Glasgow), tea

(Bristol) and slaves (Liverpool) were only the most prominent in a vast range of commercial successes which would be reabsorbed into archipelago life in the 18th century. Large amounts went into landed estates, and in one direction, commerce worked to recruit new members for the landed oligarchy. In another direction, new fortunes abroad were emulated by the improving landlords at home. "Improvement" in agriculture meant more emphasis on profit via enclosure, strict leases, better cultivation, that is, whatever would improve productivity. Agricultural improvement societies sprang up around the archipelago (Edinburgh, 1723; Dublin, 1733), and they were accompanied by a multitude of individual experiments. Among the notable efforts were the "planned villages" in Scotland (Callander, Crieff, Ormiston), where the purpose was to introduce new methods ("English husbandry"). Improvers were taking a lead from their successful commerical cousins, and they were forcing the pace of change in rural communities, which might be seen as yet another way in which the oligarchy was controlling society. However, in this case, the oligarchs clearly were not promoting stability.

The political truth about the mid-18th century empire was that it had been built on the 17th century premise of government stimulus and regulation. The old structure had never functioned as it was meant to, and insofar as it had provoked growth, it also created insoluble constitutional problems. While English ministers searched for an imperial government solution, the commercial politics of the 18th century prevented consensus as to the means and ends of empire. England attained European pre-eminence and archipelago dominance through her empire, but a mid-century crisis threatened those political achievements.

Political Crises

The empire and the archipelago experienced severe political instability in the third quarter of the 18th century. There were causal and coincidental ties between widely-separated crises: for all parts of the loosely-constructed empire were subject to the king of England; most were influenced by English political ideas, customs and personalities; and all were governed by the parliament of Great Britain, whose members and ministerial leaders for most of the 18th century were moving awkwardly toward a new constitutional relationship with the crown. This English political development was already underway when American affairs degenerated into rebellion in the 1770s; the Irish elite took a cue from America and gained some parliamentary concessions; while in India the extended powers of the merchant company and the conduct of its officers had to be regulated by Westminster. These turbulent events were caught up in the climactic crisis of 1779-84. Their combination was proof to some that the king's "influence" was too great, and prescriptions for reform were forthcoming in several styles. In the midst of these events, the issue of the king's power to choose his own ministers was fought to a paradoxical conclusion. George III apparently won with his appointment of the young William Pitt, but the son of the earl of Chatham went on to become the first recognizably modern Prime Minister.

Older histories used to bestow that title on Robert Walpole, leader of the Whig ascendancy. After Walpole left office in 1742, the Whig oligarchy held on for two more decades. But in those years there were successive strains on the once-stable system which finally gave way in the early years of George III. That king's distaste for old-fashioned factions set off a two-decade period of ministerial confusion and reform.

Walpole held power as First Lord of the Treasury and leader of the only recognized party. He was the king's choice and he wielded the king's patronage, enabling him to influence the composition and behavior of the House of Commons in his favor. This "prime" ministerial power evoked envy and distrust and by the 1740s opposition factions were strong enough to defeat Walpole in a series of votes. He resigned office, the first chief minister to step down because of loss of support in the Commons. George II appointed John Carteret in his place, but when the new minister was not able to maintain support, the king accepted his resignation in 1744. The new cabinet included some self-styled "patriots," those whose stated policy was to place national loyalty before faction or connection. The most outspoken of these was the elder William Pitt, who criticized the influence of the Hanoverian Electorate in British affairs. As the king had resisted his appointment, Pitt only obtained office in 1746. The central figures in this government were Henry Pelham and his brother Thomas, the duke of Newcastle. The latter became the sole leader when his brother died in 1754, but the duke was much less able. Pitt had left the government in 1754 and was brought back after the series of losses in war, 1756-7. As it happened,

Pitt was skillful in selecting officers and directing operations, in addition to being a popular demagogue.

George II may have had difficulty with individual ministers, but he adjusted to the system of politics. He would accept ministers he personally disliked if they could manage the machinery well enough to control the system of government. That system, including Scotland, Ireland and the colonies, was facing increasing challenges in the 1740s. We have already seen how the Jacobite uprising of 1745 gave the last hefty endorsement to Whig hegemony. The reaction helped to cement Whig control over Scottish patronage, but there was no significant reaction in Ireland. There some internal "patriot" noises were heard above the drone of the undertakers. In fact, the most dramatic (and least important?) incident was when a mob entered the Irish parliament in 1759 and demanded oaths from M.P.s against a rumored union with Britain. In India the early 50s saw the rise of the fortunes of the East India Company. In 1754 the great Anglo-French struggle opened in North America, and in 1756 there was general European war. To juggle all of these problems, George II turned to a succession of ministers with very different talents and aspirations. Meanwhile, the king himself spent much of his time in Hanover and was as concerned with the political opposition of his son, Prince Frederick, as with the elements of Whig factions. Frederick died in 1750, leaving a twelve-year old son in the tutelage of his mother and later a tutor, John Stuart, earl of Bute.

The new Prince of Wales inherited his father's generational passion against the ruling member of the family. The prince also detested the current political faction system. George was not well-endowed, but his thoughts on kingship still mattered. He took his position seriously and meant to remove the old-style politicians, presumably replacing them with some sort of idealized "patriots."

George II died in October 1760. The great war which had begun so badly in 1756 was now running heavily in favor of England. William Pitt had presided over a great series of victories in 1759, and his power as a minister was at a peak. But George III was disposed to end the fighting and to find new advisers. As of 1760, the new monarch controlled the largest amount of patronage of any 18th century ruler, as he held that of the crown and the heir apparent jointly. In addition, election contests were becoming less frequent in the general elections which were held every six or seven years. However, George misread his power and its relevance to the problems he had to solve. His was an unsophisticated view of the prerogative and of the qualifications for political leadership; meanwhile his view of faction or party was simplistic, and its application was to prove too radical. Lord Bute was brought into the government as Secretary of State in April 1761. By September Pitt had resigned. He wanted a declaration of war on Spain, but the cabinet would not support him. In fact, Spain declared war in early 1762, as Pitt had forecast, and the ministers used the plans which Pitt had prepared to defeat Spain. But King George was mainly interested in peace. Terms were agreed on late in 1762 and the Treaty of Paris was concluded in 1763. In the continental war, the status quo was restored, but overseas there was a major shift. France surrendered Canada, plus lands east of the Mississippi, while West Indian acquisitions were returned to France. Spain surrendered Florida in exchange for Havana. The predictable press attacks were made, but one was especially hostile. *The North Briton*, edited by John Wilkes and Charles Churchill, made serious allegations in its issue No. 45. The "North Briton" was a reference to Bute, the Scottish favorite, and the attack on the treaty gained extra fuel from the traditional animosity still felt on either side of the Tweed. Wilkes provoked government action. A general warrant was issued for his arrest and that of anyone connected with the publication. Wilkes successfully challenged the general warrant and his arrest as a sitting M.P. However, when he continued to publish material which was of questionable legality, he had to flee into exile.

Bute withdrew from the ministry in April 1763, apparently unable to take the pressure of office. He did however expect to remain at court and in the king's close proximity. This raised suspicions of secret influence which were worse in the eyes of politicians than any public moves Bute might have made. As for the treaty and the subsequent political situation, the possessions in North America and India were now nominally secure and the empire had attained the appearance of a mighty international enterprise.

When Bute left, King George turned to George Grenville as the new ministerial leader. In the circumstances, Grenville insisted on full royal support and the exclusion of Bute from any consultation. These terms were objectionable to the king and indeed they were improper. But the king had little recourse, at least until Grenville ran into difficulty. Given the conditions, that would not take long. In the new strategic situation, there were pressing problems. As imperial government was enlarged, it faced a doubling of debts and escalating operating costs. Grenville's solution was sensible but volatile. He would solve the fiscal problem by making the colonies pay their share. A combination of old regulation and new taxation gave a reasonable prospect of the needed revenue. Apparently Grenville did not appreciate the political and constitutional hazards, for he was introducing the first direct taxation of the colonies and thereby opening the issue of "taxation without representation."

Grenville's first steps were in the Sugar Act and Currency Act, the former regulating trade in molasses and rum, the latter banning paper currencies. These were signals of changes, the greatest of which came with the Stamp Act of 1765. The measure would have imposed stamp duties in the colonies on legal and printed documents and a list of miscellaneous items. The estimated revenue would have been about £60,000 annually. Colonial reaction was swift and severe. The most vocal elements of society were directly affected, and petitions, resolutions, embargoes were organized; more ominous still, a "Stamp Act Congress" was convened in New York in October, 1765, and there were violent acts against stamp agents, especially in Boston.

Before the news of reaction reached England, Grenville was out of office. He and the king had never been on good terms, and in the Summer of 1765 the ministry was dismissed. The new leader was the marquis of Rockingham, whose brief term in office was long enough to repeal the Stamp Act. As part of the bargain, parliament also passed a Declaratory Act. According to that, parliament had

> full power and authority to make laws and statutes of sufficient force and validity to bind the colonies and people of America, subjects of the crown of Great Britain, in all cases whatsoever.

Colonists were allowed to think that this did not include taxation, whereas members of parliament generally had the opposite interpretation. In any case the act nullified a good opportunity to demonstrate what was called "virtual representation"--the argument that M.P.s represented the interests of colonists who could not vote in parliamentary elections.

The Rockingham administration was soon replaced when the king called on William Pitt to be the new leader. He formed a non-party government, one which was weakened when he took the title earl of Chatham and left the House of Commons. In 1767 Pitt suffered a breakdown and the leadership of daily affairs was left to others. The Chancellor of the Exchequer was Charles Townshend, who introduced a plan of new duties on colonial trade. This reignited the complaints of the Stamp Act, and it constituted a more serious threat to the colonies. Now the revenues were to be used to meet the general expenses of colonial government, whereas Stamp Act proceeds had only been meant to pay for military expenses. Thus the colonists were faced with the loss of control over their governments' revenues. The Townshend duties were portrayed as new regulations, not taxes. This was a maneuver to exploit the admission of some in the colonies that they were only opposed to British exertion of taxing powers. All the same, resistance appeared in the same form as it had in the earlier crisis.

As the new duties were being applied, and as the government tried to improve colonial control (the post Secretary of State for Colonies was created in 1768), domestic politics were complicated by the return of Wilkes from exile and his election to the House of Commons for the county of Middlesex in 1768. Wilkes was arrested and jailed for his earlier offences, but he won a series of elections, each time being disqualified by the Commons, and after the fourth such election his opponent was declared the winner. Wilkes was kept in jail until 1770, only later succeeding in a career in London politics and returning to the House in 1774. Meanwhile, the affair seemed to endorse the colonists' claims of parliamentary misgovernment.

The American colonial problem was mirrored in an interesting series of developments in Ireland. When Charles Townshend went to the exchequer, his older brother was made Lord Lieutenant of Ireland. The Irish treasury then had a surplus which ministers saw as a means of aiding in the wider problem of imperial finance. George Townshend was instructed to use the surplus to increase the army establishment in Ireland. This action was a general affront in that Irish trade was excluded from enjoyment of imperial protection; in addition, Irish "undertakers" were accustomed to considerable voice in the management of affairs, and they saw their role being seriously undermined. Townshend was in fact determined to do just that. In his first session with the Irish parliament, the Octennial Act was passed, promising elections at least every eight years. This reduced the electoral control of old leaders somewhat, but the main change came when Townshend took up residence in Dublin, which had not been common practice. This made the Lord Lieutenant the key figure in Irish politics and it promised further alteration in the system.

In India, English interests had become paramount among Europeans, about the time that George III came to the throne. Here again, an ascendant overseas power became a factor in archipelago politics, in this case by way of the return of wealthy "nabobs" and by periodic requests from the company (from the late 60s) for government assistance. For as the company assumed a greater role in Indian politics, its practices and its policies were bound to be a greater concern for the home government, and when the company found its revenues inadequate, it could only resort to parliament for relief. Since its officials appeared to be looting the native princes and their own company, the demands for reform of the company's operations were hard to resist.

Thus the 1760s were a critical period in the development of empire. The original patchwork mercantilist structure was worn out, but no comprehensive replacement was installed. Instead, as problems arose, policies were fabricated without consistent principles. While London eagerly searched for more effective imperial government, colonists sought security through more autonomy. The expanding numbers of articulate subjects (lawyers, planters, agents) in the colonies gave the new communities a considerable advantage. They also inherited an ideology derived from 17th century authors like John Locke, which was useful in defending property from arbitrary rule.

The growth of imperial power was a mixed blessing. With the victory over France, there was genuine disagreement over how much more colonial territory was desirable. There were real questions about the limits of British governing capacity. Perhaps those limits were most easily seen in India, where native princes were set against warring Europeans. It was there that Robert Clive, toward the end of his great career wrote to a colleague in 1769:[6]

> Our wide and extended possessions are become too great for the mother country, or for our abilities, to manage. America is making great strides

---

[6]Cited in Angus Calder, *Revolutionary Empire* (1981), p. 698.

toward independency; so is Ireland. The East Indies also, I think, cannot remain long to us, if our present constitution be not altered.

Constitutional alteration was indeed the order of the day for all sectors of empire. This in spite of William Blackstone's popular *Commentaries* (published 1765-69) wherein the stability and balance of the system was extolled, and widely believed by later generations--of lawyers at any rate. Blackstone remains valuable as a source of the contemporary conventions which were being hardened into principles under the strain of imperial confrontation.

The man who inherited this situation was to be one of George III's most durable ministers--Frederick North, Lord North. He had succeeded Townshend as Chancellor of the Exchequer when the latter died in 1767. Then the king made North First Lord of the Treasury in Grafton's place in 1770. This was not a change of ministry, but of individual leaders. North was a competent, pleasant figure but without superior qualities or a clear policy toward the colonies.

In his first months, North gained the repeal of the Townshend duties, but kept the duty on tea as a token of parliament's power to enact such measures. But by March 1770 in an incident in Boston, a crowd was fired upon and five people were killed. The "Boston Massacre" was but one of a series of hostile acts which fuelled the propaganda efforts of Sam Adams and the "Sons of Liberty." Massachusetts was the most restive of the colonies, but its concerns were rapidly spread to the others. Colonial government in Massachusetts was virtually suspended due to a clash in which the popularly-controlled assembly and council were arrayed against the royal governor. Measures to restore the governor's power, to pay his salary and that of judges were seen as threatening by radical colonists. Most measures opposed by them were thwarted in the assembly or the town meetings--and the radical viewpoint was widely disseminated.

North was meanwhile dealing effectively with the Wilkes crisis and getting control of the Westminster politicians, when in 1773 he found himself overwhelmed by a prolonged and encompassing crisis in India. There had been serious famine in 1769-70 which may have cost 10 million lives. The company had continued its normal operations and increased its profits in spite of the conditions. Indeed, because its size was increasing and because a policy of increased remuneration had been introduced to prevent the traditional corruption of officials, the budget of the company had mushroomed. In 1772 there was a general financial crisis in most parts of the empire, and this caught the company in an exposed position. It requested loans from the government, committees were appointed to inquire into its finances, and North's government came up with a loan, and with a Regulating Act in 1773. A governor-general (Warren Hastings) was appointed, to have overall charge of affairs, official salaries were raised still further, and other reforms were made. At the same time, there was a large surplus of tea in the company warehouses, the sale of which would undoubtedly ease some of the strain. The government passed an act remitting duties on Indian tea and letting the company put its own retail agents in America. The reduced price would surely undercut the smuggled Dutch product; but the new measure was a threat to legitimate merchants as well. The "Sons of Liberty" went into action again, this time a group disguised as Indians boarded vessels in Boston and threw the first shipment of tea overboard. The British government decided to respond vigorously, not by regular course of law against accused persons, but by punitive statute against the entire community. The so-called "Intolerable Acts" closed the port of Boston and moved the custom house and seat of government to Salem; installed a nominated council and limited powers of the assembly and the town meeting; removed some capital trials and provided for quartering troops. Later parliament also attempted to settle the government of Canada in a separate legislative measure (Quebec Act). In the heat of the situation, this too was perceived as a dangerous measure: legislative powers were reduced, disabilities for Roman Catholics were removed and the frontier of Canada was determined--all of which were reasonable from the Canadian viewpoint and that of Westminster. All were apprehended as threatening to the southern colonies.

Parliament's action seemed to be an attempt to subjugate the colonies, and their response was to convene a "Continental Congress" which was a major act of rebellion (September 1774). There was discussion of Joseph Galloway's compromise federal plan at the congress, but more aggressive elements prevailed. Within months Lord North proposed self-taxation by the colonists as a way of skirting the central issue, but this offered few concessions to colonial interests. Also, the earl of Chatham and Edmund

Burke made proposals in parliament in 1775 for conciliation. The former retained too much imperial taxing power to be agreeable to the colonists; the latter had too little to be acceptable to parliament. Whether compromise might have been reached can never be known, for fighting erupted in April 1775. General Gage had sent troops to destroy the rebel supply center at Concord; the first clash was at Lexington, and after the troops completed their mission in Concord, they suffered heavy losses returning to Boston. The militia now besieged the former capital. While the Second Continental Congress was assembling, rebel forces seized the forts at Ticonderoga and Crown Point. A Continental Army was formed with George Washington as commander-in-chief. In 1776 the British evacuated Boston and shifted the main force to New York, while the colonists adopted a declaration of independence. The most serious British campaign was set for 1777, when General Burgoyne was to advance from Canada and join forces with General Howe from New York. But Burgoyne was beaten at Saratoga while Howe chose to take Philadelphia instead of advancing up the Hudson from New York. The victory at Saratoga was vital in American efforts to gain a French (and later Spanish) alliance, while the loss of Philadelphia failed to have major consequences. A commission from the British government in 1778 offered terms to the colonists which were rejected. The main British campaign shifted to the southern colonies and the West Indies (to counter the French naval threat). After limited success in the Carolinas and Georgia, the main army under Cornwallis was caught at Yorktown, cut off by the French fleet and a Franco-American army and forced to surrender in October 1781.

There was a profound political impact exerted by the American war: the archipelago felt this through direct war consequences and through reaction to the defeat. For the first, the cost in men, subsidies and supplies was significant; the direct effect of naval attacks (such as the marauding of John Paul Jones in 1778, or the related scare of Franco-Spanish invasion) was in the form of humiliation; most important, the diversion of troops and funds was directly responsible for the Volunteer Movement in Ireland. An Act was passed in 1778 authorizing an Irish militia, but there were insufficient funds to implement it. Instead, Protestant aristocrats and gentlemen formed companies of volunteers. They never entered battle, though some were used for policing; yet in the climate of the period, an armed group of 40,000 was

268

18TH CENTURY ARCHIPELAGO

Crieff

Callender

Ormiston

New Lanark

Belfast

Dungannon

Isle of Man

Liverpool   Manchester

Dublin

•Birmingham

Fishguard

Merthyr Tydfil

Bantry
Bay

Bristol   The Nore

Spithead

bound to be a political force. In fact, the volunteers met and debated current issues (free trade, catholic emancipation, parliamentary autonomy) and put pressure on the Irish Parliament. In that body, under the leadership of Henry Grattan, a talented barrister, the case was made for more Irish autonomy, and it was answered by a sympathetic English ministry at the end of the American war. Ireland was granted trade concessions, a habeas corpus act, and the repeal of Poynings' Law. Thus, by 1782 Ireland had attained a degree of legislative independence, though the colonial administration remained in place.

The loss of the American colonies brought a complex sense of anger and betrayal in Britain and America. Among the different elements, there were loyalists who suffered great losses, politicians who were looking for scape goats, plus a few reformers of more principled character. The trauma of the American revolt compounded ongoing political change at both the ministerial and the public level and the issues of patronage, franchise and selection of ministers were critical.

"Popular politics" was an incendiary idea in most circles in the late 18th century. Political decisions might be influenced by the mob but they were always made by the oligarchs. To suggest otherwise was to be exposed to charges of sedition. This accounted for the shock of Wilkes' efforts, which were but a prelude to more organized and dedicated agitations in the 1780s and later. America did not cause a new form of activity, or even give it legitimacy in most people's eyes, but it did provide valuable training, directly or vicariously. The archipelago was involved in the training process in varying degrees. London was the most active radical center, but North Yorkshire produced Christopher Wyvill's Association Movement, Dublin and Belfast had their "Volunteers," while Wales and Scotland remained relatively quiet. The advent of more organized agitation was a scattered process with few enduring successes: a series of disconnected campaigns with no major victory. The popular agitation was seriously crippled, and the conservative fear of mob violence fully vindicated, by an outburst of rioting in London in 1780. Some measures of Catholic relief had been passed in connection with army recruiting, and the Protestants formed associations to "defend" the church in England and Scotland. Lord George Gordon, a Scottish aristocrat and M.P., was a leading figure in presenting petitions to the House of

Commons against rising Catholic influence. When petitions were brought in during June, 1780, rioting broke out, and inept attempts to control it allowed the violence to run out of control for days. There were many Roman Catholic victims among the dead and the other major casualty was the death of any chance for a consensus on political reform.

In the next few years, public pressure continued through more organized channels. The Yorkshire Association was a group formed by Rev. Christopher Wyvill at a county meeting. It advocated reform of county representation in parliament and reduction of influence. The idea spread to other counties and a national committee was formed in London. Plans were made to hold a national convention and some counties formed committees of correspondence. With its essentially respectable gentry membership, this was a movement with real potential, but one which turned out to be far ahead of its time. The equally respectable Irish Volunteers held their conventions, in Dungannon in 1782 and in Dublin in 1783. They discussed ongoing constitutional changes and the prospect of major reform of Anglo-Irish relations. Splits developed over the political role of Roman Catholics, but in any event, the London government was intent on resuming full control of military forces in Ireland.

At this stage, Scottish political ambition seemed to have more limited aims. The Scots did have their organized reform groups. County reform was the subject of a convention in Edinburgh in 1782, and in 1784 about half the royal burghs were represented at a meeting on the reform of those ancient corporations. Part of the difference in Scottish activity may be attributed to the relatively tight control of patronage (in the hands of the Lord Advocate Henry Dundas after 1775). Part of the difference also came from the evident assimilating power of England (or rather London). The great social and economic distance which one might travel by moving 400 miles to the south was an irresistible temptation. It served as a form of political emasculation by compromising able Scottish leaders prior to the growth of serious democratic reform in the 19th century.

Entering the 1780's, the crises facing the ministers of George III were greater than ever. They were failing militarily in America and the West Indies, making major concessions in Ireland, fearing French and Spanish invasion, and lacking any diplomatic support in Europe. The invasion did not come, but otherwise there was little improvement in the next few years.

271

Ministers and their opponents were as always engaged in a duel to gain and hold power, but this period was one in which the grave circumstances forced some effort to define ministerial powers.

The focus of constitutional crisis in the 1780s was not in primitive bodies of associated gentry or isolated champions of franchise reform. Those were both premonitions, or perhaps in the case of the Association, a throwback to the communal ideal reflected in county meetings, assizes and quarter sessions. The principal zone of action was still around the king and his ministers. It had been widely asserted (by rebels, radicals and opposition politicians) that the crown's excessive influence was the root of failure in America (and of other evils no doubt). Portraying "Farmer George" as a despot was not easy, but it was possible to point to wicked ministers, and to the methods of their selection. There was no consensus on the correct relation of crown, ministers and commons, although there were many opinions. This uncertainty led to much of the inflamed response to defeat in America.

When Lord North was about to resign in 1782, he addressed the central question in a letter to the king:[7]

> ...the Prince on the Throne cannot, with prudence, oppose the deliberate resolution of the House of Commons. Your Royal Predecessors (particularly King William the Third and his late Majesty) were obliged to yield to it much against their wish in more instances than one; they consented to changes in their ministry which they disapproved because they found it necessary to sacrifice their private wishes, and even their opinions to the preservation of public order...

The issue of the 1780s was whether ministers would now be routinely chosen in accordance with the composition of the Commons, or whether they would continue to be the "king's friends" with the ability to use his patronage to manage his parliaments. George III made a valiant effort in this crisis to retain the royal advantage, and to some contemporaries it must have seemed that he had done so. In fact, what the king did was to exercise a veto on a ministry for the last time.

When North resigned in 1782, the new government was made up of Rockingham and his followers (Fox, Burke) and Lord Shelburne. They

---

[7]Sir John Fortescue, ed., *The Correspondence of George III* (1927-28), v. 5, p. 349.

agreed that peace and reform were paramount; they agreed on little else. Shelburne became head of the ministry when Rockingham died, and he concentrated on the completion of the peace treaty. In the meantime, parliament passed some important reforms: a Civil List Act and acts barring contractors and revenue officers from election to the House, which were seen at the time as major reductions in royal influence.

In 1783, a surprising coalition of Fox and North, once bitter enemies, defeated Shelburne in the Commons and forced his resignation. The new partners assumed office, but their alliance was widely distrusted. George III detested Fox and in particular he hated the demand that he accept a prearranged list of ministers and allow them the choice of their subordinates. This was anathema to George, and at his first opportunity he rid himself of the ministry; he did so, however, in a way which made it unlikely that it would be done again.

India was a source of continuing friction. North's Act had helped only a little, and allegations of scandal against Hastings made it easy to bring pressure for further reform. The Fox-North coalition designed a new government for the Company and its territories in India, but in their anxiety to control appointments they went too far, placing the names of new commissioners in the act, all of whom were loyal Foxites. George seized on the anger created by this and through an emissary he told the peers that anyone voting for the bill would be the king's enemy. The India Bill was beaten, George dismissed the ministers and he summoned the young William Pitt to form a ministry. From December 1783 to April 1784, Pitt governed without a majority in the Commons, and in the face of some stubborn opposition. Pitt won a major victory in the election of 1784 and remained in office for the rest of the century.

This episode might seem to be a vindication for George and the 18th century system. The correct reading is more complicated: Pitt was a spokesman of reform, not an advocate of unlimited royal power; Fox had abused momentary advantage and alienated his natural support by forming the coalition and presenting the flawed India Bill; the king had won only a respite, for Pitt set about acquiring discreetly all the control which Fox had reached for in haste. After building a parliamentary majority (using patronage and partisan issues) and making himself indispensible (the king's alternative was the hated Fox), Pitt established the ministerial control which became the hallmark of the modern prime minister. He dismantled some of the 18th century system, by attrition, by auditing and administrative reforms. He drew back from early franchise reform proposals, but continued to fortify the place of the minister as the leader of the parliamentary majority.

The crisis of the early 80s had made a public issue of the place and powers of the crown; this itself was significant. Parliamentary debates had only recently become publicized; essential political processes were starting to open up, an apparent prelude to further reform. But these efforts were to be swamped by more dramatic and dangerous events. The reform of the constitution was going to be a longer and more circuitous process as a result, and when it came it would be only a distant cousin of the reform of the 1780s.

18th Century Revolutions

The archipelago was a unique setting for a remarkable confluence of revolutions at the end of the 18th century. This powerful imperial state had vast resources around the globe and it had unusually free and open political discussion, sharply underlined by the American rebellion. In this setting, radical political and economic impulses were widely felt but readily channeled and controlled. But while the political outcome was in doubt, there were signs of fear among the ruling classes, fear which was itself partly responsible for the cautious, reforming consensus that began to emerge in the early years of the 19th century.

The revolution in France had a dramatic impact on the contemporary archipelago, and reactions there were significantly varied. The early, constitutional phase of the revolution was welcomed by many, but conservative opinion anticipated the regicide and republic. With those events came war with France, and the war created an anti-Jacobin majority in the archipelago. Frightened officials found more than enough subversives, and a series of treason trials and repressive laws were the result (1793-99). Attempted French assaults on the archipelago (1796-98) only produced localized military action, but that was enough to inspire the Act of Union (1800) which formally amalgamated the legislatures of Britain and Ireland. When the French enemy was transformed into the Napoleonic Empire, there was a reduced ideological pressure against reform. Well before Waterloo there were new signs of agitation, though these were shadowed by the spectre of democracy.

Concurrent industrial revolution touched many more lives in the archipelago more directly than the events in France. Industry was accelerated by war, and war was followed by contraction and chaos in the economy. Among the most important political consequences, the archipelago's political geography was altered by the development of resources and by population shifts linked to industrial growth, while social change was forced by the growth of the industrial classes -- owners and workers.

While it was hard for contemporaries to grasp, perhaps the most influential revolution was in population growth. Historians cannot explain why this began in the 1760s, though a set of plausible reasons can be given. The consequences, across the archipelago, were more plain. Growth was enough of a concern at the turn of the century to prompt the first formal census. Current economic thinking moved in the direction of a growth-oriented philosophy. The evident changes in the degree of urbanized and mobile social life put pressure on older forms of social control. Together the effects of population growth pointed to a need for new political measures.

The political upheaval which overthrew the French monarchy was the most dramatic event in the 18th century European politics. The onset of revolution was connected to the strains of imperial wars against Britain. Later the republic and the Napoleonic Empire both unsuccessfully made war on the British Empire. Moreover, the wars and political turmoil in France had significant impact on domestic politics in all parts of the archipelago. The fall of absolutism inspired rhetorical flourishes and fledging radical organizations, some including working class elements. The establishment read the radical literature and the reports of its spies with growing alarm, seeing in them a prospect of revolution which was probably never there. But with its massive repression in the 1790s, the British government may have insured the survival of reform incentive, and aided its tentative island-wide connections.

While some commercial gains were made in relation to Britain, France paid dearly for its support of American rebels. The *ancien regime* was manifestly arbitrary and unfair. Where English experience in America had forced commercial and financial reform in the 1780s, French ministers were unable to move against the dead weight of privilege and property. This became painfully obvious when an Assembly of Notables (1787) refused tax increases which were needed to rescue the crown from bankruptcy. The stalemate forced the radical move to summon an Estates-General for the first time since 1614.

The Estates met in May, 1789 and confusion over its composition and procedure resulted in the Third Estate taking the initiative and forming the National Assembly, in which it was soon joined by the clergy and the nobility. Shortly the first major violence erupted with the storming of the Bastille, after which radicals took control of Paris. Sympathetic outbursts in the provinces in July and August brought the surrender of feudal rights by the nobility, and later in August the Declaration of the Rights of Man was adopted. This statement drew on English and American precedent as well as the ideas of the 18th century philosophes. Radical action continued to force events, while a new constitution was being written (and re-written). In 1791 the King tried to flee but was captured; over the next year, France's neighbors, Austria and Prussia intervened and French radical leaders seized control, formed a national army and created a republic. The governing body was a National Convention (1792-95) which executed Louis XVI (January 1793) and declared war on Great Britain (Febuary 1793).

The events in France were a profound shock to archipelago politics. At first there was complacent approval, exemplified by the sermon of Richard Price, Welsh-born dissenting minister and philosopher, to the London Revolution Society. That body commemorated the revolution of 1688, and Price and others assumed that the French revolt was about to accomplish the same ends. The contrary reaction of conservatives was typified by Edmund Burke's *Reflections on the Revolution in France* which warned of bloodshed and chaos and military dictatorship. At first, Burke was answered by a number of liberal or radical apologists, including James Mackintosh (*Vindiciae Gallicae*, 1791) and Thomas Paine (*The Rights of Man*, 1791-2). Initially there was little new organization and mainly literary reactions. In 1791 two ominous incidents pointed to more serious developments. A mob in Birmingham rioted and burned the homes of dissenting leaders, including Joseph Priestley. In October, the Society of United Irishmen was founded, with a general goal of radical political reform.

More organizing took place in 1792. In January the London Corresponding Society was established, with Thomas Hardy, a shoemaker with a Scottish background as secretary. In Ireland, the moderate Catholic Committee was taken over by radicals and held a convention in Dublin which sent a petition to George III for Catholic emancipation. In April, Fox and others formed an elite organization, "The Friends of the People," which demonstrated the breadth of backing, if not the revolutionary spirit, in English society. A group of the same name, but of very much broader social composition, was formed in Edinburgh in July, and it called a convention for December. At that meeting, a young advocate from Glasgow, Thomas Muir, introduced a fiery message from the United Irishmen which offered grounds for his arrest in January 1793. While free on bail, Muir visited London and Paris, and returned *via* Ireland. His trial on charges of sedition was poorly conducted, as was Muir's own defense. He was given an unusually harsh sentence of 14 years' transportation and sent to Botany Bay.

The trials of Muir and others marked a watershed in the political reaction to the French revolution. In the year preceding, the shock of the bloodshed in France, the execution of the king and the declaration of war had firmly and effectively hardened the attitude against "Jacobins." In 1793 the government moved to suppress the London Corresponding Society, it authorized the formation of an Irish militia and it set the stage for a new series of treason trials in England.

The trials of Hardy and his associates were held in 1794. They were acquitted by London juries. However, there were more weapons in the government's arsenal: the habeas corpus act was suspended in 1794, a new Treasonable Practices Act and Seditious Meetings Act (1795) substantially broadened the legal definitions involved. In 1796 an Insurrection Act in Ireland was aimed at the United Irishmen (it made illegal oaths a capital offence and allowed the Lord Lieutenant to declare special powers in "disturbed districts.") In 1797, a Scottish militia was formed, aiming at securing better control, but in fact provoking serious rioting.

The level of high politics saw a concentration of support for ministers; Fox's Whig faction shrivelled and by 1797, seceded from the House of Commons in a futile gesture. There was thus general hostility and apprehension toward suspected "Jacobin" elements. It is true that the groups of the 1790s were more radical in their *language* than earlier reformers; their groups had generally broader social composition and they had unfortunate habits of advocating extreme political change such as universal suffrage, annual parliaments and democratic education. The government spies who reported on these groups were hardly worth their pay, since most "rebels" were intent on proclaiming their views to the public, and few of them seem to have had any plan for overthrowing the government, unless it was by inundation with speeches.

Indeed, when we consider the most dangerous episodes of the 1790s, there often were measures of repression beforehand. In 1792 there were proclamations against meetings before the famous Edinburgh convention which set the stage for Thomas Muir's trial and transportation. After the suspension of habeas corpus in England (and its rough equivalent in Scotland) in 1794, the authorities in Edinburgh discovered a cache of pikeheads and there were more treason trials and one execution. This so-called "Pike Plot" was greatly exaggerated in its extent, for at this time radical groups were already disintegrating.

The establishment of Irish and Scottish militias were both intended to replace army regulars in their function of riot control. The Acts had more to do with causing riots, especially in Scotland. In the Irish case, the causal factors were harder to separate. By 1795 the Orange Order had been organized to oppose the radicals, and it conducted a terror campaign against Ulster catholics while the authorities pursued radicals like Wolfe Tone. At this point Tone went into voluntary exile and eventually went to France and succeeded in gaining support for an Irish expedition. The scares of 1796-98 were real but insignificant. The arrival of a French force in Bantry Bay in December 1796 was but a fraction of the fleet which set out, and it failed to make a landing. In 1797 a small irregular unit landed near Fishguard in Wales with no serious effect. In 1798 there were several landings or attempts to land in Ireland, too late to affect the outcome of rebellion which broke out in the Spring.

Perhaps the most serious potential of all was in the naval mutinies of 1797. The fleets at Spithead and the Nore both were briefly under control of mutineers (May-June). In one case the government met the main demands regarding pay and conditions; in the other, where there was evidence of political motives, the ringleaders were summarily punished. Within months, the navy was in action and had defeated the French at Camperdown (October 1797) and the next year saw Nelson's major victory in the "Battle of the

Nile." In other words, it would be hard to prove that political agitation had reduced fleet effectiveness.

In general terms, the 1790s saw important political developments which may be somewhat obscured by the furor over Jacobins. In party terms, the events certainly solidified a strong Tory group and seriously reduced the Whig element, almost a reversal of the ascendancy of the early 18th century. In ideology, there were signs of "British" and "Irish" radicalism: there was some unity on the matter of republicanism, but the common ground between Richard Price, Thomas Hardy, Wolfe Tone and Major Cartwright was not very broad. Some migration of individual radicals and a few general principles did not compose a "movement." In constitutional terms, the 1790s led to the formation of the United Kingdom, which we will discuss in detail in the next chapter. Overall, it would seem fair to say that the actual political consequences of the decade were considerably less than the rhetoric of both sides promised.

The archipelago and its inhabitants meanwhile were beginning "the most fundamental transformation of human life in the history of the world."[8] The age of the industrial revolution witnessed extensive alteration in all facets of social life. As Thomas Ashton described it, "the face of England changed." With enclosed fields, new factories in new towns, and roads and canals linking them together, there was a visible change in the physical structure of the country. Ashton added that[9]

> Parallel changes took place in the structure of society. The number of people increased vastly, and the proportion of children and young people probably rose. The growth of new communities shifted the balance of population from the South and East to the North and Midlands; enterprising Scots headed a procession the end of which is not yet in sight; and a flood of unskilled, but vigorous, Irish poured in, not without effect on the health and ways of life of Englishmen.

Of course Ashton was describing the changing "face" (and economic body) of the archipelago, but as in so many other cases, the whole was rendered synonymous with "England." The truncated view produces some distortion. Here it is only possible to suggest the outlines of the collective experience, a subject which needs much more research.

---

[8]E.J. Hobsbawm, *Industry and Empire* (1968), p. 13.
[9]Thomas S. Ashton, *The Industrial Revolution* (1964) p. 3.

There were long-standing ties in agriculture, trade, investment and industry between the regions of the archipelago. Relations were erratic and certainly there was no planning for an archipelago economy, for so far as government influenced economic life it was traditionally concerned with the communities and interests which made up the separate nations. Agricultural change in the early 18th century helped to increase output in England and lowland Scotland. In the latter the changes were striking. Where production was poor at the end of the 17th century, Scottish agriculture was "transformed" fifty years later, a change more impressive when compared with the concurrent slow development in Ireland. The improving landlord was a ubiquitous figure. In fact he and his kind had begun to receive publicity from the likes of the itinerant reporter, Arthur Young.[10] The effect of his work was to tie journalism to the improving movement and multiply its impact. Similar work was done by Sir John Sinclair (*Statistical Account of Scotland*) and by the two together in connection with the Board of Agriculture. Naturally the results varied from one region to another. The most prosperous areas tended to profit more than those already 'backward.' Absentee landlords often found it easier not to force modernizing on unwilling tenants; in some cases, the modernization involved serious social disruption, from the early 'planned villages' to the notorious 'clearances' of the early 19th century in Scotland.

The archipelago became Europe's largest free-trade area as a result of the parliamentary unions of 1707 and 1801. This kind of economic unification was an important ingredient in industrial expansion, but the commerce of the Atlantic Archipelago involved connections of very long standing and considerable significance even before the 18th century. Of course some of the trading activity, such as that which made the Isle of Man a notable smugglers' haven, does not show in the historians' sketchy records. Elsewhere trade was a source of political hostility more than economic gain, e.g. the Darien episode. Still there was great and growing profit. Ireland exported provisions (livestock, dairy, grain) and textiles (wool and linen); Scotland likewise produced a surplus of commodities and was the major European importer of tobacco (until 1776); Wales exported coal and cattle;

---

[10]*Farmer's Letters to the People of England* (1767); *Political Arithmetic* (1774); *Tour of Ireland* (1780) *Annals of Agriculture* (1784-1809); *Travels in France* (1792)

England shipped a long list of colonial imports and manufactured goods, while profiting from her earnings as the shipper and broker for an expanding global trade emporium.

Investment in the archipelago was revolutionized by colonial trade. For some centuries there had been networks of landowning families. These were invaded by merchants from an early date, but at no time was there an intrusion as marked as in the 18th century. Planters, nabobs, shareholders and captains of trade returned large fortunes, which in one way or another were invested in the archipelago economy. An estimated £3 million from returning India merchants in the first half of the century rose to £15 million in the period 1751-1784.[11]

Figures such as these may never be more than wild guesses, but taking all probable returns on colonial activity together, there must have been sizeable amounts ready for investment in the archipelago. These injections plus others from domestic profits produced a growing financial community. The Scottish financier, William Paterson, was instrumental in organizing the Bank of England (1694) and the Bank of Scotland (1695). These institutions put capital at the disposal of a war-oriented government, which was happy to provide a reliable return on the investment. From this beginning, the banks went on to become central agencies for money and credit. Later the development of provincial banks helped to convert land and commercial capital into industrial investment, as well as offering currency and credit for the growing domestic markets of the industrial era. While Scottish banking was separately organized, the activity of the financial community did pool assets from different regions.

The earliest forms of industrial activity in the 18th century were localized: mining, shipbuilding, brewing and milling. Yet the marketing of coal or the regulation of trade brought political forces into play, within regions and between parts of the archipelago. Early intervention frequently came in the form of trade restriction, such as the ban on import of calicoes (1700) or export of Irish woollens (1699). In the opposite direction, the formation of the Irish Linen Board (1711) was supposed to promote the manufacture and sale of that product. These acts reflected the pressure of special interests, within a general framework of mercantile regulation.

---

[11]Calder, *Revolutionary Empire*, p. 700.

That regulatory framework was being widely ignored or evaded in the early 18th century. Such neglect accounts for the spirited reaction to George Grenville's policies. Economically, neglect meant that there was less control and less taxing of the economy, which helped (or did not thwart) accumulation and early industrial change.

One of the obvious early needs of the archipelago economy was improved overland transport. At first, there were isolated efforts at improvement such as General Wade's road-building in Scotland in the 1720s. Soon local groups were finding a more profitable solution, namely the formation of "turnpike trusts," which became a widespread practice from the middle of the century. The trust put up funds for construction, collected tolls from users and maintained a section of road, by authority of an act of Parliament. These helped to some extent to improve the facilities for carrying bulk goods (grain, minerals, construction materials). Such development had to precede the expansion of agricultural or other markets. The turnpike helped to reduce cost and increase efficiency, but at the same time the canal was being used to the same end. Here too corporate investors were needed, as was some amount of technical skill in construction. The coincidence of these transport "revolutions" was perhaps vital, creating a competitive environment. Road and canal builders were key figures of the early industrial era. One of the foremost was Thomas Telford, son of a Scottish shepherd who became the first president of the Institute of Civil Engineers (1818).

The basic power of the industrial age was produced by the conjunction of coal, iron and steam. The catalyst for expansion was cotton. In this pivotal context there were some important archipelago connections, mainly on an individual (not an aggregate) basis. For example, John Wilkinson was a pioneer ironmaster with works in the Midlands and Wales. His father was a Cumbrian ironworker who leased an establishment at Bersham, where John was his manager. They prospered with large wartime munitions orders in the 50s and 60s (including customers such as France, Turkey and Russia). By the 1770s Wilkinson had a patented cannon-boring process which brought him the attention of an important machine firm.

James Watt was a Scottish instrument-maker who became the foremost machinery designer of his day. He made a series of startling improvements for the old Newcomen steam engine, in use since the beginning of the

282

century. With a condenser, rotary motion and a governor, the new engines were efficient and had many new applications. Watt went into partnership with an English manufacturer, Matthew Boulton. The firm used Wilkinson's method to bore cylinders for their engines, and from about 1775, their production grew. Refinements in design permitted the application of steam power to more and more operations, and Boulton and Watt produced some 500 engines by the end of the century.

The most important application of steam power was in cotton textiles. In part, the reason was timing. Cotton manufacture had been retarded, due to the interference of woollen and linen interests. By the second half of the century there was a growing demand for cheap textiles, old regulations were not working and so cotton manufacture was comparatively free of restriction. The centers of production were at first located by the availability of water-power and moist climate. From Lancashire to Glasgow to Belfast there was a growing circle of activity. In the third quarter of the century, a set of technological developments occurred which revolutionized spinning; at the turn of the century, the weaving process began to feel the mechanizing impact. By the 1830s the industry as a whole was run by steam, and the output over the previous half-century had grown incredibly. All areas partook of the early stages of this transformation; Ireland was the first to be eliminated, Scotland followed by 1850.

An interesting case of "British" industrial development came in 1784 when Richard Arkwright, a pioneer of the water frame, teamed up with David Dale to build a factory at New Lanark, accompanied by its own village and facilities. The mill employed hundreds of women and children, and it was widely-known even before its new manager, the Welsh-born Robert Owen, came in 1800. While it was not typical, New Lanark was one of a number of Scottish mills which made up a good-sized sector of the new industry, but which were remotely located because of the old need for water-power. Their situations would soon become a liability.

Irish manufacture of cotton grew slowly until the 1770s, and while it might have looked for help from Grattan's Parliament in the next decade, it found instead a set of obstacles from British manufacturers. Their opposition to Pitt's "Commercial Propositions" of 1785 was moved in part by fear of free trade in cotton and other goods (and the assumed Irish advantage of low labor costs). With access to British markets blocked, there was retarded development in Ireland, and even when an opening came after 1800 with the union, the fledgling Irish cotton industry could not survive the financial crisis of the 1820s.

Only the first stage of industrial growth was complete by 1800; many indicators were advancing but others barely showed any change. And at the end of the century, the small body of data available was distorted in many places by the war. From the first spinning mill (1771) to the power loom (1787) and weaving mill (1806) the mechanized process was perceived as the origin of a "factory system." Although such a term is a misnomer before the later 19th century, there were major examples of a new order in the workplace. The arrival of the factory was readily interpreted by the worker as a more demanding and more profitable mode of employment. The location of these centers of new industry would clearly affect archipelago economic development. Historians generally assume that only England and the lowlands of Scotland (plus Monmouthshire, somewhere between England and Wales) were instrumental in the industrial revolution. Even in that restricted view, we need more than an English assessment. But industry did reach more widely still; resources were used from large areas, labor was taken from the whole of the archipelago as was capital, and so the phenomenon ought to be studied further in this context.

Sustained population increase in the archipelago began some time after 1760. This phenomenon was not entirely clear to contemporaries until the turn of the century, until uncertainty was resolved with the initiation of a formal census in 1801 (1821 in Ireland). Allied to the general increase in population were migrations and concentrations which triggered important social changes. Higher birth rates and lower death rates combined to bring growth. Change in diet and age of marriage produced the first, better medical and environmental conditions the second. There has been a great deal of speculation about these changes, but there will never be any certainty because there were few contemporary records that shed light on population. Indeed, observers in 1800 did not know what the population was; estimates had been attempted for more than a century, but it was only now becoming acceptable to have a true statistical measure, and it was arguably premature for such a process in terms of methodology. But reports like those in John Sinclair's *Statistical Account* whetted the appetite for information. In 1801 the first Census was commissioned by Act of Parliament. In English and Welsh parishes the overseers of the poor were to return figures; in Scotland it was the task of schoolteachers. All were also required to return figures for earlier years, based on parish records. Much of the latter was erratic as the keeping of parish registers was an old but often neglected function. Only when civil registration of births, deaths and marriages was begun in England and Wales (1837), Scotland (1855) and Ireland (1864) could there begin to be real confidence in the collection of population data.

Dramatic population growth after 1760 was one reason for the growth of towns and the increase in emigration. The two movements together indicate growing mobility and their impact was of considerable social importance. Before 1700 only the exceptional city had more than 3,000 people. By 1800, changes were striking. Birmingham had doubled between 1760 and 1800; Manchester tripled in size in the last three decades of the century; Merthyr "a small hamlet in 1760" reached 7,700 in the first census; Glasgow with an estimated 27,000 in 1755 grew to three times that size by 1800.

Emigration was increasing, in and from the archipelago. Here the data are more elusive; tramping laborers were joined by the factory hands and occasionally by surges of military and colonial emigration. What was clear was the sudden increase in Irish population in Glasgow, Liverpool and Manchester; the continuing drift of Scots to Ulster, the movement of English workers to South Wales, and the large emigration from the Highlands. No simple explanation can cover these; together they constitute an object for further study.

The emerging industrial society soon was reflected in political relationships and events. Some indication of the impact was in social legislation and the increased involvement of "manufacturers" (employers and workers) in politics. Deeper and wider effects showed in the transition from the old paternal social order to the new alignment of social classes and in the manner in which the young industrial society (with its commercial parent) manufactured an impressive economic performance to finance the military victory over Napoleon.

Industrial growth helped to force social legislation into new channels, through the pressure of interested parties or by weakening old social controls. Broadly speaking, there were some innovative measures to regulate the conditions of employment and to deal with the consequences of unemployment. Landowning M.P.'s and magistrates (in Harold Perkin's words)[12]

> had sold their souls to economic development long before the industrial revolution and as the most important precondition of it. When it came they were more than ready to accept its logic, the freedom of industrial employment from state regulation...

Such "freedom" might assume different shapes in different circumstances. The demand for coal, especially in the 1790s, made Scottish mineowners anxious to resolve a labor shortage, so anxious that they gave up the system of servile mine labour, first dealt with by statute in 1774. In 1799 the system was abolished, but alas there was no flood of new workers to the mines. English employers were also freeing workmen from old acts of wage regulation, yet the workers failed to appreciate this gesture. Yorkshire weavers petitioned for enforcement of the old laws, as did many other crafts and trades. Parliament responded by suspending and then repealing the old acts on apprentices and wages (1803-09).

In apparent contradiction to the "laissez faire" approach, some manufacturers supported the "Health and Morals of Apprentices Act" of 1802, which made regulations for cotton and woollen mills and factories in Great Britain and Ireland. Clothing, working hours, education and amenities for the parish apprentice employed in the mills were the chief objects of the Act. Since these unfortunate individuals were usually sent from large cities to some of the more remote and less advanced factories, whose low labor cost was a source of great annoyance to other producers, we can see something more than altruism at work here.

Adult workers were surely not being given such tender treatment by legislators. In 1799 and 1800 the "Combination Acts" codified existing limits on efforts to "combine in restraint of trade," as the common law phrase had it. There had been earlier laws in specific trades, and this generalized the practice, setting jail terms for violators. These laws (repealed in 1824-25) mainly served to drive workers into more secretive associations and certainly did not stop (though they may have slowed down) the growth of trade unions.

---

[12]Harold Perkin, *The Origins of Modern English Society, 1780-1880* (1969),p. 187.

While employers feared some associations, they encouraged others with less political potential. The "Friendly Society" was a form of mutual benevolent association, encouraged--and registered--by the government from 1793. The groups did obtain legal recognition under the act of that year, and in the first decade some 10,000 were formed, claiming a membership of 700,000. Plainly one of the motives for the societies was reduction of the burden of poor relief, but it is doubtful that that goal was ever in sight. Meanwhile the societies did offer a lawful form of worker organization. Provision for the victims of poverty was one of the archipelago's inconsistent features. In Ireland there was heavy reliance on charity before the 18th century. In Scotland the poor were aided primarily by church-administered relief, with some tax support (mainly localized) and with some forced employment for able-bodied poor. In England and Wales the Elizabethan poor law provided a parochial "system" of rate-aided relief funds, administered locally, alongside occasional private charity and church alms. Able-bodied poor might find work in a workhouse or be farmed out. But in large cities, or in times of distress, that option was foreclosed. Thus in 1795, with harvest failure and general distress, in some southern English counties, a system of 'outdoor relief' or wage-subsidy was adopted. The idea was highly controversial, for it was a compromise between regulated wages and abandonment of paternalism. In the short run it was humane; but within a few years, sharp rises in the cost of aiding the poor fuelled a movement to abolish the rates entirely. That was only prevented by a measure of uncharitable reform in 1834, one which had side-effects in Scotland and Ireland.

The industrial revolution was the solvent which eroded the old social order. That set of ranks, in a well-defined but reasonably porous hierarchy, depended for its stability upon general consent (deference) toward arbitrary but hardly despotic oligarchs. As the latter were joined by or deserted to the ranks of industrial entrepreneurs, the old system shifted toward a society of classes. In that shifting, and in the new framework, there was more latent hostility and more explosive economic rivalry.

As the social order reflected new impulses, we might expect to see representatives of industry taking a greater role in political life. Landowners would not welcome this, although they or their relatives might belong to the new group. But just as the princes of commerce and the planter and nabob had made their way, now the manufacturer was following the well- marked trail. His numbers would be very small until the mid-point of the next century, but men such as Robert Peel, Robert Owen, Josiah Wedgwood and others were anxious to take a public role, although some of them were too sanguine of their ability to deal with social and political matters as effectively as they built factories or produced goods.

Workers' activity in politics in the late 18th century was another matter. Here was evidence of a profound change. There had been intermittent popular violence and scattered efforts of a more articulate kind since the late middle ages. Now political organization was being attempted among workers. It is significant that scholars speak of the "origins" of the working *class* between 1780-1830. What is meant is of course the appearance of self-conscious, politically-active workers. Their early numbers were tiny, as was their immediate impact. Perhaps their very weakness encouraged some communication and cooperation between the areas of the archipelago. Most of those active in worker politics were skilled artisans, a so-called 'labour aristocracy.' All their organizing efforts were ipso facto "political," because of ordinary political views and because of the sensitive condition of the years after 1789. It was equally natural that acts against sedition or illegal oaths tended to stimulate opposition and more effective (secret) organization. The worker was excluded from political life in the narrow sense. The old tradition of public violence overlapped the new mode of secret organization. Machine-breaking "Luddites" were not far removed from the "Hearts of Oak." The last English agrarian uprising (Captain "Swing") was in 1830, the first industrial violence was that of the Glasgow spinners in 1812. The spokesmen for workers' grievances likewise came from different worlds. William Cobbett (1762-1835) was a garrulous champion of a lost paternal society. He wrote in his autobiography:[13]

> The truth is, that the system which has been pursued in England, from the time of the Revolution, the system of government debt, is a system which begins by totally debasing the labouring classes, and that ends by producing its own overthrow, and, generally, that of the state along with it. It draws property into great masses; it gives to cunning the superiority over industry; it makes agriculture a subject of adventure; it puts down all small

---

[13]*The Autobiography of William Cobbett: The Progress of a Plough-boy to a Seat in Parliament*, ed. William Reitzel (1947), p. 16.

cultivators; it encloses every inch of that land which God himself seems to have intended for the poor.

From a totally different perspective, the Scottish Professor of Classics, William Ogilvie, who had experimented with agricultural improvements, and who was a supporter of 18th century revolutions, wrote in 1781, "whoever enjoys any revenue, not proportioned to industry or exertion of his own, or of his ancestors, is a freebooter who has found means to cheat and rob the public."[14] Ogilvie carried some traces of 17th century radical ideas but the explicit labor theory of value was to be the engine of powerful future protest when taken up by large numbers of workers, willing and able to press for political recognition.

The effect of industry was also visible in the external face of politics. Mechanical power and the financial capacity of the archipelago were greatly enhanced in the space of one generation (1790-1815). Warfare with France was a familiar situation, and the commercial-colonial strategy was a familiar strategy. However, the monumental scale and the ideological environment were critical new features, both of which were fortified by industrial society.

The French wars brought a major extension and affirmation of the "second empire." Trade figures multiplied, as did revenues of customs and new income and property taxes. Public debt was astronomical by old standards (increasing 2 1/2 times during the wars). The United Kingdom took ports in the Indies, West Indian islands, the Cape of Good Hope, and Mediterranean and African islands and outposts. Her naval supremacy was now unchallengeable and would remain so for the rest of the 19th century. The British strategy had been to subsidize continental allies while maintaining her maritime and commercial security. Napoleon gave the British government a serious setback by instituting the "Continental System," an embargo on all British imports to Europe's markets. But it could not be fully enforced. The British decision to occupy Lisbon and move against the French in Spain (1809), seen as a shift in strategy, should also be seen as a pre-emptive strike aimed at preventing the loss of Spanish and colonial markets to France.

In the Atlantic Archipelago, there were major political consequences from French republicanism and French military advances. The former inspired the first serious subversive activity (the United Irishmen in

---

[14]*Essay on right of Property in Land,* cited in Perkin, *Origins,* p. 233.

particular), the latter spread tension throughout all classes, in meeting the cost of war (debt, taxes, suspending gold payments). The continued growth of trade and industry and the confidence of investors were vital in keeping the economy strong during its long trial, and these elements persisted.

If the government of the United Kingdom was successful in war, many of its subjects were not. Serious harvest failures, industrial crises and outbursts of radical violence were too common. Under wartime conditions they called forth more repression than might otherwise have been applied. That in turn produced an anti-establishment feeling which lasted long after fighting had stopped.

The revolutions of the 18th century brought a new age of British politics. There was repression and reform. The power of repression was sometimes reckless, uneven and transitory. Thus the ideals of scattered and ineffective reformers endured. The politics of the Atlantic Archipelago began to form a pattern which lasted into the 20th century: the constitutional union, two major political parties and a periodic confrontation with reform. These were ingredients in the "United Kingdom" which grew out of the 18th century revolutions. That kingdom was at the center of a newly-strengthened, growing commercial empire, which drew power from the world's first industrial state whose policy was already moving toward "free trade." In its structure, the empire would not be stronger than its predecessor, and soon there would be signs of devolution within it.

The archipelago and the empire achieved a prosperous position at the start of the 19th century, but the residue of revolutions could not be erased. The empire was to be an asset in keeping the island union from instability (through emigration and trade) and providing a symbol of higher political loyalty. However, the task of uniting the British Isles politically was not addressed in a timely manner, partly because of the illusion of imperial greatness.

CHAPTER 8

UNION AND EMPIRE

> ...as applied and administered in the succeeding century, [the Act of Union] had manifestly failed to create a 'nation' corresponding to the whole British Isles capable of cementing the allegiance of either Catholics or Protestants with the emotional adhesive of nationality.
>
> (D. W. Miller, *Queen's Rebels*, 1978, p. 10)

The Atlantic Archipelago was formally united for one hundred and twenty years after 1801. Political historians have not been interested in the story of this entity, except for the event of its creation and the saga of its disruption by Irish Home Rule. This neglect is understandable because there was a de facto political union long before 1801; there was very little in the way of union politics aside from Irish opposition; and the larger political questions of the 19th century have been conventionally treated within an English or an imperial framework. Nevertheless, there was a political life in the United Kingdom which merits historical reconstruction.

The problem of governing the United Kingdom was shaped by the nature of the original act and by the severe distractions of war and economic pressure in the first years of its existence, which together produced an Anglocentric imperial league of cultural provinces with a common legislature and a confused administrative structure.

Once established, the governance of the union was complicated by the growth of reform, especially from the 1830s. The net contribution of this widespread phenomenon to the union was negative. The main arguments for reform came from evangelical religion, enlightened social thought and egalitarian political ideas. However, the typical reform scenario owed more to constellations of interests than to "democracy" or "laissez faire" or "vital religion." Both the interests and the ideas gave little room to the union and in some cases it was an embarrassment when reform in one area led to anomaly in another.

The chief area of discussion of the union evoked strong feelings. Irish semi-colonial status blocked the resolution of serious questions of religious

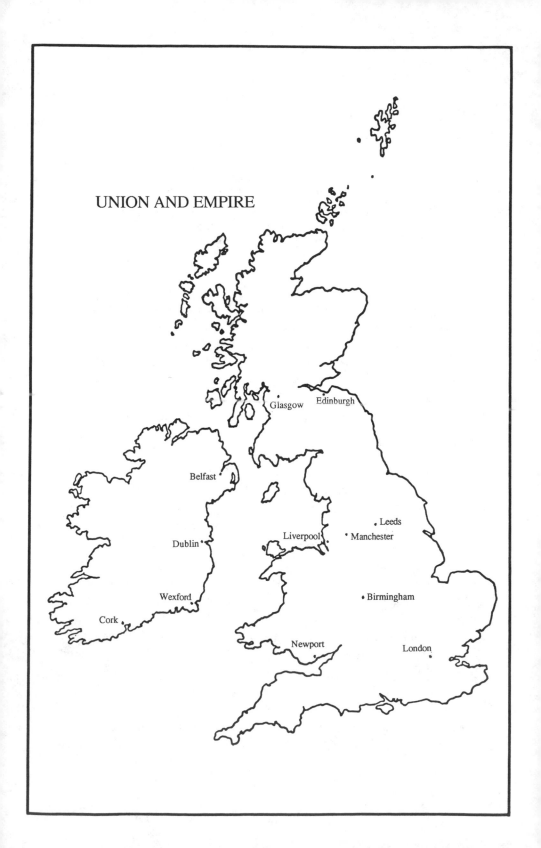

UNION AND EMPIRE

toleration, landholding and public order; the treatment of those issues was entangled with fundamental questioning of the constitutional order of 1801, and in turn that questioning provoked the formed argument for "unionism" and the exposition of "Home Rule" sentiments in Scotland and Wales.

A United Kingdom ought to have been a vital center for the growing Empire. But as in the 18th century, the empire seemed to grow of its own accord. Central rule was out of favor for two or three generations, while cheap government and free trade were popular objectives. After the 1860s, imperial policy became more aggressive in the face of competing European powers, and the later years of the century saw intensive efforts to justify the global enterprise, by analogy to Greece and Rome, by invention of a "Greater Britain," and by assorted schemes of imperial federation. This array of plans and parallels suggested that the empire's constitution was as loose and untidy as that of the archipelago. In neither had the development of constitutional forms received serious attention before the second half of the 19th century.

Uniting the Kingdom

The United Kingdom of Great Britain and Ireland was the product of a wartime emergency and civil disorder in Ireland in 1798-99. The formation of the union did little to address the problems which inspired it; the war which was its occasion and the economic stress which was the major concurrent problem in the archipelago, combined to prevent a fuller campaign to resolve the constitutional problem. The resulting amalgam in the British Isles was an awkward polity with a common sovereign and common legislature, but otherwise diversified institutions and disjointed political life. Legislative action continued to be primarily regional in scope. There were broadly similar party outlines in the several areas. Alignments tended to be formed in England and reflected throughout the archipelago, but every region and community had some impact through local issues on personnel and policies. Patronage ties also crossed the internal frontiers, and while economical reform reduced old sinecures, the expanding peerage and growing functions of government provided new tools of influence.

Irish politics in the crisis before union had taken alarming shape. The formation of United Irishmen into groups of reform agitators in Belfast and Dublin from 1791 and the creation of the Protestant and conservative Orange

Order from 1795 were portents of conflict. The threat of French military intervention also entered the picture and was countered by British political and military moves. The establishment of a Protestant yeomanry and paid militia forces, plus suspension of habeas corpus and the toleration of a vigilante campaign by the Orange Order created a crisis situation. The main confrontation came in 1798. Plans had been laid for concurrent uprisings of the United Irishmen, but the plot was exposed, the Dublin leaders were apprehended and rebels came out only in Wexford, Down and Antrim. The uprising was defeated by the government forces within about six weeks. Then a small French force landed in Connaught in August, but it was surrounded and forced to surrender. Later in the year, another invading force was intercepted and beaten. The net effect of these episodes was to aggravate insecurity in the minds of the Anglo-Irish and their superiors in London.

An act of union was introduced in the Irish parliament in 1799, but it was beaten by Irish 'patriots' who were Protestant and loyal to the crown, but were afraid of losing their position as minority rulers. Pitt's original plan had been to combine Catholic Empancipation with the union, so as to bind a large loyal Irish Catholic element to the government. Even with this feature removed, the Irish ruling class wanted to be duly compensated for its compliance. Much of 1799 was spent in negotiation. The Chief Secretary, Robert Stewart, viscount Castlereagh, finally produced a majority, helped a good deal by compensation. Each seat in the Irish parliament not moved to Westminster was worth £15,000. The total public expense was over £1 million. The Irish parliament voted itself out of existence on 6 February 1800 and the new United Kingdom parliament was formed on 1 January 1801.

For the new House of Commons, 100 Irish members were to be added (2 per county, 2 for Dublin and for Cork, 1 each for 31 other towns, plus 1 for the University of Dublin). The House of Lords received 4 spiritual peers and 28 temporal peers, elected for life.

The union joined the established churches into "The United Church of England and Ireland" as "an essential and fundamental part of the union." A free trade area including Britain and Ireland was projected with gradual removal of protection for Irish products. The finances of the two countries were not joined at once, but a plan was included whereby Irish obligations on the debt of the U.K. were calculated, and a provision for the later union of the two exchequers was agreed. The final article said that laws in force and courts in operation would not be affected, except that cases pending in the Irish House of Lords were to be transferred to the House of Lords in Westminster.

The war which was Pitt's pretext for union continued to threaten the security of the U.K. until 1815. There was a brief peace in 1802-3 and then a return to coalitions and commercial warfare. Renewed invasion fears were put to rest only with the great naval victory at Trafalgar in 1805, though evidently the relative naval strength of the two powers was decidedly in favor of Britain throughout. For the final phase, war was fought on two "fronts". The first was the struggle against Napoleon's "Continental System", which imposed a European embargo on English goods. The second was the action by British forces and their allies in the Iberian Peninsula (1809-1813). Victory came after Napoleon's retreat from Russia and his defeats by the allied forces in 1814 and again in 1815 at Waterloo.

In fighting this war the English crown called upon all its reserves, colonial and domestic. Fighting men, material and finance were all drawn from the corners of the archipelago and empire. The phrase on William Pitt's memorial said that "he rallied the loyal, the sober-minded and the good around the venerable structure of the English monarchy." The choice of words was apt, for Pitt and the cause were identified with England, not with the archipelago, though the fortunes of both were bound together.

Fighting did not erase the basic problems of governing the union, in fact it may have exacerbated some of them. The "Peace Preservation Force," (flying squads of police and soldiers and judges) was created for Ireland in 1814 to restore order in "disturbed districts." The outbreaks of agrarian crime and industrial violence which disfigured the last ten years of war were one measure of the deep problems which union government inherited, and there was no early evidence that union offered any new solutions.

Domestic disorder grew out of economic problems which bore the contemporary label "distress." Some of the economic difficulty was war-related, but probably none was originally caused by the war. Finance, trade and employment were all affected, though the problems and solutions in different parts of the archipelago were not the same. The general malaise was all too familiar: traditional harvest-cycles were overlaid by business cycles which were in turn aggravated by wartime expenditure, taxes and debt. Therefore very sharp swings in employment, prices and investment might occur unevenly across the archipelago and across occupational and class categories. For most of the years of actual fighting, the demand for supplies and weapons sustained economic activity. But events such as the imposition of Napoleon's Continental system and the response of British Orders in Council seriously disrupted British trade. Poor harvests brought extremely high prices and threatened to produce the type of economic chaos which the French had sought. The basic wealth of the U.K. was however enough to tide it over the crisis. Inflation was serious, and some prices reached 19th century highs between 1811 and 1814. The cost of the war was met in part by the radical innovation of an income tax, imposed in 1799 and abolished in 1816. In its later years of operation, the income tax came to supply a third of tax revenue. Customs and excise produced more, and more regressive collections. Even so, by 1815 half of government expenditure went to pay the interest on the national debt.

The political consequences of these economic conditions were severe. Essentially the war pitted several interests quite openly against one another: financier vs. wage earner, agriculturalist vs. manufacturer, merchant vs. rentier. In addition, the war meant further distortions as between economic regions. For example, the agricultural sector generally prospered, in that high food prices and resulting high rents were a common feature of the war years. Expansion of acreage to marginal lands with poor yields was encouraged by the same conditions. In Lowland Scotland and Southern England these trends were not excessively risky. In Ireland and the poorer farming districts in Britain this over-extension was critical. Coupled with rapid population growth, there was real danger of a Malthusian crisis even as Parson Malthus composed his *Essay on Population*. In some areas, landlords took vigorous steps to manage the local economies: the most widely-known instances were the "Highland Clearances" which began during the war years. Overpopulation in some areas coincided with economic gains to be made from high-priced livestock or war-inflated alkali (from kelp). The combination of factors encouraged emigration or relocation of tenants, much of which was undertaken in brutal or insensitive fashion.

In industrial sectors there were also serious distortions and discontents. The new industrial cities continued to grow during the war years, with the predictable stresses of urban expansion. In addition, the economic fluctuations of the war often produced sharp swings in unemployment, and they served to highlight the inadequate condition of the poor law. There were inquiries into distress, there was serious criticism of the old poor law (aiming at its abolition or fundamental revision). Beyond these general or common problems, there were specific cases of technological unemployment. The handloom weavers constituted the most extreme case; their condition was influenced at first favorably, and then unfavorably, by the war. The slow rate of mechanization in weaving was due partly to investment decline in the war. But that mechanization came inexorably and it cost the weaver dearly in falling prices and vanishing employment. The weavers had been able to enjoy the high demand for work but later "paid" for the previous advantage. Inquiry into their plight could only underline their essentially powerless position. The Glasgow weavers in 1812 obtained a court ruling that J.P.s should set adequate wage levels, but the justices were able to block this tactic, forcing a large and utterly unsuccessful weavers' strike in 1812-13.

There were no "UK" solutions for these economic problems, in fact there were hardly any solutions since the ordinarily passive government was being encouraged by the classical economist to leave economic life "free." Still, there were some ways in which the union had an economic face, if not an economic policy. This free trade area could usually succeed in feeding itself in spite of rapid population growth; the connected industrial plant could produce Europe's best cannons and other weapons and it could sustain a growing fleet of naval and merchant vessels. Finally, its infrastructure had developed enough financial strength to equip it for the strains of war.

In its political experience in the years 1815-1830, the United Kingdom had to work out the political and constitutional ramifications of earlier British and English traditions, but it also faced new challenges. The union brought dissimilar communities into an enlarged legislative body. How was that body organized and how did it govern the newly-unified entity? The enlarged House of Commons nominally represented the whole archipelago. None of the countries enjoyed anything like proportional representation or consistently large electorates; the ratio of M.P.s to total population was decisively in England's favor in 1801:

England	1: 17,597
Wales	1: 22,692
Scotland	1: 35,555
Ireland	1: 52,000

England had the lowest ratio of "rotten boroughs", i.e. those districts where elections were under the control of a proprietor. Also, there were more open county constituencies in England; finally, England had, with about 54% of all voters, nearly 75% of the seats in the House.

The new House of Commons made little or no change in procedure. The party situation in 1800 gave an overwhelming majority to the ministers. Although the Whigs had seceded from the Commons in 1797, there was still some semblance of party identification, and each party had its affiliates in the Irish parliament and was also visible in constituencies in Wales and Scotland. Non-English members were sometimes led by an agent--Henry Dundas of Scotland was the worst example of such a henchman, leading about 40 of the 45 Scottish M.P.s and all 16 of the peers. Otherwise, there were few signs of corporate life in the non-English groups; parliamentary committees were as yet not systematized and not available as a vehicle for regional issues. Of course individual members and regional groups usually were granted a certain amount of attention when legislation directly affected their districts. It never became common practice to legislate for the U.K. as a whole, except for subjects of "imperial" scope such as foreign and military affairs, colonies and public accounts. National legislation was the norm for Scotland, Ireland and England.[1] Needless to say, the majority of voting members on all measures was apt to be English.

In the House of Lords there were now five types of peers: English, Scottish, Irish, British and U.K. titles were included, with the Scots and Irish being "representative" peers. Scottish and Irish peers who were not elected to the House of Lords were eligible for election to the House of Commons. The enlargement of the House of Lords had in fact begun before the Act of Union. Peerage creations had always been an important means of bestowing honor and recognition and the new creations represented more varied social backgrounds by the late 18th century. No doubt the rising numbers had some connection to the decline in the number of "places" available to ministers (these had fallen by 1820 to about one-third of the level of 1780). According to one recent study, the years 1780-1830 saw 23 Scottish and 59 Irish creations as peers of Great Britain or the United

---

[1]"England" usually included Wales; an Act of 1747 stated that whenever "England hath been or shall be mentioned in any Act of Parliament, the same shall be deemed to comprehend the Dominion of Wales." (21 George II c. 10).

Kingdom.[2] To some degree these creations made the House of Lords a better reflection of the power structure in the U.K. The aristocracy historically had some amount of common education, social life and economic interest. However, the descendants of clan chiefs and Tudor houses were now mingling with princes of commerce. It was not clear how much the union would increase the integration of aristocratic interests, or how much the aristocracy would serve to advance the united government of the archipelago.

In 1801 the Lords were far from the end of their political role: it is often noted that the reform ministry of Earl Grey in 1830 had more peers than any other 19th century government. The influence and the active part of noblemen was still quite significant. One mode in which the role was potentially important for the archipelago was the House of Lords' place as a final court of appeal. The Act of Union gave formal authority over Irish appeals; the Act of 1707 had not been definite, but in practice, Scottish appeals were heard, even though the Lord Chancellor of England, who presided in the House, often had no legal training in the Scottish system. This anomaly underlined a broader problem in the constitutional structure, namely that the Lords in general were not competent to sit as judges in matters of law. In fact, they soon surrendered this power to their legal brethren. In 1844 a case involving the Irish barrister Daniel O'Connell served to affirm the convention. One of the Lords, not a lawyer, voted on the verdict, and his vote was pointedly not counted. In a later reform, the formal position of "law lord" was recognized and the anomaly was removed (1873).

The appellate role of the House of Lords could have been a unifying feature at one level of government, but the cases were few and random, and the position of the peers was awkward. The spiritual peers added yet another odd dimension. There were of course bishops and archbishops from dioceses in England, Wales and Ireland. Notorious as state servants at some periods, the prelates might also be outspoken evangelical reformers. In any case, the position of the legislating clergyman remained prominent, even in the more secularized air of the 19th century.

In the administrative corridors of government, 1801 was an insignificant date. The union was not reflected in a single immediate or drastic official renovation. There would be changes, some soon and a few of substance, but

[2]M.W. McCahill, "Peerage Creations and the Changing Character of the British Nobility 1750-1830" *English Historical Review* 96 (April 1981): 259-84.

initially there was business as usual. When alterations came, they were most often connected to the rising tide of new functions and new officials--the product of administrative reform in the 1830s. In the new offices, and in some private organizations, there was some evidence of a desire to form comprehensive bodies for the whole of the archipelago, but these were exceptions.

The Act of Union left the existing administrative machinery in Dublin Castle. That was no accident, and it undermined the nominal goal of incorporation. Certainly colonial control was not meant to lapse. Particular offices of Irish government did change over the next generation, the general concept did not. Three areas of Irish government showed the most early amalgamation: the church, the army and the exchequer were joined to their English counterparts in the early 19th century. These compounds were supposed to strengthen the Irish Protestant elite. The mergers were not designed to test or perfect multinational offices, with any sort of plan for future development of federal jurisdictions. In general, each exercise displayed the same English assertion of superiority which underlay the whole ethos of government in the imperial archipelago.

With novel enterprises, on the other hand, there were some opportunities for administration of wider scope. The early 19th century saw such attempts with the work on agricultural problems, public records and mapping of the British Isles.

A widespread interest in agricultural improvement had been evident for over a century, but it was addressed in private fashion, through local, regional and national groups. This movement did result in the formation of the "Board of Agriculture and Internal Improvement"--which was not a public body. The Board produced a series of county reports detailing the topography, resources and problems of individual areas. The remarkable Sir John Sinclair was president of the Board. He had produced the *Statistical Account of Scotland* , a compilation of returns from parochial clergy which gave detailed information on all parts of Scotland. In one sense, such surveys followed in a long tradition of topographical studies of the countryside, antiquarian perhaps, but vital in assembling the empirical base for certain kinds of analysis. In another sense, the works of the later 18th and early 19th century were quite new, as they aimed at more systematic conclusions; information was not collected for its own sake so much as it was to be used to explain conditions or suggest solutions to problems. By 1801 we are approaching the age of modern statistical information. This had sizeable implications, for while the U.K. did not become the common "unit" of data, the new constitution required the combination of some basic numbers such as population, imports and exports, and public accounts.

The recovery and classification of public records was an area of recognized deficiency in 1801. In that year a royal commission was established to begin this work for England and Wales. Scotland and Ireland were brought within the scope of the Commission in 1808-1812. Since the needs and problems of each national area were quite different, there was not much centralized work for the U.K. The motive was the same: legal and historical desire for the retention and preservation of authentic records. There was some saving by the use of a single commission, but there was also some evidence that record-keeping was a recognized problem long before 1800. A generation earlier Robert Adam designed and the city of Edinburgh built the famous Register House as a repository for official Scottish records. Perhaps the most significant feature was that under the U.K. there was more healthy and less predatory interest in public records. The Scots and the Welsh must have retained some memory of those medieval incidents when their regal or princely records had been roughly treated by the English sovereign. Those days were now gone, although the 19th century and the 20th would see some confusing movement of Welsh legal records from one repository to another, until a settled collection was established in the National Library of Wales.

The physical face of the United Kingdom was studied and carefully reconstructed through the work of another one of the few administrative bodies dealing with the whole of the archipelago. The Ordnance Survey undertook the energetic business of mapping the whole of the British Isles. The need was recognized in the 18th century, and as part of the defense of the realm from 1720 to 1750 there were some early surveys. Surveying and mapping had been going through significant improvements in methods of triangulation in the later 18th century. At first there was an Anglo-French project, interrupted by the war, which in its turn put a premium on better maps. The Army Ordnance office was in charge of engineers, and it conducted the survey in the early 19th century. The work on England was completed first, then Wales, Scotland and Ireland. The obvious strategic value of the survey was its original purpose; along the way it was going to affect topographical understanding, to alter traditional place-names, anglicizing some, and stimulating native reaction in other cases. Accurate maps and information were vital to the army and to many other groups. The survey had limited political importance at the national level, but in drawing boundaries for taxes, tithes and elections, it meant a great deal at the local level.

There was slight evidence in the structure of administration that a unified government entity existed in the 19th century archipelago. Several factors account for this: governing processes were still simple, and they were still carried on mainly by local officials and by 'amateurs', gentry or clergy. Agrarian society remained a potent model while its relative size retreated before industrial growth. The great transitional process from the old rural order was accompanied by continuing acceptance of small-scale, local, deferential administration. This is one reason why so many private, unofficial groups were formed to deal with social problems. Without the modern disposition to find governmental solutions, yet moved by the impulses of enlightenment or evangelicalism, there was wide resort to "associations" and "societies" for innumerable specific causes. Some of the myriad groupings crossed the frontiers in the archipelago. Missionary groups were bounded by sects, not nations; reformers like the Abolition Society, the Liberation Society, the Peace Society were pointing toward transcendant values; on a mundane level, professional organizations such as the British Association for the Advancement of Science or the Social Science Association wanted to draw on all communities.

The personnel of government were never strictly limited to native geographic areas. There was always a certain amount of 'official' migration-- either imperial officers sent out from the center, or provincial candidates drawn to the locus of power. There was easy entry to government via patrons, for the affluent, skillful or well-recommended individual. A sizeable prejudice was encountered by non-nationals in all areas. It might be possible to tally the number of cabinet ministers, judges, clergymen and military officers from the four national areas of the archipelago and compare those figures to the corresponding place of occupation. It is doubtful that these rosters could be readily interpreted. The nagging question always would be whether the presence of a Lord Chancellor with a Scottish education, or a general with an Anglo-Irish background or a Welsh bishop signified social integration, individual accomplishment and/or any degree of convergence in the several island traditions. Did such migration signify the loss of the individual's heritage or his transmission of some of it into a new multinational character? The puzzle of the interlocking societies resembles, on smaller scale and with narrower gaps in culture, the problem of imperial integration. That comparison suggests that the mere migration of individuals, whatever high office they might hold, was no substitute for bonds of culture and institutions.

Given the nature of government and the shifting social scene, we ought to look at the ranks of political outsiders for another dimension of integration. Those actively hostile to government were divisible into "seditious persons" and what we might call "lobbyists." Government made it as difficult as it could for agitators to organize, yet it may be that the earliest and most effective bodies were, like the corresponding societies, multinational radical groups. It is true here, as with government, that the most common form of organization was local and small--unions, secret societies, industrial and agrarian radicals, those clearly outside the law were inhibited from large membership--knowing how vulnerable even their small cells might be to infiltration and exposure. On the other hand, some organizers openly formed networks, an untypical example being Major Cartwright's travels in Scotland and England to establish "Hampden Clubs" for the cause of political reform in the early 19th century.

By the 1820s and 1830s there were large and significant reformist organizations: the Catholic Association of Daniel O'Connell in Ireland (1824); Robert Owen's Grand National Consolidated Trades Union (1834); the Anti-Corn Law League (1836) and the widely-dispersed branches of the Chartist Association (1839). Among the interesting aspects of these developments was some international activity which brought together recruits from varied protest backgrounds, so that tactical problems in one area might be solved with borrowed methods. There was no hesitation on the part of the outcast agitators to use their colleagues in other parts of the U.K. Measuring the effect of this communication may be impossible, but its existence was important to early reformers.

On the whole, governing the United Kingdom was not undertaken as a federal enterprise except in the few cases where such an approach was more convenient or less obstructed by tradition. The "King of England" was the sovereign, and in the case of George III there was no special effort to identify him with the larger unit. George IV made highly-publicized state visits to Dublin and Edinburgh, demonstrating that the crown was able, under the right circumstances, to foster loyalty to an integral union. In fact, the political order was entering a period of significant reform by the later 1820s, a period in which there would be further testing of the idea of a United Kingdom.

Reform in the United Kingdom

Reform was a prominent theme in the 19th century and it affected all parts of the archipelago. Local and national communities were touched by it in different ways, but there was a common experience of oligarchic decline, government remodelling and movement toward democracy. Yet this general development did not produce a "more perfect union." Specific reform measures were designed for specific problems and regions, and some attempts at reform (Scottish law, Welsh education, Irish police) backfired when national lines were crossed unwarily. These episodes indicated the continuing strength of national identity, and they demonstrated that reformers had no greater perception of or plan to deal with archipelago unity than did the leaders of the establishment.

The oligarchs who managed the political life of the 18th century saw their authority begin to crumble in the first decades after Waterloo. The ensuing changes have been attributed to "abdication of the governors" or to "revolt" of the classes below them. Both elements were behind the changes, the net effect of which was to postpone genuine democracy and to preserve a major part of establishment power. The monarchy was never seriously threatened; parliamentary sovereignty was never directly challenged; legal institutions were strong throughout. The first and foremost inroad of reform came in political, legal and economic challenges to the structure of established religion.

Conventional accounts of reform have concentrated on the role of parliamentary representation, an emphasis which originated in historians' fascination with the contrast between continental revolutions and British reform. It is likely that contemporaries were just as familiar with Wilberforce, Chalmers and Newman as they were with Bentham, Russell and Mill; with the debates on the state of the church as much as the state of the franchise. Religion was of central importance in the early reform years, from early victories for toleration in the 1820s, through evangelical reaction to further reform in the 30s, to battles over disestablishment by mid-century. The archipelago of course presented a wide and varied field for the discussion of these issues.

In the first half of the 19th century there was widespread debate over matters which touched the place of the church in society: economic issues (endowment, tithes, rates); education (school construction, funding and sectarian instruction); and social questions (slavery, charity, lunacy and crime). Significant steps in each area had been taken by the 1830s, which steps tended to reduce the formal role of the church, even while the bulk of the political community still believed in moral solutions to social problems.

Church establishment lost considerable ground in the second half of the 18th century, and expressions of loyalty and support in the revolutionary period did not alter the fundamental trend. Political power was in the hands of Anglicans (and Scottish Presbyterians), but Dissenters and Catholics had cause to expect early entry into a more effective political life. Annual indemnity for Dissenters in the 18th century was made permanent in 1778, that is, special exception to penal laws was made while leaving the laws on the books. In 1793, Catholics were enfranchised, and in 1800 there was an attempt to allow them to hold public office. The growth of nondenominational religious activity, by Methodists and other itinerant preachers, and by a growing number of societies to promote religious and moral causes, further tended to reduce the power of established religion.

The slippage of establishment authority, usually linked to the French Revolution, was not of such a precipitous nature in the archipelago. That was not simply due to innate conservatism, either Anglican or, as some would have it, Methodist. The establishment in the archipelago had seen erosion--and competition--for a long period of time. The Anglican domination of English politics (King, Lords, Commons, local magistrates, parish vestries) did not extend to Scotland; it was imposed on a Catholic majority in Ireland; and it faced a rising Dissenting element in Wales. In other words, there was a tradition of religious pluralism since the 17th century which derived from the memory of the religious warfare of that earlier era and contributed to de facto toleration.

Nevertheless, the road was not smooth, and establishment never gladly surrendered. The stubborn resistance to emancipation at the time of the Act of Union (1801) symbolized the weakness of the establishment. Instead of adding a phalanx of Catholic supporters to the crown, the frightened Anglicans in the Church of Ireland were given an illusory sense of permanence, and the Irish Catholics were given a cause to rally opposition. The union was a provocation to the Irish majority, but that body only found an effective means of expression when Daniel O'Connell succeeded in organizing the Catholic Association. Supported by penny contributions and assisted by parish priests, the travelling barrister used his network of contacts to build the first effective popular political organization in the archipelago-- "the first parliamentary party of the modern era."[3] Organized voting behavior gave the association its power. O'Connell himself stood for parliament in a bye-election in County Clare, against Vesey Fitzgerald, a Protestant who was a supporter of emancipation. When O'Connell won, the victory forced the government of Wellington and Peel to contemplate a series of such victories and widespread unrest. They chose to surrender on emancipation, but they followed that measure with a new franchise act which raised the voter qualification to £10 and thus reduced the total number of Irish voters from 90,000 to 45,000.

The year before this, the Dissenters had been granted relief from the penal laws, that is, the provisions of the Test and Corporation Acts. They still had to face the nuisances of tithes, bars to university degrees and monopoly of recognized marriage and burial ceremonies. Each of these proscriptions would fall in the course of the next generation and it may be that the establishment's privileges served as a kind of incentive. In any case, Dissenting congregations grew and prospered in England and in Wales. In 1811 the Calvinistic Methodists broke from the Anglicans in Wales and entered a period of rapid growth. The numbers of Welsh Dissenters rose with particular speed in some mining communities. By 1851 the Dissenters outnumbered Anglicans in Wales by about 3 to 1, and there was a distinctive pattern in that this delayed surge of non-conformity contributed to its lower-class and native-speaking tendencies.[4]

---

[3] Oliver MacDonagh, *Ireland: The Union and its Aftermath* (1977), p. 54.
[4] Kenneth O. Morgan, *Wales in British Politics, 1868-1922*, 3rd. ed. (1980), pp. 14f.

In Scotland, religious issues were just as significant though they followed different channels. When the repeal of the Test and Corporation Acts was being debated, the bill brought the resignation of the 2nd viscount Melville and the end of the old system of management in Scotland's parliamentary delegation (1827). But Scotland also experienced its own forms of internal religious dissent, disputes often serious enough to have important political impact. In 1834 the General Assembly passed two important measures of church governance, a Chapel Act (allowing redrawing of some parish boundaries) and a Veto Act (allowing a majority of male worshippers to veto a ministerial candidate). The acts were brought in response to the pressure of populous and evangelized congregations, but they only set the stage for further confrontation with older, traditional elements. A series of legal cases based on the acts climaxed in 1843 in the "Disruption," a split in which some 470 of the 1200 ministers of the kirk seceded to form a new establishment--the "Free Church of Scotland."

The mood of "disruption" was widespread by the 1840s. In every sector there had been serious challenges to the religious establishment and strong counteraction as well. In Ireland this assumed the grim shape of physical violence in the so-called "Tithe War" of 1830-34. A program of passive resistance to tithe payments (still legally owed by Anglicans and non-Anglicans) prompted the use of constables and troops to collect, which in turn provoked armed resistance and violent retaliation. In the end, most tithes went unpaid, with a fraction being covered by government compensation. The Whig government which took office (with O'Connell's help) in 1835, did make some headway with a Tithe Commutation Act in 1838. But the issue was not soluble, and severe damage was already done. For instance, in 1833, in order to meet some of the financial difficulties, the government suppressed ten Irish bishoprics and diverted their funds. This action was denounced by John Keble and Edward Pusey who were among the clergy who formed the "Oxford Movement." They protested the state's intervention and along with that, the general decline of respect for authority, especially in their series of essays, "Tracts for the Times."

The "tractarians" had much to protest. In the 1830s there were several inquiries into church affairs and the creation of an Ecclesiastical Commission (1836) empowered to redistribute bishops' income, reform cathedral organization and correct abuses such as non-residence. The commission was dominated by bishops, yet the impression created was one of emphatic state intervention.

While its moral dominance faltered, the oligarchy was forced to share its political ascendance with a mixed elite of owners, employers and intellectuals. The change has been conventionally placed between 1832 and 1835 due to the reform of parliamentary and municipal franchises. These were central issues, and they were the focus of wide public interest in the political process. It is less often noted that reform was applied across the archipelago, affecting the several oligarchies and producing some very different results.

In 1832 parliamentary reform was achieved with the enactment of three bills (England and Wales, Scotland and Ireland). This peaceful alteration of the political structure contained long-awaited reforms of the composition of the Commons and the electorate. After the hiatus of the French wars and the anxiety of the postwar era, the reform issue returned with redoubled support from large industrial cities and radical political leaders. The adoption of reform by the aristocratic Whig leadership was a calculated step to seize a strong issue and to exploit its power while trimming its impact. The uniform franchise was based on a property test; removal of "rotten" boroughs was selective; and there was no surrender to any of the more radical demands for reform (ballot, universal suffrage, annual parliaments). Looking across the archipelago, the results of reform showed interesting variations.

In the broadest terms, it has been calculated that one of five English and Welsh adult males was able to vote in 1832, about one out of eight Scots, and somewhere near one out of twenty Irishmen. In the details of the several reform acts there were a number of variations. In England there was very extensive overhaul. Eighty-six boroughs lost one or both seats, thirty-seven counties gained a seat as did forty-three cities and towns. Ministers insisted that population was not the principle for representation, and the end result was not a system of evenly-distributed seats. Many of the worst "rotten" boroughs were eliminated; borough voting was put on a uniform £10 franchise for free-holders in the U.K. The net increase in English voters was approximately 80%. Further, by establishing a property requirement, the law made way for a system of voter registration, which encouraged some primitive party organization via registration committees. In Wales there were six new M.P.s and a slight increase in the number of borough voters overall, while there were a few cases of dramatic increase in individual boroughs.

The effect of reform was greatest in Scotland. Eight new seats were created, but the principal impact came in the increased electorate. From a total of about 4,500, the application of the £10 franchise caused a jump to about 65,000. Voting was made somewhat more democratic in the Scottish burghs, somewhat less in the counties. The effect on Scottish politics was emphatic as there was a dramatic turn from the old system of patronage toward open political contests.

In Ireland, the act of 1829 had just revised the franchise upward and the number of voters downward. Members were not eager to reverse that measure but the reforms in Britain made it necessary to make some improvement for the Irish electorate. Their number was restored to about the 1828 level. Some boroughs were reformed and five seats were added to Ireland's total.

Public excitement in the 1830s was generated by changes in franchise, and the last election on the unreformed franchise was the first issue-oriented campaign (April 1831). But the first election under the new dispensation produced a House of Commons not easily distinguished from its predecessors: over 200 sons of peers and some 500 landowners' representatives peopled the reformed House of Commons. Behind this exterior, however, the process of registration, the increasing number of contests and the increasing public involvement in political campaigns were contriving to open the system. In addition, more rapid changes in the composition of borough governments reinforced political changes at all levels. The reform of local government was drawn along by parliamentary reform, though the local versions also followed separate channels in each country. In general, municipal corporations were bodies of co-opted membership whose role was that of trustees for a community and its property owners, rather than officials responsible to the general public.

In 1833 the Scottish burghs were placed on a £10 franchise in local elections and this transformed the local oligarchies. In England and Wales a commission of inquiry studied the municipal corporations in 1833-34. The resulting Municipal Corporations Act (1835) suppressed 178 corporations and substituted elected councils with limited powers, chosen by resident ratepayers (regardless of property values). Those councils then chose a mayor and aldermen.

Ireland had to wait until 1840 for a far less significant reform: ten elective borough councils (on a £10 franchise) and suppression of 48 old corporations. In fact the Irish act was held up for a number of reasons, one of which was the revamping of local law enforcement, which in Ireland meant the creation of the first effective constabulary forces in the archipelago. In Ireland public order came ahead of political reform in the priorities of English policy-makers.

The oligarchs were still powerful political figures in 1835 in all parts of the archipelago. However, the basis of their power was remodelled in such a way that the interests of oligarchy could no longer command the strength necessary to outweigh the public interest. For one thing the basic direction of political reform spelled trouble for the old system of patronage. That system, which had great potential for centralization, had been under fire for half a century, and by 1830 the results of years of criticism were beginning to show. Needless to say, as patronage and old officialdom were retired, novel administration took their place, often performing new kinds of government functions. There was potential here for unification, indeed one author has seen "with the passing of management after 1827 and increased centralization Scotland came to be treated as a province rather than a partner." [5] The contrast is exaggerated but real. We need to assess the degree to which centralizing was common to other parts of the U.K. under the new dispensation.

Clearly patronage was not eliminated at a stroke. Old habits were slow to die, and of course nomination and influence are not unknown today. What was evident in the 1830s and 40s was more than normal hostility to the system and its patent inequity. This more intense attitude may have been the product of the very acts of removing "abuses" such as sinecures and rotten boroughs. Moreover, the reform of patronage was overtaken by new conditions. Industrial society created new problems, new agencies, and in its own way, *new patronage.* For to the eyes of contemporaries, the boards, committees and offices of state were "jobs" just like the old ones. It was more important that debate was joined over the proper role of government. In trade, industry or public health, there were serious disagreements over the role which public authorities should have. Public interest demanded

---

[5] William Ferguson, *Scotland: 1689 to the Present* (1968), p. 319.

protection or regulation; private interest demanded "laissez faire"; the results were mixed, but certainly there was growth in the size and capacity of government--"increasing experiment in state supervision, intervention and control." [6]

If the Victorian state intervened more regularly, it still had to deal with the variety of communities and traditions in the archipelago. We can get an idea of how well it dealt with them by examining some of the more important reform issues of the century. Again the dominant theme was area legislation and variable results.

Full-time police forces were not used until 19th century urban society created sufficient fear to make the police a tolerable means of social control. Occasional force, army or militia, had been adequate once. In fact, the initial reforms came in agrarian Ireland with the "Peace Preservation Force" of 1814, a variation on militia and martial law. Within a decade the organized constabulary was created, with paid magistrates as the keystone. The force was used in lieu of regular army units in Ireland, and there were actual savings in cost, and near equality in effectiveness in reducing agrarian crime. Peel was the Chief Secretary when the P.P.F. was introduced. He may well have had the Irish constabulary in mind when he advocated the Metropolitan Police for London in 1829--though the mention of an Irish precedent would hardly have helped the cause. At the time, Peel observed that there were forty or fifty local authorities with some police jurisdiction in the metropolitan area. What he proposed was a paid, professional force to take their place, but this was a local body. Though professionalizing began in the late 18th century, local initiative was most important, and remained so, even down to the Constabulary Act of 1842 which enabled J.P.'s to hire constabulary personnel in England and Wales on local option.

Provisions for public elementary education varied widely: Scotland had a parochial school system which, if underfunded, stood out as the most egalitarian in the archipelago. In the 18th century there were assorted schemes for Irish education on charitable foundations, some of which had scandalous malfunctions. By the turn of the century, there were more reputable and even nondenominational private efforts on foot. Once emancipation was passed, there was wide agreement that more public action

---

[6]Norman Gash, *Aristocracy and People* (1981), p. 49.

was needed. Lord Stanley supported a plan which created a board of governors and a national elementary system. No denominational instruction was to be compulsory; there was to be central organization, provision of textbooks and inspection of operations. However, Protestant and Catholic clergy were soon dissatisfied with the schools, and they managed to convert them to denominational institutions within a generation. All the same, the school facilities continued to perform, if on a totally different footing than was intended.

The Irish in that sense may have been more fortunate than the English. The competition between Dissenter and Anglican prevented the full enactment of an English elementary education system until 1870. Mutual suspicion and fears about religious instruction (or its absence) meant that the roughly equal political strength of the two camps was neutralized. Only small and intermittent funding came through the Committee on Education of the Privy Council. When Forster's Act finally passed, it was a tepid measure, providing for local tax-supported school construction and local elected school boards in those communities in which there was a deficiency of facilities.

The least fortunate sector was Wales. There had been exemplary effort by reformers, but in the 19th century public funding was held up by the English standoff. Meanwhile, in 1847 an inquiry into the condition of schooling led to the publication of a report which had explosive results. The English inspectors denounced the condition of the Welsh schools, but more to the point, they denounced the use of the Welsh language and blamed it for retarded school conditions. This indictment aroused a public outcry and stimulated Welsh interest in educational reform, and at the same time gave a boost to political activists. In the second half of the 19th century, Welsh education was significantly altered with elementary, secondary and higher education all receiving major institutional improvements.

In every part of the archipelago there were mixed provisions for the relief of the poor. The oldest forms were in church and private charitable donations. Since the 17th century, England and Wales used rate-supported funding on a parochial basis under the Elizabethan Poor Law (codified in 1601). That law, by 1800, was the subject of extensive discussion, for in the economic conditions of the war years and early industrial growth, poverty was intensified. The cost of the old law rose to around £7 million in the post-war years with its later variations like the "Speenhamland System" of outdoor relief. This made it the target of those who wanted to reduce the cost or even abolish the system altogether.

A royal commission created in 1832 produced a doctrinaire English (or Southern English) solution. Workhouses would be provided and made "less eligible" than the lowest level of outside employment. The law enacted in 1834 created a central board of commissioners who governed the work of some 600 poor law unions and their local "guardians," thus taking away the responsibility of J.P.s and parish officers. The system had some hope of working in rural areas, but none in large industrial towns. The plan became the model for a similar system in Ireland (1838) in spite of the contrary recommendations of another commission. A Dublin central board was created, under the supervision of the English commissioners, and some 130 Irish poor law unions were formed by 1846. The Scottish situation was one in which the kirk and leaders of the community maintained that the old charitable system was superior to the English poor law. Certainly from the standpoint of expense that was true. The workers' claim on public support was largely denied, except in some Scottish urban and industrial communities where assessments were required to supplement the voluntary donations. This mixed system and the role of the kirk in supporting traditional charity slowed down poor law reform in Scotland. In 1845 an act was passed which left the matter of assessment on a local option basis and formed a central Board of Supervision with limited powers. The expenditures on the poor increased over the early years of the new system but these were also years of serious economic distress in many parts of the archipelago.

Poor law reform was a case of English models being applied to different communities with indifferent success, indeed, not working at all well in parts of northern England. There was no effort to create a United Kingdom system, either out of respect to local differences or fear of international drain on the resources. In fact, specific provision was made in the Scottish reform for repatriation of English and Irish poor who had not established a claim on the parish where they tried to obtain relief.

The repeal of tariffs on grain, the "corn laws," offered another instructive example of reform. Corn laws had been on the books since the 17th century, but with the post-war depresson after 1815, producers hoped to support prices and retain the large acreage still under the plow owing to wartime expansion of agriculture. This policy was attacked as an artificial price support. Needless to say, the producers were better represented in parliament; for a time there was a ban on imports when the price fell to a certain level; then in 1822 and 1828, "sliding scales" allowed imports on a graduated basis but these had little effect. By the 1830s, the economists and industrialists formed a lobbying group known as the "Anti-Corn Law League." Its first base was in Manchester, but it grew to a national organization, built around twelve districts with agents and a number of local chapters throughout England and Wales. The league was well-organized and financed. It operated largely as a speakers' bureau and information center, its aims were clearcut--and negative. In seven years of operation the league conducted what was probably the first successful extraparliamentary lobby. We have to say "probably," because repeal of the law was actually brought about by the League's main foe, Robert Peel, conservative prime minister, in the midst of the terrible famine in Ireland. The League did not "cause" repeal, but it did make the issue so prominent that the conditions of the famine left no alternative. The potato crop failed in successive years on the continent and in the archipelago. For parts of rural Scotland, this meant extreme hardship; for most of rural Ireland, it meant disaster. There was no way to justify continuing a policy which prevented duty-free grain imports in time of famine. There was also a powerful impulse to provide relief to those in distress. Since about 1 million people died and another million emigrated (1845-49), there can be no claim of success; indeed, every aspect of British policy in the crisis was tinged with failure. Peel secretly ordered the purchase of American maize (£100,000), a government relief commission was organized (November 1845) and public works schemes in the early days seemed to be successful. But public expenditures were heartily opposed (by Whigs especially), until distress forced government purchase of food through the poor law machinery (1847). A special Central Board of Health tried to operate a network of emergency hospitals to deal with epidemic disease. The efforts were small and scattered and they could not save the country from disaster. The blight of the potato was never eradicated from Anglo-Irish relations. Moreover, population in Ireland continued to fall in absolute numbers until the 20th century.

While the issues of the poor law, corn law and social reform were prominent in the 1830s and 40s, there was a popular political movement which reached much of Britain but which fell short of its goal of a democratic political structure. The Chartists were active in many parts of England, Wales and Scotland. Among the membership were radicals who had experience in the disputes over trade unions, or the resistance to the new poor law, and those who had agitated for parliamentary reform and felt that the Act of 1832 was a betrayal of the working class. In 1838 the leaders of the London Working Men's Association drafted what was called "The People's Charter." In its six main points, this document set out a plan of democratic political reform: universal (male) suffrage, 300 equal (U.K.) districts, secret ballot, pay for members, removal of property qualifications and annual parliaments. The Birmingham Political Union under Thomas Attwood played a key role, and both main English centers sent "missionaries" to other towns in the U.K. The sense of "mission" was appropriate in that Welsh and Scottish support was particularly oriented to sectarian members and there were close ties to congregations as well as to temperance groups, Chartist schools, co-operative stores and publications.

The political potential in the movement lay in its planned national conventions, the first of which met in London in 1839, timed to coincide with the opening of the session of parliament. Delegates attended from many parts of Britain, and the threat to established institutions was very real to some observers. However, the bulk of the Chartists were committed to "moral force" --a theme endorsed by a large Scottish meeting in Edinburgh (1838). The "physical force" element of the movement was perhaps always a minority, but it produced continuous wrangling as to proper tactics within local chapters and national gatherings. There were calls for a general strike and some attempts to arm and drill members. The one serious armed incident was a clash in Newport in November 1839, in which 14 were killed and the leaders were sentenced to die, but not executed. William Lovett, leader of the L.W.M.A., criticized the "Irish braggadocio about arming and fighting" of Feargus O'Connor, leader of the physical force wing and editor of the *Northern Star*, a leading paper of the Chartists.

The most publicized acts of the Chartists were the "monster" petitions presented to the House of Commons on behalf of the Charter. Reportedly containing over a million signatures, the petitions (in 1839, 1842 and 1848) proved the constitutional character of the movement and its faith in the power of gradual reform. To later observers it seemed that the Chartists were naïve and ineffective. Their last major demonstration in 1848 sputtered out in a

315

Spring rainstorm, as a gathering of supporters of the petition was prevented from marching on the House of Commons by a body of middle-class special constables. It is true that the House rejected all of the Chartist petitions and that there were few supporters of the People's Charter in government. Yet within the next generation the Chartist measures began to appear on the statute book. No one can say whether or how far the campaigns of the 30s and 40s provided the foundation for the later acceptance of democratic measures, but it would be erroneous to dismiss the movement and its contribution.

The U.K. dimension of the Chartist movement should not be exaggerated; in fact, it is a good illustration of some of the difficulties facing reformers. While active groups formed in all parts, the Chartists who marched on Newport, those who assembled in Edinburgh, and those who met in London, were naturally concerned with both local and national issues. When they convened in larger gatherings, they not only disagreed on general strategy, they also brought complicated backgrounds into a setting which was not apt to encourage easy cooperation. Some members even brought distinctly separatist views with them. In Scotland the principal Chartist papers were *The Scottish Patriot* and the *True Scotsman* . When the national dimension was added to disputes over physical force and the compound of local issues, there was little hope for a coherent U.K. Chartist movement.

In the middle of the century, political reform efforts only continued in spasmodic and limited fashion. In part this was owing to improved economic conditions, in part it was the consequence of the disappointment with earlier reforms and movements. Occasional bills for further franchise reform were introduced, but the general support for change which pushed early reform did not reappear until the later 1860s. At that point, the process entered its third and democratic phase, in which a wider franchise and broadly liberal constitution were constructed. There were three important steps in the opening of politics: (1) the wider franchise of 1867 and attendant political party development; (2) the liberal impact of Irish Disestablishment (1869), elementary education reform (1870) and the movement toward Welsh University establishment; and (3) a further franchise and distribution reform (1884-85) which pointed unmistakably toward political democracy (for men). It was no accident that the last measure was soon followed by separatist moves and other repercussions. For these steps toward democracy were also effective in bringing out fundamental differences between regions and political classes. They were not apt to be sources of U.K. harmony.

The Second Reform Act (1867) was a curious political event, for it was a major reform not really sought by any party. One successful effort at further franchise reform occurred in the 1850s in Ireland, where some effective change was made by tripling the number of county voters. Otherwise, there was little activity in the field of electoral reform until the later 60s. The Liberals were defeated on a reform proposal in 1866, and a minority Conservative government under Lord Derby, with Benjamin Disraeli as Leader of the House of Commons took office. They introduced a reform measure in 1867, and when the Liberals sought to embarrass them by proposing radical amendments, Disraeli surprised them by accepting the amendments, and the electorate was nearly doubled. Scotland gained seven seats and Wales one, while 44 were redistributed from corrupt English boroughs to underrepresented counties and towns (plus a third seat to Birmingham, Manchester, Leeds, and Liverpool). Disraeli showed his mastery of tactics during the bill's passage, but the newly-enlarged electorate failed to recognize his skill. In 1868, it returned Gladstone with a majority of 112 seats.

The enlarged electorate, heavily laced with urban workers, was clearly outside the grasp of the old political management system, and a major change in politics was begun with the creation of new national political parties (1868-1878). Liberal and Conservative were not the same as the old Whig and Tory. The central party headquarters, local constituency committees and formal organization for England, Wales, Scotland and Ireland brought significant changes in political life. Other changes followed: rhetorical duels (Gladstone and Disraeli); growth of the press and mass circulation; plus voter management as in the famous "Birmingham Caucus" of Joseph Chamberlain, where the Liberals were organized enough to win all of the three seats in the 1868 alignment.

Since any householder who paid the rates was eligible to vote, there was considerable fear of new voters on the part of the old ruling classes. At the same time, the new voters did not feel entirely free. Some landlords were not above the use of intimidation to influence voting, and the extreme form of this technique was shown in Wales in 1859 and 1868, where a number of tenants were evicted because of their voting behavior. In 1872, the Ballot Act introduced the secret ballot into parliamentary elections in all of the U.K.. The impact seems to have varied, and the Welsh and Irish voters showed the most obvious changes in voting behavior. Irish Home Rulers and Welsh radicals gained considerable momentum in the 1870s as a result.

The larger voting public after 1867 required liberalization of the religious-educational scheme. First, Irish Disestablishment in 1869 recognized the minority position of the Church of Ireland and therefore severed its political support. That act provided considerable fuel for forces elsewhere which were against establishment. The Education Act of 1870 seemed to surmount the roadblock of the previous 40 years, and it offered public support to existing schools and created machinery for erecting new schools under local supervision with central financial assistance in England and Wales. Schooling and establishment were especially volatile issues in Welsh politics, and they helped to push some of its leaders into nationalist positions and promoted the most extensive educational reform effort in the archipelago in the 19th century.

In 1884 the Third Reform Act extended the franchise in the counties and raised the English/Welsh electorate by 67%, while Scottish seats increased to 72. The principle of equal, single-member constituencies, added to effective campaign-spending reform in 1883, produced a system clearly headed toward a democratic goal.

It may seem ironic that an early sequel to such fair-minded reform was an outburst of national separatism. The first Irish Home Rule Bill (1886) and its echoes in Scotland and Wales were in fact a logical response to a wider and freer franchise. Only the timing was fortuitous. Gladstone had been moving toward a Home Rule position, but for the sake of his party's cohesion he would have preferred a gradual approach. Events forced his hand and precipitated a constitutional crisis, one which proved more than any other that reform was inimical to the concept of union.

The Irish Question

"The Irish Question" was a phrase which hinted at the disdain of English (and some Scottish and Welsh) politicians toward the other island. It probably did not occur to them that treating Ireland as a nuisance instead of as part of the union would encourage separation. From the other side, separatism only attracted extremist support at first. Advocates of "Repeal" or of "Home Rule" wanted to maintain a modified imperial constitution. But the unionist was unwilling or unable to make these distinctions. The debate on the constitutional position of Ireland naturally evoked Scottish and Welsh imitators, and it might be better to call the "Irish Question" the "U.K. question."

The issues which were central to Irish politics were the role of the Catholic population, the control of political violence, the rights of tenants, and the (re)creation of an Irish parliament. On all of these issues there were important collateral questions across the archipelago, but the central matter which colored all of them was the fact that they were debated and decided in the imperial parliament.[7]

> Irish problems remained distinct; but now they had to be thrashed out in the imperial parliament, where they often exercised a decisive influence and consumed a disproportionate amount of parliamentary time. The growth of a strong Irish party upset the political balance: relations between the two great British parties were embittered, and a disruptive element was introduced within the parties themselves.

Catholic Emancipation was the first case of profound constitutional importance, for it aimed at the base of the union, or rather at one of its flaws. For the right of Catholics to hold office was pointedly denied in 1801. As we have seen, that was the reason for organizing the Catholic Association and the achievement of emancipation in 1829 was vital in breaking down the Tory barrier to political reform. In turn, the admission of the Irish majority to office-holding encouraged further political activity and further reduction of the ascendancy, the next major step being disestablishment of the Church of Ireland (1869).

The issue of Catholic Emancipation was not exclusively "Irish," but it was brought to a head by Irish political leaders. At first an aristocratic agitation (1808-1814), the issue was kept alive by Grattan (to 1821), and support in parliament gradually increased. With O'Connell and the Catholic Association, the social tenor of the issue changed and the parish clergy were involved in gathering a popular following. As such, the organization was alarming to some, more so as the ordinary peasant tended to see equality and

[7]Beckett, *Short History of Ireland*, p. 136.

freedom as attainable goals, mirages which O'Connell's rhetoric did little to discourage. Government attempted to prosecute O'Connell and suppress the association, but these actions probably increased his support. In 1826 the membership was mobilized to vote for "emancipation" candidates with some success. In 1828 O'Connell won his bye-election victory and forced the issue. The resulting Emancipation Act allowed Catholics to hold office (except that of Regent, Lord Lieutenant or Lord Chancellor of England or Ireland), provided only that they take an oath denying the civil authority of the pope and vowing to uphold the current establishment. With this, the Catholic Association was suppressed and the viceroy was empowered to remove similar groups in the future.

Emancipation was thus a victory for the Irish majority and one which confirmed their hostility to English rulers and resident overseers. It was an impressive illustration of the power of public opinion from an unlikely quarter. It was also a victory for Catholics elsewhere in the archipelago, though nowhere else were their numbers sufficient to have major electoral impact or to offset the collateral adverse effects on the remainder of the body politic. Also, the emancipation measure began the re-entry of the Catholic church into politics, a slow and laborious process. The hierarchy was conservative and cautious, but by the 1850s, first on education and then on economic issues, it became a meaningful political force.

With the achievement of emancipation, constitutional action was ratified as a viable strategy. The remainder of the 19th century saw several varieties, beginning with the open opposition to the union which was presented by O'Connell's Repeal movement (1840s) which was stifled by government opposition and by economic calamity. After the famine, there were more secret and violent organizations, which were unable to attract a large public base until an alliance was made between the Land League and the Home Rule Party in 1879. Meanwhile, small ideological efforts such as the Young Ireland movement of the 1840s and the Fenian Brotherhood of the 50s and 60s had advocated violent opposition to English rule, with relatively little effect.

A much more significant development for the fate of the union was the disestablishment of the Church of Ireland in 1869. Gladstone was moved to declare that his "mission was to pacify Ireland" in 1868. His first step was to disendow the Anglican church there. On its merits, this was a sound decision, for there was clearly inequitable distribution of funds to an unpopular church. Yet the constitutional implications were serious and destabilizing.

After the Church of Ireland was disabled, the main prop left for the ascendancy was landownership. The great majority of owners were Protestant, and while a few were, like Parnell, progressive and even radical, most were conservative. The issue of land was one which epitomized the problem of government. Irish custom had been overlaid with English law. The rights of tenants were differently construed in the two cultures, the economics of the 19th century gave little room for compromise, and even after the horrible 'remedy' of famine, the Irish rural population remained in a tenuous position, on the edge of starvation. Large families, small plots of land, poor crops, high rents and insecure tenancy were fuel for endless conflicts.

In the last quarter of the century, the farmers of the archipelago, or most of them, experienced a series of depressions. The Irish tenant farmer was not immune, and scarcity as always meant inability to pay rent, followed by the familiar sequence of eviction, protest and violence. The landholding system was the subject of a series of reforms, culminating in government funding to buy out landlords and create an "independent" Irish peasantry. If this sort of policy plus emancipation had been employed in 1800, there might have been an answer to the " Irish question." As it was, by the 1880s it was too late.

The legislators in Westminster tried to meet these problems, but they could do little to remove generations of bitterness. In outline, Gladstone's Land Act (1870) gave some protection to tenants who made improvements, protected tenants from eviction and made a limited effort to assist tenant purchases. Most of the provisions were flawed, and all were easily circumvented. Yet government had taken a radical if ineffective step. The agricultural decline of the next decade would push through a major resolution. A second land act in 1881 went much further in behalf of tenants. But by this time the issues of the 60s and 70s had been outdated by economic troubles. Tenants who could not pay rents could not be permanently helped by legal protection of tenant status. State-aided land purchase was instituted on a large scale in 1885 and extended in 1891, 1896 and 1903. Of course the measures were designed to bail out landlords as much as they were aimed at helping tenants.

Radical land policies in Ireland were paralleled by widespread economic stress and sympathetic land reform acts across the archipelago. In simple terms, the power of the landowner was undermined by falling land values, increased voting power of rural workers, and the declining role of landowners within the aristocracy and society as a whole. The now-usual claque of leagues, societies and associations surrounded land reform. Touting peasant ownership, public ownership or special taxation, these advocates were less influential than the depressed landlord in bringing measures such as the Agricultural Holdings Act (1875), Irish Land purchase (1885), the Scottish Crofters' Commission (1886), or the Royal Commission on Welsh Land (1894-96).

Although there was close coincidence in the formation of protest groups and legislative remedies, the land reform episode proved again that the archipelago was a collection of disparate communities. The Scottish crofter, the Welsh farmer, the English "yeoman" and the Irish peasant inhabited different rural worlds--all suffering in the depressed economy of the later 19th century, sharing experiences and solutions, but usually developing distinct regional remedies, implemented through their common political machinery. The most emphatic underlining of this separateness came in the evolution of the movements for "Home Rule."

The concept of "Home Rule for Ireland" was a revival of the effort to repeal the Act of Union in the 1840s, and it was aimed at the restoration of an Irish parliament on the lines of 1782-1800. Of course a new Irish legislature would contain Roman Catholic members and would be based on a much more democratic franchise. Although the fate of Dublin Castle was uncertain, the place of the Protestant Ascendancy could be expected to be further diminished.

From about 1870, the political balance had shifted: the most powerful church, the leading political party and the populist radical groups seemed to coalesce on a position of Irish reform; the outstanding problem was finding the means to introduce Home Rule into British politics. The Liberals and Conservatives were equally likely to support Irish reform--but neither would be genuinely eager to do it, for the obvious political risks were great. As this consensus was developing, its opposite was also taking shape. Protestant landowning and manufacturing interests, Anglican and Presbyterian, grew nervous and then openly rebellious in defense of their status. The union was their symbolic salvation, and in all its essentials, they had watched it being undermined in the course of the 19th century.

The "Home Government for Ireland Association" was founded in 1870 by the Protestant Dublin attorney Isaac Butt. It was a moderate group until the end of the decade, when under Charles Stewart Parnell it moved into alliance with land reform activists and toward alliance with nationalists and the Catholic church. Soon the party had the overwhelming majority of Ireland's seats in parliament. It may not have been much more coherent than other parties, but its aims gave it such an appearance. Certainly the open advocacy of "Home Rule" produced the first coherent expression of "unionist" political argument. "Unionism" was a hybrid political creed which drew upon the ideals of 17th century theory and the circumstances of 19th century empire. Its essence was loyalty to the crown; but it was a conditional loyalty which required performance of the contractual obligation, usually symbolized by the guarantees of the Act of Union. Quite naturally, the Irish Protestant saw the acts of emancipation, disestablishment and land reform as an erosion of his guarantees. This erosion was even more intolerable in that peculiar region where the Protestant (Presbyterian) Irishman was in the majority--in Ulster.

With the growth of Irish Home Rule sentiment and the appearance of its corollary of Irish nationalism, the unionist response was altogether predictable. What was not so obvious was the rate at which its strength would grow, both in Ulster and in its ties to the political structure elsewhere in the U.K. Ireland had not historically had strong English party links; Tory and Liberal labels were in use, but in the 1880s they paled before the "Irish" parties. From 1885, "Home Rulers" dominated the returns for the South, while "Unionists" carried about half of the seats in the North.

The parliamentary setting in late 1885 was novel: an 85-vote margin separated Gladstone's victorious Liberals from the Conservatives; the Irish party had won 86 seats, giving it the most potential influence it had yet had. At some point in the latter days of 1885, Gladstone decided to put the support of his ministry behind a Home Rule Bill. This decision was taken without full consultation, and the leadership of the Liberals was badly split. In June 1886, the Home Rule Bill was defeated when Joseph Chamberlain led a mass defection of Liberals to vote against their leader. Gladstone was forced to call an election, in which the voters soundly defeated his party.

Gladstone had devised a measure which grappled with some thorny constitutional problems. That his bill failed to provide a satisfactory solution is usually overlooked because of the defeat of the bill and the subsequent defeat at the polls. Yet this point has some importance for our discussion in that a potentially workable Home Rule Bill meant a very different future for Ireland and the rest of the union. In fact, none of the three Home Rule Bills (1886, 1892, 1912-14) could solve the contradictory issues of taxation and representation which arose when devolution was attempted. In 1886, Irish members were to be removed from Westminster, but sizeable Irish revenues would still have gone to the imperial exchequer. Later versions gave the Irish some representation in Westminster in addition to their own parliament, but this created other legislative anomalies. The basic problem was that "Home Rule" meant very different things to different politicians. Most Irish supporters saw it as a dominion similar to Canada; the English Liberals did not intend any loss of parliamentary supremacy; and of course the unionists were quite sure that it would result in both.

Debate on Home Rule for Ireland generated discussion of similar measures for Scotland and Wales, along with discussion of imperial federation and "Home Rule all round." The size and shape of these other Home Rule efforts emphasized the distance between political goals of Irish and other activists. Still, the existence of the movements served to show the residual power of regional or national sentiment.

Cymru Fydd (Young Wales) was formed in 1886, and significantly its first chapters were organized in London and Liverpool. The group's principal objectives were in the realm of cultural nationalism and it lacked either motives or leadership on the Irish model. The Liberals of North and South Wales disagreed on the issue of recognition. With the advent of county councils (1889), the return of many activist leaders meant the overthrow of the old governing class, and this "blunted the wider objective of Welsh Home Rule." [8] Some measures were introduced in parliament: the proposal for a Welsh Committee in 1888; for a Secretary of State for Wales, 1890; for a Welsh National Council, 1892. Such measures did not arouse strong support in the Welsh electorate, and they were easily defeated at Westminster. There were too many other issues of greater significance to Welsh voters.

---

[8] Morgan, *Wales in British Politics*, p. 107.

The "Scottish Home Rule Association" was founded in 1886 as well. But the Scottish background was quite different. Since the early 19th century there had been evidence of Scottish revival, cultural and social, whether in the literature of Scott, the work of varied reformers, or the popularity of Highland custom and symbolism. In the 50s there was a National Association for the Vindication of Scottish Rights, more interested in heraldry than politics. In the early 1880s there was discussion of the renewal of the post of Scottish Secretary (lapsed since 1746), and that step was taken in 1885 by Lord Salisbury. In 1888 the Scottish Liberal Party adopted a Home Rule policy, but it may have been out of desperation as the party was losing ground, and certainly there was no radical sentiment comparable to that of Ireland, or even Wales.

Still, a Scottish Grand Committee was created in 1894, allowing all Scottish M.P.s to consider legislation affecting Scotland at the committee stage. Between 1886 and 1924 there were 14 Home Rule Bills introduced for Scotland, but none passed. This consistent rejection of devolution helped to keep support alive for a more vigorous Scottish nationalism, but it also demonstrated the grip of the major parties and of unionist sentiment. At the same time, more radical opinion in Scotland was being diverted into the work of the rising labor political movement.

The question of "Home Rule" also received occasional attention on a broader basis, that of "Home Rule all round." This entailed a federal scheme with regional parliaments for Ireland, Wales, Scotland (and in some cases, English regions as well). The idea was suggested by Joseph Chamberlain in 1886. It was adopted briefly by Lloyd George in 1895 and Herbert Roberts in 1898. In later years it was discussed in the Liberal cabinet in 1911-12 as the third Irish Home Rule Bill was coming forward; finally it was the topic of a Speaker's Conference in 1919, in the midst of the civil war in Ireland and as the issue of partition was being legislated. No one seriously expected federalism to become a reality, for its adoption would have been a renunciation of the central concept of the English unitary state--the supreme parliament. The unionists could see fundamental conflict with loyalty to the crown, while the regions themselves would have had their own objections. In any case, the tactical reality was that Home Rule all round was a device to dilute or confuse separatist opinion. There was never a strong and serious campaign in its behalf.

What the entire Home Rule debate contributed was a much more conscious and much more critical view of the politics of the U.K. That this came at the end of the 19th century, and in the context of economic problems and political instability, spelled trouble for the archipelago government. Another reason why the union was being more closely regarded at the end of the century was the state of affairs in the empire. There too, national aspirations and problems of economy and diplomacy were becoming serious.

Imperial Mission

The domestic political importance of the British Empire was as an outlet and a symbol. An outlet for people and goods, ideas and invesment; a symbol of power, progress and racial identity. The empire remained a focus of internal debate in the 19th century. The cost, the value and the purpose of colonial ventures were widely discussed. Few politicians wanted or expected to restrict the growth of empire, all politicians had remedies for its ills, but no one party or leader could effect a total blueprint for its reform.

The "great migration" was an unparalleled export of humanity. Some 13 million emigrants left British ports between 1815 and 1905 for destinations outside Europe, a number equivalent to the entire population of the archipelago in 1780. The largest portion went from Ireland, and the chief destination at most periods was the U.S. The outflow coincided with rapid increase in the population--about 2 1/2 times or 23.7 million for the 19th century. Underlying the migration were sharp natural increases after 1760 and radically improved (and cheapened) transport by 1850. Serious economic stress and deliberate government inducement were significant factors at some points.

The primitive state of record-keeping and the difficulty of documenting migrants (emigrating individuals may have moved any number of times before departure) mean that we can never get a full picture. We can still work with the political significance of migration, and the principal aspects of the subject which concern us are the circumstances of emigrating, the politics of the emigrant, and the persistence of personal and emotional connections to the British body politic.

The causes of emigration were preeminently economic. Uprooting of families and individuals was no longer essential for the survival of a religious

326

minority; social or political stigma only touched a handful. But the impact of growing, urbanizing and rapidly industrializing population was altogether more disruptive. At the same time, availability of colonial space and shortage of colonial population were receiving more attention. The odd figure of Edward Gibbon Wakefield, rake, writer and political gadfly, espoused what he called "systematic colonization," i.e. the deliberate 'planting' of settlers, given certain economic liberties and providing certain revenues for the mother country. His theories were not fully applied, but after much discussion in the 1830s, and after the famous report on Canada by Lord Durham, stronger government involvement ensued. The Colonial Land and Emigration Commissioners (1840-1878) undertook to regulate ports and ships and manage large-scale movement of emigrants and of workers between different parts of the empire. The Wakefield principle called for a high price on land, remitted to the Crown, to pay for this managerial work, and to keep emigrant labor from quickly establishing economic independence. All the same, from the 1850s, colonies tended to take over their own lands and land policies. In this and other respects, the political significance of emigration and the policies around it become complicated. A few obvious forms of political impact may be mentioned. In the first place, some observers felt that departing emigrants were a kind of safety-valve. In 1851 the *Glasgow Herald* commented on the emigration of Irish peasants from County Mayo:[9] "If the country continue to be thinned...we may yet have the power...of establishing a British population in Ireland and rendering real the Union of the United Kingdom."

The attraction exerted by the U.S., Canada and Australia was significant. These progressive states were favorites of Irish emigrants and continuing contacts included James Stephens, Michael Devoy, Parnell and others among those who used the American connection for fund-raising and for recruiting.

In the opposite direction, there was evidence of strong and persistent loyalty. The empire became a part of many families through emigration, temporary or permanent. A select group of entrepreneurs were the latter-day "nabobs" who infused large amounts of cash and patriotism from the frontiers of imperial expansion.

---

[9]Cited in Patrick O'Farrell, *England and Ireland since 1800* (1975), p. 1.

Large movements of population were not uncommon in the 19th century world. They were byproducts of industry and the world economy which emerged in the third quarter of the century. To the archipelago, the movement offered an escape route to economic survival for most, with riches for a few, while the panorama of global activity offered powerful diversions from domestic political problems.

The British empire functioned as a giant international marketing system, incorporating the emigrant, white European settler and the native of Asia, Africa and the Near East. In this capacity, the U.K. enjoyed an unrivalled free trade empire until the last decades of the century. Most of the archipelago benefitted from this, but by 1870, new industrial competitors (U.S., Germany, France) and old imperial governments (Russia, Turkey, China) began to contest for colonial markets and colonial political power even as colonial populations themselves were beginning to follow precocious national liberation movements.

British overseas trade became a mammoth source of wealth in the middle of the 19th century--a source of wealth with several vital political dimensions. Between Peel's trade reform (1842) and Disraeli's Crystal Palace speech (1872), exports rose from £60 million to £312 million per annum. The value of foreign trade in that period went from £130m. to £669m. British trade was benefiting from large-scale export of machines and capital. By 1875 an estimated £2 million was invested overseas. In the short run these both produced handsome profit; in the long run, machinery and investments helped to build future industrial competition. The involvement in this bonanza was shared by some Scottish and Welsh industrialists but hardly enough to affect the power-distribution in the archipelago.

The 19th century was the golden age of "free trade." The navigation laws were eliminated in 1849, and tariffs were not a significant feature of British trade again until the 1930s. This condition was and is confused with the advent of "laissez faire," but in fact there was a good deal of economic and social regulation in the same period; the key was as always in the relative political strength of the several interests involved. The slave trade was abolished (1807) and later the practice of slavery (1833); factories were regulated and inspected (1833), passenger ships and railroads were subject to inspection and regulation. Generally, it was advantageous for British merchants not to have tariffs, hence they were removed.

The question of colonial government was cause for considerable debate, especially as domestic political reform proceeded in the archipelago. While direct analogies were rare, there was a general aura of reform in the concept of "responsible government" not unlike "home rule." There was a basic distinction made between white settlement colonies (extensions of English or British "civilization") and the territories dominated by black or brown races who were "not ready" for self-government. The former were on their way to becoming semi-autonomous dominions by the middle of the century. The latter required a long apprenticeship, to be converted by missionaries, educated in English law and customs and otherwise rehabilitated. There were significant signs of resistance, for example the Great Mutiny in India in 1857. Such events were not often interpreted as indications that anything was wrong with basic imperial policy. The government of colonies overseas received a great deal more attention and discussion on constitutional terms than the United Kingdom itself. The simple reason was that colonies were newer, more remote, and harder to control than the home islands.

The colonial service was only organized in consequence of its first regulations, adopted in 1837. The staff, from governors down to lesser clerks, were the physical structure of empire. The service attracted personnel from all parts of the archipelago, especially England and Scotland. Whether James Mill was right to call it a "system of outdoor relief for the middle classes" will remain a matter of opinion. The growth of a regulated service and special educational programs were signs of health in the internal structure.

Exact distributions can never be recovered, but a few figures may act as guides. The students appointed to Haileybury for the first half of the century have been analyzed.[10] Their backgrounds were well-mixed, over half from England (a quarter from the London area); about 13% Scottish and 5% Irish. Nearly a fourth were born in India. In this case, the stereotypical non-English presence was quite a bit less than other sources suggest. If it were common, we might find that the Civil Service (or I.C.S.) exams or other factors tended to favor the English applicants, or those with English connections.

---

[10]Bernard S. Cohn, "Recruitment and Training of British Civil Servants in India, 1600-1860" in *Asian Bureaucratic Systems* ed. Ralph Braibanti (1966), p. 108.

Colonial governments and all aspects of colonial policy were standard fare for 19th century parliamentary debates. Down to about 1850 there was a strong presumption that colonial governments were temporary institutions (either because of economy, free trade, pacifism or reform ideas, one might support such a position). The middle of the century saw a firmer notion of imperial positions, tied to the remarkable economic growth and displayed in an emerging sense of *pax Britannica* . From about 1870, there was more emphasis on aggressive imperialism, the idea of a "Greater Britain" and the more mechanical ideas of imperial federation were mooted; the demonstrative moves such as the Royal Titles Act (1876) naming Victoria "Empress of India," and her later jubilee celebrations (1887, 1897) were symptomatic of a more competitive and combative view of empire.

There were several conceptual visions of a world federation, a "greater Britain" which attracted a wide (white) audience in the heyday of imperialism (1875-95). Federation was the political side of England's "mission" to civilize those massive red stretches on the globe. Numerous self-analyses of this expansive activity ranged from racial superiority, to classical allusions to self-doubt and socialist denunciation.

The more aggressive phase of imperialism began to take shape in the 1860s. Charles Dilke, a Cambridge graduate and a proponent of the Great Exhibition of 1851, made a global tour in 1866 and told of his experience in a volume entitled *Greater Britain*. Dilke extolled those parts of the world which had been exposed to British civilization. He predicted that "AngloSaxondom" held the key to world progress, and he visualized a future world-state of Anglo-American design. While there was no mass following for such an ambitious vision, there soon were signs of an imperial revival, one which has conventionally been tied to Disraeli's speech at the Crystal Palace in 1872, whence his name was linked with "imperialism," and with a more aggressive foreign policy.

A confident vision of empire captured the minds of most by the 1880s, for while events in Egypt, Sudan, and South Africa drew criticism, there was a feeling in many quarters that the empire only needed some remodelling. In 1884 the Imperial Federation League was founded to pursue plans for the better government of empire, and in 1887 the first of a series of Imperial Conferences was held. Unfortunately for the optimistic planners, these years also brought strong imperial competition.

Imperialism was shared by Liberals and Conservatives. In one sense, all of the imperial schemes were nationalist ideas drawn on an oversized canvas. They were intensely popular, "jingoist" in moments of crisis, and always a bit ambiguous. For example, Alfred Milner once wrote[1]

> I am a Nationalist...a British (indeed primarily an English) Nationalist. If I am also an Imperialist it is because [of] the destiny of the English race...I am a British Race Patriot...The British State must follow the race."

The interpretation and the implementation of imperial policy were complex and consuming tasks, and it was by no means a simple matter for the British state to "follow the race." Indeed, the legal and practical forms of that sort of activity lagged behind the artistic. From the rhetorical inspiration of John Ruskin to the evocative but concrete works of Edward Freeman (*Greater Greece and Greater Britain* , 1886) or James Bryce (*The Roman Empire and the British Empire in India* 1901), these interpreters found fruitful analogies which appealed to wide audiences, especially English. More objective were John Seeley's works, *The Expansion of England* (1883) and *The Growth of British Policy* (1895). Both concentrated on the political/diplomatic evolution which produced an extended English/British polity, books which, like their contemporaries, emphasised narration and offered relatively little analysis; the eventual English supremacy was, by implication, the inevitable outcome of both processes.

The imperial mission was composed of a vast outpouring of people, products and power which spread "British" influence to all corners of the globe. The energy which went into this expansion had to divert efforts from building an archipelago nation, or at least to complicate them by combining the archipelago with an imperial federation. More seriously, overseas investment diverted funds from British industry and the profits from the investment compounded interests of the most extensive kind.

When the term "imperialism" was first used to malign Disraeli, it was a pejorative usually reserved for French, Prussian or Russian expansionists. Before the end of the century, Lord Rosebery called it "a larger patriotism." Indeed, it had become a compound loyalty to the old territorial base of dynastic power and to the expansive economic and political structure of

---

[1]Cited in R. R. James, *British Revolution* (1977), p. 25.

formal and informal empire. The union and the empire were interdependent entities, whose constitutions both faced serious challenges by 1890.

CHAPTER 9

IMPERIAL FINALE

> In an independent world, England is more dependent than most major nations. Instead of England leading the world as in Victorian times, international political and economic constraints today severely limit the government's scope for action. An empire turned into a multiracial Commonwealth now poses problems too. The arrival of more than a million new Commonwealth immigrants faces England with the problem of adapting a formerly all-white society to multiracial life. Within the United Kingdom, expressions of nationalism in different ways in Northern Ireland, Scotland, and Wales have forced Her Majesty's government to think about the means by which a single parliament at Westminster can govern a multinational system.
>
> (Richard Rose, *Politics in England*, 1986, p. 30)

In the 20th century the British Empire disintegrated and the archipelago was politically and constitutionally divided, while the combined forces of totalitarianism, social democracy and nationalism were altering the shape of world politics. Although the empire made some impressive contributions in the world wars, neither its weapons nor its ideology were a match for the combined strength of American and European rivals. Economic power which had been the empire's basis was being overtaken as early as the 1880s, and its political structure barely lasted into the second half of the 20th century. As that structure was dismantled, a compound of political divisions in the archipelago appeared. These events at home and abroad were interdependent, but their courses tended to drift apart, particularly after the great watershed of the Second World War.

The first broad crisis in government occurred between 1890 and 1914. In the 90s there was increasing international rivalry, racial and national tension and social democratic protest. One manifestation of the crisis appeared in South Africa, with war between white settlers apparently engineered by British agents. The fighting had mixed results, and victory did

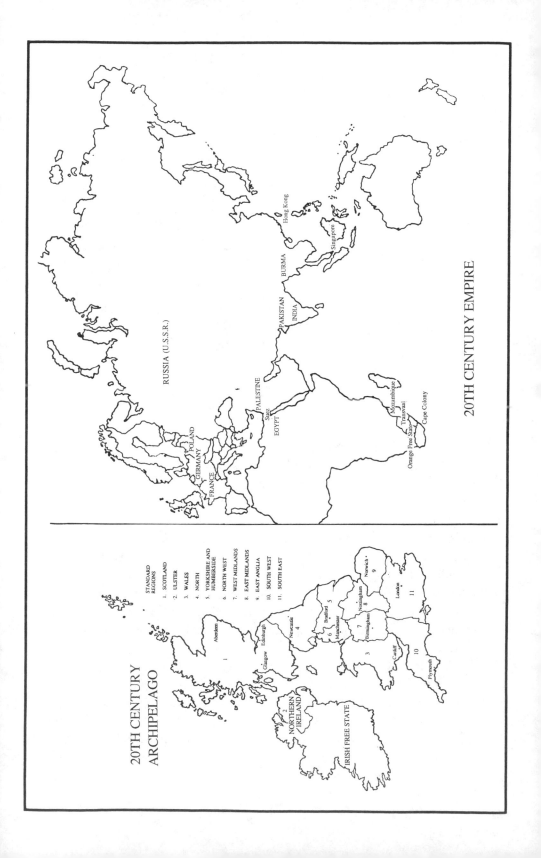

20TH CENTURY ARCHIPELAGO

STANDARD REGIONS

1. SCOTLAND
2. ULSTER
3. WALES
4. NORTH
5. YORKSHIRE AND HUMBERSIDE
6. NORTH WEST
7. WEST MIDLANDS
8. EAST MIDLANDS
9. EAST ANGLIA
10. SOUTH WEST
11. SOUTH EAST

Aberdeen

Glasgow
Edinburgh
Newcastle
4
Bradford 5
6 Manchester
3 7 Birmingham 8 Nottingham
Cardiff 9 Norwich
10 London 11
Plymouth

2
NORTHERN IRELAND

IRISH FREE STATE

20TH CENTURY EMPIRE

RUSSIA (U.S.S.R.)

GERMANY
POLAND
FRANCE

PALESTINE
Suez
EGYPT

PAKISTAN
INDIA
BURMA
Hong Kong
Singapore

Mozambique
Transvaal
Orange Free State
Cape Colony

not produce uniform response. Indeed the imperial consensus broke down, followed by the liberal consensus in domestic affairs. There was growing domestic political violence and a constitutional crisis over the House of Lords.

The domestic crisis was overwhelmed by European and world war. The Empire was unprepared, in military, diplomatic and political terms, especially for the war which Britain had to fight. The major campaigns were in Europe, where the combatants were mauled in four years of trench warfare, after which they tried to solve the divisive issues of the day at the Peace Conference in Paris (1919). In the archipelago the war stalled a constitutional Irish Home Rule measure and a possible rebellion in Ulster. Dublin's "Easter Rebellion" (1916) changed the question into one of armed force. Hostilities (1918-21) led to a truce and treaty (1921); dominion constitutions were settled on the North and the Irish Free State, though in the latter the sequel was internal violence between Irish parties (1922-25). Partition of Ireland was no solution, for both sides were frustrated by the partial disruption of the union. In the 1920s small nationalist parties appeared in Scotland and Wales, but they were overshadowed by the advance of the Labour party, which attracted large blocs of "Celtic fringe" votes on the way to its first electoral plurality in 1929.

The next two decades saw imperial collapse: depression, war and anti-colonialism were key factors. The empire actually reached its greatest extent around 1930 and the Statute of Westminster (1931) defined a global empire and commonwealth which appeared to be a shrewd compromise of colonial and responsible government. Yet the real structure and power were already eroding, and no amount of written constitutional phrases would halt the march of events.

The second war, even more than the first, involved the civilian population and forced political leaders to promise generous reconstruction programs. As these had been neglected in 1919, the government could not do so again, even though the cost of the second war had a more shattering effect on the British and imperial economy. The great Labour majority of 1945 was a vote for reconstruction, and the 'welfare state' thus inaugurated was based on national insurance and nationalized industry.

In external affairs, Britain changed the most: the ambiguity of the Commonwealth was increased, the Anglo-American alliance was emphasized, and the European Economic Community which at first was boycotted out of pride, was later joined out of necessity. Within a decade of the war's end, moreover, the global strategic power of Britain was drastically reduced, as shown by the 1956 crisis over the Suez Canal.

Meanwhile vital changes occurred in the internal constitution of the archipelago. Centralism was enshrined in the growing social service agencies and economic management machinery, but that picture was modified by regional organization. Scotland, Wales, Northern Ireland and regions of England were made the basis for economic plans and programs. In a way, these divisions recalled the early 20th century schemes for "home rule all round," schemes which had been among the casualties of postwar Irish violence. But just as regional federalism had been a distraction from "home rule," its reincarnation was a useful foil for resurgent Scottish and Welsh nationalism in the 1960s and 70s. The political base for the national movements, especially in Wales, was very narrow, but sentiment (or major party fear) was strong enough to produce a royal commission study of "devolution," a series of legislative measures, and referenda in 1979 which defeated the proposals for Scottish and Welsh assemblies. In the meantime changes went on in local government and in the national political system, changes which promised that the constitution would continue to evolve.

In 1980 the archipelago displayed a compound of features of union and division: regional economics, cultural loyalties and administrative separation were offset by royalism and tradition, parliamentary supremacy and the ideal of the unitary state. Without its imperial shell, how would this political federation adjust? In what direction would continuing tension, most visible in the army presence in Ulster, push political change? How would the mix of external ties to the North Atlantic Treaty Organization and the European Economic Community and the American colossus affect the political future?

Democracy and Confrontation

The last generation of the 19th century saw the formal achievement of political democracy and the bitter evolution of political confrontations at all levels. The two were interdependent in that the lure of democracy could inspire extreme behavior, and the more direct confrontations could force more democratic reform. In the context of the empire and archipelago, of course, these interactions became more complicated.

In spite of the progressive direction of franchise reform, the main lines of party policy were dictated by powerful leaders, some of whom seemed to control electoral baronies, and all of whom maneuvered for power within an elite circle of political chiefs. The most important contests were not at the polls. The ascendancy of Salisbury over Randolph Churchill (and his "Fourth Party") and the stubborn resistance by Gladstone to the challenge of Joseph Chamberlain were critical personal struggles. Both leaders affirmed their positions, and one consequence was to force Chamberlain and Liberal Unionists to look for ways to work with the Conservatives. Such a coalition did in fact hold power for most of the two decades before 1906. This unsettled party political scene contributed to the spreading and escalating incidents of confrontation. Collectively these incidents paint an unflattering picture of the first generation of democracy; imperial war in South Africa fought for dubious reasons; constitutional battle over the House of Lords when its leaders opposed the will of the electorate; renewed Irish Home Rule efforts which inspired Unionist rebellion; and agitations by workers and women for further extension of "democracy."

The shape of democracy in the 1890s was such that about 20% of adult males still could not vote, and women could not vote in parliamentary elections. Since 1869 it had been possible for unmarried women to vote in borough elections (followed by school boards in 1870 and county councils, 1888). The vote was still essentially a property-based privilege: for rate-payers, for householders, for lodgers who occupied premises of £10 annual value. This limited democracy had more egalitarian expressions in mass education, popular journalism and the expansion of organized labor. The operation of the working-class vote could be detected in social policies adopted before the end of the century: workmen's compensation, the eight-hour day for coal miners, housing, public health and trade union measures. On the other hand, the landed aristocrats experienced some recession of their hereditary strength, due to the effect of depression on rents and due to political moves. The buy-out of Irish landlords continued (1885-1903), and the English and Welsh county governing structure was significantly altered (though the persons governing changed only slightly) by the County

Councils Act which supplanted the local governing powers of the Justice of the Peace (1888).

The latter part of the 19th century was the period when the first "national" political party organizations came into being. These have been overrated in their impact. When viewed across the archipelago, they were regionally-bound (North and South Wales Liberals, eastern and western Scottish bodies; the renowned "Birmingham caucus," etc.) There was perhaps no genuine "U.K." political party, even the "Conservative and Unionist" organization was made up of very different types of unionists. Another form of internal complication is shown by the evolving Labour Party, composed of main elements from trade unions (by no means monolithic) and socialist groups with their inherent individuality: the Social Democratic Federation (1881), Fabian Society (1884), Crofter Independent Party (1885), Scottish Labour Party (1888), and Independent Labour Party (1893).

The imperial ideas of the 70s and 80s had conjured up a "greater Britain" with a steadily-developing federal structure, but imperialists of the 1890s were forced to confront a more realistic assessment of Britain's place in the world. Her European competitors had made their claims in Africa and Asia in the 1880s, and the emphasis now shifted to the allocation of "spheres of influence." At the same time, the democratized political scene changed the media and the tone of imperial discussion. With a growing mass-circulation press, with a more literate, book-buying populace, the global activity of the U.K. was becoming the property of the public.

That public was addressed in language which was shot through with outspoken, quasi-scientific racism. According to Joseph Chamberlain, "the British race was the greatest of governing races that the world has ever seen." This was the attitude which disposed people to believe that there was a "white man's burden," nobly to be borne for the advance of civilization. This attitude stalled colonial self-government in non-white territories until well into the 20th century. Yet those populations were not deterred from their own national sentiments and from the formation of political movements to express their views and advance their causes.

Colonial nationalism was evident in the revolt of Egyptian army officers in 1881, it was present in diluted form in the Indian National Congress (1884) and it was apparent in more strident form in the Boer Republics in

338

South Africa. Imperialists saw these manifestations as nuisances, or even as further signs that colonies were not "ready" for self-government. This view was most inappropriate for South Africa, where a decade of fast-moving imperial activity ended in a bitter war which totally changed the imperial consensus in the Atlantic Archipelago.

Since the Napoleonic period, Britain interfered for strategic purposes in the Cape Colony. When Boer farmers moved away to evade slavery abolition, the British followed them and periodically threatened their governments in the Orange River Colony and the Transvaal. Later 19th century discoveries of diamonds (1870) and gold (1886) insured continuing interest in their affairs. The Cape Colony, under Prime Minister Cecil Rhodes, tried to form a territorial barrier around them, but Transvaal President Paul Kruger succeeded in building a railway link to the sea through Mozambique, and his state was on its way to becoming the strongest power in South Africa. Transvaal mining was done by immigrant whites who outnumbered the Boer population. Rhodes tried to exploit the lack of political rights of the *uitlanders* to foment rebellion and seize power on behalf of the Cape Colony. A raid in 1895 was thwarted, Rhodes was forced to resign, and Joseph Chamberlain the Colonial Secretary was embarrassed but able to cover up his role in the episode. The new British High Commissioner, Alfred Milner (1897-1905) was determined to achieve British ascendancy, and his negotiations with Kruger were destined to fail. After a Boer ultimatum in October 1899, war was declared.

For several months Boer forces had the initiative, besieging several forts and threatening some major towns. After British reinforcements arrived, the centers were recaptured and a British offensive began. Conventional warfare ended in a Boer defeat in October 1900. There ensued a guerilla campaign which led to ugly reprisals, concentration camps and widespread misery before a treaty was signed in May, 1902. The Cape Colony annexed the Republics, an oath of allegiance to Edward VII was required, and reparations of some £3 million were made to the Boers. The total cost of the war for Britain was some £250 million. About 22,000 imperial soldiers died, only 5,800 in battle (compared with estimated Boer battle deaths of 4,000). But another 20,000 women and children died from disease in the concentration camps. Such shocking mortality was a sobering statistic. As tempers began to cool, the political impact of the war was visible in many ways.

First the war showed that Britain was isolated and held in contempt by world opinion. A more disturbing form of opposition was the support given by Kaiser Wilhelm for Kruger's government, support which was seen as a corollary of new German naval construction programs.

The domestic political effect of the Boer War was quite as important as any other consequence. The divisions of the Liberal Party were compounded and aggravated and the wider electorate was split on an imperial issue as it had rarely been before. The main element of the Liberals was behind the government through the better part of the actual hostilities; but reports and recriminations continued after the war, and by 1901 Campbell-Bannerman (who had succeeded Lord Rosebery as leader in 1898), publicly opposed the "Liberal Imperialist" position. The young Welsh M.P. David Lloyd George was one of the more outspoken "pro-Boers," and he was once threatened by an angry mob of 30,000 in Birmingham. That sort of public behavior suggested a stronger support for the war than may have actually existed. Even at its height, when the Conservatives called the "khaki election" of 1900, the voters only added four seats to the number of Tories, in spite of considerable division and confusion among the Liberals.

In South Africa itself, the postwar settlement was a target of loud recrimination. If Britain had been fighting for "votes for Uitlanders" she had lost. Mineowners now tried to exclude white labor entirely, hoping to avoid future conflicts. But their haste contributed to political disputes. Milner authorized the import of Chinese laborers for the mines (1904-05), and this move brought vehement charges of "slavery." Meanwhile, the annexation of the Boer Republics with the Cape went ahead, and fairly swift settlement of dominion status (giving no political rights to black or Asian inhabitants) formed the climax to this unhappy chapter of the Empire. In South Africa "the imperial idea had thus suffered a contraction, a loss of moral content, from which it never completely recovered."[1] Popular support and public acceptance of empire, the glory and the righteousness of England (Britain) were no longer self-evident and non-partisan.

Arthur Balfour succeeded his uncle Lord Salisbury as Prime Minister in 1902. Besides being an outstanding intellectual of his day, Balfour had the unusual experience of having served as Secretary for Scotland and Chief

---

[1]A.P. Thornton, *The Imperial Idea and its Enemies*, (1958) p. 125.

Secretary for Ireland. His government had to deal with postwar settlement in South Africa and important domestic questions such as education reform (1902) and the culmination of Irish land purchase (1903). On top of these issues, the government was faced with the new initiative of imperial preference (i.e. tariff reform) introduced by Joseph Chamberlain in 1903.

The Liberals' internal fractures over home rule and empire were measurably healed by the fundamental challenge to their gospel of "free trade." That traditional position was small comfort to exporters in the current world economy, but it was a tonic to the tattered political party. And on another front, the weak Liberal position on workers' political organization was covered by a secret pact in 1903, whereby Liberal and Labour candidates were to avoid contesting the same seats, in effect forming an alliance against the Conservatives. For the moment, this caused no damage to the Liberals, but they lost an opportunity to recapture what was once their "Lib-Lab" wing, and what now was the most rapidly developing and potentially powerful electoral force. After 1900, Labour's ranks were growing and there was unprecedented co-operation between the essentially hostile trade unions and doctrinaire socialists. By 1906, with only a modest steering committee in place, they took 29 seats, and the new M.P.s adopted a parliamentary party constitution.

The real news of the 1906 election was the Liberal victory in 400 seats, against only 157 for the Unionists. Liberal strength was widespread, in rural and urban districts, and with special concentrations in Wales and Scotland (but only three seats in Ireland). However, it seems likely that the voters had registered an opinion *against* Tories and *against* past measures, more than for the Liberals or for social democracy. Whatever the voters wanted in 1906, they were given a startling political performance in the next eight years. Major social reform, serious constitutional confrontation bringing two elections in one year (1910), and a surprising assortment of extreme political tactics by workers and women, by army officers and aristocrats.

The Liberals who were victorious in 1906 were unlike the team which left office in 1895, and quite alien to those who held power in 1885. New progressive views on pensions, land reform and health insurance were a reflection of the enlarged electorate after 1885. However, the House of Lords had changed in the opposite direction over the same period. In 1868 there had been a Tory majority of 60; by 1906 that majority had swollen to

341

nearly 400. This change was magnified by the fact that it occurred when the issues being discussed were increasingly popular or democratic in content-- hence the parliamentary political setting was explosive. When the Liberals won the election in 1906, Balfour said that "the great Unionist party should still control, whether in power or whether in opposition, the destinies of this great empire." Such a comment suggested that he planned to use Tory strength in the House of Lords to defy the electorate--so at least it would be read by a Liberal.

In the first three years of the new parliament only a few major pieces of legislation were adopted. The Trades Disputes Act (1906) granted important legal immunity to trade unions; the Old Age Pensions Act of 1908 established the principle of state-aided support for the elderly. But other measures were either rejected or heavily amended by the peers. Some proposals for curbing the peers' power were brought forward, but easily sidetracked. In 1908 the ministry was reorganized. Herbert Asquith became the new Prime Minister and Lloyd George the new Chancellor of the Exchequer. In 1909 the new leadership brought in what was called the "People's Budget." New taxes, especially on land, would pay for more social programs and more new navy vessels. The budget had become the province of the Commons alone since the end of the 17th century, and according to convention, the Lords could not intervene. It may be that the Liberals chose to provoke the peers this way, or it may be that the peers' success in their earlier maneuvers encouraged them to take their tactics one step further. In either case, the Lords voted against the budget in November 1909.

At first it was uncertain what the vote meant. Tories maintained that the adverse vote required a new election; Liberals upheld the Commons' priority and insisted that the election be a referendum on the budget. In the event, the voters went to the polls in January 1910 and took away the Liberal majority, made a virtual tie with Unionists (275-273) and gave the balance of power to Irish Home Rulers (82) and Labour (40). This meant that in further constitutional votes the government would have to rely on Irish support. The first order of business was the budget, which passed in April. But already the focus of attention was on the constitution--what would be done about the peers? Would the crown create sufficient new peers to give a Liberal majority? King Edward VII died in May, 1910, and it was obviously indelicate to force the question on George V; in any case, the number of new titles would have been too great to contemplate. A party conference (June-November) tried to work out a solution, and when none was found, a new election was called in December. This result was a tie (272) with 84 Irish and 42 Labour M.P.s. The Liberals remained in office and prepared to introduce their bill to reform the Lords.

Introduced in February 1911, the Parliament Act passed in May (after 900 amendments and a threat to create peers). The act created a two-year "suspensive veto"--i.e., the Lords might only halt a measure two years running. If the Commons passed an identical bill in three consecutive sessions, it would become law. In addition, the Lords could not amend a "money bill" (so designated by the Speaker of the House). The other main provision was to reduce the maximum term of parliament from seven to five years. The measure finally made its way through the Lords in August. The crisis surrounding the Parliament Act showed a grave weakening of political convention and loss of traditional restraint. Outside parliament, the years 1906-1914 witnessed a decline of stable political discourse and the frequent resort to violent methods of persuasion. The foremost example was in the battle between the Irish Home Rule (alias nationalist) movement and the hard line Ulster Unionists. This issue nearly resulted in a rebellion (1912-14) before the Great War, and midway through that holocaust there was a revolt. In 1886 and 1893 there had been violent agitation in Ulster against pending schemes for Home Rule. The parliamentary defeats silenced the agitation temporarily. But when the Parliament Act passed with Irish support, there was a clear prospect of Home Rule. This in turn produced more determined outside opposition. An "Ulster Covenant" was signed by 500,000 Protestants who vowed to resist Home Rule by any means. From 1911, units of volunteers had been drilling illegally, arms were being smuggled into Ulster, and in 1913 the "Ulster Volunteer Force" was organized, eventually reaching some 100,000 men, with cavalry and motorized units (but without artillery or aircraft). This was paralleled by a provisional Ulster government. It had sympathetic support from British army officers, who at one point turned in mass resignations rather than carry out a policy which was aimed at suppressing the Ulster loyalists. German arms were landed in Ulster in early 1914, where gun-running had been an open activity, but when a shipment of arms for Irish volunteers in the South was landed, there was government intervention and loss of life. Meanwhile, the Conservative and Unionist party endorsed the Ulster cause. Party leaders Andrew Bonar Law, Walter Long and Edward Carson attended a mass review of the volunteers in 1912, and they spoke publicly and freely of resisting a Home Rule measure. There was evidence that they gave covert encouragement to mutinous army officers in 1914. In the end, Asquith gave in and offered Ulster a six-month exemption from the operation of the Home Rule Act. A conference was summoned by the king in July 1914 to find a compromise; no solution was negotiated, but the law (due to go into effect in September) was put aside by general agreement when war was declared.

During the crisis, the South had raised volunteers, and they were being armed and drilled. The conventional idea of Home Rule was being overtaken by vigorous nationalism, republicanism and socialism. Since the unionists vowed resistance, there was strong likelihood of civil war; it might be postponed by a larger war abroad, but the threat would remain.

There were other forms of brutality in politics which were not connected to the Irish question. The campaign for "Votes for Women" reached its peak in 1913. Over the preceding half century there had been statutory concessions but there had also been stubborn political and judicial resistance, evoking more vigorous agitation. It might seem that denial of the parliamentary franchise could not go on much longer, but such expectations were overheated by a radically new agitation, which itself became a central part of the issue. Emmaline Pankhurst and her daughters Sylvia and Christabel were not shy of the notoriety which soon came to the Women's Social and Political Union. Founded in 1903, the women campaigned in moderate fashion at first, but by 1908 the members resorted to heckling speakers and to physical obstruction. When some of their number were roughly handled by police, the tactics were broadened to include hunger strikes, vandalism and more dramatic protests. The center of active agitation was in southern England (where it would have the greatest effect). Only a few incidents were reported in Edinburgh and in Wales, and only in Scotland were there traces of organization similar to that in England. Several attempts were made to push through legislative endorsement of the female vote, but leaders like Asquith had been alienated and challenged, and they became hostile to the suffragettes. Here again, the war brought a suspension, but it also brought large-scale female employment and a social upheaval which was reflected in the Representation of the People Act (1918) which first gave votes to women in parliamentary elections. It is difficult to account for the radical tactics of the suffragettes. Their action must be seen as part of a move beyond the 19th century issue of franchise reform, toward the 20th century reshaping of politics. Direct action, that which bypassed the parliamentary course, or was designed to sweep it along on a wave of popular emotion, emerged as a new and disturbing part of the political scene, one which induced a wide range of public demonstrations, and one which provoked an impressive government response designed to subdue opposition. These newer expressions (parades, strikes, mass meetings) seemed traditional enough, and they appeared to be logical extensions of the 19th century reforms. However, new groups and tactics took political action in new directions.

A major instance of the new direction was provided by the development of organized labor and working mens' political parties in the archipelago. From about 1880, the less skilled and more numerous workers (dockers, seamen, etc.) were being organized, and these new unions tended to have more radical and aggressive leaders than the older craft unions. There were still significantly different traditions and conditions in different parts of the archipelago, and aside from migrating leaders, there were no extensive international bodies before 1900. Indeed, a Trades Union Congress had been set up in England in the 1860s, and a counterpart in Scotland in 1897, while most union activity in Ireland and Wales lagged behind, due to different cultural and political interests. Meanwhile, workers' political action was moving ahead in other areas. Two general forms may be sketched here: socialist parties and trade union activities.

The Scottish Labour Party was formed in 1888, a small and localized group. A conference was held in Bradford (1893) which formed the Independent Labour Party, a body which has been called "intrinsically regional in character."[2] In 1896 James Connolly formed the Irish Socialist Republican Party. By the turn of the century a few labor candidates were finding success in parliamentary elections, and in 1900 an important conference in London brought labor union and socialist leaders together to form a joint Labour Representation Committee. Other parties continued to appear, such as the Scottish Socialist Labour Party in 1903. By the 1906

---

[2]Morgan, *Wales in British Politics*, p. 199.

election, the candidates endorsed by the L.R.C. formed a large enough bloc in the Commons to constitute themselves as a national (U.K.) party.

The existence of the new parliamentary party did not mean the end of the smaller doctrinaire or regional parties. Nor did it affect the other forms of labor political action which were becoming more prominent in the early years of the 20th century. The use of strike action entered a new phase of political significance, primarily because of the new levels of worker mobilization (new unions and syndicalist theory) and because of the new strategies adopted by governments to cope with labor unrest. A small selection from the disputes of these years shows the nature of change. In 1900 there was a strike against the Taff Vale Railway in Wales by the Amalgamated Society of Railway Servants. The union was held liable for damages occurring in the strike, to an amount which meant bankruptcy. This decision on an appeal to the House of Lords seemed to threaten the right to strike, and it aroused widespread labor opposition. In 1906 the new Liberal government passed a Trades Disputes Act which was meant to prevent future liability of this kind. Meanwhile, the more elementary purpose of striking was being tested. An unsuccessful six-month miners' strike in Wales (1898) was but one instance in which the owners seemed to have the upper hand. In response, some organizers looked to larger, more powerful union organization, and tougher, more direct political action. In reply, the government was willing to intervene, as in the riotous setting at Tonypandy (November 1910) when troops were sent in to quell the violence. To its credit, the government also offered mediation. Under legislation of 1896, supplemented in 1911, there were procedures for resolving disputes, and the number of arbitration boards rose from 64 in 1894 to 325 in 1913.[3] The unions meanwhile were being influenced by notions of syndicalist action, and were forming larger bodies such as the National Transport Workers Federation (dockers and seamen, 1910) and a "Triple Alliance" of transport, mine and railway workers (1914).

The oversized union groups were perhaps less of a threat than they appeared to be. Still, there were some very serious and challenging forms of labor organization in various parts of the archipelago. In 1913 the Irish Transport and General Workers' Union staged a bitter five-month strike. In the same year, James Connolly began to organize his "Citizen Army" in

---

[3]Henry Pelling, *A History of British Trade Unionism* (1976), p. 142.

Dublin, a radical workers' group which eventually participated in armed rebellion. This and other incidents suggest that it is too simple to see the labor discontent of this period being suppressed by the war and a burst of patriotism. In 1915 there was serious trouble on the Clyde; in 1918 there was a dispute in the ranks of the London police; in sum, the new century and its escalating political militance pointed to a renovation of domestic politics. Yet that change has been hard to discern through the smoke and carnage which fell on Europe in 1914.

Empire Goes to War

The British Empire was tested in the devastation of the Great War, and although the nation gained a military victory, its political system suffered heavy casualties. The war was a political event of the first magnitude, requiring full-scale mobilization and control, disarray and disuse of political parties and a radical postwar settlement. These were serious enough, but during the war the stage was set for brutal fighting in Ireland and the forcible partition so long resisted there. These violent events caused what Winston Churchill called the "liquefaction" of politics in the 20s: shifting major parties, and serious constitutional debates within a greatly enlarged and demanding electorate and empire.

British involvement in World War One is difficult to explain, for there were few obvious grounds for war with Germany. Yet preparation for such a war seemed to have been on the agenda for some time. In the diplomatic realignment at the beginning of the century, Britain had engaged in strategic agreements with Japan (1902), France (1904) and Russia (1907). During these years military policies and programs were being overhauled, a new planning agency was created (the Committee for Imperial Defence, 1902), the fleet was reassigned to home waters, a new army organization was worked out, and secret military talks were held with the French, as a strategy centered on a continental expeditionary force was developed. What was behind these actions? Around the end of the 19th century there was a growing sense of the loss of British dominance in spite of her massive naval and economic power. European competition in both spheres was a novel and frightening condition, no doubt one which was exaggerated beyond its true proportions. There were occasions in the 80s and 90s when political "panic" set in on the question of preparedness--or rather, lack of it. In 1884 there was a French naval scare, the German navy act of 1898 brought tension, and the army losses in South Africa were hardly reassuring.

The most unnerving development was the German fleet program, perhaps because its existence was a novelty and its potential was unknown. Certainly it was a serious challenge to the "two-power standard," which conventional rule told British officials that they had to have as many capital ships as the next two strongest powers. This could not be maintained after 1900. In fact, the technological changes from 1870 to 1914 were so great that they disabled most calculations based on a simple count of ships. After so many years of reduced spending, there were relatively low levels of manning, armament and preparation. Occasional spurts of politically-inspired activity, such as naval construction in 1884, 1889 and 1904 had not dispersed a pervasive lethargy and overconfidence. The unpleasant corollary to weak naval leadership was lack of innovation. The submarine, the screw propeller and the rifled gun barrel were not warmly received by most of the admirals.

By 1906, the British made arrangements in secret military talks with France which were indicative of the decline of her naval power. The countries agreed that, in the event of hostilities, France would have responsibility for Mediterranean sectors, the British for the Atlantic and North Sea. While H.M. vessels made a presence felt around the globe, limits on the power of the fleet were clearly visible in Admiral Fisher's reorganization which shifted main battleship strength to home waters in 1905. The British army was a volunteer force with a combination of professional and territorial (militia) units. The South African war had been a humbling experience, after which there was some reform, but hardly enough. At the same time the desire to reduce spending was costly in terms of technological advance, force levels and general strategy.

The diplomatic problem in Europe before 1914 arose from a compound of military alliances, military plans and preparations and rival national and imperial aspirations. Russia, Austria and Turkey presided over declining continental empires, while Germany, France and Italy had expansive policies as ambitious new regimes. Since 1885, Germany, Austria and Italy were members of the Triple Alliance. To counter this, France and Russia became allies in 1894. Both alliances were designed for mutual protection and each

348

probably induced greater risk of war in a given crisis. The crises which culminated in war began in a series of conflicts and outrages in the Balkans, chiefly territory between Austria and Turkey in which several nations were seeking international recognition, usually with outside help. British engagement was slow, awkward and inconclusive; by 1895 she had dropped the defense of Constantinople in favor of a strong Egyptian base; by 1902 she made an alliance with Japan, who three years later removed Russia from seapower competition. Meanwhile there were pacific gestures to France from 1903. By 1904, Admiral Fisher was beginning his reassignment of the fleet. Between 1906 and 1913 there were regular diplomatic crises involving the major powers, usually triggered by a military or diplomatic incident in the Balkans. In each case there were prompt steps taken through diplomatic channels to bring matters to negotiation.

The 1914 crisis was a bizarre set of events, even when we only consider European state relations. Earlier crises from about 1908 had been settled by conferences and treaties. Somehow, the crisis after the assassination of the heir to the Austrian throne (Archduke Franz Ferdinand) was uncontainable. Austria gave the Serbs an ultimatum, which Russia urged the Serbs to accept. When Austria declared war, Russia ordered mobilization, Germany gave an ultimatum to Russia to desist and then mobilized herself, putting into operation the famous general staff orders (the "Schlieffen Plan") which required a German invasion of France before attacking Russia. The German attack violated neutral Belgium, and gave the British ministers the way out of their dilemma, wherein they had committed Britain to defend France without telling most of their colleagues. The war which began in 1914 was not the one for which strategists were prepared. It consumed 20 million lives and mountains of treasure before it ended. Primarily a European war, it involved the empire and the U.S. in a limited and peripheral fashion. The major initial power alterations were European, but the long-term effects of the war reached around the globe. In this chapter we must emphasize the war's political aspects, and readers will have to look elsewhere for battles and strategy. The conduct and impact of the European war, the conduct of war in Ireland, and the postwar politics of the 1920s (imperial and domestic) are our chief concerns.

The "Great War" had three major political aspects in the archipelago: the mass mobilization, common to all combatants; the constitutional strain on a democratic state at war; and the party political repercussions of the struggle. The impact was similar around the archipelago, though some responses bore the marks of historic regional variation. Mass mobilization drew resources from all parts; unprecedented regulation was imposed by war needs; and notable patriotic fervor was created, at least in the first few years of fighting.

There was general and enthusiastic support for the British war effort at first (even from Ireland, North and South). Due to enlistments there were shortages in some critical occupations (e.g. Scots coalminers). Popular support was blunted naturally enough by the carnage of 1914-16, and in the latter year conscription was introduced in Britain. It appears in retrospect that voluntary enlistment might have been enough to sustain the war effort, though no one would have guessed that in the later months of 1916. Some six million were eventually in uniform. These needs were totally unforeseen, and the expeditionary force had been expected home before the end of 1914. By then, however, there were new demands for recruits and the drain on workers forced hiring of women and unskilled workers.

An important corollary to the manpower question was that organized labor was strengthened while it grew more radical in some areas. Union membership doubled during the war from four to eight million. Strikes were nominally renounced in 1915, but this was actually an abdication by national leaders, after which shop stewards took it upon themselves to lead sporadic stoppages. In general the time lost on strike was limited, and the war effort often gave added leverage to workers. In the case of a necessity like coal, government subsidized the mine owners and the miners' wages in order to avoid strike action. All the same, workers in some areas gave ample evidence of increasing radicalism (e.g. Clydeside shipworkers and South Wales miners). The workers' main grievance was wartime inflation but owners feared revolutionary tendencies. Actually the capitalists' tactics for managing the war economy were not calculated to make socialists less optimistic about plans for nationalized industry and social policy.

War industry was erratically brought under government supervision and basic production (coal, iron, steel, shipping) was accelerated, while special production (munitions in particular) was taken over by central authority. Late in the war, shipping, railroads and food supply were brought under emergency direction by the London government. Most measures were taken without any debate or discussion, all of them extended to the whole archipelago, and radical economic interventions were accepted as a necessary wartime measure.

The general constitutional image of wartime government was that of suspended democracy and militarized administration. By statute or prerogative the chief ministers and officers of the crown waged war as it had never been waged before. A War Council was succeeded in 1917 by a War Cabinet (five members) each body having secretariats to implement their elaborate directives. Ordinary liberties were suspended, a course generally accepted by the population. Out of approximately 16,000 conscientious objectors about 1,300 served terms in jail. As for traditional politics, the leaders of all parties accepted a moratorium on regular opposition. The main statutory power used by the government in the war was the Defence of the Realm Act. It gave broad powers to carry out whatever measures were deemed necessary "for the public safety and defence of the realm," and it included wide authority to deal with persons opposing or impeding the government's action or those giving any aid to the enemies of the crown. One of the more ominous measures, initiated after it was clear that the war would be of long duration, was the National Register of all Persons in August 1915--how successful it was is uncertain; how totalitarian it was is obvious.

After the first bout of patriotism, the war took its toll on the morale of society. The long casualty lists, the indecisive but terribly costly battles, all were bound to be discouraging. There were two forms of information control: censorship and propaganda. The uses at first were simple and innocuous. But before the war was over, the government had imposed heavy censorship, while it brought in heavy subsidies for newspapers to offset falling advertising revenues. In 1918 a Ministry of Information was formed to coordinate and disseminate war-related stories.

Thus most of the constitutional action during the war was understandable but disturbingly illiberal. These measures were tied to the warmaking process; and the government felt obliged to promise compensatory postwar measures (pensions, education, housing, voting rights). Franchise reform was the only promise effectively fulfilled. The Act of 1918 gave the vote to most adult males (excepting only peers, criminals and the insane). It added six million women over 30. Even if it was a grudging concession, the result was indeed important. The franchise issue was practically settled as the Liberal era came to an end.

When voters went to the polls in 1918, it was for the first time in eight years. By resolutions in the Commons the required election of 1915 had simply been postponed. This was not a serious constitutional lapse, as it turned out; there was never much danger that elections would not be resumed, but there was plenty of reason for concern over what happened in their absence. If the voters were inactive, leaders certainly were not.

The Liberal government of Herbert Asquith began the war. At first it enjoyed ample support, but within nine months there was a threat of conservative opposition when it appeared that artillery shells had run out and there were rumors of a major internal dispute at the Admiralty (between Churchill and Fisher). In May 1915 the government was reorganized as a coalition, with Bonar Law and Balfour joining Asquith, Lloyd George and Arthur Henderson, the token Labour representative, as members of the cabinet. This arrangement lasted until December 1916, when once again the conservatives became restive under Asquith's leadership. A complicated coup was staged in which Lloyd George was made the head of a new coalition. In his first War Cabinet were Bonar Law, Curzon, Milner and Henderson. Lloyd George made a strong impression as an effective leader in the Ministry of Munitions and then as Secretary for War. From a stance close to pacifism in 1914, he had shifted rapidly and decisively toward the role of a vigorous war leader. His advent marked the highest level of government ever attained by a Welsh politician, but nationality had ceased to be major theme in his politics as early as 1900. Lloyd George remained in power for nearly six years, holding together his wartime coalition until 1922 and at the same time dealing a heavy blow to the Liberal Party by creating and continuing a deep personal rivalry at the top.

The change in 1916 produced a unified and invigorated coalition which "won" the war, negotiated the peace and managed the transition to "normalcy." In war more than other times, we focus on the command centers of politics, as indeed we must. However, political life did go on elsewhere, and it had more life in the local communities than in the moribund House of Commons. But the local focus was also on the war; issues of devolution or disestablishment were temporarily muted, but those and other sectional issues were not forgotten.

With the armistice in 1918, politics revived, but in a strange and "un-British" form. The franchise act was too late to have an effect on the outcome, and Lloyd George managed the election with what Asquith derisively called the "Coupon." Each Coalition candidate got a letter of endorsement from the Prime Minister, which Asquith likened to a ration coupon, implying that both were wartime expedients, both symbolized government restriction, and both ought to be jettisoned since peace had arrived. The coalition won a decisive victory, some of it on a vindictive platform of "making Germany pay" and some of it on the more humane (if no less impractical) promise of postwar reconstruction of a "land fit for heroes to live in."

Immediately after this victory, Lloyd George set out for Paris and the Peace Conference at the head of the empire delegation. In fact, the dominions began to receive greater recognition of their autonomy at the conference and they would demand more in the years ahead. The election of 1918 had one especially ominous result. The Sinn Fein winners (73 in all) did not take their seats at Westminster. Those who were out of jail remained in Dublin, proclaimed the Irish Republic and met as the "Dáil Éirann" in January 1919. The Irish revolution was underway, as were other European upheavals, in the wake of the great international conflict.

The "Irish Question" was unanswered in 1914, and when the British government returned to it, the question was totally different. The change was accomplished by the events of 1916-18 and the gestation of the first popular revolutionary movement in southern Ireland. To understand its rise, we have to go back to the fate of the Home Rule Act of 1914.

John Redmond had inherited the Parnell legacy, but he was not able to reunite the Home Rule party until 1900, by which time other forces were gaining strength rapidly. Redmond's methods were moderate and constitutional, and in the early 20th century he was overtaken by violent events and radical leaders. This became evident from 1898 on with Sinn Fein, labor and socialist groups. In 1911, when passage of Home Rule seemed assured, the organization of armed forces and provisional government in Ulster, complete with rousing gestures such as the Ulster Covenant, brought the issue to the brink of rebellion. The famous gun-running incidents of 1914 and the drilling of volunteers in North and South were clear enough signs. John Redmond used his influence to assume a leading role with the southern volunteers. When war broke out, Redmond urged support for the British cause and accepted the postponement of the Home Rule Act. There was a significant response to the call for recruits in the south and even more in the north of Ireland. But one segment of "National Volunteers" had never been true supporters of Redmond. The Irish Republican Brotherhood had hoped to infiltrate and influence the volunteer movement. The war created the setting for their desperate "Easter Rebellion" in 1916.

A small section of the radical wing of the volunteers, numbering no more than 1,500 men, occupied the Dublin Post Office and other public buildings on April 24, 1916. They had tried to obtain German arms, and in fact a shipment was intercepted and a British Foreign Service Officer, Roger Casement, was captured when he tried to land and call off the rebellion. Casement and 15 others were executed, and it was those executions (not unusual for wartime enemies) which began to reverse the mood of the Irish public.

Lloyd George summoned a convention in 1917 to discuss the Home Rule question, hoping that if Irish partisans could not find a solution, they would at least neutralize one another in the process. Sinn Fein and other groups boycotted the convention, and their political strength continued to grow, especially when the British government announced that it was instituting conscription for the armed forces in Ireland. The Irish party thereupon withdrew from the House of Commons and a broad-based opposition developed in Ireland, an opposition which was strengthened by British efforts to arrest and deport its leaders. Sinn Fein won a series of bye-election victories leading up to its dramatic success in November 1918, when Home Rulers won only six seats and Unionists twenty-six.

With the establishment of the *Dáil* and the declaration of the Irish Republic, the goal of 1916 seemed to be in sight, but an undeclared war went on until 1921, and serious internal feuding lasted several years more. The terrorism of the I.R.A. was met by reprisals by the Royal Irish Constabulary and its reinforcements. In 1920 the Government of Ireland Act created parliaments in North and South, both of which were to come into existence at the end of that year. Fighting continued until a truce in the summer of 1921, when negotiations were opened with the British government. After one breakdown, the talks were renewed in October. The Irish delegation was led by Michael Collins and Arthur Griffith. After long and difficult sessions, Lloyd George delivered an ultimatum: either a treaty or renewed war. In December, the Irish delegates accepted partition and dominion status. In bitter debate in the *Dáil* in the following month, the treaty was ratified by a margin of 64 to 57. The anti-treaty faction withdrew and began a terrorist campaign against its former colleagues. The fighting after the treaty (1922-25) resulted in significant casualties, heavy expenditure by the fledgling dominion government and a prolonged political crisis. Some 60,000 British troops were stationed in Ulster to prevent full-scale civil war.

In April 1922, a group of I.R.A. dissidents seized the Four Courts building in Dublin. The anti-treaty forces wanted an election on the issue of the agreement, and in June the voters endorsed the agreement by a margin of three to one. But resistance continued. The insurgents held out, and they were shelled by government forces in late June, causing heavy damage to the Four Courts and great losses of public records by fire. By now there were several rival factions. A series of outrages (kidnapping, robberies and murders) invited reprisals which were more tragic now, for they were between fellow-citizens, even kinsmen. Michael Collins died in an ambush, two deputies to the *Dáil* were murdered, and another 650 people lost their lives between September 1922 and July 1923. For several years there was no hope of normal politics in the Irish Free State.

One of the crowning ironies in a history replete with twists was that the Home Rule measure for Ulster was a fair copy of the versions once suggested for all Ireland (sending representatives to Westminster and keeping its own, local-issue parliament). From 1921 to 1969, there was a high degree of independence in Stormont, as the Northern Parliament was known.

The empire was deeply affected by winning the war. Dominion contributions had been great, with about 2.5 million subjects in arms and approximately 200,000 lives lost. Those losses produced a greater incentive for independence and an aversion to future overseas commitments, and even without the losses, it was certain that participation in events such as the Paris Peace Conference or the League of Nations would elevate the national aspirations of dominion governments. They could hardly debate the national rights of Czechs and Slavs and not be reminded of their own imperial subservience. Canada, Australia, New Zealand and South Africa wanted to abstain from security pacts such as the one contemplated between Britain,

France and the U.S. The dominions were also concerned about British mandates and their potential for even more imperial political power in the middle east and Africa, while British troops were actively engaged in fighting Bolshevism in Russia and nationalism in Ireland. All of these issues were bound to move the dominions to seek more autonomy with regard to Britain, even if the individual leaders wanted to maintain close formal ties with the empire.

Britain had seemed on the verge of reversing her long-standing aloofness in foreign policy. As part of the settlement at Versailles, the League of Nations was created, with French acceptance conditioned upon the postwar alliance with Britain and the U.S. Actual fulfillment of this pledge was avoided when the U.S. Senate refused to ratify the treaty.

On a more positive note, internal reforms within the empire seemed promising. Power-sharing ideas such as Lord Lugard's "dual mandate" in Africa, or the joint administration under "dyarchy" in India looked like steps toward political reform. Such concessions were a sign of retreat, but so slow as to possibly make the result worse than prompt withdrawal. This was complicated by promises made in the war, to Zionists, and to Arab and Indian nationalists, which appeared to be major concessions. Many of these promises were ignored in the postwar period. As for the dominions, by the 1926 Imperial Conference they had earned a new definition as "autonomous communities within the British Empire, equal in status, in no way subordinate to one another" but uniformly loyal to the crown. This was formalized in the Statute of Westminster in 1931.

Domestic politics had no Statute of Westminster. Deep and fundamental shifts occurred, sometimes without the benefit of formal signposts. Wartime centralization had been dismantled quickly, but its constitutional dimension was left behind. The war and its lure of "reconstruction" was but one impulse toward new social policy. In another sense, political life was revolutionized; in 1918 there were 21.8 million voters where in 1900 there had been 6.7 million. Since 1911 there had been salaries for M.P.s and there was no more effective veto power in the Lords. Finally, the political parties came out of the war in a confused state. A dozen minor parties contested the election of 1918, and the majors (Conservative Unionist, Liberal, Labour) were divided into "coalition" and regular groups. The first "traditional" postwar election was held in 1923, and then Labour managed to pull into second place overall, thanks largely to victories in the old Liberal strongholds in Wales and Scotland.

Coupling these changes with the physical experience and social impact of the war (levelling of class, occupational and educational distinctions) created a new vista of electoral politics. Political life was also altered by the not so constitutional elevation of the Prime Minister. Lloyd George became a dictatorial figure from the latter stages of the war. Making decisions with several close associates, meeting only occasionally with his cabinet, and disdaining attendance in the House of Commons, Lloyd George's wartime habits carried over into the next four years. So also did the Cabinet Secretariat, the first permanent body created for and by the cabinet and producing the first connected set of records of cabinet decisions. In general the new offices created in the war were not likely to survive. Some ten new ministries and 160 boards or commissions were created, only a few of which lasted beyond 1919. But the war marked a break with the past. The break took several forms--a comprehensive but unsuccessful reconstruction program which signalled a basic shift in political philosophy; a constitutional change in the achievement of a genuine electoral democracy (1918-1929); and a party change in the rise of Labour to second position, plus its first experience in office as the ruling party.

There was a strong social democratic impulse to centralization which paralleled the postwar promise of reconstruction. Ironically, the centralization came and the social benefits for the most part did not. Public housing and education were promised, but the government would not provide the funds. Nationalized coal, rails and electricity were flirted with, and in one or two instances attempted, but there was still an overriding fear of such control. The area of unemployment insurance saw the most progressive development in that the government felt obliged to give veterans increasing protection against unemployment, and the resulting expenditure, especially when the economy turned sour in 1921, became a central issue for the rest of the decade. In the 1920s, there were few acts for the "heroes" and the depressed economy could not support large trade union activity for political ends. The brief and futile General Strike of 1926 showed that organized labor was far from ready for effective national action.

The revolution in electoral politics was masked by the war and the peace settlement. There were of course several perspectives. After 80 years of reform, one-fourth of all adults still could not vote. Looking back from the 1920s, the dominant impression might be amazement at the staying power of the aristocracy. Only in 1923 when Stanley Baldwin was chosen to lead the Tories (passing over Lord Curzon because of his rank) was there a clear sign that democracy had reached into the highest levels.

The widened electorate might have been expected to shape the issues and the organization of parties as had apparently happened in the past. There were some shifts in issues and organization, but their origins are not too clear. The number of political parties and the shift of support to the party of working men may be the best indicators of popular influence. The myth of the "two-party" system had only slight relevance before 1914: it was blown apart by the wartime and postwar changes. There were three major parties over the period and there were more years of coalition than of single-party government (1914-45). At the same time, multiplying minor parties seemed to be a reflection of the mushrooming electorate (nationalists, socialists, communists, and fascists).

Oddly enough, the Irish Free State had the most traditional form of two-party system (if their behavior was slightly untraditional). The *Fianna Fail* and *Fine Gael* parties divided power in the years 1925-1939, in a system which was based on proportional representation (a deliberate effort to move away from British electoral procedure). The Irish anomaly was in Ulster where a single-party regime held power at Stormont for nearly half a century.

The major British political parties (Conservative, Liberal and Labour) saw their relationships shift markedly in the interwar years. The Conservative-Unionists were nominally defeated by the Government of Ireland Act (1920) which gave in on the issue of Irish Home Rule; but "unionism" and "empire" continued to draw heavy political support for many years to come. The true strength of the party for the next generation came from its tactical success in exploiting coalition government and wartime problems; together these had withered its opponents without an electoral contest, and in 1918 the Conservatives won a victory as impressive as the Liberal triumph in 1906 (and one with as little substance). The "coalition effect" might be said to have lasted through 1945; for Liberal and Labour were dividing the non-Tory vote (which averaged about 55% from 1919-1939) while the Tories were in office for all but three or four of those years.

The Liberal Party was disorganized and confused after the war; there was not much left of 19th century liberalism--in the sense that electoral reform was virtually complete, and in the sense that collectivism (Bolshevik, or Fascist or Fabian) was in the ascendant. Liberals had in fact been too close to Tories all along. With a popular electorate, there was no room for a "whiggish" party, and the Liberals could not arrive at a consensus on a reformed model.

The dramatic effect of Labour politics on the Liberals was no more clearly shown than in the strongholds of Scotland and Wales. There the 19th century Liberal had seemed to synthesize the hope of populist, nationalist and evangelist, but it is clear in retrospect that as the Liberal organization was the only alternative of national (U.K.) scope, it drew the anti-government vote. When Labour appeared, it soon added these votes to a number of commited ideological voters who would never be Liberals. Only a handful of working class M.P.s had entered parliament before 1906. The arrival then of 29 new members (plus 24 who adhered to the old Lib-Lab connection) was a first. No party had ever been organized in the way that Labour was, and it enjoyed the benefit of falling support for the Liberals from 1918 on, which soon put it in the second position in overall strength. Labour still depended upon Liberal support during its first two times in office (1924, 1929), but it had risen in those same years to become the "loyal opposition."

LABOUR M.P.S	1918	1924	1929	1945
WALES	9	16	25	25
SCOTLAND	6	26	36	37
ENGLAND	42	109	226	331
TOTAL	57	151	287	393

Finally our discussion of postwar politics has to explain why the national parties formed in Scotland and Wales did not enjoy more success at the expense of Liberal decline than the growing Labour party. That explanation has two levels. The U.K. dimension was that "home rule" and its comprehensive ("all round") counterpart were effectively dismissed in the wake of the Speakers' Conference (1920) and because of the violent and dramatic conclusion of the Irish crisis. On the level of internal politics in Scotland and Wales, neither community would support an activist national movement in the 1920s. In Scotland the main reason was historical satisfaction with traditional institutions, to which was added a growing Scottish administrative capacity. In Wales, the absence of historical institutions was coupled to economic and social depression (unemployment, emigration and the removal of the established church as a focal issue). The small national parties, *Plaid Cymru* (1925) and the National Party of Scotland (1928), were responses to manifold signs of assimilation which had not yet become large enough issues to move the electorates.

Imperial Retreat

The Great Depression, the cost of the Second World War and potent anti-colonial forces combined to bring a generally voluntary retreat of British imperial authority by the 1950s. It was not without anguish and bitter debate, and the withdrawal was paralleled by major anomalies in internal politics. These concurrent political events need more systematic study, but we may sketch some suggestive relations between the Irish republic, regional devolution and economic reorganization as they were related to imperial retreat. More dramatic of course was the shape of global politics in the 1930s and 40s. The "Axis" of Germany, Italy and Japan was defeated by a "united nations" alliance, led by Britain, the U.S. and Russia (and aided by the "Free French" and Nationalist China). Postwar political rivalry turned into "Cold War" between the U.S. and the U.S.S.R., and Britain shed her global commitments and became a favored satellite of the U.S.

The 1930s will long be remembered as a period of mass unemployment, political insecurity and imperial uncertainty. In fact, most of these features were well established before 1919. There had been high unemployment in Britain (over 10%) since 1921. Major political crises in Poland (1920) and the Ruhr (1923) coincided with the construction of "collective security" machinery. The League of Nations has been the target of too much criticism; its ideal was peace; its agents were people and diplomacy, not armies and navies. When the Geneva Protocol on binding arbitration was turned down

(1924), the League probably lost its last chance to pursue peace effectively; disarmament talks were slow to begin and quick to fall apart; League sanctions were unenforceable since League members were afraid to alienate some of their colleagues and most of their own economic interests.

The effect of this first experiment in internationalism was bound to be disruptive for an empire with its roots in the 17th century. The concurrent motions of dominions to stake their claims to autonomy were part of a world full of nationalist claims and counterclaims, laid out for general inspection at Versailles, and on the agenda ever since. Reforms in India, Egypt and Africa were grudgingly undertaken, less out of desire to "free" the colonies than to appease the public at home and around the world.

The tone of the 30s was set by the financial collapse of 1929-31, the chaos in international markets and the tension and fear that these produced. Translated in domestic political language, by gold standard economics, this meant retrenchment and a depressed economy. This classic "remedy" was not well received in a popular electorate with some taste of social service expenditures, yet the leaders of government and their economic advisers had no experience with any other strategy. When his Labour cabinet blocked budget cuts, Ramsay MacDonald simply resigned as Labour Prime Minister and formed a coalition with the Conservatives in 1931. This "palace coup" caused bitter denunciations and internal divisions which disabled Labour as a national force until 1945. During the interval, the Conservative-dominated coalition marked a hiatus in party politics similar to that of 1915-22. The National Government took steps which economic orthodoxy said could not be done. The gold standard was discarded (September 1931), the principle of free trade was killed by the Import Duties Bill (February 1932) and later that year "Imperial Preference" was adopted at the Ottawa Imperial Conference. The political impact of these heresies was obscured by the coalition, but it amounted to the death of liberal economics. In fact, there had been significant inroads on that body of doctrine during and since the war. Industrialists chose to "rationalize" with cartels in steel and cotton, and electricity distribution was centralized as was the management of transport in London.

Economic recovery was the justification for these measures, but there were few bright spots before the end of the decade. Unemployment did not drop significantly until about 1934, and even in 1939 the level (1.5 million or nearly 12% of insured workers) was close to that of the postwar slump (1921-22). As always, the impact of unemployment was uneven. This was recognized by the designation of "distressed areas" (politely renamed "special areas" in 1934). The common affliction of these areas was industrial specialization, which left few outlets for alternative employment. Most such areas were situated in Scotland, South Wales and Northern Ireland, as well as the North and the Midlands of England. With worldwide economic depressions, the great staple industries of coal and shipbuilding and iron and steel and textiles were forced into painful contractions. The policies and resources of the government were unable to make headway against the crisis. One strategy was the 19th century remedy of emigration. About 430,000 people left Wales between 1921-1940; about 465,000 left Scotland and another 75,000 left Northern Ireland. The high rates of unemployment persisted, and "there appeared to be no economic strategy at all for reviving the staple industries of Wales," even in the Labour government of 1929-31.[4] Over the next few years, there were the more radical steps already noted in finance, and there were some timid moves toward government intervention to revive industry. As of 1939, the Commissioner for Special Areas had spent nearly £5 million in Scotland, but this could barely offset the effects of Scottish industrial subordination which had become so clear after the war. The steps which were taken to encourage public housing or to open industrial estates were more significant in pointing toward future policies than in their immediate economic impact.

The political consequences of depression and dislocation were surprisingly slight. In depressed areas there was prevailing apathy, and the occasional hunger march was a pathetic gesture which underlined the political weakness of the unemployed. Trade union membership fell from 6.6 million in 1921 with the trend only reversing in 1933-34 and regaining its former level in 1939. Radical political groups were unable to capitalize on the faillure of the major parties to cope with the economy; apart from successes in municipal elections, there were few parliamentary victories for communists and none for fascists. In the depth of national crisis, the "national government" coalition had more appeal to voters than radical ideological solutions, either John Middleton Murry's *Necessity of Communism* or

---

[4]Kenneth Morgan, *Rebirth of a Nation: Wales, 1880-1980* (1981), p. 222.

Oswald Mosley's fascist *Greater Britain* , both published in 1932. The main political consequence of the thirties seems to have been the delayed reaction visible in the election of 1945, when Labour won an overwhelming victory. But during the decade the results were confused and essentially non-partisan at the national level, therefore without any clear direction.

Severe economic problems bedevilled the world economy, and it was there that the next stage of imperial retreat occurred. The British Commonwealth undertook trade restrictions at Ottawa in 1932. A commission recommended responsible government for India on a federal scheme. There were conferences to develop those terms and they were put in statutory form in 1935. Although elections were held in 1937, the opposition from the Congress Party prevented implementation. In the Near East, Egyptian independence had been announced in 1922, but reservations were attached which made it unattainable. After the crisis of Italian intervention in Ethiopia, a treaty was negotiated which left a Canal Zone force and preserved British rights to bases, but Britain would otherwise withdraw, and Egypt would become a member of the League of Nations (1936-37). In 1930 the British government tried to restrict Jewish immigration to Palestine, but under pressure it relented, and the immigrant population doubled between 1931 and 1936. In these circumstances the mandate requiring British assurance of equal rights to all groups was steadily being eroded by a growing settlement colony which would not recognize British authority.

The broader setting for British withdrawal was the crisis in world affairs being actuated by militant governments in Germany, Italy and Japan. Whereas the early 1920s had promised a reform of international relations, the League and its members had nothing to give but promises. A measure of self-interested naval disarmament was the sole achievement in limiting weapons, and that took place outside the League. Diplomatic alignments, which should have been contained within the international forum, grew more numerous and demonstrated the decline of confidence in collective security.

With ruthless suddenness, Adolf Hitler and the Nazi party seized power in Germany in 1933. Determined to attack the terms of the Versailles treaty, and to find "living space" for his new *reich,* Hitler led the nation toward rearming and expansion. The British and French policy of "appeasement"

363

was a compound of concessions on the treaty with rearmament and preparation for the war which they hoped to avoid.

Appeasement grew from recognition of the relative decline of British power and the absence of an alternative alliance. The policy was nourished by fear: the revulsion at the horror of the previous war, and the terror of the prospect of the next. The naval agreement with Germany in 1935 was an interesting example of the workings of appeasement. In March of that year a government White Paper called for British rearmament. Two weeks later, Hitler used this as a pretext to announce conscription; in April the "Stresa front," (Britain, France and Italy) made vague warnings about aggression. In June, Britain reached the naval agreement, sanctioning a German buildup to 35% of British strength and 45% in submarines. The basis for agreement was the admiralty's desire to maintain some assurance of security in the Atlantic and Pacific, in spite of dwindling fleet size. But in fact the British became accomplices in undermining the Versailles Treaty, failure of disarmament was ratified, and little was gained, except an increase in French distrust owing to Britain's unilateral action.

The Ethiopian crisis brought economic sanctions against Italy by the League, which France and Britain privately agreed to sabotage. In 1936 there was no armed opposition to German reoccupation of the demilitarized Rhineland. By 1938, in his boldest moves to date, Hitler annexed Austria (March) and occupied parts of the Czech borderlands (October) after discussion with Chamberlain and Daladier in Munich, which lent the move a spurious legitimacy. In March 1939, Hitler occupied the rest of Czechoslovakia and the illusion of appeasement collapsed. Britain made a formal commitment to defend Poland. The move was a futile gesture in view of the Nazi-Soviet Non-Aggression Pact (August 23, 1939). For the latter was designed to protect Germany and Russia from each other while they jointly devoured Poland.

While Britain was unable to halt the advance of Germany, the British imperial structure was showing more signs of decay. In 1938 the Anglo-Irish tariff war concluded. It had begun when President de Valera refused payments promised in 1926, the British imposed high tariffs and the Irish Free State responded in kind. In 1937, at the death of George V, the Irish government adopted a new constitution deleting reference to the crown. In negotiations the following year, Ireland agreed to make a £10 million payment and received back three naval bases which Britain had retained under the 1921 treaty. Both sides had made concessions, and in the end Britain had gained a benevolent Irish neutrality.   In India, when the new federal government was stymied by native opposition, it was necessary for the Governor-General to declare war by proclamation, even though the legislative assembly was then in session. Indian political leaders refused to defend the British Empire in the face of Japanese imperial expansion. India remained neutral, even when the war widened in the Pacific in 1941.

War plans were more advanced than in 1914, but by 1939 the nation and the empire were weaker than before. What Winston Churchill called "their finest hour" in 1940-41 was rendered dramatic by the fact that British power very nearly collapsed. There was no imperial force of consequence in the Pacific, there were daily air raids on London in 1940, and a severe submarine blockade reached its peak in 1941. Only a desperate defense of the archipelago kept Britain in the war until attacks on the U.S.S.R. and the U.S. created active major allies for Britain in the second half of 1941.

The Committee for Imperial Defence had prepared a War Book which outlined steps for civilian and military mobilization. It provided for registration of manpower (and womenpower) plus ministries for food, shipping and information. Air raid precautions were under discussion from 1935, civil defense and evacuation plans were in the works from 1937, and a sort of trial of these was run during the Czech crisis in May 1938. Air raid shelters, private and public, and other defense measures were made ready. In stark contrast to 1914, the first phase of fighting was over in a matter of weeks in the Fall of 1939, and no British forces were actively engaged.

Poland fell between her powerful neighbors, and a lull followed. This "twilight war" or "phony war" was possible because there were no plans for a British or French counter-offensive, due to the ruling French defensive strategy, based on the famous "Maginot Line." Britain had neither the means nor the will to enforce an alternate strategy.

In April 1940, Germany successfully invaded Denmark and Norway. In the latter case, British units were engaged and were forced to withdraw. This defeat triggered a political crisis, and Chamberlain had to resign. Winston Churchill became Prime Minister just as Hitler launched his major offensive into Belguim, the Netherlands and France in early May. Within six weeks, France surrendered. Only shortly before, Mussolini had entered the conflict, sensing Hitler's victory. The only bright spot for Britain in this period was the successful evacuation from Dunkirk of 334,000 men at the beginning of June.

The first bombs to land on British soil fell near Canterbury on May 10th. London was hit in June, but it was not until August that Hitler ordered "Operation Eagle"--an allout attack on the R.A.F. preparatory to a cross-channel invasion. After a month of bombing, Hitler shifted the attack to London and the other population centers, but the R.A.F. was not yet disabled. The "blitz" was thus a military mistake. Bombing of major cities produced little significant military advantage and a great deal of popular animosity and will to resist. In spite of this, Bomber Command made the same error on the British side, for the air commanders evidently all overrated their capacity to demoralize the enemy.

While the air war went on, the "Battle of the Atlantic" took a heavy toll in ships, supplies and morale. While fighting alone (May 1940-December 1941) Britain lost over one-third of her merchant ships and half of the crewmen. In April 1941 alone she lost 195 ships. The U.S. swapped 50 overage destroyers for leases on British bases in the western Atlantic in September 1940. By 1941 the U.S. had adopted its lend-lease program and President Roosevelt ordered naval patrols in the western Atlantic, extending to Greenland's coastal waters in April.

The Russian and American entry into the war in 1941 by no means made victory certain, for both were brought in under conditions of grave danger to themselves. Still, the attacks had the effect of forging a Russian alliance more quickly and effectively than could have been done any other way. The U.S. and Britain, on the other hand, already had a *de facto* alliance and a set of (secret) joint military plans. When the three states became allies in the winter of 1941-42, the fall of Singapore and Rommel's offensive in North Africa meant that the tide was still running against them.

In 1942 there were some promising signs. In Pacific naval battles (Coral Sea and Midway) the Japanese advance was stemmed. At El Alamein the British turned the tide in Egypt, and soon there was a successful invasion in Morocco. There followed the stirring Soviet victory at Stalingrad, which was the final push on Churchill's "hinge of fate." The next two years saw a remarkable series of counter-attacks, which finally brought unconditional surrender in 1945.

The management of this intense and profound effort was obviously a matter of much stricter controls than the war of 1914-18. The Emergency Powers Act (1939) created martial law; aerial bombing made air raid precautions an important if overrated part of the war; monetary controls, food subsidies and industrial "constriction" were examples of greater control.

Churchill created a War Cabinet (Halifax, Chamberlain, Attlee, Greenwood), and there was marked centralization of decision-making. There was demonstrable need for secure channels in regard to defense measures, like radar or the "ultra" code secret, and latterly for the joint plans for allied offensives in the Mediterranean and eventually in France. As a war leader, Churchill by his personality helped to convey courage and commitment which were priceless assets. He also had the eccentricity which had been his political hallmark. The latter returned to plague him when, at the close of fighting, he made overzealous allegations in the electoral campaign which helped the Labour Party gain its one-sided victory in July 1945.

Domestic administration during the war was highly controlled, but there were some odd differences in application. Scotland had been gaining administrative autonomy in the 1930s. Thomas Johnston, the wartime Secretary of State of Scotland, won Churchill's approval for a Scottish Council of State (all former Secretaries for Scotland, forming a quasi-cabinet), plus a Scottish Council on Industry and a North of Scotland Hydroelectricity Board (1943). This administrative devolution was a wartime expedient which did a great deal to revitalize the region's economy. Wales was run entirely from London during the war and there were no steps similar to those taken in Scotland. A large influx of English evacuees was Wales' reward, though the same was bestowed on rural counties in England and Scotland. In Ulster there was a patriotic response to the declaration of war, and the Stormont government made a significant contribution in proportion to its resources.

The archipelago was run by rigorous wartime methods for six years, and reconstruction was once again a topic of great interest, in this case from as early as 1940. By 1942 there were elaborate discussions of the plans which might be used to reorder society at war's end. The major elements included an employment policy, education expansion, social insurance and town and country planning. How far the wartime centralization helped to advance the peacetime equivalents (or to retard them) is impossible to pin down. After the war, there was considerable interest in retaining some of the controls, and there was a strong desire to demobilize.

Politically there was a more stable condition than there had been in the 1914-18 war, but minor parties did contest bye-elections and there was a gradual appearance of opposition to Churchill's government. When Germany surrendered, Labour withdrew from the coalition and went into formal opposition. This necessitated a general election, overdue since 1940. During the crisis, there had been considerable solidarity, especially with the Soviet Union as a major ally. When the guns were silenced and the "people's war" ended, political opposition was restored, and the popular support for the wartime coalition deteriorated.

The war meant a massive drain on the British economy, the cost running to something like one-fourth of the national wealth. A large share (50%) of the burden was borne by the taxpayer through purchase taxes, surtax and excess profits taxes. About 300,000 military deaths and 60,000 civilian fatalities were a heavy blow. Some 500,000 homes were destroyed and another four million badly damaged; shipping losses were huge (16 million tons) and there was heavy damage to railroads. Debts of £3,355 million (at an interest charge of £73 million) combined with a need to borrow heavily for some time after the fighting ended. Restoration of a productive peacetime economy was to be a major challenge.

The course of the war also demonstrated the fundamental weakness of the empire-commonwealth. Canada, South Africa, Australia and New Zealand all came to the aid of Britain in some degree, sending troops to Europe, North Africa or Asia. Yet the dominions were now acting as independent states and were much less subservient to British leadership. While wartime meetings of the "Big Three" sustained Britain's image as a great power, events in and after 1945 brought a new picture. Canada was a major power with the fifth largest army in the world. Other dominions were diplomatically independent, and a trend toward establishment of republics in former colonies (Burma, Ireland, India) was soon evident. The formation of the United Nations (in concept as early as 1941 and in structure in 1945) produced a new international forum. Britain's permanent seat on the Security

Council was a token of past power more than an estimate of current importance.

The United Kingdom faced economic and political crises in several parts of the empire. The decision to leave India had been made in 1935, and was stalled for ten years by internal and international conflict. In 1945, the *Raj* had completely lost its reputation, and sudden American victory over Japan made any British revival in East Asia impossible. The best to be made of the situation was prompt withdrawal. Rival factions (basically Hindu vs. Muslim) sought federal vs. partitioned settlement, and debates on the issue grew more heated and violent as the act of withdrawal became more certain. The British government declared that the latest date of departure would be June 1, 1948. Lord Mountbatten took office as Governor-General and pushed the date up to August 1947.

The growing pressure of Zionists in Palestine was overpowering in the wake of Hitler's "Final Solution," and British proposals for joint rule were pushed aside. The mandate ended ingloriously in May 1948 with war between Jews and Arabs followed by the formation of the state of Israel. Military withdrawal from Egypt (1946-7) was expected to permit continued alliance, but nationalist overthrow of the monarchy ended those plans.

Erosion of British power had been visible to some since 1918 when promises of liberation were made under duress. The general population was not prepared for such change, and the seemingly swift departures after 1945 were startling and disturbing to many. On the other side, colonial nationalists usually had the backing of the United Nations, the added support of the United States and the anti-imperialist rhetoric of the Soviet Union. Acquiescence of H.M. government permitted the maintenance of "commonwealth relations" in many cases, though these were often strained. In 1952 the "British" Commonwealth became "the Commonwealth of Nations."

In the Middle East, Britain had its most intricate relations as an imperial power, with few instances of full sovereignty and paradoxically difficult problems of withdrawal. On the other hand, withdrawal from India in 1947 might have been expected to remove the perennial British strategic motive for a presence in the eastern Mediterranean. In 1954, Col. Nasser took power in Egypt and the British withdrawal from the Suez was begun. Britain looked for security in the area through such devices as the Baghdad Pact (1955).

Nasser looked for support to the Soviet Union, China and their satellites. When the U.S. and Britain withdrew financial aid for Nasser's Aswan Dam, he moved to nationalize the Canal (July 1956). Anthony Eden proposed to use force to stop Nasser, but he was rebuffed by the U.S. and the U.N. In October, Israel made a pre-emptive attack, Great Britain and France (by pre-arrangement) called for a cease-fire and when that call was ignored, the two intervened (without Commonwealth consultation by Britain). Port Said was bombed and Nasser retaliated by sinking vessels to block the Canal. The U.N. called for withdrawal and sent in a peace-keeping force. In two weeks the operation was over; Britain had forfeited its influence in the Arab world, the Canal was closed until British and French forces withdrew, and when it reopened it was under Egyptian control. This entire operation was successful in one regard; it marked quite clearly the end of British imperial power. Hereafter, the withdrawal syndrome was dominant and barely questioned. India and Pakistan sought and were granted republican status in 1953, retaining ties with the Commmonwealth. In 1957, Ghana became the first black African Commonwealth member. In the same year, Ceylon declared neutrality and Singapore obtained self-government. The next surge of 'liberation' was between 1961 and 1965 when twenty states were granted autonomy, and by that stage the final result was certain.

The global strategic view of these changes was one in which Britain gave up "great power" status but kept some of the symbols of that status. The only general conference at the end of the war was the U.N. meeting in San Francisco. There was no treaty. On the other hand, there were several occupation zones where the victors governed the defeated foe or related areas. It was in these zones the "Cold War" soon became evident. The two superpowers drew lines around the globe and lesser states hurried to enlist (or to be drafted) on one side or the other. The U.S. supplied money and weapons and assumed command of the "free world." Britain held out for a place as a special partner, sharing atomic secrets and a historical connection. That connection was at the root of the unique prewar and postwar cooperation (Lend-Lease, Joint Military plans, Marshall Plan). By 1949 these were succeeded, as a result of the cold war by the U.S.-dominated North Atlantic

Treaty Organiztion, and beside it, a "special relationship" between the U.S. and the U.K.

While the U.K. adjusted to its international demotion, the domestic postwar picture seemed to be one of revolutionary change, or so many regarded the work of the Labour government (1945-51). Actually the domestic reform was a continuation of wartime centralism and policies which had been endorsed in the early 20th century. Few measures were actual inventions of the postwar government. The main expressions of the theme were the "welfare state" and nationalized industry.

Industry had serious problems at the end of the war: capital was scarce, exports had fallen, and plants had been badly damaged or run down. Many areas still bore the scars of the 1930s. There were some aggressive measures needed, and a few were taken. Factories were converted from war production and development of new industries was encouraged. Industry was assisted in moving to locations where labor was in good supply. This represented a major shift from prewar ideas, when workers were forced to retrain or relocate. In the early postwar years 179 new factories (112 with government aid) were located in Wales alone.

In Eire postwar growth was fostered by tax incentives and grants. Here there had been earlier and more dramatic innovation. "State companies" were authorized in the 1937 constitution; an Electricity Supply Board had been operating since 1927; thirteen state corporations were formed during the "war" with Britain in the 1930s.

All of these activities form a context in which we can more readily understand the "nationalization" of the postwar years. In its manifesto, Labour made it plain that a number of services and industries were judged to be in the public domain. The changes were all made by legislative enactment, with full compensation for owners and continued rights of collective bargaining and strike for the workers.

Nationalized industry was no panacea for economic inefficiency or regional inequality. Coal, rails, road transport, gas, electricity and steel were taken over. Results varied between industries and regions. Public ownership promised the return of profits to public owners; yet the industries were often unable to make profits. There were deficiencies in some cases at the time of takeover and there were later errors or defects in management. The National Coal Board, for example, inherited a large number of uneconomical units and there was a steady closure of pits, especially in Wales and Scotland. The difficulty in making public corporations efficient and accountable and conflicting regional needs (Welsh railways, Scottish mines, Ulster factories) further complicated the new regime. Management decisions mainly emanated from London and compounded some of the problems. At best it may be said that national economic organization demanded more coherent planning, and that in turn forced attention on the several regions of the U.K.

The welfare state was the other half of the so-called revolution of 1945. The main enactments were national insurance and the National Health Service (1946-48). These too had a substantial pedigree, wide discussion and broad public endorsement. The famous Beveridge Report of 1942 had caught the imagination of the public, fatigued by war and haunted by Depression memories. Sir William had begun work on an inter-agency committee (1941) but the formal support of government was later withdrawn. Nevertheless, his report was a wartime best-seller, with over 600,000 copies being published. It called for a "national minimum" of income, guaranteed through a system of flat rate contribution and benefits, under a new Ministry of Social Security.

The acts of the 1940s were consolidations and extensions of existing law, based upon a new principle of universal coverage. Administration was centralized, with important regional and local divisions. There was nominal uniformity of benefit across the U.K., but due to variable living standards and employment and wage rates, some inequality of contribution and demand were bound to creep in.

In summary, the postwar decade saw concurrent change in the external power of the U.K. and in the internal socio-political structure. These changes were largely independent of political party policies and actions, or rather the respective parties were not responsible as much as they were responsive to powerful popular political forces outside their control, both anti-colonial and egalitarian.

Archipelago Without Empire

The post-imperial archipelago has experienced economic decline, has engaged in fundamental constitutional debate and may be undergoing major political realignment. Amid these events, there has appeared a more precise approach to United Kingdom politics. In 1970, Richard Rose noted that "many who write about British politics confuse England, the largest part, with the whole of the United Kingdom, or ignore any possibility of differences within it."[5] Since then, he and his colleagues have labored to put an end to that. There is now better recognition of the diversity of cultures, communities and concepts in archipelago political life. These are solidly held together by the crown in parliament and by a complex of devolved administration and shared political ideals. The loss of imperial power, therefore, was not fatal and may have been therapeutic, by encouraging introspection and reform.

The U.K. completed its retreat from empire in 1971. In the final years it was negotiating entry into the Common Market while trying to readjust its relations with the Commonwealth. Since 1961 there was a non-European majority, and it was no coincidence that South Africa left the Commonwealth at that point. In 1964 Southern Rhodesia was not invited to attend the Commonwealth meeting, and the following year saw her unilateral declaration of independence. British control of affairs between member states was weak; war between India and Pakistan (1965) plus secessions and inactive members helped to poison the atmosphere of the 1966 meeting.

Another milestone was reached in 1968 when H.M. government announced the withdrawal of military forces "east of Suez", specifically the bases in Aden and Singapore. In the next few years, British interest shifted perceptibly toward European markets and alliances. British departures and accompanying violence (Malaya 1957-63, Nigeria 1960, Kenya 1963) were a steady drain on a weak central financial structure. That edifice, the "sterling area," had once been a proud emblem of imperial strength. Evolved in the 1920s and 30s, the area included countries where sterling was the principal currency after the departure from the gold standard in 1931. This was made formal by treaty at the outbreak of war in 1939, but these arrangements ended in 1971.

One of the most troubling issues in this period of transition, and one which literally transports us into archipelago politics, was the matter of commonwealth immigration. Historically, all residents of the empire-

---

[5]"The United Kingdom as a Multi-National State," (University of Strathclyde, Occasional Paper, no. 6; revised and reprinted in Richard Rose, ed., *Studies in British Politics,* 1979). A more extended treatment is in *The Territorial Dimension of Goverment* (1982).

commonwealth could migrate freely, and for many years the balance of movement had been outward from the archipelago. After a rapid increase in Indian and Pakistani immigration, a voucher system was begun in 1962. When Asians in Kenya were forced out in 1967, those holding U.K. passports tried to enter, and a new law in 1968 interrupted that migration. The movement of non-whites to the U.K. after 1945 was significant in its impact on a predominantly white society, even though the numbers were small. The assimilation of residents of former colonies was doubly difficult while employment in Britain was artificially supported by a policy of "full employment" and well before there was positive public racial understanding. Some organized efforts to promote toleration (Race Relations Board, 1965; Commission on Racial Equality, 1976) barely offset the efforts of promoters of racial discrimination.

In the 1950s and 1960s the domestic political picture was dominated by economic concerns, as declining industrial power was competing with social democratic goals for attention. Foreign relations were shaped by the military, diplomatic and financial consequences of declining imperial power. The European Economic Community was the creation of the Treaty of Rome (1957), in which six nations formally pooled their resources and accepted the principle of common economic policy as a prelude to political community. To the latter, the British reaction was negative, and she led the formation of the European Free Trade Area (1959). That alignment was later abandoned, but the distrust endured, cutting across all parties and penetrating through most levels of society.

The opponents of the Common Market were rescued by Gen. De Gaulle, who blocked the British bids for entry in 1963 and again in 1967. In 1971 the third application succeeded, and the United Kingdom and the Republic of Ireland joined at the same time. There was still vociferous opposition at home and the Treaty of Brussels (1972) had to be renegotiated. Facing continued resistance, the Labour government submitted the question of membership to a referendum (1975) in which 60% favored membership. The economic problems of the U.K. were not solved by the Common Market, nor had they all been made worse by the termination of empire. Roots of weakness went deep: industrial inflexibility, trade deficiencies, and monetary instability combined to retard growth and productivity. In the early postwar years there was reliance on borrowing and on commonwealth support; these were replaced in the 1960s by expected help from the EEC, and in the 70s by faith in North Sea oil revenues. Until 1979, there was a consensus among major parties that Keynesian fiscal management would eventually solve the problems. In that year, a Tory victory brought a new 'monetarist' approach: by freeing most aspects of the economy and by controlling the money supply, the government would draw back to its proper level of economic interference and there would be general recovery. The early results of those policies were rising unemployment and interest rates beside declining inflation and production.

While divergent economic philosophies were engaged in rhetorical and real conflict, new forms of economic control were developed. A whole new approach to regional economic planning was shaped by the Depression and wartime efforts. The lagging regions were re-named "development areas," and a National Economic Development Council worked on serious economic disparities. Some remedies were severe (the Beeching study proposed drastic cuts in service in order to allow British Rail to break even). Industry was to be reallocated, development in the one active area--the Southeast--was to be retarded, in Wales and Scotland it was to be subsidized. Persistent imbalance in employment rates was a major reason for this policy, but the policy may not have had the desired effect.

In the years 1960-1980, planning failed to demonstrate its expected benefits. While there were plenty of external scapegoats, the planning approach was also the victim of excessive hopes and mediocre to dismal performance records. A Department of Economic Affairs (created by Labour in 1966, as a counterweight to the Treasury) was ineffective. The regional planning bodies were not coordinated and had too many overlapping competitors. In the bitter atmosphere of failure (1971-74) labor unions exerted heavy pressure for benefits, many companies were under extreme pressure, taxes and prices rose rapidly.

By 1980, the picture was marginally better on inflation and significantly poorer on unemployment. There was a contradiction between planned growth and democratic politics: the latter demanded quick results and the former was an unproven innovation trying to solve riddles which had never been untangled in industrial society. Thus there were improvements in living standards *and* noticeable growth in public discontent.

Postwar social policy did not bring the millenium. Class interests did not go away when the welfare state arrived. In the 50s and 60s the momentum of wartime egalitarianism was exhausted. It did produce or help the growth of education. The University Grants Committee centralized funding, access was promised to all qualified students, new universities were built and the Open University employed television to broaden higher education. At the secondary level, "comprehensive" schools were expected to undermine the exclusive public school, but they also brought periodic angry debates and shifting local and national policies.

The National Health Service and national insurance and public housing were all facets of the new order. In general these were so popular that Tories for some time were afraid to risk political disaster in opposing them. Similarly, in Eire although the Roman Catholic Church opposed the plan, the Health Act of 1947 and subsequent efforts attested to similar popularity, if not at the same level of funding.

There was indeed considerable variation in the levels of social spending around the archipelago. An analysis of government spending *per capita* along regional lines showed significant differences in the mid-60s.

	Net Government Social Expenditure (£)	Gross Domestic Product (% of U.K. average)
England (South East)	-39	113
England (North West)	+5	98
Wales	+45	88
Scotland	+32	86
Northern Ireland	+82	66

Source: Commission on the Constitution, *Research Paper* no. 10 (1973), p. 72.

It should be noted that these differential amounts were recorded in the decade *before* there was active political effort for devolved constitutional forms of government, and that over the next decade there was noticeable levelling, especially in regional G.D.P. An interesting sidelight here is that regional statistics are a recent phenomenon. In fact, "Parliament has never sought to require the production of United Kingdom statistics according to a standard pattern throughout the United Kingdom."[6]

In this archipelago without an empire, constitutional change was a dominant if incoherent theme in the 1960s and 1970s. Jostling for attention were the bloody conflict in Northern Ireland and the less dangerous debates on Welsh and Scottish devolution. The longest effort at devolved authority within the U.K. was in the six counties of Northern Ireland since 1920. One-party rule by the Unionists there had maintained a quiet order until the later 1960s. Then there were increasing protests on behalf of Roman Catholics in Ulster, civil rights demonstrations, violent incidents, and finally the summoning of the British army to restore order in 1969. The presence of the latter led to escalating protest, attacks by the I.R.A. in Ulster and in England, and in 1972 the dissolution of the Stormont regime and the return of direct rule by Westminster. Successive British governments have tried to invent constitutional solutions, but all of them encountered deep division within the Ulster community. In 1985 a consultative body was created which for the first time allowed a measure of involvement by the government of the Republic in the affairs of Ulster.

The questions of Welsh and Scottish nationalism seem tame by comparison. There were no deaths attributed to devolution. The support for full-fledged (i.e. separatist) nationalism was tiny. Often confused or conflated with it was support for the various forms of "devolution," which were always designed to *maintain* the union. Indeed, in a longer view, historians of the future may be surprised at the weakness of national sentiment, since the period of imperial withdrawal saw so many instances where sovereignty was granted to communities with far less claim than Scotland or Wales. Those were also communities much farther away and harder to rule; and large majorities in Scotland and Wales felt that their security was greater in a United Kingdom.

Nevertheless, the constitution was made the subject of a Royal Commission of Inquiry, and the results reflected the ambiguity of the public. The Kilbrandon Commission was established in 1969, and it looked at various models of devolution but could not come to an agreed conclusion.

---

[6]Richard Rose and Ian McAllister, eds., *United Kingdom Facts* (1982), p. 142.

The majority report in 1973 recommended devolution for Scotland and Wales, without settling on the form it should take. A minority report suggested the creation of seven regional authorities in the U.K. The indecision was an opportunity for politicians to take no action. But the election results of 1974 showed significant nationalist gains, and thus the government returned to the matter with proposals for legislation in 1975. After many diversions, measures were passed in 1978 which gave a legislative body to Scotland and an assembly to Wales. Both were conditional upon the approval of 40% of the registered voters in the respective areas. In March 1979 the Scots voted favorably, but only 33% of the electorate were in that group (and nearly 32% voted No). In Wales the measure only gained about 12%, and 47% voted No. Devolution had been supported by the Labour government, and within a short time, it lost a vote of confidence and resigned.

In the General Election of May 1979, Margaret Thatcher won an impressive victory at the head of the Conservative party, thus becoming the first female Prime Minister in British history. She called her victory a "watershed," and certainly she was entitled to do so. Her party's opposition to devolution was successful, and as the voters' attention returned to economic issues, she convinced them to support a broad set of measures reversing economic policy, restricting trade unions, and vigorously pushing U.K. interests in the Common Market.

The post-imperial era had wrestled with constitutional remedies, but there was no common diagnosis of the patient's ailment. Three opposing constitutional ideas were present in the late 20th century archipelago. The dominant one was that of a unitary (English) monarchy entitled (through parliament) to allegiance from all of the U.K. Beside this was the Ulster unionist idea of "contractarian" sovereignty, where loyalty to the crown was separated from total obedience to the Westminster parliament. Finally there was the republican nationalist idea, realized in Eire, but only expressed in small political parties in Wales and Scotland, and the small but lethal terrorist organization in Northern Ireland.

Historians of English politics have always admitted the people of the periphery when they seemed to earn some attention. As rebels, as targets, and later as new adjuncts to parliament, it was sufficient to take note of the Welsh in the 16th century, the Scots in the 17th and 18th, and the Irish in the

19th and 20th centuries. It was not necessary to study the heritage of these societies and their continuing connections with England and the empire. English parliamentary government had proven that it was able to conquer the globe and plant its institutions everywhere. This confident picture dissolved with the empire and the nervous sequel of constitution-tampering. Now the Englishman and his history deserve to be reviewed together with the stories of his archipelago neighbors.

APPENDIX

THE ATLANTIC ARCHIPELAGO
AND THE HISTORIANS

> The history of the two islands interpenetrate. The history of the British Isles is not a mosaic but a painting in which the colours run into one another and overlap.
>
> (Sir George Clark, *English History: A Survey*, 1971, p.5)

> ... something in the national mentality is liable to deflect the historiography of every country--each people making its own peculiar kind of mistakes.
>
> (Herbert Butterfield, *Man on his Past*, 1955, p. 2)

The Atlantic Archipelago has been dominated by a Latin, Christian and Anglocentric historical tradition. The impressive range of sources and practitioners in this tradition overshadow all but the archeological evidence of the Celtic cultures. Although interest in Scottish, Irish and Welsh history has grown over the last generation, it is for the most part an interest shaped by the same Latin and Christian tradition. There has been little demand for study of Celtic history and historians, and most of the history of the "fringe" has been written in the context of or in contrast to the dominant Anglocentric mode. In more recent years, a few historians have looked at the history of the whole archipelago, but this work has not yet affected the prevailing view. Our task here is to reconstruct the evolution of historical writing in the archipelago in order to comprehend its variety. It is evident that when we speak today of "England," or "Ireland," or "Wales" or "Scotland," we mean both a territory and a political community. That was not always the case. Each area and people has known stages of tribal identity, national development and imperial government, albeit stages of different duration and circumstance. In telling about the past, historians were attuned to these communal conditions, and the nature of their stories varied accordingly. One kind of history was no better or worse than another, only more or less appropriate to its particular audience. However, rivalry between historical visions has been a potent adjunct to political rivalry, and an active ingredient in maintaining distinct identities in the archipelago.

Early historians were relatively indifferent to political boundaries. The base of the political order was personal, familial and tribal--not territorial. The historian's subject was people, especially real or legendary heroes, political and spiritual. Their stories were intended to edify. Literal accuracy was secondary to the didactic purpose, and when miracle or myth supplied the correct instruction, they were the best "evidence." The early histories (of "the Angles," "Kings of the British," or "Dukes of the Normans") were collected anecdotes, mixing fable and fact and having little or no regard for territorial nations. The first signs of a changing orientation began to appear in the 12th century and became widespread by the 14th century. After 1500, the national church and the unitary state of the Tudors helped the national idea to advance at the expense of the older, folkish image of political community. The long period of medieval national gestation produced distinct forms of historical consciousness in Ireland, Scotland and Wales, which were accentuated by the impact of Reformation. But neither the "elect nation" of Scottish reformers nor the bardic tradition of Wales and Ireland could compete with the spread of English scholarship by the late 17th century. The Anglocentric result was fortified in the 18th and 19th centuries and reached its zenith. Only when imperial power receded in the 20th century was there space for recovery of the Celtic and national traditions and dawning interest in a neutral comprehensive approach.

Historians in the Medieval Archipelago

The oldest history was oral transmission of memorable events and their heroes. Celtic poets were well-schooled and revered figures of a magical, even spiritual authority. As one author put it, they had "the shadow of a high-ranking pagan priest or druid" behind them.[1] Court poets had practical functions as remembrancers, entertainers and advisers. Later evidence suggests that learned families might have developed privileged positions at a

---

[1] James Carney, *The Irish Bardic Poet* (1967), p. 8; cited in J.E.C. Williams, "The Court Poet in Medieval Ireland," *Proceedings of the British Academy* 57 (1971): 86.

very early date.[2] In any case, bardic culture was not entirely displaced in the medieval period, especially outside southern Britannia. When Christian influence entered the archipelago, it adjusted to Celtic ways and it later converted the Saxons and Danes. The early Christian historian therefore worked in a world which accommodated barbarian poets, pagan Roman historians and scriptural authority. The simple yet vital achievement of clerical writers in the early years was the accumulation of chronological records.

The monastic historian only slowly advanced beyond the rudimentary function of recording dates of major events. These records evolved into annals and chronicles. The collected "deeds" of a king or bishop became a biography, while similar collections for a group of rulers or clerics formed an elementary narrative. The rare or exceptional author might criticize sources and analyze their contents. The most advanced early historian in the archipelago was Bede, but even in his *Historia ecclesiastica gentis anglorum*, Bede's political vision was conventional. He said of Britannia:[3]

> This island at present, following the number of books in which the Divine law was written, contains five nations, the English, Britons, Scots, Picts and Latins, each in its own peculiar   dialect cultivating the sublime study of Divine truth.

Bede described the Anglo-Saxon migrations with a reference to the "swarms of the aforesaid nations," showing that his was a dynamic definition, while perhaps disguising his modest amount of factual information for events which occurred centuries earlier.

By the time that Bede was writing in the eighth century, annals and chronicles were being kept in several monastic centers in the archipelago. We know of their existence from critical study of the surviving manuscripts of much later versions. Annals evidently appeared first, as dates entered into the margins of Easter-tables. Sometime later, separate copies of these, and continuations of lists of kings, prelates and notable events, formed the base for a chronicle. What we know as the *Anglo-Saxon Chronicle* was begun in the ninth century, probably under the direction of King Alfred of Wessex,

---

[2]Kenneth Nicholls, *Gaelic and Gaelicised Ireland in the Middle Ages* (1972) points out that "Most of the learned families first appear in history in the thirteenth century" and "it is possible that some of the poetic families had in fact expressed their craft since pagan times." (p. 80).

[3]*The Ecclesiastical History of the English Nation* (Everyman Edition, 954), p. 5.

with an eye to the preservation of the historical record of political events in Wessex. This was a considerable departure, full of political and historiographic significance. A vernacular chronicle, under royal patronage, kept for nearly three centuries in a period of striking political instability, was a surprising achievement, made more significant by the fact that the incoming Danes, from Guthrum to Cnut, did not leave a record of their side of the story.

With the advent of the Normans in the 11th century, there was a reversal of roles. The Normans could be called a history-conscious people, perhaps more self-congratulatory than most.[4] Be that as it may, the Norman conquerors had many able historical writers in their employ, and their chronicles and histories left a sizeable pro-Norman account of the 11th and 12th century. This writing (William of Jumièges, William of Poitiers, Orderic Vitalis) is of interest in illuminating the stage of national-political thinking which we have reached. For these historians, the Normans had an identity which was both tribal and territorial: a descent from folk heroes and a kinship with Norman soil. Those qualities somehow were supposed to be transferable, either into England or Sicily. The migration was successful in the minds of Norman writers, if not so tidily accomplished in the real world.

William of Malmesbury and Geoffrey of Monmouth were contemporaries, writing in the 1120s and 30s after a half-century of Norman rule. Both were churchmen, but each had a different approach to history. William saw himself as a successor to Bede; Geoffrey was the story-teller who supplied a plausible legend for the years down to Bede's lifetime, from the side of the British native instead of the Saxon or Norman invader.

William wrote surveys of political and ecclesiastical events (*Gesta regum anglorum; Gesta pontificum anglorum*) which explained the background of the present Anglo-Norman community (c. 1125). He also wrote a contemporary *Historia Novella* near the end of his life. William's work was serious historical research and writing--involving considerable travel and study, and showing scholarly attributes. Of English and Norman parents, William tried to blend the Saxon and Norman strands of both church and political history. No clear national orientation was likely since William was

---

[4] R.H.C. Davies, *The Normans and their Myth* (1976).

more interested in monastic politics and since the matter of Anglo-Norman integration was politically unresolved.

The other view was that of the "Briton." Geoffrey of Monmouth, whatever his defects as a historian, was a great success in telling stories, and his *Historia regum britanniae* was a medieval best-seller. Geoffrey was a native of Brittany, later a bishop, and his fabulous account invented an illustrious origin, in Brutus of Troy, whose sons divided the islands among them. The romantic legends of great kings and battles, combining real and mythical figures, captivated their audience for centuries. Geoffrey's work was so successful, especially in its sections on Arthurian "history," that it spawned a host of literary imitations and derivations, in the archipelago and on the continent.

A recent historian has suggested that Geoffrey's work "had a marked influence in subduing the social animosities of the Britons, Anglo-Saxons and Normans and drawing them together into a single nation." He had invented a myth useful to Plantagenets and Tudors, an antidote to Norman myth perhaps. As the story of a pre-English dynasty, the "British history" also proved nourishing to national ideas other than English. If Geoffrey made Arthur the "hero of a composite people, uniting Britons, Saxons, and Normans," he also preserved an idea of the several component peoples[5]

Monastic compilations of Irish myth and historical record coincided with the reform of secular and regular clergy in 12th century Ireland. Transcription of law tracts, annals and other materials was inspired by antiquarian motives more than patriotism. Nevertheless its critical importance for future historians is obvious. The literary sources for early Irish history even so are very limited. One authority estimated that the number of extant Gaelic manuscripts prior to 1600 was probably "not more than 200."[6]

Another form of national interaction was represented by the work of Gerald "of Wales." Descended from Anglo-Norman and Welsh lines, *Giraldus Cambrensis* was a skilled writer with a typical "international" clerical career. He was looking to advancement in the Angevin court, where his Welsh background was a liability. His education and continental cultural affliations tended to make his work critical of his Celtic kinsmen. He wrote a

---

[5]Hugh A. MacDougall, *Racial Myth in English History* (1982), pp. 7, 13.

[6]Brian O Cuiv, "Literary Creation and Irish Historical Tradition," *Proceedings of the British Academy* 49 (1963) :58.

Topography of Ireland (1188), an *Itinerary of Wales* (1191), a *Description of Wales* (1194), and his best-known *Conquest of Ireland (Expugnatio Hibernica)* around 1199. Gerald also composed a number of biographies and shorter works. At first he was a dutiful court writer for Henry II, but later Gerald became a supporter of the French invaders in 1216-17. His most consistent theme was support of the family interests, which were identified with marcher society. Gerald was an ambiguous Welsh nationalist, but nevertheless a pioneer in national historiography. His maligning of barbarous Irish and Welsh custom may have been a result of courtly obligation, but whatever its source, this commentary did not alter the fact that Gerald was composing a literary base for national histories yet to be written?

The most significant historical work in 13th century England was that of Matthew Paris, monk of St. Albans (?1200-1259). His *Chronica majora* told the history of the world down to 1259, but only the last 23 years were independent of other sources; the earlier parts relied heavily on Roger of Wendover and others. Matthew's consistent theme was a criticism of royal and papal power-- or abuse thereof. Part of this of course reflected the selfish interest of the Benedictine house, or of Matthew himself. In part, the theme was a nationalistic reaction to political trends in the first half of the 13th century. Papal authority in England increased noticeably, and there was continuing tension between royal and baronial power. Matthew was engaged in writing the most detailed "current history" yet composed; St. Albans was near the royal center of power and so the monks had frequent visits and ample information--plus a certain insulation from the court.

The 13th century saw growing variation in chronicle sites. The new medicant orders produced their own accounts, and the first town chronicle appeared in London before the end of the century. Also, in the reign of Edward I, a number of chronicles began to deal with the rise of national issues, provoked by Edward's campaigns in Wales, Scotland and Gascony.

As Bruce Webster noted, "The chroniclers who wrote the only accounts we have of Scotland in the twelfth and thirteenth centuries, though they were monks in Scottish monasteries, hardly seem to have conceived of Scotland as a separate country....they include only English and universal history until the

---

[7]Robert Bartlett, *Gerald of Wales, 1146-1223* (1982).

point when their orders reached Scotland." [8] Webster said that this was not proof that Scottish national feeling only came in response the the assault of Edward I, but that monks or court historians wrote history to suit their situation; only when the historian felt an identity with a nation was there an opportunity for what we would define as national history. Writers generally were working for a king, an abbey or an order, none of which actively cultivated territorial national identity in earlier centuries. In many cases the reverse was true: anglicizing Scottish rulers, Welsh aristocrats seeking dominion in Ireland, or an Angevin sovereign trying to exert authority over both, were unlikely patrons for territorial national history.

What changed between the 13th and 14th centuries was the basic political context. Edward I was not the Norman ruler his predecessors had been, and he was a greater menace to the neighboring royal and marcher/aristocratic houses. His campaigns in Wales and Scotland were not simply expeditions for loot, they were well-prepared political and military campaigns. As such, they helped to inspire, in Scotland at least, the beginnings of a national historiography. Wales, on the other hand, was too quickly conquered for it to enjoy a historical revival. Moreover, Edward went out of his way to demonstrate that Arthur was dead, by disinterring his alleged remains at Glastonbury. The king also seized a purported crown of the legendary ruler, and later he invested his own son with the title Prince of Wales.

In the 14th century we have a late example of the old chronicle tradition from Ranulph Higden, Benedictine monk of Chester, whose Universal Chronicle (*Polychronicon*) was written in the 1320s. [9] It was translated into English in the 1380s, which was itself notable. The *Polychronicon* was popular and influential. Its political geography drew upon older sources as well as the work of Gerald on Wales and Ireland. Higden's geography received lengthier treatment than earlier political narrators had offered. He had separate sections for Scotland, Wales and Ireland. His longest section was on England, with an imbalance toward the North, reflecting his own orientation and interest.

---

[8] *Scotland from the Eleventh Century to 1603* (1975), p. 13.
[9] John Taylor, *The Universal Chronicle of Ranulph Higden* (1966).

But by the 14th century, a number of examples of "national" histories appeared. English translations of the *Brut*, derivations from Geoffrey of Monmouth's *British History* (by way of French verse chronicles or romances) were turning up from the 1330s. These contained the Trojan origin myth, the stories of Arthur, and more recent sections on the history of the English. Behind this development was a larger transition, namely the increase of writers outside the court or cloister, and outside religious orders: chronicles of aristocrats or of municipalities, having begun earlier on the continent, were well in evidence in parts of the archipelago by the 14th century. The wars of the 14th and 15th century helped to separate what had been fairly close connections between the historiography of England and France; while the diversity of authors' social backgrounds, plus the decline in the traditional Latin Chronicle, completed the outline of a major alteration.

In early 14th century Ireland, the confusing circumstances of the Bruce invasion and the resurgence of the Gaelic community were responsible for political pressures unlike those in the other parts of the archipelago. The Anglo-Irish view of events was given in the *Annals of Ireland* ascribed to Friar John Clyn of Kilkenny, which included sections of English history but was chiefly an account of Irish affairs. The native side was shown in the *Triumphs of Turlough* by John Magrath (c. 1350), with epic battle stories and heroic tales of Gaelic leaders (ed. S.H. O'Grady, Irish Text Society, vols. 26 & 27, 1929).

The first surviving Scottish vernacular historical work was John Barbour's *Bruce*, written in the 1370s. Barbour was Archdeacon of Aberdeen, and his verse epic was a notable landmark in Scottish national historiography. In the same generation, John of Fordun compiled the more traditional *Chronica gentis scotorum* , bringing Scottish history down to the 13th century. While other chronicles had been composed in Scotland, their focus had not previously been so clearly upon the land in which they were being written. In sum, the 14th century saw the origin of a distinctly Scottish view of the nation's history, partly in response to the impulse of English invasion.

At the end of the century in Wales, we find a figure reminiscent of Gerald: the lawyer and royal servant Adam of Usk. His *Chronicle* nominally covered the period 1377-1421, though only its middle decade was extensively treated.[10]   Adam was also a product of marcher society (Monmouthshire). His career took him to the continent in royal service, and in later years he returned to Wales and was out of favor by the time of the Glyn Dwr rebellion. Therefore the account of Adam was not simply a "Welsh" history, but it was a uniquely non-English one. At the same time, Usk's *Chronicle* was one of a growing number of 15th century works which departed from old conventions. Municipal accounts became more numerous (though most of them employed a version of the *Brut* for introductory matter); some English writers worked on antiquities with a more scholarly approach (John Rous and William Worcester); there was a continuing appeal in romantic verse such as Henry the Minstrel's account of *William Wallace, his Life and Deeds*; and more modern political and constitutional analysis was evident in work such as Sir John Fortescue's *De laudibus legum Angliae* (1459).

In the last quarter of the century, more telling signs of alteration were evident. Among the most important were the introduction of mechanical printing (1475), the appearance of a new royal dynasty of Welsh origin, and the arrival of the first continental humanist influences, particularly in England and Scotland. The impact of these changes would be several generations in development. Now it is possible to see that historical writing was entering a period of major alteration. In 1500 that was by no means so clear. The historians of the early 16th century continued many traditional forms, but as we shall see, they were writing from different vantage points and with different objectives. These variations were significant for the wider history of the archipelago and for the immature history of its constituent national communities.

Modern Historians and English Hegemony

All of the ingredients of what we regard as "modern" historiography appeared in the archipelago sometime before 1600. Collecting and publishing sources, critical analysis of their contents, and sceptical views of authority were mixed in varied quantities, as each part of the archipelago experienced what is loosely termed the "Tudor" historical revolution. We

---

[10]*Chronicon Adae de Usk*, ed. E.M. Thompson (1904).

will follow the consequences of those changes from the 16th to the 19th centuries, a period in which convincing English hegemony was formed, but like the political world which spawned it, the history never completely shed its Celtic or colonial elements. After the 16th century origins, our sketch will examine three segments of Anglocentric evolution: the crude superiority foisted on the archipelago during the conquests of the 17th century; the commercial and rational empire of the 18th century, and finally the zenith of Anglocentric history in the professionalized setting of the 19th century.

The chronicles of English history, which were relatively neglected in the 15th century, had a period of renewed popularity in the 16th. Richard Fabyan, Edward Hall and Richard Grafton continued the chronicle tradition of compilation, from the *Brut*, to the *Polychronicon*, the later local accounts, and more recent addenda. These authors accepted most of Geoffrey's account, and they were almost as credulous as their medieval predecessors. As the century progressed, there were some signs of new direction. The so-called "Holinshed" Chronicle (1577) was a composite description of England, Scotland and Ireland, done by different authors, but from an essentially English viewpoint. Still, its descriptions of the several countries were in the manner of compilation. These and other chronicles would remain staple fare, and perhaps their popularity was enhanced by the "histories" of Elizabethan dramatists.

There was relatively late humanist influence on historical writing in the archipelago. The first signs were in the second quarter of the 16th century, and they came in the work of two non-English writers. John Major was a Scot who had been educated in Paris and later taught at St. Andrews. His *Historia Maioris Britanniae* was published in 1521. It was a pioneering effort to prune the mythology from Scotland's early history, and it included a scathing rejection of the fabulous story of Brutus and the Trojans and the prophecies of Merlin. An even more telling critique of Geoffrey of Monmouth came from the pen of Polydore Vergil, an Italian cleric who lived in England. His *Anglica Historia* (1534) exposed Geoffrey's faulty classical allusions and fabricated characters, drawing on a wide range of classical authors to refute many of the tales of Arthur and other rulers. In its contemporary setting, Vergil's work has been called "an up-to-date history justifying the Tudors in Latin to the Latin-reading humanists of the West."[11] His theme was English monarchy, his books corresponded to the several reigns, the whole placed in a providential pattern. Vergil was a fine publicist for the anglicizing Tudors. He drew angry replies from several defenders of the British History, such as that of Sir John Price (*Historiae Britannicae Defensio*) composed in the 1540s and published in 1573. Another defender was the English antiquarian, John Leland.

Students of the past had always been interested in physical remains, and in the 16th century the study of antiquities seemed to take on new life, sometimes a new urgency during the reformation. Some important early groundwork was done by John Leland and John Bale. While pursuing the dispersed collections of monastic libraries, Leland travelled extensively in England and Wales. He projected a set of works (a dictionary of authors, a general history and a record of British families) all of which he failed to complete when he lost his sanity. Subsequently most of his papers were dispersed, but his colleague and continuator, John Bale, completed a *Catalog of British Writers*.

Caught up in the tempest of reform, Bale traced monastic authors and their works, but much of his collection was lost when his library in Ireland was attacked (where he had just become Bishop of Ossory in 1552). The work of collection and publication was forwarded by the efforts of Archbishop Matthew Parker. He and others founded the first Society of Antiquaries (1586), and Parker patronized publications designed to authenticate the antiquity of the English church and to develop studies of Saxon ancestors.

English and Anglican self-consciousness was the main force in the reformation of historical work. It was a potent engine of national unity for Englishmen, and it was simultaneously a force for several directions of development in historical thinking outside England. We can see the impact of the "Anglican revolution" transmitted in various ways. In Wales, the Elizabethan government decided to sponsor a Welsh-language translation of the Holy Bible (1563-1588). This may or may not have been due to the Welsh ancestry of the Tudors, but whatever the source, "vernacular translations and the Protestant view of history, taken together, worked more

---

[11]Denys Hay, *Annalists and Historians* (1977), p. 119.

potently for Welsh culture and patriotism than they were to do for English."[12] Where formerly the "bards had been the custodians of the national memory," the new Bible supplied a vehicle for cultural and historical identity.

The deeply-divided state of Ireland had a less happy experience. The Anglo-Irish found effective modern spokesmen in the works of Edmund Campion (*Historie of Ireland*, 1571) and his continuator, Richard Stanihurst. But the Gaelic historians were victims of the political and cultural warfare which escalated in the second half of the century. The Elizabethan conquest meant the suppression of the *filid* along with their Catholic ecclesiastical counterparts.[13]

The historical impact of reformation in Scotland was in a positive nationalist direction. There were contacts of long standing and cultural similarities of great significance between England and Scotland, and so the result was not a simple rejection of things English.[14] George Buchanan's *History of Scotland* (1582), the leading example, gives some idea of the complexity involved. An inveterate foe of Mary, Queen of Scots, Buchanan was also the young king James's tutor. The *History* was perhaps unavoidably steeped in current controversy, and Buchanan said he was aiming to combat "English lies and Scottish vanity."[15] He faced a tall order, for his contemporaries in England and Wales were taking issue with the very essence of Scottish identity.[16]

The Welsh antiquarian Humphry Llwyd had asserted Welsh mythology against the Scottish variety, and in the process he insisted quite persuasively that the Scots did not appear in history before the 5th century.

---

[12]P.R. Roberts, "The Union with England and the Indentity of 'Anglican Wales'" Royal Historical Society, *Transactions* 5s., v. 11 (1972), p. 69.

[13]R. Dudley Edwards, *Ireland in the Age of the Tudors* (1977) gives an excellent overview of "Historians in Sixteenth Century Ireland" pp. 185-94. The Annals in the several provinces terminated between 1541 and 1590. Also see R.W. Dudley Edwards and Mary O'Dowd, eds., *Sources for Early Modern Irish History, 1534-1641* (1985).

[14]Gordon Donaldson, "Foundations of Anglo-Scottish Union," in *Elizabethan Government and Society*, S.T. Bindoff *et al.*, eds. (1961).

[15]The phrase is found in Buchanan's *Vernacular Writings*, cited in W.A. Gatherer, *The Tyrranous Reign of Mary Stuart* (1958), p. 11.

[16]Arthur H. Williamson, *Scottish National Consciousness in the Age of James VI* (1979), p. 126.

William Camden echoed this critique and denied a separate identity to the lowland Scots. His *Britannia, or a chorographical description of the most flourishing kingdoms, England, Scotland and Ireland, and the islands adjoining* was published in 1586. Camden presented a geographical and historical sketch, a discussion of British origins, of the orders of society and government, and a county by county description of Great Britain and Ireland. He drew on many sources, using Leland's work, and the geographic work of continental scholars. Camden said:[17]

> I got some insight into the old British and Saxon tongues for my assistance; I have travell'd almost all over England and have consulted in each county the persons of best skill and knowledge in these matters. I have diligently perus'd our own writers; as well as the Greek and Latin who mention the least tittle of Britain. I have examin'd the public records of the kingdom, ecclesiastical registers, and libraries, and the acts, monuments and memorials of churches and cities.

Despite its title, *Britannia* was English in orientation, like its chronicle predecessors. Its method was modern, and the sources were extensive and critically evaluated. Because of these strengths, *Britannia* formed a solid footing for modern Anglocentric historiography.

During the 17th century a combined process of political, legal and literary development was reshaping and further anglicizing archipelago history. The union of crowns, the legal ascendancy of the English and the literary renaissance of Anglo-Saxon and Anglican sources overshadowed the rest. Only a small amount of Scottish, Gaelic or Welsh historical work survived these unfavorable conditions, and some that did was under colonial patronage or supervision.

The regal union under James naturally influenced the writing of political history. Francis Bacon criticized modern histories, noting "the unworthiness of the history of England in the main continuance thereof, and the partiality and obliquity of that of Scotland," in the work of George Buchanan. Bacon supposed[18]

---

[17]*Britannia* (1722 edition), as cited in May McKisack, *Medieval History in the Tudor Age* (1971), p. 152.

[18]*The Advancement of Learning* (ed. Arthur Johnston, 1974) Book 2.II.8.

that it would be an honour for your Majesty, and a work very memorable, if
this island of Great Brittany, as it is now joined in monarchy for the ages to
come, so were joined in one history for the times passed.

But he added a telling note. "If it shall seem that the greatness of this work
may make it less exactly performed, there is an excellent period of a much
smaller compass of time, as to the story of England," namely that of the
Tudor dynasty.

Another proponent of combined history was Sir Thomas Craig. He
called for "a new history of Britain which shall be written with the utmost
regard to accuracy." What he meant by accuracy was that "as far as possible
the public annals of the two countries should be revised. Errors and irritating
expressions must be expunged." [19] John Clapham had just completed a
Historie of England dealing with the Roman period (1602) which he
republished as *The Historie of Great Britanie* in 1606. It omitted Scottish
history, however, since "there should be severall histories of the English and
Scottish nation." [20] Clapham may have only wanted to add a fashionable
title, and his geographic embarrassment evidently was no great matter. New
works took the larger realm into account, as for instance John Speed's
geographic and historical work, *Theatre of the Empire of Great Britaine*
(1611).

Anglocentric development was advanced by the leading modern political
historians. Camden's *Annals of Great Britain in the Reign of Queen
Elizabeth* (1615-1627), and Francis Bacon's *History of the Reign of King
Henry the Seventh* (1622) were examples. The *Annals* were partly formed
on that model of annular summary. They related the political circumstances
in great detail, and the focus on the English queen quite naturally relegated
other areas to a minor place. Bacon in his turn composed a similarly full and
court-centered narrative, focusing on the nature of Henry Tudor's relation to
the dynastic and national unions.[21]

---

[19]*De unione regnorum Britanniae tractatus* (1608), Scottish History Society,
Publications, v. 60 (1909), p. 468.

[20]*Historie of Great Britanie*, p. A3; see Levy, *Tudor Historical Thought* (1967),
p. 185.

[21]*Henry the Seventh*, p. [ii].

that king to whom both unions may in a sort refer: that of the Roses being in him consummate, and that of the kingdoms by him begunne.

Both authors used the English monarch's "deeds" as a central theme, presenting a readable, continuous, documented story. While these were examples of the higher style of writing, lesser authors were equally drawn to the English focus. In *The Glory of England* (1618), Thomas Gainsford compared English political development to that of continental states--and to Canaan. In his subtitle, Gainsford promised "a true description of many excellent prerogatives and remarkable blessings whereby she [England] triumpheth over all the nations of the world." It was just such notions of "triumph" which were at the root of political and academic differences. One of the most important areas where this clash appeared, and one which profoundly affected historical understanding, was in the law.

One immediate source of inspiration for historical legal argument was the claim by James I to regal ownership of the entire kingdom after the Norman manner. Coming from a Scottish ruler, this hardly appealed to his land-conscious English subjects, particularly when they were discovering what they thought was the parliamentary government of early Saxons. The main proponents of this theme were the common lawyers, whose arguments based on precedent did not need to take strict account of chronology. The wide public use of their "case" must have given a similarly extended audience to the racial-political thrust: that it was Saxon institutions which were at the core of the historical culture, and these were now threatened by an outsider.

Legal studies made a major contribution to new directions in historical writing. Inspired first by the attempt to trace the early church and its laws, the theme reached a new level of achievement with John Selden's *History of Tithes* (1617). Legal scholarship had an impact on political history quite early in the archipelago context. As Attorney-General for Ireland, Sir John Davies studied the case of the Anglo-Irish in their awkward position between two cultures and wrote "the most outstanding piece of historical writing achieved by an Englishman in James I's reign."[22] This cross-cultural view of the legal issues of the day explained the failure of English efforts to anglicize

---

[22]*Discovery of the True Causes why Ireland was not Entirely Subdued* (1612) J.G.A. Pocock, *The Ancient Constitution and the Feudal Law* (1957), p. 62.

Ireland. It was one of a growing number of historical studies of legal subjects.

Sir Henry Spelman's *Archeologus* was a lexicon of legal terms (1626), and his *Feuds and Tenures by Knight Service* (1639) redefined the medieval past as a wholly different social and political order. This view clashed with the static impressions of common lawyers. Spelman's work required outward-looking examination of continental institutions. The work of Edward Coke demanded insular concentration upon the English legal past. Spelman's work was not generally available to the scholarly community, some of it not published until long after his death in 1641. Coke, on the other hand, was in the thick of political activity, his theme was shared widely in the legal profession, and its effect was to retard the development of historical thought and to enhance other anglicizing tendencies. Only much later, with the maturer view of one such as Matthew Hale (d. 1675) in his *History of the Common Law* (1715) was it perceived that the law was constant while it was in constant flux. The law[23]

> must needs receive diverse Accessions from the laws of those people that were thus intermingled with the ancient Britains or Saxons.... And hence grew those several denominations of the Saxon, Mercian, and Danish laws, out of which the Confessor extracted his body of the Common Law.

English legal scholarship was attaining some intellectual maturity while it maintained a practical ascendancy over neighboring systems. The Welsh had been subjugated in the 16th century, the Irish at the beginning of the 17th, and although the Scots regained their distinct system, it only began to take formal shape toward the end of the 17th century, especially with the publication of Lord Stair's *Institutions of the Law of Scotland* (1681). While the 17th century saw English victory and political hegemony, the result in religion was quite different. The several faiths survived, and with them the incentive to produce correct accounts of the past. This pluralism also meant that the history of the civil government would no longer be tied so closely to that of the church. For these reasons, there was a rapid growth of "church history" in the early 17th century, especially by the 1650s. John Ussher, Archbishop of Armagh, is mainly remembered for the chronology "deduced from the origin of time," in his *Annals of the World* (1658), but he was an

---

[23]pp. 62-3.

important collector of manuscripts and he recognized the need for Irish-language sources to write the history of Ireland. Archbishop John Spottiswoode had begun his *History of the Church of Scotland* under the patronage of James I, but it was not published until 1655. In that year the first volume of Thomas Fuller's *Church-History of Britain* appeared. It was in fact English in focus and regal in arrangement. In the same period, William Dugdale, the herald and antiquary, began publishing his *Monasticon Anglicanum*, with its detailed records of orders and houses in England and Wales (1655-73).

While churches had the capacity to sustain a continuing tradition in the 17th century, subordinate political communities were not so well-equipped. The efforts of the first half of the century to collect and organize historical material in many parts of the archipelago were most successful in England. The famous collections of Robert Cotton which were to provide a foundation for the British Museum were being brought together before the wars. Dugdale was publishing his monastic collections, and in 1659 the *Historical Collections* of John Rushworth began to appear in print. Elsewhere, Geoffrey Keating had compiled a manuscript history in Irish (*Foras feasa ar Eirinn*),[24] and Sir James Ware produced *De Scriptoribus Hiberniae* (1639) and *Librorum Manuscriptorum* (1648), while John Colgan edited the *Acta Sanctorum Hiberniae* (1645). But these works were relatively scarce and inaccessible, compared to Rushworth, and to later publications like Thomas Rymer's *Foedera* (1702) and John Strype's *Annals of the Reformation* (1700-31). In fact, many works of non-English origin were not published until the 19th century.[25]

The richness of sources lay behind the striking accomplishment of the later 17th century in English historiography. As David Douglas described it:[26]

> Between 1660 and 1730 a long succession of highly distinguished Englishmen brought to its proper culmination the best sustained and the

---

[24]D. Comyn and P.S. Dineen, eds., *The History of Ireland*, 4 vols. (1902-14).

[25]John Spalding, *History of the Troubles, 1624-1645* 2 vols. (1792); Sir James Balfour, *Historical Works* [1604-1652] 4 vols. (1825); Michael O'Clery, *The Annals of the Kingdom of Ireland to 1616* (1848); Sir Richard Bellings, *History of the Irish Confederation and War in Ireland* [1641-9] 7 vols. (1882-91).

[26]*English Scholars, 1660-1730* 2nd ed. (1951), p. 13.

most prolific movement of historical scholarship which this country has ever seen.

This process resulted from scholastic effort and political hegemony. Given its advantages, the Anglocentric interpretation was understandably dominant, and it became increasingly preoccupied with English and imperial politics.

In the last third of the 17th century, historical writing became more sophisticated and rigorous even as it became more partisan. John Milton was an early exemplar of a mature style in his *History of Britain, that part especially now call'd England* (1669). This work only reached the Norman Conquest; in it Milton's approach was quite modern, for instance in his discussion of national origins. His curiously-worded title was a reflection of the times; "Britain" had lately been a political reality, but the restored monarchy had reverted to the several kingdoms with England dominant.

With the growing constitutional debate in the 1680s, historical interpretation was sure to be affected. Robert Brady wrote a *Compleat History of England* (1685) in which he advanced a strong statement of the Tory view of monarchic power based on a rereading of Norman and medieval history. As a result of the Glorious Revolution, however, Brady was supplanted by William Petyt as Keeper of the Records in the Tower, and a popular view of the Germanic antiquity of parliament prevailed. While important as a chapter in the long debate over Norman vs. Saxon influence, this episode was also significant since it anchored historical discussion in a framework of English political events.

In the final decades of the century and the opening years of the 18th, a more mature view of the wars only reinforced the English domination. Sir Roger Manley wrote one of the best early accounts of events, a relatively balanced and comprehensive sketch. It included the several sectors of fighting and it looked at the whole as one might expect from a royalist raised at court.[27] Manley had been in exile and then served as governor of Jersey. He was well-equipped to see a broader picture. But his contemporaries began to focus more narrowly on England.

We find a good example of the late 17th century style in Sir William Temple, diplomat and scholar, who published his *Introduction to the History*

---

[27]*History of the Rebellions in England, Scotland and Ireland* [1640-1685] (1691).

of England in 1695. Temple complained in his preface that "so ancient and noble a nation as ours" had not produced "one good or approved general history of England." While other countries boasted modern accounts,

> ours have been written by such mean and vulgar authors, so tedious in their relations, so injudicious in their choice of what was fit to be told or to be left alone, with so little order and in so wretched a style; that as it is a shame to be ignorant in the affairs of our own country, so tis hardly worth the time or pains to be informed, since for that end a man must read over a library rather than a book, and after all, must be content to forget more than he remembers.

Temple presented his work as part of a projected survey, this volume only reaching the Normans. As to the British History, "Those tales...are covered with the rust of time, or involved in the vanity of fables, or pretended traditions." Temple concentrated on the Norman era, in which he found a stirring tale of assimilation and increased power. "England grew much greater both in Dominion and power abroad, and also in dignity and state at home." [28]

After the turn of the century, the great narrative of Edward Hyde, earl of Clarendon, was published.[29] Written in the 1640s and 1660s, this eyewitness account was a striking contribution. Clarendon's grasp of events was exceptional, his treatment was quite fair for one who had become a devoted royalist. In earlier sections he dealt fully with the three kingdoms, but reaching the war years his view was confined more and more to the court's perspective. He called the rebellion "a general combination, and universal apostasy in the whole nation from their religion and allegiance." Clarendon wrote with a sure grasp of events and keen critical insight on all sides. While he offered little new evidence, he stood well above his contemporaries in style. His narrowing scope, which tended to shut out events not English, was shared by all but a few continental writers. As a recent student observed: [30]

> The insularity with which the English historians regard the continent finds an echo in the lack of understanding, and even curiosity so often evident in

---

[28]*Introduction*, preface and p. 313.

[29]*The History of the Rebellion and Civil Wars in England* 3 vols. (1702-1704).

[30]Royce MacGillivray, *Restoration Historians and the English Civil War* (1974), p. 231.

their treatment of Scotland and Ireland. For most of the historians, these two closely neighboring nations were very far away indeed.

In 1661 Percy Enderbie wrote his *Cambria Triumphans, or Brittain in its perfect lustre, shewing the origin and antiquity of that illustrious nation.* What the author really meant to show was a Welsh genealogy for Charles II and a tolerant view of the old British History and its appropriation by the Stuart dynasty. Edmund Borlase in *The Reduction of Ireland to the Crown of England* (1675) arranged his story around the successive "Governors" of Ireland and included a section on the late insurrection. His view was that "it seems strange (scarce credible) that after so many years possession of Ireland, any should dare question the right of England to that part of its just Empire."[31] Part of the reason it seemed strange was that the English audience heard very little of the historical thought of the other side. Borlase probably did not have access to works like *Cambrensis Eversus* (1662) by John Lynch. In that work, Gerald of Wales was severely criticized and the same views were given a wider audience in Peter Walsh's *Prospect of the State of Ireland* in 1682. This was also the period in which Robert Ware augmented his father's collections with forged documents, to produce such revelations as *Hunting of the Romish Fox* (1683) "proving" subversion by Jesuits in 16th century Ireland. In an interesting contrast, the Dublin Philosophical Society was founded in 1683 by William Petty, William Molyneux and others, continuing a co-operative tradition of Gaelic and Anglo-Irish scholarly work. Molyneux was later involved in a printed dispute over the nature of Ireland's historic connection to England. He wrote *The Case of Ireland's being Bound by Acts of Parliament in England Stated* in 1698, and was challenged by William Atwood, a pupil of Petyt, who wrote *The History and Reasons of the Dependency of Ireland* in the same year. The debate over constitutional priority was more political than historical, and it had parallels in the essays of the Scottish author, Andrew Fletcher of Saltoun. But such protests as these were feeble enough politically, and they could not turn the historical tide which had risen in the 17th century.

There was a growing imbalance in quantity and quality of sources by the beginning of the 18th century, added to which was a growing discrepancy in access to publishers and patrons. More than ever, authors were encouraged

---

[31]*Reduction of Ireland*, p. B3.

to migrate to England and seek patronage there. Sometimes this was beneficial to non-English history. The Welshman Edward Lhuyd became Keeper of the Ashmolean Museum at Oxford. In the 1690s he travelled extensively in Celtic lands and collected information from questionnaires to parish clergy. Lhuyd was working on a four-volume *Archaeologia Britannica* which would describe language, customs, monuments and rulers, but only the first volume was complete at his death.[32]

A more ambitous expatriate might try to make his way in the employ of the Anglican Church. After the revolutions of the 17th century, that institution was still a major force in Anglocentrism. Major works in theology, history and the collection of documents were vital signs that the twice-restored establishment (saved from both republicans and reactionaries) was firmly in place.[33] One historian who did find his way to eminence by way of the church was Gilbert Burnet, who became Bishop of Salisbury. Burnet was born in Scotland, where he found the religious establishment oppressive. He migrated to England where he found preferment and further difficulty. He spent time on the continent, accompanied William of Orange to England, and credited his "zeal for the Church of England" as his motive for writing *The History of His Own Time* [1660-1713], published in 1724 and 1735. The work was an openly biased endorsement of the Glorious Revolution and the Protestant settlement, full of personal observations on the characters of the period.

Burnet's work was one of a number of histories published in the 18th century by Scottish authors which maintained the ascendancy of English events. The renowned narratives of the middle of the 18th century were written by Scottish-born men of letters striving for success in an English-dominated literary world. That fact explains why the enlightenment impulse toward universal and scientific study was sometimes overcome by Anglocentrism.

David Hume was the best-known Scottish Enlightenment historian of England. He came late to historical writing. His early failure to make a mark

---

[32]John L. Campbell and Dericks Thomson, *Edward Lhuyd in the Scottish Highlands, 1699-1700* (1963).

[33]See Strype, *Annals;* Edmund Gibson, *Codex juris anglicani* (1713), Jeremy Collier, *An Ecclesiastical History of Great Britain* (1708-14), David Wilkins and William Wake, edd. *Concilia Magnae Britanniae et Hiberniae, 446-1717* (1737).

with his philosophical works plus his appointment as Librarian to the Faculty of Advocates (1752) were instrumental, as was his discontent with works like Burnet's and that of the popular French Huguenot, Paul de Rapin-Thoyras.[34] He first wrote a volume on James I and Charles I, then on the period to 1688, after which he wrote earlier volumes on the Tudors and on medieval England (1754-1762). He challenged the prevailing Whig interpretation, disputing the dominant idea of tyrannical rule by the Stuarts. Perhaps Hume "had no special vision of a need for a national history of England," [35] but his very popular work, written in a polished narrative style, surely augmented the Anglocentric tendency.

Tobias Smollet, the Scottish novelist, wrote a "continuation of Hume" covering 1688-1748, and published a general survey in 1757-58.[36] His popular style assured Smollett of a large audience. He was said to have composed his *History* in a space of only 14 months, and he revised the whole for a new edition in 1758. Though maligned as a "Jacobite" and a "Papist," Smollett was popular with his English audience, and profitable for his English publisher. He confided to a correspondent that [37]

> I was agreeably surprised to hear that my work had met with any approbation at Glasgow for it was not at all calculated for that meridian. The last volume will, I doubt not, be severely censured by the West country Whigs of Scotland.

Robert Henry, Scottish clergyman and Moderator of the General Assembly, tried to diverge from the line of Hume and Smollett. His *History of Great Britain on a New Plan*, published in 1771, employed a systematic and topically- broadened approach to "the most important events which have happened in Great Britain...together with a distinct view of the religion, laws, learning, arts, commerce and manners of its inhabitants."[38] Henry tried to offset Anglocentricity and keep the focus on Great Britain.

---

[34]*The History of England* (1724-27) .

[35]T.P. Peardon, *The Transition in English Historical Writing, 1760-1830* (1933), p. 21.

[36]*A Complete History of England*, 4 vols.

[37]Lewis M. Knapp, *Tobias Smollett: Doctor of Men, and Manners* (1949), p. 193-4.

[38]Henry, *History of Great Britain* 5th ed., (1814), v. 1, p. [xix].

William Robertson, another Scottish cleric and principal of Edinburgh University (1762-92), is usually classed with Hume and Edward Gibbon as one of the great figures of 18th century historiography. He did not write a history of England, but his examination of the 16th century *History of Scotland* (1759) was a major work. In terms of scholarship, Robertson probably surpassed other writers in the British field, but this work was restricted to detailed narration of the later 16th century. The English queen, who in her relations with Scotland used "her craft and intrigues, affecting what the valour of her ancestors could not accomplish, reduced that kingdom to a state of dependence on England".[39] History followed in the wake of politics, and "the few compositions that Scotland produced were tried by the English standard," and by his own time "the same authors are read and admired" in both countries. That some of those authors were Scots was insufficient compensation.

Contemporary with the Enlightenment, but much closer to the ground, numerous antiquaries were at work in the 18th century archipelago.[40] The numbers involved were one reason for organization. The Society of Antiquaries was refounded in 1718; the Physico-Historical Society of Dublin was organized in 1744, the London Welsh community set up the Cymmrodorion Society in 1751, and its less exclusive counterpart, the Society of Gwyneddigion in 1771. The Royal Dublin Society formed a Committee on Antiquities in 1772, the Scottish Society of Antiquaries was formed in 1780, and the more practical Highland and Agricultural Society was established in 1784.

While antiquarians did some useful work,[41] a few of their colleagues were too anxious to produce new results. William Stukeley had helped in the reorganization of the Society of Antiquaries, and he had done some important field-work. But, as Stuart Piggott said, Stukeley "brought the Druids to

---

[39]*History of Scotland*, v. 2, p. 194.

[40]A recent survey of English antiquaries found 853 writers in the second half of the century alone (Arlene H. Eakle, "Antiquaries and the Writing of English Local History, 1750-1800," unpublished Ph.D. dissertation, University of Utah, 1985).

[41]See especially William Nicolson, *The English, Scottish and Irish Historical Libraries* (1736); Thomas Innes, *Critical Essay on the Ancient Inhabitants of the Northern Parts of Britain, or Scotland*, (1729).

Stonehenge."[42] The effect of his work lingers, but other 18th century authors were more easily refuted. In 1761 James MacPherson produced what he claimed were ancient writings of a poet named Ossian.[43] These forgeries were detected fairly soon. Meanwhile, other scholars produced more reputable edited works. Evan Evans selected *Some Specimens from the Poetry of the Ancient Welsh Bards* (1764) and Thomas Percy edited *Reliques of Ancient English Poetry* (1765).

Among the many sources of inspiration for the revived interest in early history, the internal rivalries in the archipelago played a part. In the second half of the century, the effort to introduce the terms "North Briton" and "South Briton" foundered on Anglo-Scottish mutual animosity. There was also a continuing dispute over the priority of settlement of Scotland and Ireland. An interesting contribution to this debate was made by Sylvester O'Halloran, a surgeon and antiquary of Limerick. In refuting the claim that the Scots were the original colonists of Ireland, he decried the fraudulent Ossian, spawned "under the auspices of Lord Bute, and countenanced by the nobility and gentry of Scotland." O'Halloran also answered the remark of Voltaire that the Irish were "formed for subjection to others." He said that foreigners should "strip their English biographical dictionaries of all Irish and Scotch names," in order to see the true "characteristics of England." [44] The antiquarian rivalry was a vigorous scholarly phenomenon, but it was unproductive because of its remoteness, parochialism and, at times, its unreliability. These features were not an obstacle in the growing field of imperial history, an area which would have increasing impact on archipelago historical understanding.

Historical analysis of the imperial enterprise helped to reinforce and entrench Anglocentrism. Pioneering work on political economy and colonial history drew attention toward the center of the empire and supported a trend toward reverential study of the English law and constitution.

---

[42] *The Druids* (1968), p. 125.

[43] *Fingal, an Ancient Epic Poem* (1761); *Temora, an Ancient Epic Poem* (1763); he also wrote an *Introduction to the Ancient History of Great Britain and Ireland* (1771) and a *History of Great Britain from the Restoration*, 2 vols. (1775).

[44] *An Introduction to the Study of the History and Antiquities of Ireland* (1772), pp. 298, 309, Appendix.

The study of "political economy" aimed at better understanding and improved application of economic power. At the early stage, this was still conceived in moral more than in statistical terms, the latter science only maturing after the beginning of the 19th century. But long before that there was an insatiable fascination with the material and political characteristics of the burgeoning empire. The writers who engaged in that subject were regularly drawn into historical explanations of current conditions[45]

John Campbell was born in Edinburgh but raised in England. His writing was mainly on imperial and naval subjects, though he produced *The Political State of Europe* (1750) and a *Description of the Highlands* in 1752. Campbell's last work was the product of years of labor, and it showed the potential and limitations of the political economist. The *Political Survey of Britain* (2 vols., 1774) was a detailed political geography of the archipelago, set in a general world and European historical framework. Campbell believed in the innate political strength of islands, and he proposed to enhance British power by the full and systematic exploitation of all the British Isles: "the outworks... for the Security of this great Country."(I, 454) Campbell included sections on constitutional history, the history of revenue and the history of colonies in his work.

Other economic writers were equally concerned with the strategic aspect of their subject. Thus George Chalmers produced *An Estimate of the Comparative Strength of Britain during the Present and Four Preceding Reigns* (1782). This interest was repeated in a number of other works on economic subjects.[46] On the heels of the American revolt there was an evident sense of loss and a potent demand for historical information. The crisis in America stressed the importance of colonies and intensified current interest in imperial government and its history. The "colonial historian" of the late 18th century was, like the political economist, enmeshed in current debate and not a detached observer--in fact sometimes not a very well-informed observer, unless he had travelled widely, as a few of the writers had. The first half of

---

[45]Among the more interesting mid-century works were Jonas Hanway, *An Historical Account of the British Trade over the Caspian Sea* (1753); James Postlethwayt, *The History of the Public Revenue* (1759); Adam Anderson, *An Historical and Chronological Deduction of the Origin of Commerce* (1764).

[46]John Sinclair, *History of the Public Revenue* (1782); John Phillips, *A General History of Inland Navigation* (1792); John Reeves, *History of the Law of Shipping* (1792).

the century had not seen many serious attempts at literary treatment, but that picture soon changed. William and Edmund Burke produced *An Account of the European Settlements in North America* (2 vols., 1757) which sketched the exploration and settlement by the European peoples in the mainland and island colonies over 250 years. Another important work was John Wynne's *General History of the British Empire in America* (2 vols., 1770). He offered "an historical, political and commercial view of the English settlements" believing that [47]

> nothing is more rational to suppose, than that a thorough knowledge of each other's interests may contribute to the reconciliation of both parties and be the means of once more uniting them in bonds of union and procuring for them a lasting and undisturbed repose.

While no doubt rational, Wynne's hope for "thorough knowledge" on either side was unrealistic, but colonial historians were not deterred. William Robertson produced a *History of America* in 1777, and he wrote a work on *Ancient India* in 1791. George Chalmers offered *An Introduction to the History of the Revolt of the American Colonies* in 1782, only partly completed. In the later years of the century there were topical works from other imperial sectors, for example Charles Hamilton's *Historical Relation of the...Government of the Rohilla Afgans* (1787) and Bryan Edwards' *History, Civil and Commercial, of the British Colonies in the West Indies* in 1793.

The study of the empire, even when it was critical, had to focus attention on the central institutions and draw it away from the peripheral communities in the archipelago. A critical area in which this was made evident was in the consensus on the law and the constitution. From William Blackstone's *Commentaries on the Laws of England* (4 vols. 1765-69) to Gilbert Stuart's *Historical Dissertations Concerning the Antiquity of the English Constitution* (1770) or John Millar's *An Historical View of the English Government* (1787) there was a confident sense of the historical origin of English and imperial institutions. Even the well-known public dispute between the Welshman Richard Price and his *Love for our Country* (1789) and the Anglo-Irish Edmund Burke and his *Reflections on the Revolution in France* (1790) was not a dispute over the virtue of the English constitution, but

---

[47]v. 1 p. vii.

whether it was designed to protect "civil liberty" as the American and French revolts were defining that term. All attested to the English locus of imperial authority, none seemed to challenge that fact. This condition did not mean that histories of other parts of the archipelago were not written.[48] It did mean that the history which was written was dominated by the heart of the empire. John Reeves, picking up a theme from Blackstone's sketch of legal history, claimed that his method was "wholly new", and that he would show "the true colours in which [the laws] appeared to persons who lived in earlier periods." [49] His claim was inflated to be sure, but also Reeves was not attempting to do other than Blackstone, namely, to see the *English* law as the framework of his subject.

Anglocentric history was in command during the 19th century. Once past the great political watershed of 1789, anglicized and imperial historians of the archipelago turned more and more to self-congratulatory political history. Though strong national-romantic impulses were widespread, the Welsh, Scottish and Irish practitioners were neutralized by the United Kingdom constitution and by an emerging historical establishment. By the middle of the century, the modern historical profession was clearly visible, with institutional record-keeping, professional organization, and academic establishment. In the second half of the century the great narrators of the English past--Macaulay, Stubbs, Gardiner, Green and Lecky--composed a literature which celebrated a past peopled by Saxon and Norman heroes which led inexorably to an Anglocentric present. Those writers were joined by a group of empire historians with wider but compatible objectives. Seeley, Froude, Freeman, Bryce and Trevelyan outlined the "expansion of England," which assumed the absorption of the archipelago en route to formation of the global empire. The political movements of the last decades of the century would challenge this comfortable English scenario, but conventional political history would not be seriously affected until well into the 20th century.

---

[48]John H. Wynne, *General History of Ireland* 2 vols. (1772); Thomas Leland, *The History of Ireland*, 3 vols. (1773); William Crawford, *A History of Ireland*, 2vols. (1783); Gilbert Stuart, *The History of Scotland*, 2 vols. (1782); William Warrington, *The History of Wales* (1786).

[49]*History of English Law* (1783-84) v. 1, pp. v-vi.

With the era of the French revolution, political tension brought forth romantic and nationalist historical impulses. The result was a populist form of antiquarianism, evident in many parts of the archipelago. In part it was inspired by French Jacobinism, but it also drew on a universal fondness for mythology. As Asa Briggs put it,[50]

> Our popular attitudes to history rest on myths not on facts, and the early and late Victorians, for all their increasing material sophistication, were as dependent on myths as any other generations.

With the popularizing trends of the early 19th century, this dependency may have been greater than normal. Certainly it affected historical works around the archipelago. The potent mixture of populist notions and presumed antiquity probably did not advance the study of history, but it added energy and emotion, and by doing so, some of the populist work provoked reassessment.

Thomas Oldfield described a pre-Norman government in which the Saxons held annual parliaments based upon a household franchise, in one of the more extreme versions of the Saxon myth.[51] Iolo Morganwg invented the *Gorsedd*, described by a modern writer as the "democratic elite of a new and democratic Welsh nation." [52] Robert Burns called himself a peasant, and his "form of personal radicalism" illuminated the customs and traditions of the lower classes.[53] The antiquities of Ireland were treated with an excessively romantic touch by Charles Vallancey, the French soldier, engineer and antiquary.[54]

The works of these "antique democrats" were governed by their belief in a myth of ancient "liberty" more than a trust in documentary evidence. With this weakness, the romantic democrats were soon the target of scholars who readily found the means to challenge them. For example, the work of Sharon

---

[50]*Saxons, Normans and Victorians* (1966), p. 3.

[51]*The History of the Original Constitution of Parliament from the Time of the Britons to the Present Day* (1797).

[52]Gwyn A. Williams, *The Welsh in their History* (1982), p. 51.

[53]David Craig, *Scottish Literature and the Scottish People, 1680-1830* (1961); Rosalind Mitchison, *History of Scotland* (1970) p. 362.

[54]*A Vindication of the Ancient History of Ireland* (1786), and see, Donald MacCartney, "The Writing of History in Ireland, 1800-1830," *Irish Historical Studies* 10 (1957):348.

Turner revived serious Anglo-Saxon studies in the 19th century. He said that "the subject of the Anglo-Saxon antiquities had been nearly forgotten by the British public."[55] Turner's political view was more reserved than Oldfield: [56]

> After many years consideration of the question I am inclined to believe that the Anglo-Saxon Witan-agemot very much resembled our present parliament, in the orders and persons that composed it; and that the members, who attended as representatives, were chosen by classes analogous to those who now possess the elective franchise.

In other words, the Saxon institution was a precedent, but not a precedent for political reform.

For the Scottish populist, the antidote took the shape of the Tory literary genius of Walter Scott. His novels were set in periods of major historical crisis, their characters evoking a Scottish loyalty and a laudable Scottish identity. In the realm of the scholar, the work of George Chalmers had been much more important in beginning a long process of recovery and reinterpretation of Celtic Scotland.[57]

Romantic visions of Irish antiquaries were stoutly addressed and corrected by writers such as Rev. Edward Ledwich. In *The Antiquities of Ireland* (1790) he professed reliance on valid documentary sources, though he was unable to live up to the promise. But the aim was more nearly fulfilled with the *Ecclesiastical History of Ireland* (4 vols., 1822) by John Lanigan.

By 1830, historical writing in the archipelago was advancing on several fronts, though certainly without a coherent design. Sharon Turner published a modern history (1826-29); Jonah Barrington produced *The Rise and Fall of the Irish Nation* in 1830, commemorating the era of Grattan's Parliament (1782-1800); Walter Scott's *History of Scotland* also appeared in 1830. Conventional historical work fared less well than fiction in his hands, though

---

[55]*The History of the Anglo-Saxon* 4 vols. (1799-1805) cited in J.W. Burrow, *A Liberal Descent* (1981) p. 116.

[56]ibid., p. 119.

[57]*Caledonia; or an Account, Historical and Topographic, of North Britain...* 3 vols. (1807-24).

after Scott, things would be even worse for Scotland, owing to southward migration.[58]

Sir Nicholas Harris Nicolas wrote his *Observations on the State of Historical Literature* in that same year, concluding that "Science and History cannot be neglected by this Country...the present state of both is humiliating to the nation." Ironically, what drew his censure was not total inactivity, but a generation of public efforts to restore and preserve records.[59]

> Nearly everything remains to be done that is worth doing, and it may be said, without fear of contradiction, that the Commission [on Public Records] after having existed for thirty years, and expended £200,000, has left the history of this country very nearly in the same state as it found it.

Surely the indictment was too strong, and just as surely the intrusion of official action had not brought a scholars' millenium. What had begun, however, was a major transformation in the professional approach to the study of history, and one by-product of that would be further centralizing in historical interpretation.

The first half of the 19th century was a significant period of professional development for historians. Many of the factors which were affecting professions generally were important (urbanization, prosperity and political reform). More immediately significant to historians were the changes in public records, professional organization and growing academic recognition.

The government had long had an interest in the collection and preservation of records, at least its own. Yet that interest had not been systematically pursued. In the 18th century there were signs of development, as for instance with the formation of the collections of the British Museum and with the construction of the Scottish Register House, begun in 1774. But record publication was a matter of private initiative, and even standards of preservation were not well-developed. That might not be surprising in

---

[58]Christopher Harvie comments: "The tide set decisively to the South.... Carlyle took the London coach....Social thought as much as administration or technology was to be dominated by men of Scottish birth or descent: Carlyle, Ruskin, Mill, Gladstone, T.B. Macaulay, Leslie Stephen. The dividend on past educational and social investment was impressive. But the result was an intellectual vacuum in the north." *Scotland and Nationalism* (1977), p. 135.

[59]Peardon, *Transition*, p. 303-4.

view of the fact that it was estimated in 1800 that in London alone there were some sixty offices in which records were being held.

Thus it was not premature in 1800 for the issue of a royal commission to inquire into the state of public records in England and Wales, nor for that inquiry to be extended to Scotland (1808) and Ireland (1812). The Record Commission had many critics, but its creation did mark the beginning of more or less continuous effort by the government to organize and preserve its documents. Moreover, particular individuals took some inspiration and acted decisively to advance the process. Thomas Thomson, as Deputy Clerk Register of Scotland from 1806, pioneered Scottish record organization and publication.

The work of the early record reformers was important in another way. There were massive quantities of documentary material in private collections. Discovery and publication of such "treasures" was one of the principal motives in "printing clubs" in the early 19th century. We have noted some of the national organizations which brought antiquaries together in the later 18th century, and some local bodies were also formed (Literary and Philosophical Society of Manchester-1781, Literary and Antiquarian Society of Perth-1784, Philosophical Society of Glasgow-1802). Over the next few decades these multiplied rapidly and became more specialized. The earliest of the "printing clubs" was the Roxburghe, founded in 1812. Its members subscribed and provided funds for printing of rare and valuable tracts, documents and papers. The Bannatyne (Edinburgh 1823) and the Maitland Clubs (Glasgow 1828) were early imitators. In England a number of later and more specialized bodies appeared (the Surtees Society for Northumberland, 1834; the Parker for Anglican documents, 1840; the Aelfric for Saxon materials, 1842; the Hakluyt for explorers, 1846). The Camden Society was founded in 1838 for the editing and publication of material across the United Kingdom, while a number of functional societies were founded (Numismatic, 1836; Philological, 1842; Ethnological, 1843; Archaeological, 1843). For the outlying areas, there were few, Scotland being disproportionately "represented." But the Irish Archaeological Society was begun in 1840 to be joined by the later Celtic Society (1845-53) and the Cambrian Archaeological Association was founded in 1846.[60]

It would be unrealistic to attempt a general assessment of these bodies and the real contributions they made to the understanding of history. Their numbers were evidence of a strong historical interest, as were their manifold publishing efforts. The editing standards, if not high to start, were to benefit from exercise and wider reading audiences. Those audiences in turn were receiving more serious attention at the university level in the 19th century.

Instruction in history had been a nominal part of the university curriculum since the 18th century. Regius Professors of Modern History were appointed at Oxford and Cambridge from 1724, appointments in ecclesiastical history had existed earlier at Edinburgh and Glasgow, and Trinity College had a position in history and oratory. Some of these were held as sinecures and history continued to be written chiefly by philosophers, novelists and antiquaries. Under the impetus of new foundations and new ideas in the 19th century, faculties were provided with professors of history more inclined to lecture, study and write in their field. One observer would comment that only "about 1850 modern history obtained a place in the curriculum" of Oxford and Cambridge.[61] At Durham (1831), London (1836), Belfast, Galway and Cork (1845) and Aberystwyth (1872), Cardiff (1884) and Bangor (1885) the new facilities were equipped with historians. These posts were intended primarily for the teaching of English or European history, the predominant emphasis being upon medieval subjects with topical orientations mainly along ecclesiastical or constitutional (legal) lines. An accepted feature of the new positions was the adoption of the model of the German seminar and its high standards of source-criticism. The cultural bias and the institutional structure tended to favor the already-established influence of the Anglo-Saxons.

The study of history was reshaped by much that went on outside of the university. Major documentary publication projects and important scholarly groups were corollaries of the formation of a historical "establishment."

---

[60] Abraham Hume, ed. *The Learned Societies and Printing Clubs of the United Kingdom* (1853) gives a full listing and description of each body and its publications.

[61] C.H. Firth, "The Study of Modern History in Great Britain," *Proceedings of the British Academy* 6 (1914):114.

Perhaps in imitation of Pertz's *Monumenta Germaniae Historica*, the Record Office began the publication of the famous *Rolls Series* (1856-86), edited versions of major documentary sources. The State Paper Office (joined to the Record office in 1854) began the massive task of publishing *Calendars* (lists and extracts) of the voluminous foreign, domestic and colonial documents in government custody from the middle ages.

The masses of papers held privately were recognized as a vital source, and in 1869 a royal warrant created a commission to make inquiries of the private owners, to inspect their papers and to publish periodic reports. Thus began the series of examinations and reports by the Historical Manuscripts Commission which still continues.

Another potential symbol of establishment was the formation of the Royal Historical Society. Its first meeting was in 1868, but it only obtained the "royal" designation in 1872. Indeed, its organizer, Dr. Charles Rogers, was a Scottish clergyman who had left Scotland in unpleasant circumstances and had just founded another body known as the "Grampian Club," and was secretary to some other organizations as well.[62] It was some time before the Society became a bastion of the establishment, indeed some time before a fully-developed establishment was in place. Meanwhile, a number of popular historians and some vigorous historical debates preoccupied the Victorian audience and fed its growing appetite for history.

The third quarter of the 19th century was the zenith of Anglocentric Whig history. A remarkable group of narrators compiled an impressive survey of English events, and there were few to parallel them in Scotland, Ireland or Wales.[63] Thomas Macaulay was an active politician as well as a successful historian. His *History of England from the Accession of James the Second* (1848-1855) was a great popular success. Macaulay wanted to [64]

---

[62]R.A. Humphreys, *The Royal Historical Society, 1868-1968* (1969), pp. 1-12.

[63]John Hill Burton's *History of Scotland, 1689-1748* 2 vols. (1853) and his seven-volume work prior to 1688 (1867-70) were exceptions, as was the lengthy section on Scotland in H.T. Buckle's *History of Civilization in England*, 2 vols. (1857-61). For Ireland, most works were concerned with English relations; for Wales, the first Welsh-language history in 1842 (Thomas Price, *Hanes Cymru*) and B.B. Woodward, *The History of Wales* 2 vols. (1853) and Jane Williams, *A History of Wales* (1869).

[64]*History of England*, v. 1, p. 2.

relate the history of the people as well as the history of the government, to trace the progress of useful and ornamental arts.... I shall cheerfully bear the reproach of having descended below the dignity of history, if I can succeed in placing before the English of the nineteenth century a true picture of the life of their ancestors.

Macaulay included material on non-English areas, but his views of Scottish and Irish history were much less careful and sound than his other sections.

Edward A. Freeman was one of the leading narrative historians who began to focus on more carefully defined topics, his own main interest being the Norman Conquest. He called it the "great turning point in the history of the English nation," and the "temporary overthrow of our national being," but as a recent author notes, "the Norman was a Teutonic brother," and could be assimilated. The dynasty would return to its roots with Edward I "like an old Bretwalda." [65] Freeman's more scholarly and influential contemporary was Bishop William Stubbs whose great work was his *Constitutional History of England* (3 vols. 1874-78). Stubbs was interested in breaking away from political history and its heroes, to study "the continuous development of representative institutions from the first elementary stage." In the process he wrote "the best available general history of medieval England." [66]

Samuel R. Gardiner devoted his career to the explanation of the political history of the 17th century. His early volumes were not well-received, but by the 1880s he was gaining wide recognition and acclaim. His *History of England from the Accession of James I to the Outbreak of the Civil War 1603-1642* had been written between 1863 and 1882 and was reissued in a 10-volume set in 1883-84. Gardiner chose to write a detailed chronicle of events, avoiding large analytical themes or dominating portraits.

In a unique manner, but still belonging to this class of narrators, John R. Green was tremendously successful with his *Short History of the English People* (1874). Green wanted to avoid "drum and trumpet history" and he preferred to outline social and cultural conditions. His work was a publishing coup, even outselling Macaulay in its first year.[67] Green and his

---

[65]*The History of the Norman Conquest*, 6 vols. (1867-79); Burrow, *A Liberal Descent* , p. 215.

[66]J.R. Hale, *The Evolution of British Historiography* (1964), p. 59.

[67]R.D. Altick, *The English Common Reader* (1957) cites first-year sales of 35,000 compared with Macaulay's 22,000.

wife also wrote a popular *Short Geography of the British Islands* (1879) which served as a model for the type of historical application of geography which Green advocated. At the same time, that work was the closest thing to an archipelago history written in the 19th century. Still, the dominant and indelible theme of these works was the priority of English political development. We see further proof of that in the last quarter of the century, and in the treatment of Ireland in particular.

As noted earlier, "Irish" histories in this period tended to focus on England's involvement in that island, which was a large and inescapable topic in current politics. James Anthony Froude challenged the goal of Irish political reform in the early 1870s.[68] He introduced his book with a survey of the archipelago and a vivid, one-sided account of the 1641 massacre. He found the Irish unfit for their own government and prone to stimulate English repression. Froude certainly stimulated historical debate, and the bulk of later writers were more judicious. For example, George Hill wrote a detailed study of the Ulster plantation in 1877.[69] As the Librarian of Queens College, Belfast, Hill was in a position to give a detailed account of the records of the plantation.

A careful general work on the 16th century was done by Richard Bagwell.[70] Working from State Papers, private collections and Irish chronicles, he assembled an impartial narrative of the 16th century English sovereigns and their Irish policies. More significant still was the work on the 18th century by William Lecky. He was from an Anglo-Irish family (one with some Scottish roots), and he rectified the biased attacks of writers like Froude. Lecky actually wrote a long *History of England in the Eighteenth Century* (8 vols., 1878-1890) in which there were large sections on Ireland, later extracted to form the 5-volume *History of Ireland in the Eighteenth Century* (1892). This curious pattern suggested to some that Lecky wrote the English history as a cover for his ultimate Irish interest, though that seems an unnecessary deception.

During debates over Home Rule, there were strong views from the other side. For instance, Albert Venn Dicey wrote *England's Case Against Home Rule* (1886). The existence of unionist historical works underlined the fact

---

[68]*The English in Ireland in the Eighteenth Century*, 3 vols. (1872-74).
[69]*An Historical Account of the Plantation in Ulster... 1608-1620* (1877).
[70]*Ireland under the Tudors*, 3 vols. (1885-90).

that Anglocentric history had developed somewhat absent-mindedly. The challenge of Irish claims for autonomy (with their faint echoes from Scotland and Wales) were bound to produce historical answers which bolstered the Whiggish view of England's "right" to govern the archipelago, although that imperial title had previously been hardly discussed in historical contexts outside the events of 1707 and 1801. Beside the legalistic unionism of Dicey was the dual loyalty ("national unionism"?) of one such as Lord Rosebery. He combined strong feelings of Scottish national identity with a stout-hearted vision of "an imperial race...vigorous and industrious and intrepid." [71] The strength of unionist opinion derived in part from the larger imperial sentiment being cultivated in the 1880s.

The evolution of imperial historiography dated from the 17th century. The imperial subject became a more emotional and compelling one in the late 19th century, under a combination of impulses, from economic pressure to European rivalries to racist theory. By the 1860s Charles Dilke was describing his travels in "Greater Britain," wherein he saw the future world power of "Saxondom." This essential idea was formulated in more acceptable academic fashion by the Cambridge professor John R. Seeley. In 1883 he published *The Expansion of England*, based on a set of lectures on English and imperial history from the 16th century. Seeley continued this discussion in *The Growth of British Policy* (1895), which was an attempt to explain the imperial structure in terms of political science.

The empire was a subject of great interest for historians, though at this stage its practitioners were not equipped with satisfactory archives and they tended to write polemics or projects. J. A. Froude was an active author in this field, drawn to it through his early work in Elizabethan history (*History of England* [1530-1603], 1869). He wrote *Oceana, or England and her Colonies* (1886) and *The English in the West Indies* (1888). James Bryce and George O. Trevelyan were drawn to the subject of the American colonies and their abrupt departure from the empire, perhaps as a historical object lesson to the Victorian governors.[72] The interest in the history of the empire buttressed the Anglocentric interpretation, but the rise of home rule sentiment

---

[71]Rectorial Address, University of Glasgow, Nov. 16, 1900 (John Buchan ed., *Miscellanies, Literary and Historical*, 2 vols., 1922; v. 2, p. 250).

[72]Bryce, *The American Commonwealth*, 2 vols. (1888); Trevelyan, *The American Revolution*, 6 vols. (1899-1914).

and colonial nationalism soon aroused more interest and activity in the "lesser" histories in the archipelago.

Historians in the 20th Century Archipelago

The Anglocentric pattern was well established by the beginning of the 20th century. At the same time, there were ample indications that Celtic subjects were being revived, while both national and pan-Celtic interests grew. Such growth was obscured by the continuing importance of empire (and its history) down to 1945. Since then, new trends in political history have tested many older views and begun to shape new accounts of archipelago history.

Some major projects helped to anchor the English establishment at the turn of the century, while the star performers in the profession continued to advance historical understanding within an Anglocentric pattern. In 1885 the multi-volume *Dictionary of National Biography* was inaugurated, its basic set of volumes being completed in 1900. In 1886 the *English Historical Review* began publication, one of a growing number of scholarly journals, bringing more capacity for scholarly publication and more editorial control.[73] Some important bibliographic works made their debut at the end of the century. Charles Gross edited *A Bibliography of British Municipal History* in 1897, followed by the broader and basic *Sources and Literature of English History from the Earliest Time to about 1485* (1900).[74] In the same year, a team of researchers began to produce the series of *Victoria Histories of the Counties of England*, while another group was preparing the multi-volume *Cambridge Modern History* (1902-12). These encyclopedic works attempted to gather and publish the best available summaries of their several subjects and they each had lasting value.

The scholars were generally engaged in refining and perfecting the Whig historical image of imperial England. That is not to say that there were no feuds along the way, for matters of party, sect and disposition were not

---

[73]Later there were the *Scottish Historical Review* (1903-28; 1947-); *Irish Historical Studies* (1938-); and the *Welsh History Review* (1960-).

[74]This became the initial volume of the series, *Bibliographies of British History*, sponsored by the Royal Historical Society and the American Historical Association, now consisting of six volumes.

banished from historical discussion by the alleged objectivity of the new "science." Probably the most active field of study in the years 1890-1930 was medieval history. John Horace Round gave a view of feudal society which fundamentally challenged Stubbs' portrayal and turned subsequent research toward detailed analysis of this largely alien system.[75] Frederic W. Maitland was the leading English legal scholar (founder of the Selden Society, 1887), and he wrote, with Frederick Pollock, a classic *History of English Law before the time of Edward I* (1895).

In the writing of modern history there was continuing fascination with the 17th century. Charles H. Firth completed Gardiner's magnum opus to the Restoration. He gave the Ford Lectures in 1901 which were later published as *Cromwell's Army* (1902). Firth's wide experience included editing a number of volumes for the Scottish History Society, and his long apprenticeship resulted in some classic political histories. George M. Trevelyan made his first major appearance with *England under the Stuarts* (1904). The dynastic set-piece in the standard Whig framework was marked by the young author's compelling style, and he went on to become the most popular English historian in the early 20th century.[76]

With the Great War and its attendant political and social upheaval, no profession, no part of modern society was untouched. There was a sudden and severe blow to any complacent and progressive philosophy of history, scientific or otherwise. In the 1920s there was much more evidence of revision and innovation. The major directions which emerged were the analysis of economics (Marxist or traditional), the explanation of social conditions and relations, and (especially for earlier periods) the more energetic study of cultural and archeological evidence. It is difficult to separate this activity from its occasional political links, but then the old Whig view had not been without political connections.[77] For our purposes, it is more important to gauge how much or how far these newer emphases affected the shape or the geography of archipelago history. The new breed of historian specialized in a topic or period, particularly one of a new and less

---

[75]*Feudal England* (1895).

[76]*England in the Age of Wycliffe* (1899); *British History in the Nineteenth Century* (1922); *History of England* (1926); *England Under Queen Anne* 3 vols. (1930-34).

[77]Herbert Butterfield, *The Whig Interpretation of History* (1931).

political type. As a result the work tended to share a common Anglocentric outline and a rather old political calendar, except in those cases where work was directly aimed at a non-English area, or a specific revision of old political ideas or interpretations. Moreover, the "new" historians, like their predecessors, were inclined to go to the continent for comparisons rather than looking elsewhere in the archipelago.

Among those whose work marked significant departures in political history were Sidney and Beatice Webb's *English Local Government* (9 vols., 1906-1929) which applied an exhaustive research technique to the myriad institutions and problems of 19th century administration. The pioneer work of R. H. Tawney (*Religion and the Rise of Capitalism*, 1926) put forward a seminal view of the vital role of economic forces and religion in the shaping of political history. L. B. Namier wrote provocative reassessments of the 18th century in his *Structure of Politics at the Accession of George III* (1929) and *England in the Age of the American Revolution* (1930). Namier discarded the conventions of political parties and made microscopic studies of individuals and groupings, which work transformed the study of politics thereafter.

While these authors were refurbishing the outlines of the past at the "core" of the historical establishment, there were many signs of renovation near the "periphery." A number of institutional changes from the late 19th century had affected Wales, Scotland and Ireland, creating more capacity for their historians to either emulate or separate from their English colleagues. Both routes were followed, some writing what we would call traditional (even "colonial") national history, while others developed "Celtic" awareness which appeared in both national and "pan-Celtic" works. The Welsh received their national university with the founding of three university colleges (1872-85). The symbolic value of the University of Wales was as great as its immediate educational value, but both were critical in shaping a new Welsh self-image. In the 19th century universities there was only belated recognition of the need to teach Welsh, Scottish or Irish history. In his rectorial address at Aberdeen in 1880, Rosebery said[78]

> There is an omission of part of modern history, which, strange to say, is worse than the omission of the whole. For I cannot help regarding it as a

---

[78]*Miscellanies*, v. 2, p. 48.

stain not merely on this University, but on all your Scottish Universities, that there is no provision for teaching Scottish history...the history of our native country is not merely useful and interesting, but absolutely essential.

A Professor of Scottish History was appointed at Edinburgh in 1901, and at Glasgow in 1911. A National Library of Wales was founded in 1909, and it gave a resting-place to some peripatetic public records which had been moved about in the 19th century. There was much more record collection, cataloging and publication in Scotland during the 19th century, and Irish records, chiefly of Dublin Castle, were being carefully arranged. Ireland was first with the formation of a nativist cultural movement, the Gaelic League in 1893. The aim of the League was to minimize English influence and revive the Irish language. A variety of similar efforts were made in Scotland and Wales.

William Forbes Skene was an example of a dedicated and overzealous student of poorly-understood ancient history. His editorial skills have been severely criticized, but only a few of his works have been superseded. His *Celtic Scotland* (3 vols., 1876-80) was the most important work of its kind in the later 19th century, but unfortunately it was not a model of scholarly judgment.[79]

O. M. Edwards was another student of national history called "perhaps the most powerful single personal influence upon the generation up to 1914."[80] Edwards edited a number of periodicals and made the knowledge of Welsh history much more widespread in the Welsh language. Thus, while he was not a prolific or profound scholar, Edwards made a vital contribution to the cause of his subject.

One of the founders of the Gaelic League, Eoin MacNeill was a leading figure in scholarship and in nationalist politics. The former was most important, to him and to Ireland. One author has said that[81]

To MacNeill belongs the credit of having dragged Celtic Ireland practically single-handed from the antiquarian mists into the light of history.

---

[79] James Anderson, "William Forbes Skene: Celtic Scotland v. Caledonia," *Scottish Historical Review* 46 (1967):140-50.

[80] Morgan, *Rebirth of a Nation*, p. 103.

[81] F. J. Byrne, *The Scholar Revolutionary* (1973), p. 17.

MacNeill was another popularizer, but one who had acquired impeccable credentials as an authority in ancient texts. His main published work was in learned articles and collections of lectures (*Phases of Irish History*, 1919; *Celtic Ireland*, 1921).

In the traditional category, none was more significant than John Lloyd's *History of Wales to the Edwardian Conquest* (2 vols. 1911) which is still a basic work. Lloyd was a nationalist, but a scholar first, carefully working over the Welsh Chronicles, teaching at Bangor for many years, and becoming the leading Welsh medievalist. In Scotland, a number of historians were pursuing the same objectives: Andrew Lang published his *History of Scotland from the Roman Occupation* (4 vols. 1907-29); Herbert Maxwell edited *Early Chronicles Relating to Scotland* (1912); Peter Hume Brown, having edited the *Register of the Privy Council of Scotland* (1898), produced a three-volume *History of Scotland* (1902-09), but "wrote rather apologetically, and could express little pride in Scotland's institutional achievements."[82] As if to remedy this, R. S. Rait wrote on *The Scottish Parliament* and C. S. Terry published *The Scottish Parliament* in 1905. The prolific William L. Mathieson published his first work, *Politics and Religion in Scotland* (1902) dealing with the period from the reformation to the revolution. Mathieson added four more volumes, taking his survey up to the middle of the 19th century.

By contrast, Ireland had few narrators in the early 20th century. Alice Green wrote *The Making of Ireland and its Undoing* in 1908, but "no one ventured to write a full-scale history of the period before the Norman invasion" for the next half century.[83] The Anglo-Norman period did receive a confident survey from Edmund Curtis in 1923 which held the field for the next generation.[84] Otherwise current politics seemed to absorb most attention.[85]

Perhaps because of Irish republican "victory," or perhaps because of scholarly motivation, the interwar years saw the rise of pan-Celtic studies and

---

[82]Gordon Donaldson, "Scottish History and the Scottish Nation," *Inaugural Lecture*, University of Edinburgh, 1964, p. 4.

[83]F. J. Byrne, in *Irish Historiography 1936-70*, ed. T.W. Moody (1971), p. 1.

[84]*History of Medieval Ireland* (2 ed. 1938).

[85]C.G. Duffy, *The League of North and South* (1886); William O'Brien, *An Olive Branch in Ireland* (1910); T. P. O'Connor, *The Parnell Movement* (1886); Michael Davitt, *The Fall of Feudalism in Ireland* (1904).

a consequent impulse toward wider (or more related) study in the archipelago. The work on mythology and cultural features, with its many pitfalls, had always pointed to associations, but did not always make them with precision. Linguists became more adept at amplifying the archeological record, but occasionally that erudition was a stumbling-block to accurate historical reconstruction.[86] Meanwhile, the political and cultural historians added their insights, as with David Mathew's *Celtic Peoples and Renaissance Europe* (1933) or Sir Reginald Coupland's *Welsh and Scottish Nationalism* (1954). The most ambitious pan-Celtic work was that of Nora Chadwick and Myles Dillon (*Celtic Realms,* 1970) which unlike those just mentioned, depended upon the innovative work of linguists like Kenneth Jackson (*Language and History in Early Britain,* 1953).

It may be that the most important consequence of Celtic and pan-Celtic studies has been to stretch the limits of the traditional historical framework. That process began almost unnoticed in the 1930s, and in the postwar years it has taken on a more self-conscious aspect. There were several elements to this change in its early stages: an imperial revision, a "colonial" element, and the spread of authoritative national histories.

It was obvious by the late 1930s that the empire was changing. One American scholar was moved to take a new approach. When L.H. Gipson began his study of *The British Empire before the American Revolution*, he set the stage with a volume on *The British Isles and the American Colonies: Great Britain and Ireland, 1748-1754* . In his first edition, Gipson left out Wales, which error was remedied in 1958. Yet his treatment was an odd sort of comparison between four countries, as if they were unconnected. There was here, however, a novel treatment of the participants in the empire[87]

---

[86]See for example, Thomas F. O'Rahilly, *Early Irish History and Mythology* (1946).

[87]More selective international studies were a subject of continuing interest. See W.F. Adams, *Ireland and Irish Emigration to the New World from 1815 to the Famine* (1932); A. D. Gibb, *Scottish Empire* (1937); A.H. Dodd, *The Character of Early Welsh Emigration to the U.S.* (1953); I.C.C. Graham, *Colonists from Scotland; Emigration to North America, 1707-1783* (1956); R.J. Dickson, *Ulster Emigration to Colonial America, 1718-1774* (1966); Gordon Donaldson, *The Scots Overseas* (1966); and in a different vein: Frank Clune, *The Scottish Martyrs: Their Trials and Transportation to Botany Bay* (1969) and G.A. Williams, *The Search for Beulah Land: The Welsh and the Atlantic Revolution* (1980).

After World War II, the concept of an Atlantic Community was politically popular, and J.B. Brebner made an attempt to develop the historical antecedents in his *North Atlantic Triangle: The Interplay of Canada, the United States and Great Britain* (1945). Similarities in the 18th century empire were studied by Bernard Bailyn and John Clive.[88] David B. Quinn on the other hand, examined connections between Irish and American experiences in the 16th century (*The Elizabethans and the Irish,* 1966).

While imperial history was assuming these new shapes, the historians of Scotland, Wales and Ireland were re-examining their subjects and their national studies were less apologetic and more independent. Of course English relations would always be a large portion of their story, but the approach to those relations was changing in substantial ways as the national (sometime "colonial") historian now had much more to rely on in terms of sources and scholarly support.

The first broad *History of Modern Wales* was written by David Williams in 1950. His balanced treatment of Welsh history since the 16th century concentrated on different fields (religion, education, economics) over successive periods, reflecting the book's pioneering status. In the more heavily-travelled field of Irish history, J.C. Beckett produced a remarkable *Short History of Ireland* in 1952. His synthesis was an objective and sensitive treatment of the major themes of Ireland's past. Elsewhere, Gordon Donaldson produced the first modern and objective *History of the Scottish Reformation* in 1960. Of even greater significance was his treatment of the 16th and 17th centuries in the debut of the four-volume*Edinburgh History of Scotland* (1965-75), the most comprehensive general Scottish history yet produced.

Of course the magisterial multi-volume history was familiar to England. It had been a staple item of the 20th century (e.g. William Hunt and R.L. Poole, *The Political History of England,* 12 vols. 1905-14). The best known of these was the *Oxford History of England*, which eventually ran to 15 volumes and was published over the years 1934-1965. It is worth noting that the Oxford History was broader than its title, as most volumes contained significant sections on Wales, Scotland, Ireland and the colonies. Indeed, it was during the generation of its publication that increasing attention was

---

[88]"England's Cultural Provinces: Scotland and America," *William and Mary Quarterly*, 3rd Series, 11 (1954):200-13.

being given to these several subjects, and the *Edinburgh History of Scotland* was soon joined by the first volumes of *A New History of Ireland* (1976) and *The History of Wales* (1981). In addition to these authoritative projects, inexpensive series histories for each national subject began to appear in the 1970s.

In 1968 the Oxford History Syllabus still offered[89]

"The History of England, with some attention to Scotland, Ireland, Wales, India and other Commonwealth countries so far as they are connected with the History of England."

This imperial tone was a small advance beyond the famous British Museum Catalogue entry, "For Wales--See England." The histories of the several nations were finding places of their own from the 1960s. It is unflattering to historians that they were the last to recognize the multinational reality, for it had been a commonplace of literary and social scientific study for many years.[90] In the last generation, historians have become working partners with the social scientists, a hardy breed seldom reluctant to deal with the whole of the archipelago. The geographers were probably the earliest to push toward an archipelago view. Halford Mackinder's study of *Britain and the British Seas* (1902), Cyril Fox's *Personality of Britain* (1932) and Dudley Stamp's *British Isles: A Geographic and Economic Survey* (1933) showed the value of broad interdisciplinary analysis. For the national level, E.G. Bowen's *Wales: A Study in Geography and History* (1941) had the same effect. The importance of the natural environment was taken further in the anthropological work of H.J. Fleure (*Natural History of Man in Britain*, 1951). Physical studies obviously had no problem transcending political boundaries. Similar development was evident in economic and social studies. Brinley Thomas gained some valuable insights in studying *Migration and Economic Growth: A Study of Great Britain and the Atlantic*

---

[89]Boyd C. Shafer, *Historical Study in the West* (1968) p. 134.

[90]In literature, see A.W. Pollard, G.R. Redgrave, *et al.*, *A Short-Title Catalogue of Books Printed in England, Scotland and Ireland and of English Books Printed Abroad, 1475-1640* (1926); D. G. Wing, *A Short-Title Catalogue of Books Printed in England, Scotland, Ireland, Wales and British America and English Books Printed in Other Countries, 1641-1700* (1945); and E. Dix, H. Plomer, G. Bushnell, *A Dictionary of the Printers and Booksellers who were at Work in England, Scotland and Ireland from 1726 to 1775* (1932).

Economy (1954) and Michael Hechter searched for "a theory of ethnic change" in *Internal Colonialism: The Celtic Fringe in British National Development, 1536-1966* (1975). These studies were all important to the changing view of politics, and by the 1970s the political scientists saw that the archipelago needed to be studied as a whole, or as Richard Rose described it, "The United Kingdom: A Multinational State."

The Atlantic Archipelago has only begun to regain the attention of historians in recent years. There have been varied attempts for nearly half a century, beginning with F.J.C. Hearnshaw's *Outlines of the History of the British Isles* (1938). He constructed a parallel set of narratives, with a few short analytical sections. Hearnshaw was content to demonstrate the luck or skill of Anglo-Saxons and their institutions, and made no attempt to integrate the several areas. Contemporary with him, the vigorous constitutional and legal work of H.G. Richardson and G.O. Sayles was a scholarly parallel. They concentrated on the middle ages, seeing England and Ireland in a French- dominated world by the 12th century[91]

In the 1950s there were several important contributions to the archipelago idea. J.C. Beckett's view of the war of the three kingdoms has been noted. C.V. Wedgwood's volumes on *The King's Peace* (1955) and *The King's War* (1958) saw the great rebellion centered upon the crown and involving all of its dominions. She described this extensive domain, pointing out that [92]

> events in one part of the country repeatedly influenced events in another, so that the war cannot be imaginatively understood without some idea of its infinite territorial ramifications.

Another early pioneer was G.W.S. Barrow, whose *Feudal Britain* (1956) was aimed at the whole of the larger island. He called his work[93]

> a serious attempt to trace the medieval ancestry of modern Britain, narrate the development of England from 1066 to 1307, of Scotland 1058 to 1314,

---

[91]*The Irish Parliament in the Middle Ages* (1952); *The Governance of Medieval England from the Conquest to Magna Carta* (1963).

[92]*The King's War*, p. 12.

[93]*Feudal Britain*, p. 6.

425

and of Wales in the thirteenth century, in as full a manner as possible and in relative proportion.

In the 1960s there were some interesting surveys which seemed to arise from current political interests, and took rather different approaches to the same end: an analysis of the islands and their history, collectively and extensively. In 1968 Owen Dudley Edwards wrote an analysis of *Celtic Nationalism*, followed the next year by William Greenberg, *The Flags of the Forgotten*. Also in 1969, aroused perhaps by the controversy over immigration, F. George Kay used an anthropological approach in his *The British: From Pre-History to the Present Day*. The archipelago was a sort of melting-pot, later a dispenser of migrant peoples, and lastly a closed island community.

By 1970, the wider field of study was entering a period of more rapid growth, both at the scholarly level and in the form of more general works. In 1971, Sir George Clark's *English History: A Survey* went beyond its title and gave a reasoned introduction to an English community situated in an archipelago. W. L. Warren wrote of the reign of *Henry II* (1973) and his "lordship of the British Isles." H. R. Loyn described the wide impact of the *Vikings in Britain* (1977), including Ireland. M. T. Clanchy reviewed the broad aspects of medieval political geography in *England and Its Rulers* (1981). On the empire, S. S. Webb analyzed *The Governors-General: The English Army and the Definition of the Empire (1569-1681)* in 1979. A striking new imperial survey was begun in 1981 by Angus Calder. His *Revolutionary Empire* was a broad synthesis, showing the involvement of the whole archipelago in imperial expansion.[94]

The anomalous relation of England and Britain and the U.K. has been noted often, but it has not received the thorough study of historians until the current generation. Ideas and attitudes operating behind the prevailing usage have been discussed at length. The best early work was that of Thomas Kendrick (*British Antiquity*, 1950). Eric John made some important additions in his *Orbis Britanniae* (1966). A recent book by Hugh

---

[94]Textbooks have begun to show variations on this theme. John Randle, *Understanding Britain: A History of the British People and the Culture* (1981); Michael DeL. Landon, *Erin and Britannia: The Historical Background to a Modern Tragedy* (1981); Keith Robbins, *The Eclipse of a Great Power: Modern Britain, 1870-1975* (1983). Reference works have also moved in this direction: Richard Rose and Ian MacAlister, eds., *United Kingdom Facts* (1982); Christopher Haigh, ed., *The Cambridge Historical Encyclopedia of Great Britain and Ireland* (1985).

MacDougall has looked at *Racial Myth in English History* (1982). These works confront the essential issue of the coexistence of different groups within the archipelago, their respective images of each other, and their collective historical experience. Until the latter part of this century, their history has been written from a distinctly Anglocentric perspective; the main rejoinder has been history written from the opposing national points of view; the idea of writing the history of the archipelago on comprehensive lines has but slowly gained support. Recent evidence suggests that it has a future?[95]

[95]Bernard Bailyn, "The Challenge of Modern Historiography," Presidential Address to the American Historical Association, December 1981, in *American Historical Review*, 87 (1982): 14-18; J.G.A. Pocock, "Limits and Divisions of British History," *American Historical Review*, 87 (1982): 311-36.

INDEX

431

Rhodes, Cecil, 337
Rhodri Mawr, 46
Richard I, 84, 86
Richard II, 138-40
Richard III, 153
Richard, duke of Normandy, 55
Richard, duke of York, 146-7
Richard de Clare ("Strongbow"), 83-4
Robert Bruce, king of Scotland, 115-6, 121-3
Roman Britain, 2, 5, 9, 10, 15, 16-24

St. Columba, 36
St. Germanus, 24
St. Patrick, 16, 24, 36
Saxons, 3, 9, 22, 24-35
Saxon Shore, 18, 20, 22
Scandinavia, 11, 42-65
    politics of, 46-7, 50, 54, 56
Scotland, 5, 6, 46, 88, 95, 100-03, 114-6, 122-3, 169, 171-2, 180, 182, 185-90, 198, 201, 208-15, 218, 225, 230-1, 234-5, 250, 269, 278, 343
Scots, 1, 3, 34, 49, 51
Scottish enlightenment, 255-6
Scottish monarchy, 4, 49, 51, 73, 84, 114-16, 130, 142, 154, 198
Scottish National Covenant, 206
Severus, Septimius, 18
Shetland, 1, 20, 60, 102
Simon de Montfort, 99-100
South Africa 337-8, 371
Spain, relations with, 160-2, 173-6, 193, 252, 260
Stamford Bridge, 62
Stephen of Blois, 80
Stilicho, 22
Stuart, John, earl of Bute, 259-60
Surrey, 49
Sussex, 32, 49, 52
Swanscombe man, 9
Sweden, 46, 50, 54
Sweyn Forkbeard, 50-4

Tacitus, Cornelius, 2, 19
Tertullian, 23
Theodore of Tarsus, 38
Thorfinn the Mighty, 55, 59, 64
Tostig, 63, 70-1

Unification, 49, 193-205, 217-21, 222-3, 290-301
    1604, 193, 197-201
    1707, 195, 235-6

1801, 290-3

Vikings, chapter 2, passim
    raids, 39, 42-50
    hoards, 58
    and see Scandinavia

Wales, 5, 6, 17, 19, 20, 28, 46, 63, 72, 83, 89, 96, 101, 110, 112-14, 158-9, 167-8, 189
    and see Marcher lords, Welsh princes
Walpole, Robert, 258
War of Three Kingdoms, 194, 205-6, 208-15, 196
    and see English Civil War
Wars of the Roses, 146-8
Welsh princes, 4, 46, 50, 64, 96, 101, 110, 112-14
Wentworth, Thomas, earl of Strafford, 207-09
Wessex, 3, 24, 32, 33, 47, 49, 55, 60
Whitby, Synod of, 37
Wilkes, John, 260, 264
William I, 11, 59, 69-74
William II, 78
William III, 7, 195, 228
William I, king of Scotland, 84-5
William de Briouze, 89
William the Marshal, 89
Witan, 54, 64
Wolsey, Thomas, 161-2
World War, 1914-18, 345-51, 353
World War, 1939-45, 362-5
Wulfstan, 56, 61

York, 45, 47, 48, 58, 62, 71

432

STUDIES IN BRITISH HISTORY